ORATIONS

JOSEPH CHAMBERLAIN

Orations—Volume twenty-two

ORATIONS

FROM HOMER TO WILLIAM McKINLEY

EDITED BY

MAYO W. HAZELTINE, A.M.

ILLUSTRATED

IN TWENTY-FIVE VOLUMES

VOL. XXII

NEW YORK
P. F. COLLIER AND SON
MCMII

CONTENTS

VOLUME TWENTY-TWO

ORATIONS

WHITE

THE HONORABLE THOMAS WHITE was born in Montreal in 1830, where he received his education and where his early life was spent. He studied law in Ontario, but did not engage in the practice of the profession. During a number of years he was engaged in journalism in Hamilton and subsequently in Montreal, and he was one of the most brilliant writers and platform speakers of his day. He was returned to the House of Commons for Cardwell, Ontario, in 1878, and re-elected in 1882, becoming minister of the interior in 1885; and he remained in the Macdonald government until his death in the spring of 1888. His death was a great loss to Parliament and to the Conservative party of which he was a devoted member.

TWENTY YEARS OF LIBERAL-CONSERVATIVE ADMINISTRATION IN CANADA

DELIVERED AT THE VILLAGE OF L'ORIGINAL, MARCH 5, 1874

WE are here to-day for the purpose of forming a Liberal-Conservative Association. Mr. Hamilton has told you that all through Ontario a similar course is being adopted by the party. You, gentlemen, have not been alone in the absence of proper organization. Unfortunately it has been the lot of the party generally to neglect the organization of the ranks and to depend upon the great skill and statesmanship of the leader.

We have been disposed to think, because our party has been in office for twenty years, it was impossible that it could be defeated, and we have trusted to that skill and statesmanship and to the fact of previous triumphs, rather than to our strong united effort to win the contest. To-day the party is becoming more organized than I believe it has ever been, and from one end of Ontario to the other, and in the other Provinces as well, the electors who hitherto have had Liberal-

Conservatism inscribed upon their banners are uniting, so that when the day arrives they may be ready for the contest with the certainty of success.

It has occurred to me, as we are about to organize, that if possible we should know the grounds upon which we organize. Are we as Liberal-Conservatives entitled to maintain our organization and to look forward to future party triumphs? Is the record of the past such as we may be proud of? Are the achievements of the party during its long tenure of office, such as, if we look back upon them, justify us in keeping alive our party organization, and in looking forward with confidence to the achievements of electoral triumphs in the future?

As an answer to these questions it may not be amiss, as we are about establishing this association, if I should refer, as briefly as the circumstances will permit, to the history of the last twenty years, during which the party of which we are members has held office and guided the destinies of this country. I say twenty years during which they have been in office, because although for eighteen or twenty months our opponents held the reins of power, the legislation and results of those months were such as scarcely to take from the Liberal-Conservative party the fair credit of having done whatever has been done during the last twenty years to promote the prosperity of Canada.

Let me, sir, at the outset, refer to some of the incidents connected with the formation of what to-day is the Liberal-Conservative party. Such of you as attended some of the meetings that were held during the contest will remember that one gentleman—a learned gentleman, who evidently thinks he has more knowledge than those whom he came to address, and who traversed this county from one end to the other for the purpose of explaining the political views of Mr. Hagar, the member for the county—attempted to throw ridicule upon the term "Liberal-Conservative." Not having much confidence in your education and intelligence, he told you that an eminent professor, Mr. Goldwin Smith, had declared that the term Liberal had been attached to Conservative as a deodorizer. And supposing you might not understand the meaning of that word, he kindly vouchsafed the information to you that it meant taking the offensive smell from the latter name.

Now I think it is worth while to-day to point out that we are entitled to the name upon the highest grounds of the historical record of the past, and that judged by that record that name is entitled to the respect of all who rejoice to call themselves by it.

The party which to-day calls itself the Liberal party of Canada is not the old Liberal party of the Province of Canada. As far back as 1848-49, when Robert Baldwin and Louis Lafontaine were the great leaders of that party, the restless spirits who constitute the Clear Grit and Rouge parties of to-day began to show themselves. Then it was that Mr. Malcolm Cameron and others, who were at that time in Parliament, started what is known and designated as the Clear Grit party of Canada—composed of men in the Liberal ranks, but dissatisfied with the staunch conservatism of their leaders—men not satisfied with such leaders as Baldwin and Lafontaine, who thought by going a little faster they would manage to achieve greater things and establish greater popularity for themselves. And as in Upper Canada so in Lower.

The Liberals, as they call themselves, of to-day are not the Liberals of those days. Then the Rouge party, the party of Jean Baptiste Eric Dorion and *L'Avenir*, raised the war cry against the old Liberals, and erected platforms, the planks of which were regarded as extravagant then, and are happily, as to a large number of them, considered equally extravagant to-day.

The year 1854, which saw the Liberal-Conservative party spring into existence, was memorable for the attempts of these restless spirits who to-day claim a monopoly of the liberalism of the Dominion, to break down a Liberal administration, composed of the men who had been the colleagues and were the successors, as leaders of the party, of Messrs. Baldwin and Lafontaine. In Upper Canada the malcontents were led by Mr. Brown, the present leader—or, perhaps, more properly dictator—of the so-called Liberal party, and they included such men as Messrs. Hartman and Wright, members for two of the divisions of York. In order to break down a Liberal government Mr. Brown supported in all the constituencies Conservatives in preference to old Liberals; and as a result the Conservative party was strengthened and the old Liberal party weakened.

In Lower Canada, for the first time, the Rouges appeared in numbers in Parliament. Nineteen young men, led by Mr. Dorion, some of them men of earnestness and ability, but extravagant and almost revolutionary in their opinions, were elected to the Legislative Assembly. But they were elected, not as Liberals, but as Rouges opposed to the Liberal party of the day. Thus although the Liberal government, and the party represented by it, had a large majority over any of the other parties in Parliament considered singly, they found themselves in a minority when confronted with the three parties—Conservatives, Clear Grits, and Rouges—combined, and were compelled on the meeting of Parliament to tender their resignations.

When the time thus came for the change of government, owing to the defeat of the ministry, the question that arose in the minds of the old Liberals was this:—Shall we hand over the government of this country to the men who, calling themselves Liberals, have broken down the Liberal party by the declaration of extravagant views, by the enunciation of principles far more radical and reckless than any we are prepared to accept, and by a restless ambition which we cannot approve; or shall we not rather unite with the Conservatives, who have gone to the country declaring, in reference to the great questions which then agitated it, that if the decision at the polls was against them they would no longer offer resistance to their settlement, but would, on the contrary, assist in such a solution of them as would forever remove them from the sphere of public or political agitation.

Then came the coalition of 1854; then came the union between the true Liberals of the old days and the Conservatives; then came the party which for twenty years since that time has governed us under the title of the Liberal-Conservative party of Canada. And who shall say, looking at the great benefits of their rule, that they were not entitled to the name then and since of Liberal-Conservatives?

Do you want proof of the entire acquiescence of the foremost Liberals of that day in this arrangement? I ask you to refer to a letter dated September 22, 1854, addressed by Robert Baldwin to Sir Francis Hincks, then Mr. Hincks, in which that great old Liberal leader gives in his adhesion to the celebrated coalition of parties. In that letter he indorsed the action taken, and told his old friend and colleague that the best thing that could be done for the party and for the success of its principles was what he had done.

And the bitterness with which even Robert Baldwin,

whose claim to be considered a Liberal few will now dispute, was persecuted because of his acquiescence in the measure by which the Clear Grits and Rouges have been so long kept in opposition, was exemplified shortly afterward when a number of his friends, old political opponents as well as allies, requested him to enter the legislative council as the member of the York division. Instead of acquiescing in a selection, the absolute fitness of which could not be questioned, these Clear Grits, headed by Mr. Brown, these men who claim to-day to be the Liberals of Canada, brought out a nobody, politically, in the person of Mr. Charles Romaine, to oppose him, and thus forced the old statesman, whom, however men may have differed from him politically, all were compelled to honor and respect, back into private life and soon after to a sorrowing grave.

One wonders to-day that the spirit of Robert Baldwin does not rise to rebuke the hypocrites and traitors who, having thus cast reproaches upon him in his maturer years, now venture to deck their banqueting halls with his honored name.

The party having thus been formed, let us for a moment look at questions that divided the country at that time. The two leading questions were the Clergy Reserves and the Seigniorial Tenure questions. The first was a subject which many years before was one of the elements in the rebellion of Upper Canada, and the other under which the people of Lower Canada were made to pay dues at different times contrary to and destructive of all chances of material prosperity. These questions constituted the leading issues of that time. They were large, important questions, requiring solution at the hands of the public men of the country. What was done? The Clergy Reserves were secularized; and you well remember the agitation made by the so-called Liberals, the Clear Grits, against the commutation clause of the Act of Secularization simply for this reason: that by means of that commutation clause all chances of future agitation upon the subject were swept away.

The Conservative party at that time—for the very principle of Conservatism is to destroy as far as it can the cries of agitators and the trade of demagogues—endeavored to take from the arena of public discussion mere questions of popular agitation. The commutation clauses were introduced as the Conservative element into that bill.

And by one stroke the whole question was removed from political discussion; and although the Grits got up petitions, signed by some eighty or ninety thousand people, against the clause, it was carried successfully through and became law. I venture to say that to-day there is not a man in the entire Province but rejoices that that which set neighbor against neighbor, one class against another, which placed the badge of religious inferiority upon some and the badge of superiority upon others, has been removed from the political arena. From that time to this we have heard nothing of the discussion of the Clergy Reserves.

The Seigniorial Tenure in Lower Canada was in like manner forever swept away. In this the party has been attacked by the Liberals of Lower Canada, chiefly because in the settlement of the question it had adopted principles which entirely removed it from the political arena. From that day to this men can do what they could not before. Now they can sell their lands without paying the *lods et ventes*, carry their grain to the mill without paying the rights of *banalité*, till their soil without the oppression of the *cens et rentes*, and are freed from a number of other dues which pressed and oppressed the people of that Province. Equality of religious denominations before the law and free tenure of land in Lower Canada were established as the result of the union which took place between the Liberals and Conservatives in 1854, and are among the achievements of the Liberal-Conservative party.

Well, gentlemen, these questions being removed, the agitators who had broken up their own party and who have now ventured to assume the name of the party broken up started new questions of agitation.

The first one was the question of "No Separate Schools." Realizing that in Lower Canada the union of the old Liberals and Conservatives had secured in that Province a majority to the government, they set themselves to work in the west for the purpose, if possible, of bringing from this Province a large majority against the administration of the day, and thus provoking sectional strife. They started this question of no separate schools, coupled with the Protestant cry, as one of the most effective ways of doing this; and for upwards of eight or ten years every hustings in Upper Canada rang with the cry, "No Separate Schools."

The Liberal-Conservatives, although they went to the elections and suffered defeat in many parts because of these cries raised against them, because they acted upon the principle that the man who believed that religion and education should go hand in hand was as much entitled to have his conscientious opinions respected as the man who was a Secularist in the matter of education, yet lived long enough to see their opponents acquiesce in the wisdom of their course and consent to separate schools being made a constitutional enactment, embodied in the British-American act.

Then the cry of representation by population was taken

up; and a more dishonest cry—and I am prepared to prove what I say by words from the mouth of its chief advocate—was never raised in the country. It was declared throughout Ontario that the man who would not go for representation by population was a traitor to his country; it was declared that the ministers who refused to accept it were traitors to their country; and in every public assembly the discussion was as violent as discussions well can be.

It is something for us to know that the leader of the Conservative party, a man whom I am proud to acknowledge as a leader, throughout the whole of the discussion opposed strongly what he believed to be the impracticable scheme of representation by population, and that he lived to find his opposition to it vindicated out of the mouth of his chief opponent. He suggested as a means of solving the question and meeting the demands which were made for representative reform, a union of the different Provinces, and he made the suggestion almost in the very terms of the constitution which we now possess. . . .

Then, gentlemen, the Liberal-Conservative party, in addition to the settlement of these great questions, and undoubtedly they were great questions, brought about law reform, extension of the municipal system, improvement of the school laws, and such other measures of legislation in the old Province of Canada before confederation as left us at the time of confederation with only one question to be solved by the Parliament of the country.

And what has been the career of the country since? Although not until 1864 was the question of confederation even discussed, although only in 1867 was the question of confederation finally carried, yet when the Liberal-Conservative government left office they handed to their successors a united British America, with the single exception of the colony of Newfoundland.

Contrast, sir, these performances with the most ardent hopes of the most enthusiastic speakers on the subject of confederation. Mr. Brown, and I prefer to refer to him because he can hardly be said to be a partial witness on behalf of Liberal-Conservatism, in his great speech in Parliament, after describing the extent of territory and the different Provinces which it was intended to include in the union ultimately, said:—

"Well, sir, the bold scheme in your hands is nothing less than to gather these countries into one—to organize them all under one government with the protection of the British flag and in heartiest sympathy and affection with our fellow subjects in the land that gave us birth."

"When?" shouted the incredulous member for North Hastings, Mr. Wallbridge.

"Very soon," answered the impetuous Sir George E. Cartier.

But Mr. Brown was more cautious and gauged with a keener eye the difficulties of the work:—"The honorable member for North Hastings asks when all this can be done? Sir, the whole great ends of this confederation may not be realized in the lifetime of many who now hear me. We imagine not that such a structure can be built in a month or in a year. What we propose now is but to lay the foundation of the structure, to set in motion the governmental machinery that will one day, we trust, extend from the Atlantic to the Pacific."

There was the statement of Mr. Brown as to the work before them—a statement which showed that he had no hope even within his lifetime that that could be accomplished which the skill and statesmanship of the Liberal-Conservative party have already accomplished. A confederation extending from the Atlantic to the Pacific was the dream of the far-off future for Mr. Brown. To-day we have that confederation; we have representatives from all the Provinces except one—the Province of Newfoundland—taking part in the legislation of the Dominion of Canada.

I ask you, therefore, whether, looking at the past political record of the Liberal-Conservative party of the country—looking at the important questions they have settled—we have not reason to be proud of the name and to determine to stand by the old flag whatever others may say of it, or however others may traduce it. . . .

Now let us look at the progress which the country has made in those twenty years of Liberal-Conservative administration. For the purpose of comparison I take the Provinces of Ontario and Quebec, and for this reason—that I have not been able to get access to the trade and navigation returns of the Lower Provinces previous to 1867; but, at any rate, as they were not part of Canada and as the policy of the Liberal-Conservatives had no effect upon them, they are better left out for the purpose of comparison and to show the progress made during the twenty years. In 1854, when the Liberal-Conservatives came into office, the aggregate trade of the Province of Canada was $63,548,515. In 1872, the last year for which we have full returns, the aggregate trade of the two Provinces of Ontario and Quebec amounted to $153,990,704, an increase of upwards of 142 per cent. That is progress of which any people may fairly be proud.

Then take the aggregate trade of the whole Dominion—and I give you the statement as made by the finance minister last week at Ottawa. For the year ending on the 30th of June last it amounted to $216,000,000, which, assuming the population at four millions—rather more than the population really is—represents $54 per head of the population. Well, gentlemen, the aggregate trade of the United States, which we have been in the habit of looking upon as a wonderfully prosperous country, for 1870 was $961,420,145, which, taking their population at thirty-eight millions, equals $25.30 per head for the trade of the whole of the United States, as compared with $54 per head for the aggregate trade of the Dominion of Canada. . . .

I am aware, gentlemen, that the common answer to these statements is, that the prosperity of the country springs from the industry and enterprise of the people, and is in no way due to the government. I should be sorry to take from the people of Canada, in the slightest degree, the great credit which is due to them as an enterprising and progressive people. I am too proud of my country as a native Canadian to do that.

But in a country like Canada, situated as we are in close proximity to the United States, the great element of prosperity must always be confidence in the political institutions of the country. That confidence has been more than once shaken by the political agitations of unthinking men; and only by the removal of those questions of agitation, by their solution in a manner satisfactory to the public at large, can we secure that political quiet which is the best guarantee for public confidence, and the best incentive to the introduction and investment of capital among us. To the settlement of the great questions to which I have to-day referred is due the confidence of the moneyed men of the world in the future stability of our political system, and the great prosperity which has followed that confidence. And as to the administration of the Liberal-Conservatives during the last twenty years is due the removal of those causes of agitation, to them must be fairly accorded credit for the prosperity of Canada.

During those twenty years the common mode of attack of the Opposition was to assail the personal characters of members of the government. They were called corruptionists, and I can remember that in old elections, instead of giving us the name to which we were entitled, they headed their lists "Liberals," "Corruptionists."

Where are the evidences of corruption from that time to this? Where is there a single charge made of personal corruption against any single minister of the party in the country? It is quite true that on one occasion they thought they had a case against Sir John A. Macdonald. He had dabbled in lands up at Sarnia, they said, and they thought the job would afford a good ground against him. But he made his explanation in Parliament; and what said the leader of the Opposition? Here is the report: "Mr. Foley could not let slip this the last opportunity he had in that Parliament of saying that the explanations of the honorable attorney-general met with his hearty approval."

That is the only charge of personal corruption ever brought against a member of the old government, and his vindication from that charge came from the leader of the Opposition himself.

We never heard of the Sarnia job after that day without reflecting upon the effect of assuming things upon insufficient foundation to damage the reputation of public men. Sir John A. Macdonald, at the time he entered public life, had probably the largest practice of any solicitor in Ontario, with prospects before him which could not have failed to amass for him great riches and to have made him to-day one of the wealthy men of the country. But after thirty years' service —twenty years of which were spent in an official capacity— he is out of office literally a poor man.

Is that likely to be the case with men who go into public life for the purpose of filching the public purse, taking their share in contracts and otherwise furthering their individual interests? I have in my mind's eye one public man, at any rate, who, a year or two ago, was without visible means of support, known to be in debt at every turn. Now he is rolling in wealth—but I am inclined to think that the position public life gave him helped to it—why or how I don't pretend to say.

Thank God, in the whole record of the Liberal-Conservative administration there has not been a similar instance; our ministers have left public life without the stain upon them of having taken a sixpence of the public funds. When, a couple of years ago, Sir John Macdonald, at a public meeting in the city of Hamilton, stretched forth his arms with the exclamation, "These hands are clean," he stated what was literally true With all the temptations of public and official life he has retired from office without a single stain of corruption upon his personal or public character.

The truth is, sir, that the charges of political vice, of official corruption, were made by the Clear Grits in order to conceal their own practices as a party. During the last session of Parliament we had one rather remarkable case brought forward by Mr. Mackenzie, upon which he asked the sense of Parliament, and put on record his own opinion to show how terribly reckless the old government was and how pure he was in comparison with them. Mr. Griffin, in 1872, was a post-office inspector, and he wrote a letter to a postmaster in the county of Welland, in which he simply said this: "If you cannot support Dr. King, who is the ministerial candidate, take no active part against him and give no ground of complaint against yourself."

That was a suggestion made by an officer of the government to his brother official; but it so shocked Mr. Mackenzie that he got up in the House and moved this resolution:—

"That it is highly criminal in any minister or ministers, or other servants under the crown, directly or indirectly, to use the power of office in the election of representatives to serve in Parliament; and an attempt at such influence will be at all times resisted by the House, as aimed at its own dignity, honor, and independence."

Well, gentlemen, we have just passed through a general election, and let me ask you how this has been observed. These gentlemen had scarcely obtained seats when the Ottawa mayoralty election came on. And what occurred? The deputy head of at least one department went round to his subordinates and said, "If you cannot vote for the ministerial candidate you must not vote against him."

Why? These men were paying taxes, and had as much interest in the proper management of the city of Ottawa as the government themselves. But the Liberals made a political contest out of a municipal election, and the government were found saying to their employes, "You must not vote at all unless you vote for the ministerial candidate!"

Then, in the Kingston election the finance minister visited the post-office and custom-house and told the employes to vote for Mr. Carruthers, or not to vote at all. Then, again, in the Argenteuil election letters were sent to postmasters of the county telling them to vote for Mr. Cushing, or not vote at all. The case of the Central prison at Toronto is another beautiful exemplification of the manner in which these pure ministers, these liberal-minded ministers, these ministers who record it as an offence against the dignity and honor of Parliament for members of a government, or even subordinate officials of a government to attempt to exercise influence in an election, carry out their Opposition principles when they obtain office. Mr. McKellar with his own hand wrote to the superintendent of those works ordering him to send the men to the nomination for West Toronto in order to increase the apparent majority for Mr. Moss, the ministerial candidate. In this case, not only was official and ministerial influence used, but the public exchequer was mulcted to the extent of the half day's pay of each of these men, in order to provide a party triumph.

Even in this very county we had, during the last election, some illustrations of how ministerial influence was used.

We saw here an old contractor who in times past, when the Conservative party had contracts to give, was a Conservative, traversing the country in the interests of the ministerial candidate and endeavoring by dint of his old Conservative associations to win Conservatives from the cause. If rumor be true he did not come altogether empty-handed, and he soon after received his reward. The election was scarcely well over when a contract for the Ottawa booms, awarded to one gentleman, and the work by him actually commenced, was cancelled on the technical ground that the tender was a few minutes late, although its deposit in the post-office within the specified time was attested by the postmaster, and the work was given to new contractors, one of whom was understood to be our old friend, the renegade missionary to the county of Prescott.

I have the information from undoubted sources that in

New Brunswick and Nova Scotia the most unblushing use of ministerial and official influence was made in the elections. Mr. Mackenzie has boasted in his address that he had voluntarily given up on behalf of the government the great advantage of so arranging the days of election as to make the result of one influence that of others. But what was the fact? With the influence of the two governments at his back he felt tolerably confident of Ontario, and he did fix the elections on one day in Old Canada. But in the other Provinces, where the influence of success was likely to be greatest, he deliberately so arranged them as to secure the greatest advantage.

In New Brunswick they were arranged so as to leave the elections where the Opposition was supposed to be the strongest to the last, in order that the influence of success elsewhere might have its effect in favor of the government candidates. And in Nova Scotia, where by the local law the elections must be held on one day, he so arranged that they should all take place a week after the result in Ontario and Quebec became known. And what then was seen? Why, from every hustings the most unblushing use was made of the argument that the influence of the constituency with the government would depend upon the fact of their sending a ministerialist to represent them.

The administration, it was urged, had already secured a working majority, even though the Province should go as a unit against them; and was it wise that they should voluntarily range themselves for the then coming Parliament with the ranks of a hopeless minority? Such was the cry, and its effect is unfortunately but too well known. Even the local premier, acting for and speaking for his friends in the Dominion government, went from platform to platform reminding the constituencies that their chances of ministerial favors depended upon their granting ministerial support. And by means of those influences and arguments, by means of this prostitution of official and ministerial power and patronage, in violation of the doctrine I have quoted to you as enunciated by Mr. Mackenzie in the case of the Griffin letter, a large majority of supporters was obtained for the government from the maritime Provinces.

Coming again nearer home, we have the illustration of the influence of the vacant shrievalty of this county. We know there were gentlemen who in times past had worked in the ranks with you, and who were found working on the other side.

It was said of them that they had this office dangled before them and were looking forward to the occupancy of the coveted place. The late sheriff had died some months before. Under ordinary circumstances it was the duty of the government to fill the office promptly. But it was more convenient to keep it as a bait for aspirants during the elections. We had rumors in every direction as to who the fortunate man would be, and we had either passive or active resistance on the part of some gentlemen, accounted for by the fact that they had received this much encouragement, at least, that the vacant office must be filled, and they were wonderfully clever fellows and wonderfully well qualified for the position.

Well, the election was scarcely well over and the necessity for this means of using ministerial and official influence past when a gentleman was appointed—who had at least this merit, that he had not deserted his party for the chance of an office; and I am inclined to think there are a good many sore heads in the county of Prescott to-day on account of this matter. These are but a few illustrations of how the gentlemen who are now in office can, from the Opposition benches, lay down doctrines such as those embodied in the resolution I have read to you, and then when in office can, in violation of these doctrines, prostitute ministerial influence and the patronage of the Crown to their own party interests, as was never done in Canada under any former administration.

And now, sir, let me say that I had some doubts whether in an address such as that which I am now delivering I should refer in any way to the celebrated Pacific scandal, the immediate cause of the downfall of the Liberal-Conservative government. But it occurred to me that, now that the elections are over—now that men's minds have cooled down, now that there are no votes to be got by discussing the question and denouncing the public men of the country in connection with it, now when the sober second thought must be beginning to assert itself, that now might be a good time to look at the question fairly and dispassionately and deal with it as it really deserves to be dealt with, to see what it really amounts to, and whether it was the heinous, unpardonable American connection in the matter of the Pacific Railway.

The gravamen of the charge is not that Sir Hugh Allan subscribed a large sum of money to the elections. He, as a wealthy member of the party, had a right to do this if he chose to do it. Even the pure-minded gentlemen who now sit on the ministerial benches, and who are so horrified at the idea of money being spent at elections, could, if they were for a moment seized with that rare commodity—candor—tell us of some pretty large expenditures during the last elections, and could perhaps tell us that the source of that reservoir, from which an almost never-ceasing supply ran into the different counties, is to be found in the remarkable change recently announced in their views on the subject of American connection in the matter of the Pacific Railway.

I have no doubt that Mr. R. W. Scott, who from his seat at Ottawa, sent forth his missionaries into the different counties, could tell us something. I have no doubt that throughout the country, as, for instance, in one of the divisions of Montreal, we could find evidences of expenditures which aggregated over the whole Dominion would make the contribution of Sir Hugh Allan, great as it was, appear small. The truth is, and I admit it with regret, that money does get spent at elections, and my own experience is that those who bawl most loudly for purity generally manage to spend the most.

The gravamen of this charge, I repeat, is not the mere fact of subscription by a wealthy member of the party to the election funds of the party. The gravamen of the charge is, and if that could be established it would be a damning one, that Sir John A. Macdonald, being the first minister of the crown, entered into such an agreement with Sir Hugh Allan, who was at the time both a contractor and an expectant contractor, and accepted money from him for party purposes on such terms as prevented him doing his duty to the country in regard to any contract in which Sir Hugh Allan was interested. Is there anything in the records of Parliament since the elections of 1872, or in the evidence taken before the commission, or in the well-known facts connected with the Pacific Railway charter, to justify this charge?

Take the first. It is true that Sir Hugh Allan, or rather the firm of which he is the head, was a contractor, a contractor for carrying the ocean mails. Well, what happened? The very first session after these transactions took place that contract had to be renewed, and it was renewed at half the price of the old one! Did that look like being bound by any agreement against the interests of the country?

And as to the second, we know from the testimony of a gentleman who certainly showed during the November session no disposition to befriend the late government, that Sir Hugh Allan was compelled to abandon, one after another, all the special features of the Pacific Railway charter upon which he had set his heart, and was not even consulted, but, on the contrary, his advice was actually rejected in the matter of the gentlemen who were to compose that company. I know of my own knowledge that in relation to one gentleman especially, with whom he had been acting in railroad matters, he felt deeply chagrined at not having been able to secure his presence on the board of directors. Did that look as if there had been an agreement which bound ministers to Sir Hugh Allan against their own independent conception of their duty to the country? . . .

Sir John Macdonald, gentlemen, committed a great mistake in being personally connected with any question of money for the elections and he has most grievously suffered for it. It was a mistake resulting from the absence in Canada of those political organizations which in England assume the management of these things, and it was a mistake which he committed in common with other public men of both political parties, and, if I am not greatly mistaken, in common even with members of the pure government which we have presiding over the destinies of Canada to-day.

But no man in Canada, from Prince Edward Island to Vancouver, would venture the assertion that a single sixpence had stuck to his own fingers or tended to enrich himself. The money he obtained he spent in aiding his friends throughout Ontario in their elections, and the whole amount obtained by him did not exceed what I venture to say has been spent in three elections that I would name during the late contest in this country on the Clear Grit side alone.

I venture, sir, to think that the maturer judgment, the sober second thought of the people of this country will yet vindicate the character of the great statesman who has so long presided over the destinies of this country and whose name is so eminently associated with the twenty years of Liberal-Conservative administration in Canada from the bitter aspersions which a mad jealousy and disappointed ambition have heaped upon it.

I venture, sir, to think that that judgment will shape itself after this fashion: Here is a man who, at the cost of professional prospects which might have made him one of the wealthy men of the land, entered at an early age the service of his country, and for thirty years has uninterruptedly given to that service the eminent abilities with which God has endowed him; who for twenty years has been in official life, and has during that time solved all the great questions which separated and agitated the country, and has given to it measures which have brought peace and prosperity to the people; who, finding a number of isolated Provinces with hostile tariffs and local agitations, has welded them into one great Dominion in the enjoyment of free constitutional government under the crown of Great Britain; under whose administration the people have both socially and politically and materially enjoyed a prosperity certainly not excelled by that enjoyed by any other people on the face of the earth; who has made the name of Canada known and respected the world over, and has made for himself an honored name on both sides of the Atlantic; who has received at the hands of his sovereign honors such as have never been bestowed upon any other colonial statesman; but who at a time of great political crisis, when the interests alike of his party and his country seemed at stake, was tempted to aid his friends in a contest against sectional prejudice backed by the substantial aid of large money support, by accepting from a wealthy member of his party a large subscription toward party funds; who suffered defeat from it; but who throughout all the period of these discussions remained uncharged even of personal corruption for his own advantage; who even when accepting this subscription to party funds was careful not to allow it to embarrass him in his public duty; and when the time came to deal with the wealthy donor kept himself in a position to treat with him on terms of perfect independence and with a single eye to the public interests.

And, sir, when hereafter, when the discussions of to-day have been forgotten, and the influences which prompt those discussions have passed away, the correspondence of Sir Hugh Allan with his American associates comes to be read, and from it is ascertained what Sir Hugh aimed at, and that is contrasted with what he got in the charter, it will require neither skill nor courage to vindicate the great Liberal-Conservative leader from the aspersion of having entered into an agreement to sell a valuable public franchise for gold, with which to corrupt the electors of the country. Perhaps, gentlemen, the time has not come for that sober second thought to assert itself; but that it will come I feel as certain as that I am addressing my good friends in the county of Prescott to-day.

And now, Mr. Chairman and gentlemen, why is it that we are to-day forming this association? I have shown you that the policy of the past has been sufficient to solve all the great questions which have agitated the country during the last quarter of a century. I have shown you that the party which has just attained to office after years of agitation has not one single reform which it can call its own upon which to appeal for public sympathy and support. If, then, the great questions which have agitated parties in the past have been settled, why should we have a party organization such as is now proposed?

We must not forget that under the constitutional system which we happily possess in Canada, based as it is on the model of that of the mother-land, government by party is essential to the well-being and the proper government of the State. An opposition in Parliament is as essential as a government and performs almost as important a function in the administration of the affairs of the country. Not an opposition influenced simply by a factious desire to upset the administration or embarrass it in its work. That is not the ordinary work which a party out of office has to perform. The gentlemen now in power and their friends did their best when in opposition to bring our entire constitutional system into disrepute by forgetting this sound rule. Every measure of the old government was opposed with all the bitterness they could bring to bear upon it, and that from their peculiar temperament was not a little. And yet to-day we have the statement from ministerial lips, that the policy of the new government will be in the main the same as that of the old.

The duty which is before us as Liberal-Conservatives is to illustrate by our conduct what a constitutional opposition is, as the party when in office presented the spectacle of a constitutional government. The duty of an opposition is not to obstruct, but to assist the government in carrying on the affairs of the country. That does not imply that the government should be supported, but it does imply that all measures submitted by them and all acts of administration committed by them shall be subjected to such fair and candid criticism as will tend to produce as nearly a perfect government as it is possible to have. And it is because of the necessity for this opposition in the interests of good government that the Liberal-Conservatives should organize in every part of the Dominion as you are proposing to do here to-day. Such an organization will prove to the government that it is certain to be subject to a careful vigilance; and it will give to the minority elected to fight the battle of the Opposition in Parliament the encouragement of knowing that although the representation of the party in Parliament has been greatly reduced, there is a stalwart body of men in all the constituencies upon whose intelligence and political firmness and integrity they can rely for support.

The difficulty which may present itself in the formation of these associations is a definition of distinct principles. But there is one principle, and I name it not as distinguishing us from our opponents, for that would imply a charge I should be very sorry to make, viz.: the principle of British connection, which should constitute a first plank in any platform the party may adopt.

You know, gentlemen, at this moment efforts are being made in different parts of the country to start new parties. We have in the city of Toronto one party taking as its motto "Canada First," and another taking as its motto "Empire First." From my point of view both titles are admirable as mere mottoes, but neither by itself meets the requirements of the country. "Canada First"—let that be our motto in everything affecting the interests and prosperity and well-being of this country; let it be our motto in making the name of Canada an honored name, whether in legislation or commerce, the world over; let it be our motto in the dissemination of such information relating to our institutions and resources as will make the Dominion an attraction for the emigrating millions of the Old World. "Canada First!"

Let that be our motto so far as the interests of the Dominion, separate and distinct from those of the mother country, so far as they can be so, are concerned. "Empire First!" Let that be our motto so far as the interests of the glorious empire with which we are connected are concerned. "Empire First!" Let that be our motto in our reverence for the dear old flag and in our prayer that it may be borne as loftily in the future as it has been in the past. And if at any time danger should threaten it, and we should be called upon to vindicate in other form than by words our loyalty to the throne, then let "Empire First" be the guiding star under which we shall illustrate that the Queen has in this new Dominion as loyal, stalwart sons and as devoted and fair daughters as in any other part of her vast realms.

But let us take neither to the exclusion of the other. Both are mottoes worthy of our respect and worthy of being accepted by us. Our great object should be as a party to so conduct our public discussions, to so maintain our principles and views, that when the time of electoral struggle comes as come it must before long, we shall be able to show such a front as to save us from the defeats of the past and secure for us the triumphs of the future.

SULLIVAN

ALEXANDER MARTIN SULLIVAN, a popular Irish journalist, was born at Castletown, County Cork, Ireland, in 1830. When a young man he went to Dublin and engaged in the work of illustrating books and periodicals. In 1855 he became editor and proprietor of "The Nation," and a few years later, having indulged in bold utterances that were considered seditious, he was thrown into prison. The following year, on the 23d of November, 1867, three Irishmen named Allen, Larkin, and O'Brien, known as the "Manchester Martyrs," were executed in front of Salford jail for the murder of a police officer during the rescue of two Fenian leaders, Col. Kelly and Capt. Deasy, and for an article on the executions which appeared in the "Weekly News" Sullivan was sentenced in February, 1868, to six months' imprisonment, but was released when half the term had expired. In 1874 he was elected member of Parliament for Louth, and in 1876 was called to the London bar. In 1880 he was chosen to represent Meath. He died October 17, 1884, at Dublin, and was interred, amid impressive demonstrations of national grief, in the "O'Connell Circle" of Glasnevin cemetery. His principal publications were "The Story of Ireland," a delightful compendium of history issued in 1870 and still enjoying an immense circulation among the Irish at home and abroad; "New Ireland," a series of vivid sketches of Irish life, published in 1877; and "A Nutshell History of Ireland," which was brought out in 1883. As an orator he enjoyed great popularity, and an interesting collection of his speeches in Parliament, on the platform, and at the bar, was published in 1884.

"DISESTEEM OF THE LAW"

SPEECH DELIVERED FROM THE DOCK AT DUBLIN, FEBRUARY 20, 1868

MY LORDS AND GENTLEMEN OF THE JURY,—I rise to address you under circumstances of embarrassment which will, I hope, secure for me a little consideration and indulgence at your hands. I have to ask you at the outset, to banish any prejudice that might arise in your minds against a man who adopts the singular course—who undertakes the serious responsibility—of pleading his own defence. Such a proceeding might be thought to be dictated either by disparagement of the ordinary legal advocacy, by some poor idea of personal vanity, or by way of reflection on the tribunal before which the defence is made. My conduct is dictated by neither of these considerations or influences.

Last of all men living should I reflect upon the ability, zeal, and fidelity of the bar of Ireland, represented as it has been in my own behalf within the past two days by a man whose heart and genius are, thank God, still left to the service of our country, and represented, too, as it has been here this day by that gifted young advocate[1] the echoes of whose eloquence still resound in this court and place me at a disadvantage in immediately following him.

And assuredly I design no disrespect to this court; either to the tribunal in the abstract, or to the individual judges who preside; from one of whom I heard two days ago delivered in my own case a charge of which I shall say—though followed by a verdict which already consigns me to a prison—that it was, judging it as a whole, the fairest, the clearest, the most just and impartial ever given, to my knowledge, in a political case of this kind in Ireland, between the subject and the Crown.

No; I stand here in my own defence to-day, because long since I formed the opinion that on many grounds, in such a prosecution as this, such a course would be the most fair and most consistent for a man like me. That resolution I was, for the sake of others, induced to depart from, on Saturday last, in the first prosecution against me. When it came to be seen that I was the first to be tried out of two journalists prosecuted, it was strongly urged on me that my course, and the result of my trial, might largely affect the case of the

[1] Michael T. Crean.

other journalist to be tried after me, and that I ought to waive my individual views and feelings and have the utmost legal ability brought to bear in behalf of the case of the national press at the first point of conflict. I did so. I was defended by a bar not to be surpassed in the kingdom for ability and earnest zeal; yet the result was what I anticipated.

For I knew—so I had held all along—that in a case like this, where law and fact are left to the jury, legal ability is of no avail if the Crown comes in with its arbitrary power of molding the jury. In that case, as in this one, I openly, publicly, and distinctly announced that I, for my part, would challenge no one, whether with cause or without cause. Yet the Crown—in the face of this fact—and in a case where they knew that at least the accused had no like power of peremptory challenge—did not venture to meet me on equal footing; did not venture to abstain from their practice of absolute challenge; in fine, did not dare to trust their case to twelve men "indifferently chosen," as the constitution supposes a jury to be.

Now, gentlemen, before I enter further upon this jury question, let me say that with me this is no complaint merely against the Tories. On this, as well as on numerous other subjects, it is well known that it has been my unfortunate lot to arraign both Whigs and Tories. I say further, that I care not a jot whether the twelve men selected or permitted by the Crown to try me, or rather to convict me, be twelve of my own co-religionists and political compatriots, or twelve Protestants, Conservatives, Tories, or Orangemen.

Understand me clearly on this. My objection is not to the individuals comprising the jury. You may be all Catholics, or you may be all Protestants, for aught that affects my protest, which is against the mode by which you are selected—selected by the Crown—their choice for their own ends—and not "indifferently chosen" between the Crown and the accused. You may disappoint, or you may justify the calculations of the Crown official who has picked you out from the panel by negative or positive choice (I being silent and powerless)—you may or may not be all he supposes—the outrage on the spirit of the constitution is the same. I say by such a system of picking a jury by the Crown I am not put upon my country.

Gentlemen, from the first moment these proceedings were commenced against me, I think it will be admitted that I endeavored to meet them fairly and squarely, promptly and directly. I have never once turned to the right or to the left, but gone straight to the issue. I have from the outset declared my perfect readiness to meet the charges of the Crown. I did not care when or where they tried me. I said I would avail of no technicality—that I would object to no juror—Catholic, Protestant, or Dissenter. All I asked—all I demanded—was to be "put upon my country," in the real, fair, and full sense and spirit of the constitution. All I asked was that the Crown would keep its hand off the panel, as I would keep off mine.

I had lived fifteen years in this city; and I should have lived in vain if, among the men that knew me in that time, whatever might be their political or religious creed, I feared to have my acts, my conduct, or principles tried. It is the first and most original condition of society that a man shall subordinate his public acts to the welfare of the community, or at least acknowledge the right of those among whom his lot is cast to judge him on such an issue as this.

Freely I acknowledge that right. Readily I have responded to the call to submit to the judgment of my country the question whether, in demonstrating my sorrow and sympathy for misfortune, my admiration for fortitude, my vehement indignation against what I considered to be injustice, I had gone too far and invaded the rights of the community.

Gentlemen, I desire in all that I have to say, to keep or be kept within what is regular and seemly, and, above all, to utter nothing wanting in respect for the court; but I do say, and I do protest, that I have not got trial by jury according to the spirit and meaning of the constitution. It is as representatives of the general community, not as representatives of the Crown officials, the constitution supposes you to sit in that box. If you do not fairly represent the community, and if you are not impanelled indifferently in that sense, you are no jury in the spirit of the constitution. I care not how the Crown practice may be within the technical letter of the law; it violates the intent and meaning of the constitution, and it is not "trial by jury."

Let us suppose the scene removed, say to France. A hundred names are returned on what is called a panel, by a state functionary, for the trial of a journalist charged with sedition. The accused is powerless to remove any name from the list, unless for over-age or non-residence. But the imperial prosecutor has the arbitrary power of ordering as many as he pleases to "stand aside." By this means he puts or allows on the jury only whomsoever he pleases. He can, beforehand, select the twelve, and, by wiping out, if it suits him, the eighty-eight other names, put the twelve of his own choosing into the box. Can this be called trial by jury? Would not it be the same thing, in a more straightforward way, to let the Crown solicitor send out a policeman and collect twelve well-accredited persons of his own mind and opinion? For my own part, I would prefer this plain dealing, and consider far preferable the more rude but honest hostility of a drum-head court-martial.

Again I say, understand me well, I am objecting to the principle, the system, the practice, and not to the twelve gentlemen now before me as individuals. Personally, I am confident that being citizens of Dublin, whatever your views or opinions, you are honorable and conscientious men. You may have strong prejudices against me or my principles in public life—very likely you have; but I doubt not that though these may unconsciously tinge your judgment and influence your verdict, you will not consciously violate the obligations of your oath. And I care not whether the Crown, in permitting you to be the twelve, ordered three, or thirteen, or thirty others to "stand by"—or whether those thus arbitrarily put aside were Catholics or Protestants, Liberals, Conservatives, or Nationalists—the moment the Crown put its finger at all on the panel, in a case where the accused had no equal right, the essential character of the jury was changed, and the spirit of the constitution was outraged.

And now, what is the charge against my fellow traversers and myself? The Solicitor-General put it very pithily a while ago when he said our crime was "glorifying the cause of murder." The story of the Crown is a very terrible, a very startling one. It alleges a state of things which could hardly be supposed to exist among the Thugs of India. It depicts a population so hideously depraved that thirty thousand of them in one place, and tens of thousands in various other places, arrayed themselves publicly in procession to honor and glorify murder—to sympathize with murderers as murderers. Yes, gentlemen, that is the Crown case, or they have no case at all—that the funeral procession in Dublin on the eighth of December last was a demonstration of sympathy with murder as murder. For you will have noted that never once in this smart narration of the Crown story did Mr. Harrison allow even the faintest glimmer to appear of any other possible complexion or construction of our conduct.

Why, I could have imagined it easy for him not merely to state his own case, but to state ours too, and show where we failed, and where his own side prevailed. I could easily imagine Mr. Harrison stating our view of the matter and combating it. But he never once dared to even mention our case. His whole aim was to hide it from you and to fasten, as best such efforts of his could fasten, in your minds this one miserable refrain—"They glorified the cause of murder and assassination."

But this is no new trick. It is the old story of the maligners of our people. They call the Irish a turbulent, riotous, crime-loving, law-hating race. They are forever pointing to the unhappy fact—for, gentlemen, it is a fact—that between the Irish people and the laws under which they now live there is little or no sympathy, but the bitter estrangement and hostility of feeling or of action. Bear with me if I examine this charge, since an undertaking of it is necessary in order to judge our conduct on the eighth of December last. I am driven upon this extent of defence by the singular conduct of the Solicitor-General, who, with a temerity which he will repent, actually opened the page of Irish history, going back upon it just so far as it served his own purpose and no farther. Ah! fatal hour for my prosecutors when they appealed to history, for assuredly that is the tribunal that will vindicate the Irish people and confound those who malign them as sympathizers with assassination and glorifiers of murder——"

[The Solicitor-General.—" My lord, I must really call upon you—I deny that I ever——"

Mr. Justice Fitzgerald.—" Proceed, Mr. Sullivan."]

My lords, I took down the Solicitor-General's words. I quote them accurately as he spoke them, and he cannot get rid of them now. " Glorifiers of the cause of murder " was his designation of my fellow traversers and myself and our fifty thousand fellow mourners in the funeral procession; and before I sit down I will make him rue the utterance.

Gentlemen of the jury, if British law be held in " disesteem "—as the Crown prosecutors phrase it—here in Ireland, there is an explanation for that fact other than that supplied by the Solicitor-General,—namely, the wickedness of seditious persons like myself and the criminal sympathies of people ever ready to " glorify the cause of murder." Mournful, most mournful, is the lot of that land where the laws are not respected—nay, revered by the people. No greater curse could befall a country than to have the laws estranged from popular esteem or in antagonism with the national sentiment. Everything goes wrong under such a state of things.

The ivy will cling to the oak and the tendrils of the vine reach forth toward strong support. But more anxiously and naturally still does the human heart instinctively seek an object of reverence and love, as well as of protection and support, in law, authority, sovereignty. At least, among a virtuous people like ours, there is ever a yearning for these relations, which are and ought to be as natural between a people and their government as between the children and the parent.

I say for myself, and I firmly believe I speak the sentiments of most Irishmen when I say, that so far from experiencing satisfaction we experience pain in our present relations with the law and governing power; and we long for the day when happier relations may be restored between the laws and the national sentiment in Ireland. We Irish are no race of assassins or "glorifiers of murder." From the most remote ages, in all centuries, it has been told of our people that they were pre-eminently a justice-loving people. Two hundred and fifty years ago the predecessor of the Solicitor-General—an English Attorney-General—it may be necessary to tell the learned gentleman that his name was Sir John Davis (for historical as well as geographical knowledge seem to be rather scarce amongst the present law officers of the Crown),—held a very different opinion of them from that put forth to-day by the Solicitor-General. Sir John Davis said no people in the world loved equal justice more than the Irish, even where the decision was against themselves. That character the Irish have ever borne, and bear still.

But if you want the explanation of this "disesteem" and hostility for British law, you must trace effect to cause. It will not do to stand by the river-side near where it flows into the sea, and wonder why the water continues to run by. Not I—not my fellow traversers—not my fellow countrymen—are accountable for the antagonism between law and popular sentiment in this country. Take up the sad story where you will—yesterday, last month, last year, last century—two centuries ago, three centuries, five centuries, six centuries—and what will you find? English law presenting itself to the Irish people in a guise forbidding sympathy or respect, and evoking fear and resentment. Take it at its birth in this country. Shake your minds free of legal theories and legal fictions, and deal with facts.

This court, where I now stand, is the legal and political heir, descendant, and representative of the first law court of the Pale six or seven centuries ago. Within that Pale were a few thousand English settlers, and of them alone did the law take cognizance. The Irish nation—the millions outside the Pale—were known only as "the king's Irish enemie." The law classed them with the wild beasts of nature, whom it was lawful to slay.

Later on in our history we find the Irish near the Pale sometimes asking to be admitted to the benefits of English law, since they were forbidden to have any of their own; but their petitions were refused. Gentlemen, this was English law as it stood toward the Irish people for centuries; and wonder, if you will, that the Irish people held it in "disesteem":

"The Irish were denied the right of bringing actions in any of the English courts in Ireland for trespasses to their lands, or for assaults or batteries to their persons. Accordingly it was answer enough to the action in such a case to say that the plaintiff was an Irishman, unless he could produce a special charter giving him the rights of an Englishman. If he sought damage against an Englishman for turning him off his land, for the seduction of his daughter Nora, or for the beating of his wife Devorgil, or for the driving off of his cattle, it was a good defence to say he was a mere Irishman. And if an Englishman was indicted for manslaughter, if the man slain was an Irishman, he pleaded that the deceased was of the Irish nation and that it was no felony to kill an Irishman. For this, however, there was a fine of five marks, payable to the king; but mostly they killed us for nothing. If it happened that the man killed was a servant of an Englishman, he added to the plea of the deceased being an Irishman that if the master should ever demand damages he would be ready to satisfy him."

That was the egg of English law in Ireland. That was the seed—that was the plant—do you wonder if the tree is not now esteemed and loved? If you poison a stream at its source, will you marvel if down through all its courses the deadly element is present?

Now trace from this, its birth, English law in Ireland—trace down to this hour—and examine when or where it ever set itself to a reconciliation with the Irish people. Observe the plain relevancy of this to my case. I, and men like me, are held accountable for bringing law into hatred and contempt in Ireland; and in presenting this charge against me the Solicitor-General appealed to history.

I retort the charge on my accusers; and I will trace down to our own day the relations of hostility which English law itself established between itself and the people of Ireland. Gentlemen, for four hundred years—down to 1607—the Irish people had no existence in the eye of the law; or rather, much worse, were viewed by it as "the king's Irish enemie." But even within the Pale, how did it recommend itself to popular reverence and affection?

Ah, gentlemen, I will show that in those days, just as there have been in our own, there were executions and scaffold-scenes which invoked popular horror and resentment—though they were all "according to law," and not to be questioned unless by "seditionists." The scaffold streamed with the blood of those whom the people loved and revered—how could they love and revere the scaffold? Yet, 'twas all "according to law." The sanctuary was profaned and rifled; the priest was slain or banished—'twas all "according to law," no doubt, and to hold law in "disesteem" is "sedition."

Men were convicted and executed "according to law;" yet the people demonstrated sympathy for them and resentment against their executioners—most perversely, as a solicitor-general doubtless would say. And, indeed, the State papers contain accounts of those demonstrations, written by Crown officials, which sound very like the Solicitor-General's speech to-day. Take, for instance, the execution—"according to law"—of the "popish bishop" O'Hurley. Here is the letter of a State functionary on the subject:

"I could not before now so impart to her Majesty as to know her mind touching the same for your lordship's direction. Wherefore, she having at length resolved, I have accordingly, by her commandment, to signify her Majesty's pleasure unto you touching Hurley, which is this: That the man being so notorious and ill a subject, as appeareth by all the circumstances of his cause he is, you proceed, if it may be, to his execution by ordinary trial of him for it. Howbeit, in case you shall find the effect of his course doubtful by reason of the affection of such as shall be on his jury, and by reason of the supposal conceived by the lawyers of that country that he can hardly be found guilty for his treason committed in foreign parts against her Majesty, then her pleasure is to take a shorter way with him, by martial law. So, as you may see, it is referred to your discretion whether of those two ways your lordship will take with him, and the man being so resolute to reveal no more matter, it is thought best to have no further tortures used against him, but that you proceed forthwith to his execution in manner aforesaid. As for her Majesty's good acceptation of your careful travail in this matter of Hurley, you need nothing to doubt, and for your better assurance thereof she has commanded me to let your lordship understand that, as well as in all others the like as in the case of Hurley, she cannot but greatly allow and commend your doings."

Well, they put his feet into tin boots filled with oil and then placed him standing in the fire. Eventually they cut off his head, tore out his bowels, and cut the limbs from his body. Gentlemen, 'twas all "according to law;" and to demonstrate sympathy for him and "disesteem" of that law was "sedition." But do you wonder greatly that law of that complexion failed to secure popular sympathy and respect?

One more illustration, gentlemen; taken from a period somewhat later on. It is the execution—"according to law," gentlemen, entirely "according to law"—of another popish bishop named O'Devany. The account is that of a Crown official of the time—some most worthy predecessor of the Solicitor-General. I read it from the recently published work of the Rev. C. P. Meehan:

"On the twenty-eighth of January the bishop and priest, being arraigned at the king's bench, were each condemned of treason and adjudged to be executed the Saturday following; which day being come, a priest or two of the Pope's brood, with holy water and other holy stuffs——"

no sneer was that at all, gentlemen; no sneer at Catholic practices, for a Crown official never sneers at Catholic practices——

"were sent to sanctify the gallows whereon they were to die. About two o'clock P.M. the traitors were delivered to the sheriffs of Dublin, who placed them in a small car, which was followed by a great multitude. As the car progressed the spectators knelt down; but the bishop, sitting still like a block, would not vouchsafe them a word or turn his head aside. The multitude, however, following the car, made such a dole and lamentation after him as the heavens themselves resounded the echoes of their outcries."

Actually, a seditious funeral procession—made up of the

ancestors of those thirty thousand men, women, and children who, according to the Solicitor-General, glorified the cause of murder on the eighth of last December.

"Being come to the gallows, whither they were followed by troops of the citizens, men and women of all classes, most of the best being present, the latter kept up such a shrieking, such a howling, and such a hallooing, as, if St. Patrick himself had been gone to the gallows, could not have made greater signs of grief; but when they saw him turned from off the gallows, the raised the *whobub* with such a main cry as if the rebel had come to rifle the city. Being ready to mount the ladder, when he was pressed by some of the bystanders to speak, he repeated frequently, *Sine me quæso.* The executioner had no sooner taken off the bishop's head than the townsmen of Dublin began to flock about him, some taking up the head with pitying aspect, accompanied with sobs and sighs; some kissed it with as religious an appetite as ever they kissed the Pax; some cut away all the hair from the head, which they preserved for a relic; some others were practisers to steal the head away, but the executioner gave notice to the sheriffs. Now, when he began to quarter the body, the women thronged about him, and happy was she that could get but her handkerchief dipped in the blood of the traitor; and, the body being once dissevered in four quarters, they neither left finger nor toe, but they cut them off and carried them away; and some others that could get no holy monuments that appertained to his person, with their knives they shaved off chips from the hallowed gallows; neither could they omit the halter wherewith he was hanged, but it was rescued for holy uses. The same night after the execution a great crowd flocked about the gallows and there spent the fore part of the night in heathenish howling and performing many popish ceremonies; and after midnight, being then Candlemas Day, in the morning having their priests present in readiness, they had Mass after Mass till, daylight being come, they departed to their own houses."

There was "sympathy with sedition" for you, gentlemen. No wonder the Crown official who tells the story—some worthy predecessor of Mr. Harrison—should be horrified at such a demonstration. I will sadden you with no further illustrations of English law, but I think it will be admitted that after centuries of such law one need not wonder if the people hold it in "hatred and contempt."

With the opening of the seventeenth century, however, came a golden and glorious opportunity for ending that melancholy—that terrible state of things. In the reign of James I, English law for the first time extended to every corner of this kingdom. The Irish came into the new order of things frankly and in good faith; and if wise counsels prevailed then amongst our rulers, oh, what a blessed ending there might have been to the bloody feud of centuries. The Irish submitted to the Gaelic king to whom had come the English crown. In their eyes he was of a friendly, nay, of a kindred race. He was of a line of Gaelic kings that had often befriended Ireland. Submitting to him was not yielding to the brutal Tudor.

Yes, that was the hour, the blessed opportunity for laying the foundation of a real union between the three kingdoms; a union of equal national rights under the one crown. This was what the Irish expected; and in this sense they in that hour accepted the new dynasty. And it is remarkable that from that day to this, though England has seen bloody revolutions and violent changes of rulers, Ireland has ever held faithfully—too faithfully—to the sovereignty thus adopted. But how were they received? How were their expectations met? By persecution, proscription, and wholesale plunder, even by that miserable Stuart. His son came to the throne. Disaffection broke out in England and Scotland. . . . How did the Irish meanwhile act? They stood true to their allegiance. They took the field for the king.

What was the result? They were given over to slaughter and plunder by the brutal soldiery of the English Fenians. Their nobles and gentry were beggared and proscribed; their children were sold as white slaves to West Indian planters; and their gallant struggles for the king, their sympathy for the royalist cause, was actually denounced by the English Fenians as "sedition," "rebellion," "lawlessness," "sympathy with crime."

Ah, gentlemen, the evils thus planted in our midst will survive and work their influence; yet some men wonder that English law is held in "disesteem" in Ireland. Time went on, gentlemen; time went on. Another James sat on the throne; and again English Protestant Fenianism conspired for the overthrow of their sovereign. . . . King James came here and opened his Irish Parliament in person. Oh, who will say in that brief hour at least the Irish nation was not reconciled to the throne and laws? King, Parliament, and people were blended in one element of enthusiasm, joy, and hope, the first time for ages Ireland had known such a joy. Yes—

> "We, too, had our day—it was brief, it is ended—
> When a king dwelt among us—no strange king—but ours.
> When the shout of a people delivered ascended
> And shook the green banner that hung on yon towers.
> We saw it like leaves in the summer time shiver;
> We read the gold legend that blazoned it o'er—
> 'To-day—now or never: to-day and forever'—
> Oh, God! have we seen it to see it no more!"

Once more the Irish people bled and sacrificed for their loyalty to the throne and laws. Once more confiscation devastated the land, and the blood of the loyal and true was poured like rain. The English Fenians and the foreign emissaries triumphed, aided by the brave Protestant rebels of Ulster. King William came to the throne—a prince whose character is greatly misunderstood in Ireland: a brave, courageous soldier, and a tolerant man, could he have had his way. The Irish who had fought and lost submitted on terms, and, had law even now been just or tolerant, it was open to the revolutionary *régime* to have made the Irish good subjects.

But what took place? The penal code came, in all its horror, to fill the Irish heart with hatred and resistance. I will read for you what a Protestant historian—a man of learning and ability—who is now listening to me in this court—has written of that code. I quote "Godkin's History," published by Cassel of London:

"The eighteenth century was the era of persecution, in which the law did the work of the sword more effectually and more safely. Then was established a code framed with almost diabolical ingenuity to extinguish natural affection—to foster perfidy and hypocrisy—to petrify conscience—to perpetuate brutal ignorance—to facilitate the work of tyranny—by rendering the vices of slavery inherent and natural in the Irish character and to make Protestantism almost irredeemably odious as the monstrous incarnation of all moral perversions."

Gentlemen, in that fell spirit English law addressed itself to a dreadful purpose here in Ireland; and, mark you, that code prevailed down to our own time; down to this very generation. "Law" called on the son to sell his father; called on the flock to betray the pastor. "Law" forbade us to educate—forbade us to worship God in the faith of our fathers. "Law" made us outcasts—scourged us—trampled us, plundered us—do you marvel that, among the Irish people, law has been held in "disesteem?" Do you think this feeling arises from "sympathy with assassination or murder?" . . .

And lo! once more, for a bright, brief day, Irish national sentiment was in warm sympathy and heartfelt accord with the laws. "Eighty-two" came. Irish Protestant patriotism, backed by the hearty sympathy of the Catholic millions, raised up Ireland to a proud and glorious position; lifted our country from the ground, where she lay prostrate under the sword of England—but what do I say? This is "sedition." It has this week been decreed sedition to picture Ireland thus.[1]

Well, then, they rescued her from what I will call the loving embrace of her dear sister, Britannia, and enthroned her in her rightful place, a queen among the nations. . . . But sad is the story. Our independent national legislature was torn from us by means the iniquity of which, even among English writers, is now proclaimed and execrated. By fraud and by force that outrage on law, on right, on justice, was consummated. In speaking thus I speak "sedition." No one can write the facts of Irish history without committing sedition. . . .

Look at the lessons—unhappy lessons—taught our people by that London legislature where their own will is overborne. Concessions refused and resisted as long as they durst be withheld, and, when granted at all, granted only after passion has been aroused and the whole nation been embittered. The Irish people sought Emancipation. Their great leader was dogged at every step by hostile government proclamations and Crown prosecutions.

Coercion act over coercion act was rained upon us; yet O'Connell triumphed. But how and in what spirit was Emancipation granted? Ah, there never was a speech more preg-

---

[1] For publishing an illustration in the "Weekly News," thus picturing England's policy of coercion, Mr. Sullivan had been found guilty of seditious libel on the previous trial.

nant with mischief, with sedition, with revolutionary teaching—never words tended more to bring law and government into contempt—than the words of the English premier when he declared Emancipation must, sorely against his will, be granted, if England would not face a civil war. That was a bad lesson to teach Irishmen. Worse still was taught them. O'Connell, the great constitutional leader, a man with whom loyalty and respect for the laws was a fundamental principle of action, led the people toward further liberation—the liberation, not of a creed, but a nation.

What did he seek? To bring once more the laws and the national will into accord; to reconcile the people and the laws by restoring the constitution of queen, lords, and commons. How was he met by the government?

By the flourish of the sword; by the drawn sabre and the shotted gun in the market-place and the highway. "Law" finally grasped him as a conspirator, and a picked jury gave the Crown then, as now, such verdict as was required. The venerable apostle of constitutional doctrines was consigned to prison, while a sorrowing—ay, a maddened nation wept for him outside. Do you marvel that they held in "disesteem" the law and government that acted thus? Do you marvel that to-day in Ireland, as in every century of all those through which I have traced this state of things, the people and the law scowl upon each other? . . .

Gentlemen, the present prosecution arises directly out of what is known as the Manchester tragedy. The Solicitor-General gave you his version—his fanciful sketch—of that sad affair; but it will be my duty to give you the true facts, which differ considerably from the Crown story. The Solicitor-General began with telling us about "the broad summer's sun of the eighteenth of September." Gentlemen, it seems very clear that the summer goes far into the year for those who enjoy the sweets of office; nay, I am sure it is summer "all the year round" with the Solicitor-General while the present ministry remain in. A goodly golden harvest he and his colleagues are making in this summer of prosecutions; and they seem very well inclined to get up enough of them.

Well, gentlemen, I'm not complaining of that, but I will tell you who complain loudly—the "outs," with whom it is midwinter, while the Solicitor-General and his friends are enjoying this summer. Well, gentlemen, some time last September two prominent leaders of the Fenian movement—alleged to be so, at least—named Kelly and Deasey, were arrested in Manchester. In Manchester there is a considerable Irish population, and among them it was known those men had sympathizers. They were brought up at the police court—and now, gentlemen, pray attentively mark this. The Irish executive that morning telegraphed to the Manchester authorities a strong warning of an attempted rescue. The Manchester police had full notice—how did they treat the timely warning sent from Dublin; a warning which, if heeded, would have averted all this sad and terrible business which followed upon that day? Gentlemen, the Manchester police authorities scoffed at the warning. They derided it as a "Hirish" alarm. What! The idea of low "Hirish" hodmen or laborers rescuing prisoners from them, the valiant and the brave!

Why, gentlemen, the "Seth Bromleys" of the "force" in Manchester waxed hilarious and derisive over the idea. They would not even ask a truncheon to put to flight even a thousand of those despised "Hirish;" and so, despite specific warning from Dublin, the van containing the two Fenian leaders, guarded by eleven police officers, set out from the police office to the jail. Now, gentlemen, I charge on the stolid vaingloriousness in the first instance, and the contemptible pusillanimity in the second instance, of the Manchester police—the valiant Seth Bromleys—all that followed.

On the skirts of the city the van was attacked by some eighteen Irish youths, having three revolvers—three revolvers, gentlemen, and no more—among them. The valor of the Manchester eleven vanished at the sight of those three revolvers—some of them, it seems, loaded with blank cartridge! The Seth Bromleys took to their heels. They abandoned the van. Now, gentlemen, do not understand me to call those policemen cowards. It is hard to blame an unarmed man who runs away from a pointed revolver, which, whether loaded or unloaded, is a powerful persuasion to—— depart.

But I do say that I believe in my soul that if that had occurred here in Dublin, eleven men of our metropolitan police would have taken those three revolvers or perished in the attempt. Oh, if eleven Irish policemen had run away like that from a few poor English lads with barely three revolvers, how the press of England would yell in fierce denunciation—why, they would trample to scorn the name of Irishmen. [Applause in the court, which the officials vainly tried to silence.]

I am sorry, my lord, for the interruption; though not sorry the people should indorse my estimate of the police. Well, gentlemen, the van was abandoned by its valiant guard; but there remained inside one brave and faithful fellow, Brett by name. I am now giving you the facts as I in my conscience and soul believe they occurred—and as millions of my countrymen—ay, and thousands of Englishmen, too—solemnly believe them to have occurred, though they differ in one item widely from the Crown version. Brett refused to give up the key of the van, which he held; and the attacking party commenced various endeavors to break it open. At length one of them called out to fire a pistol into the lock, and thus burst it open. The unfortunate Brett at that moment was looking through the keyhole, endeavoring to get a view of the inexplicable scene outside, when he received the bullet, and fell dead. Gentlemen, that may be the true or it may be the mistaken version. . . .

But even suppose your view differs sincerely from mine, will you, can you, hold that I, thus conscientiously persuaded, sympathize with murder because I sympathize with men hanged for that which I contend was accident and not murder? That is exactly the issue in this case. Well, the rescued Fenian leaders got away; and then, when all was over—when the danger was passed—valor tremendous returned to the fleet-of-foot Manchester police.

Oh, but they wreaked their vengeance that night on the houses of the poor Irish in Manchester! By a savage *razzia* they soon filled the jails with our poor countrymen, seized on suspicion. And then broke forth all over England that shout of anger and passion which none of us will ever forget. The national pride had been sorely wounded; the national power had been openly and humiliatingly defied; the national fury was aroused. On all sides resounded the hoarse shout for vengeance, swift and strong. Then was seen a sight, the most shameful of its kind that this century has exhibited—a sight at thought of which Englishmen will yet hang their heads for shame, and which the English historian will chronicle with reddened cheek—those poor and humble Irish youths led into the Manchester dock in chains! In chains! . . .

For what were those chains put on untried prisoners? Gentlemen, it was at this point exactly that Irish sympathy came to the side of those prisoners. It was when we saw them thus used, and saw that, innocent or guilty, they would be immolated,—sacrificed to glut the passion of the hour,—that our feelings rose high and strong in their behalf.

Even in England there were men—noble-hearted Englishmen, for England is never without such men—who saw that if tried in the midst of this national frenzy those victims would be sacrificed; and accordingly efforts were made for a postponement of the trial. But the roar of passion carried its way. Not even till the ordinary assizes would the trial be postponed. A Special Commission was sped to do the work while Manchester jurors were in a white heat of panic, indignation, and fury. Then came the trial, which was just what might be expected. Witnesses swore ahead without compunction, and jurors believed them without hesitation. Five men arraigned together as principals—Allen, Larkin, O'Brien, Shore, and Maguire—were found guilty, and, the judge concurring in the verdict, were sentenced to death. Five men—not three men, gentlemen—five men in the one verdict, not five separate verdicts. Five men by the same evidence and the same jury in the same verdict. Was that a just verdict? The case of the Crown here to-day is that it was—that it is "sedition" to impeach that verdict. . . .

The very evening those men were sentenced, thirty newspaper reporters sent the Home Secretary a petition protesting that—the evidence of the witnesses and the verdict of the jury notwithstanding—there was at least one innocent man thus marked for execution. The government felt that the reporters were right and the jurors wrong. They pardoned Maguire as an innocent man,—that same Maguire whose legal conviction is here put in as evidence that he and four others were truly murderers, to sympathize with whom is to commit sedition—nay, "to glorify the cause of murder." . . .

But now arose in redoubled fury the savage cry for blood. In vain good men, noble and humane men, in England tried to save the national honor by breasting this horrible outburst of passion. They were overborne. Petitioners for mercy were mobbed and hooted in the streets. We saw all this—we saw all this; and think you it did not sink into our hearts? Fancy if you can our feelings when we heard that yet another man out of five was respited—ah, he was an American, gentlemen—an American, not an Irishman—but that the three Irishmen, Allen, Larkin, and O'Brien, were to die—were to be put to death on a verdict and on evidence that would not hang a dog in England!

We refused to the last to credit it; and, thus incredulous, deemed it idle to make any effort to save their lives. But it was true; it was deadly true. And then, gentlemen, the doomed three appeared in a new character. Then they rose into the dignity and heroism of martyrs. The manner in which they bore themselves through the dreadful ordeal ennobled them forever. It was then we all learned to love and revere them as patriots and Christians. . . .

Yes; in that hour they told us they were innocent, but were ready to die; and we believed them. We believe them still. Aye, do we! They did not go to meet their God with a falsehood on their lips. On that night before their execution, oh, what a scene! What a picture did England present at the foot of the Manchester scaffold! The brutal populace thronged thither in tens of thousands. They danced; they sang; they blasphemed; they chorused "Rule Britannia," and "God Save the Queen," by way of taunt and defiance of the men whose death-agonies they had come to see!

Their shouts and brutal cries disturbed the doomed victims inside the prison, as in their cells they prepared in prayer and meditation to meet their Creator and their God. Twice the police had to remove the crowd from around that wing of the prison, so that our poor brothers might in peace go through their last preparations for eternity, undisturbed by the yells of the multitude outside.

Oh, gentlemen, gentlemen—that scene! That scene in the gray cold morning, when those innocent men were led out to die—to die an ignominious death before that wolfish mob! With blood on fire—with bursting hearts—we read the dreadful story here in Ireland. We knew that these men would never have been thus sacrificed had not their offence been political, and had it not been that in their own way they represented the old struggle of the Irish race. . . .

All this we felt, yet we were silent till we heard the press that had hounded those men to death falsely declaring that our silence was acquiescence in the deed that consigned them to murderers' graves. Of this I have personal knowledge, that, here in Dublin at least, nothing was done or intended until the "Evening Mail" declared that popular feeling, which had ample time to declare itself, if it felt otherwise, quite recognized the justice of the execution.

Then we resolved to make answer. Then Ireland made answer. For what monarch, the loftiest in the world, would such demonstrations be made, the voluntary offerings of a people's grief! Think you it was "sympathy for murder" called us forth, or caused the priests of the Catholic Church to drape their churches? It is a libel to utter the base charge.

No, no! With the acts of those men at that rescue we had nought to say. Of their innocence of murder we were convinced. Their patriotic feelings, their religious devotion, we saw proved in the noble, the edifying manner of their death. We believed them to have been unjustly sacrificed in a moment of national passion; and we resolved to rescue their memory from the foul stains of their maligners and make it a proud one forever with Irishmen.

Sympathy with murder, indeed! What I am about to say will be believed; for I think I have shown no fear of consequences in standing by my acts and principles—I say for myself, and for the priests and people of Ireland, who are affected by this case, that sooner would we burn our right hands to cinders than to express, directly or indirectly, sympathy with murder; and that our sympathy for Allen, Larkin, and O'Brien is based upon the conviction that they were innocent of any such crime. . . .

Now, gentlemen, judge ye me on this whole case; for I have done. I have spoken at great length, but I plead not merely my own cause, but the cause of my country. For myself, I care little. I stand before you here with the manacles, I might say, on my hands. Already a prison cell awaits me in Kilmainham. My doom, in any event, is sealed. Already a conviction has been obtained against me for my opinions. . . .

Sedition, in a rightly ordered community, is indeed a crime. But who is it that challenges me? Who is it that demands my loyalty? Who is it that calls out to me, "Oh, ingrate son, where is the filial affection, the respect, the obedience, the support, that is my due? Unnatural, seditious, and rebellious child, a dungeon shall punish your crime!"

I look in the face of my accuser, who thus holds me to the duty of a son. I turn to see if there I can recognize the features of that mother whom indeed I love, my own dear Ireland. I look into that accusing face, and there I see a scowl and not a smile. I miss the soft, fond voice, the tender clasp, the loving word. I look upon the hands reached out to grasp me—to punish me; and lo, great stains, blood-red, upon those hands; and my sad heart tells me it is the blood of my widowed mother, Ireland. Then I answer to my accusers—"You have no claim on me—on my love, my duty, my allegiance. You are not my mother. You sit indeed in the place where she should reign. You wear the regal garments torn from her limbs, while she now sits in the dust, uncrowned and overthrown, and bleeding from many a wound. But my heart is with her still. Her claim alone is recognized by me. She still commands my love, my duty, my allegiance; and whatever the penalty may be, be it prison chains, be it exile or death, to her I will be true."

But, gentlemen of the jury, what is that Irish nation to which my allegiance turns? Do I thereby mean a party, or a class, or creed? Do I mean only those who think and feel as I do on public questions? Oh, no. It is the whole people of this land—the nobles, the peasants, the clergy, the merchants, the gentry, the traders, the professions—the Catholic, the Protestant, the Dissenter. Yes. I am loyal to all that a good and patriotic citizen should be loyal to; I am ready, not merely to obey, but to support with heartfelt allegiance, the constitution of my own country—the Queen as Queen of Ireland, and the free Parliament of Ireland, once more constituted in our national senate-house in College Green.

And reconstituted once more it will be. In that hour the laws will again be reconciled with national feeling and popular reverence. In that hour there will be no more disesteem, or hatred, or contempt for the laws; for, howsoever a people may dislike and resent laws imposed upon them against their will by a subjugating power, no nation disesteems the laws of its own making. That day, that blessed day, of peace and reconciliation, and joy and liberty, I hope to see. And when it comes, as come it will, in that hour it will be remembered for me that I stood here to face the trying ordeal, ready to suffer for my country—walking with bared feet over red-hot ploughshares, like the victims of old. Yes; in that day it will be remembered for me, though a prison awaits me now, that I was one of those journalists of the people who, through constant sacrifice and self-immolation, fought the battle of the people and won every vestige of liberty remaining in the land.

SALISBURY

ROBERT ARTHUR TALBOT GASCOYNE CECIL, Marquis of Salisbury, a distinguished English statesman, was born at Hatfield, Hertfordshire, February 10, 1830, and educated at Eton and Christ Church College, Oxford. He entered Parliament for Stamford in 1853 as Lord Robert Cecil, and was soon known as one of the ablest speakers in the House of Commons on the Conservative side. On the death of his elder brother in 1865 he assumed the title of Viscount Cranbourne. He was secretary of state for India, 1866-67, but resigned from the cabinet on account of his unwillingness to support the Reform Bill upon which the other ministers were agreed. By the death of his father in 1868 he succeeded to the title of Marquis of Salisbury and took his seat in the House of Lords. In November of the next year he followed Lord Derby as chancellor of the University of Oxford, and on the return of Disraeli to the premiership in February, 1874, he again became secretary of state. He was appointed special ambassador to Turkey in November, 1876, and in 1878 received the appointment of minister of foreign affairs. Since the death of Disraeli in 1881 Salisbury has been the recognized leader of the Conservatives. From June to November, 1885, he was prime minister and after a brief Liberal administration was again at the helm as premier in 1886, remaining such until 1892. His conduct of affairs was marked by an aggressive foreign policy and repression in Ireland, the ministry finally succumbing on the Home Rule question. In 1895 the Marquis became premier for the third time, the most important event occurring within his latest administration being the war with the Boer republics in South Africa. Salisbury is an able and impressive, but not persuasive, orator, and the occurrence of an injudicious phrase here and there sometimes destroys the effect which his speech was desired to produce. He is an enthusiast in scientific matters and his inaugural address before the British Association at Oxford in 1894 attracted general attention for its arraignment of Darwinism.

TAMPERING WITH THE CONSTITUTION

SPEECH DELIVERED IN 1875 TO THE MIDDLESEX CONSERVATIVE ASSOCIATION

MY LORD MAYOR, LADIES AND GENTLEMEN, — I listened to the resolutions which were read one after another from the various deputations which constitute this very remarkable, significant, and representative meeting, and I could not help wondering why it was that the truths which seemed to be so obvious had not made their impression upon her Majesty's government. Why, having this great work to do, did they deliberately depart from the practice of all which had gone before them and raise up gratuitous difficulties in their way?

It was not from any ignorance on their part of the importance of redistribution as an integral portion of reform. I need only quote that sentence of Mr. Bright's which has been quoted again and again, but which I should like to see prefixed as a sort of text to every conservative sermon.

"Repudiate without mercy any bill that any government whatever may introduce, whatever its seeming concessions may be, if it does not redistribute the seats that are obtained from the extinction of small boroughs amongst the large towns."

But their knowledge was not such ancient history as that. Mr. Bright seems to imagine that he has entirely explained away his utterance given publicly in 1859 by reciting a private note which he says he wrote to Lord Beaconsfield in 1867, and he concludes in the most self-satisfied way that he has entirely explained his previous declaration.

But his colleague on the platform was not less conscious of the necessity of a redistribution of seats. Only on Saturday Lord Hartington is reported to have said, "We admit the inconvenience which will arise if a dissolution should take place."

If a dissolution should take place, as if Mr. Chamberlain and the wire-pullers were not perfectly resolved on that matter!

"We admit the inconvenience which will arise if any dissolution should take place with the extended numbers of the existing constituencies. We know that that will be no fair representation of the people."

Well, at least Lord Hartington knew perfectly well what he was about. Then, what was the motive which induced them to undertake this eccentric and abnormal plan of reform? Well, we had some difficulty in measuring it at first. We were told that it was the extraordinary block in the House of Commons, as if blocks in the House of Commons had never existed before the year 1884.

But, fortunately, as the controversy went on candor increased. It is one of the advantages of the thorough discussion which I hope this question will receive between this and November that all false pretences and all hollow pretexts will be dissipated, and the cause which logically and constitutionally is in the right will be triumphantly established.

You know that Mr. Gladstone at the Foreign Office told us that it was necessary that some pressure should be applied to the House of Commons, that he could not hope to pass his Redistribution Bill unless it was put before them in such a manner that they were to understand that if they had no Redistribution Bill they should have to go to the existing constituencies with the new franchise.

That speech of Mr. Gladstone's at the Foreign Office has been apologized for and slurred over. People intimate that he was not exactly possessed of his usual presence of mind when he made it, and that indeed must have been the case, or otherwise how could he deliberately impute to me words which I never uttered, and not only impute them, but make them the basis of a long, and elaborate, and most injurious indictment? He could not have made that statement if his memory had been in its usual condition.

But now Lord Hartington comes forward and explains to us that it was not merely some spontaneous exuberance of

Mr. Gladstone's indignation that produced this explanation. It was the deliberate purpose of the government to establish a machine for controlling and coercing the judgment of the House of Commons and of the House of Lords. Lord Hartington on Saturday said,

"We know that the passing of any really rational or fair Redistribution Bill is an impossibility unless Parliament and all shades of political opinion are acting under some pressure and compulsion, and that compulsion to the House of Commons and to the House of Lords was to be applied by the creature of Parliament, the prime minister of the day."

Such a pretension has never before been made in our history. The most encroaching monarchs have never made it. It has never been pretended that any man, however high his pretensions and great his authority, should have the power given to him of applying pressure and compulsion to Parliament in the discharge of its legislative duties. Well, it is a tremendous claim.

Let us look what grounds have we for believing that such a power, so unexampled, so without parallel in English history, will be exercised with equity and with justice. Mr. Gladstone — I do not wish to use any harsh language in the matter, but this lies on the surface of current history — Mr. Gladstone has been pre-eminent among statesmen for the rigor with which he has used a victory when he has obtained it; for the determination with which he has pressed to the utmost limit any advantage he has obtained over those opposed to him.

It is not, therefore, to his hands that we should like to trust ourselves, without condition and without defence. And if we look to his past conduct, to the past conduct of the Liberal party, or to the professions which they now put forward in respect to this very question of redistribution, it does not exalt our confidence.

I should like to remind you of a little incident in the last redistribution that took place — the redistribution of 1868 — which throws a flood of light on Mr. Bright's views of justice in this matter. There is a certain suburb of Birmingham which is named Aston. It runs in the counties of North Warwickshire and East Worcestershire. At the last redistribution the commissioners — impartially selected men — recommended that this, which was a suburb of Birmingham, and was in continuity with it, and was simply part of the town, should be made part of the borough of Birmingham.

The matter came before the House of Commons. The Liberal party, though the Opposition, were in a majority. Distinctly because this suburb of Aston might have the effect of influencing in the direction which he wished the counties of North Warwickshire and East Worcestershire, distinctly because it belonged to a community in which the ideas that he admired prevailed, Mr. Bright insisted that the recommendation of the commissioners should be discarded, and that Aston — though it was really part of Birmingham — should be thrown into North Warwickshire and East Worcestershire, for the purpose of controlling, by a population which he hoped was devoted to him and imbued with his ideas, a population that he had reason to think was adverse to him. He was supported by the Liberal party, and a majority reversed the decision of the commissioners.

Now, we do not often have a case which shows the precise spirit in which the leading statesman of the dominant party will approach a question of that kind; but that particular case of Aston might be multiplied a hundred times. It involves the whole question of the separation of interests in this coun-

incomplete any measure of reform is without it, I should like to compare the representation of the communities represented in this room with the representation of that favored county where Mr. Gladstone lives to which I have just referred — the principality of Wales.

Whereas the principality represents some 1,400,000 inhabitants, we in this room represent some 5,000,000. Is it possible with that fact before you, to go forward with a Reform Bill that shall not include redistribution? Is it possible that, knowing that Mr. Gladstone has laid down a principle that will uplift Wales and depress the metropolis, we should feel confidence and allow him to draw up his own Redistribution Bill? And we have heard something of blank checks; but this is not merely a blank check — this is a blank disposal of all that we possess for all time, given into the hands of a man who, by the previous conduct of his party and by his own previous utterances, has given us every reason to mistrust him.

I meet with the statement that it is very unconstitutional for the House of Lords to indicate when her Majesty's government may in their wisdom please to dissolve Parliament. Well, I should have said, as a matter of constitutional law, that the person who dissolves Parliament is her Majesty the Queen, and that that is one of the few cases in which necessarily, by the hypothesis of the minister being in issue, or being supposed to be in issue with the people, it is precisely one of the cases in which the Sovereign cannot abandon her will absolutely to the guidance of her advisers.

But now there is the question, how far it is legitimate for the House of Lords to press for a dissolution. Well, I think that any such claim on the part of the House of Lords simply would not be justified by the constitution. But the House of Lords has a right to say this — "We do not approve of the measure you bring before us. If you like to accept its rejection, well and good; if you object to its rejection your remedy is to appeal to the people." And we do not think that under the constitution there is any other remedy than that.

But with respect to the right, not only in the House of Lords but in all of us, of pressing for a dissolution of Parliament, I admit that if it was to be done in respect to ordinary measures of controversy, or the ordinary legislation on which we have to decide, it would be matter of considerable inconvenience if we were to interfere with the discretion which is ordinarily reposed in the advisers of the crown. But the fallacy, the fundamental fallacy, of all the reasonings of ministerial arguers upon this point is that they ignore the fact that it is not a common question of legislation, it is a vital question, it is a question of the revision of the constitution. And in neither of the other popularly governed countries is the revision of the constitution treated even so lightly as we desire and are content to treat it.

Look at what they do in France. In France they have, curiously enough, the contemporaneous phenomenon of a Liberal minister who is trying to alter the constitution of the country in the hopes that it may affect agreeably the constitution of the next assembly that he has to meet. I presume that that is a characeristic of Liberal ministers all over the world. That whenever they don't know how to get a majority in any other way they try to revise the constitution; but it cannot be done by a simple bill in France as it can in England. There is an elaborate process of revision. A congress must be called under certain guarantees, and guarantees of a tolerably stringent character. It is not treated in an ordinary manner, and the very fullest recognition is given to the right of the second Chamber to make its own opinions heard and felt in the conduct of that revision.

Well, but we pass from France, with which we have only a certain point of analogy, and go to our kith and kin on the other side of the Atlantic, who, full of English traditions, but cut off by circumstances from monarchy, set up a republic according to their own judgment for themselves. What did they do? They surrounded the question of the revision of the constitution with the most minute and elaborate guarantees. It can only be proposed, in the first instance, by a two thirds majority in both of the Houses of the legislature, and when it has been proposed that is not sufficient. It has to be submitted to each State of the country, and passed there by three fourths of the States.

That is the amount of security which the Anglo-Saxon mind, by circumstances cast loose from tradition, has judged to be absolutely necessary in the conduct of a popular government. And now, because the House of Lords interposes, and says that by a vote of a House of Commons, in the fifth year of its existence, passed at the bidding of a dictatorial minister — and thrown into an unprecedented form — because the House of Lords demurs to such a measure passing into law without the people having been consulted, you are told that they have been guilty of some strange and intolerable arrogance.

Just consider for a moment what the authority of the House of Commons is. I wish to speak of the House of Commons with the highest respect, and there is no doubt that, for ordinary purposes, dealing with ordinary bills, its authority is full and unquestioned to the term of its natural career; but when it lays hands upon the constitution for the purpose of revising it, a very different state of things arises, and then you cannot turn away your attention from the fact that it is a House of Commons on the decline — that it has already existed longer than the average of Parliaments which have been since the Reform Bill of 1832 — the average is four years and two months, and we have passed that — and that its action is discredited and disavowed by every election that takes place in those constituencies which this bill is intended to affect.

You tell me that this bill has been passed by the representatives of the people. In a legal sense they are the representatives of the people — in a legal sense every act of Parliament is submitted to the unfettered will of the Sovereign, the House of Lords, and the House of Commons; but if you pass from a legal to an actual sense they are not the representatives of the people, they are the representatives of what the people were five years ago. And between that day and this there is an absolute gulf, so completely has the whole surface of the political world changed, so entirely different are all the objects of political controversy and interest, so utterly have passed away the burning questions upon which the last election was decided.

Now Mr. Bright tries to dispose of the House of Lords by saying that it is a Tory caucus. He tries to give you the impression that it was a Tory caucus under Lord Aberdeen and Lord Palmertson, for he mentions their names. But my memory, I think, is as fresh as Mr. Bright's. I can perfectly remember what took place in the House of Lords, for instance. We will not deal with Lord Aberdeen's government. We will deal with Lord Palmerston's. There were two great questions which shook the ministry and closely divided the House of Commons. They were two of the most burning questions of the day. They were the questions of the Chinese war and the Danish war.

The decision of one of them forced Lord Palmerston to dissolve. The decision of the other in his favor was regarded as the great victory of his administration. How did the House of Lords, this Tory caucus, vote? On both occasions the lords assembled at Westminster voted in favor of Lord Palmerston.

The truth is, that until Mr. Gladstone became a leading figure — became the leader of the Liberal party — there was no talk about this permanent majority in the House of Lords, and my belief is that if ever Mr. Gladstone ceases to be the leader of the Liberal party there will then be no longer that decided Tory majority in the House of Lords.

For whatever else you may say about his legislation, at least there can be no doubt of this, that he has applied principles to the rights of property of his fellow subjects which we never heard of in this England of ours before. Whether they were right or wrong, they were absolutely new, and they seemed to lead not only to gross injustice in the present, but to an illimitable horizon of spoliation in the future, and therefore it is that in the legislative body which has special charge of those interests and those rights, and to watch over the conservance and the protection of those rights of our fellow citizens — that in them that alarm at Mr. Gladstone's proceedings has spread and increased with every year.

I told you when Lord Palmerston was in office he was able on great critical questions to obtain a majority in the House of Lords. Since that time fifty-one Liberal peers have been created against only thirty-one Conservatives, and yet the normal majority is between fifty and seventy against the government in the House of Lords. Is it surprising that the lords have felt something of that apprehension which has spread to every class and interest and industry in this country?

Look around, where will you find men who count on a secure and certain future in the history of trade? Everywhere you will hear of industry languishing, of commerce unable to find profitable channels, of the hearts of men of business failing them for fear, of banks refusing to receive money on deposit because they do not know where to invest it — every sign of the presence over the community of a great apprehension, of the disappearance of that old security which made property in England seem as solid as the rocks upon which England herself was founded. That time has passed away. Men will not invest as they formerly would; men are not employed as they formerly were; capitalists do not gain profit; the working classes are ceasing in many places to gain livelihoods. Is it surprising that this apprehension, which has reached so many classes of their countrymen, should deeply infect the peers as well, and that the shadow of Mr. Gladstone's formidable individuality should be thrown alike upon the judgment and the apprehensions of English peers as upon the industry, the commerce, and the labor upon which this country depends?

Well, Mr. Bright tells us that he does not go into the question whether the House of Lords has done right or wrong; he seems to abuse the House of Lords, and to desire to prove that they are a very disreputable body of men, who hold a title which he wishes to discredit. But I venture to say, and I submit it to the judgment of those who wish to consider this controversy impartially, that the merits of the House of Lords have nothing whatever to do with the case. The question is, not what the House of Lords are, or how they got there, but whether they did right or wrong.

It would be no excuse for them if they had not done their duty, to say they have some doubts about the validity of their title to be there. That distinguished assembly over which my right honorable friend the Lord Mayor presides in the city of London, have at least this in common with the House of Lords, that they have been doomed by a distinguished statesman. The decree has gone forth from the lips of Sir William Harcourt that the one shall cease to exist as the decree has gone forth from the lips of Mr. Bright that the House of Lords shall cease to exist; and I think it is quite possible that both assemblies will continue to exist to do useful work for a very long time. If the corporation were to refuse to assemble to-morrow and to perform their ordinary duties, would it be any excuse for them to say, "Oh, we are condemned by Sir William Harcourt, or by any other statesman, and it is perfectly impossible that we can go on performing our duties."

Well, if the House of Lords had not performed what, I think, I have shown to you to be the elementary duty of a second Chamber, to prevent the first Chamber from using its power to filch a perpetuity of political predominance for one party in the state, if the House of Lords had refused to do its duty, on the ground that some Radicals thought that the country had an objection to the principles on which it is formed, would it not have been guilty of the most cowardly and craven action that you can positively conceive? It is a question which we shall be ready to argue when the time comes — the question as to the constitution of the second Chamber, and what is the best way in which it shall be upheld, and whatever its present theoretical difficulties, you will not in practice much improve upon the House of Lords.

That has nothing to do with the question we have in hand. The question is, if the House of Lords does its duty, could it have acted otherwise than we have done? What is it after all that we have done? We have seen this strange and sinister spectacle of a minister claiming to resist by the compulsion of the House of Commons the action of the House of Lords. We have seen him applying that principle, not to ordinary principles of legislation, but to the most vital matter in which a deliberative assembly can be engaged — the reform of the constitution. We have seen him tampering with the very springs of political power. We have seen him do that in a manner unexampled and without precedent, and the House of Lords said to him, "You shall not exercise this unprecedented power; you shall not claim this right of compulsion; you shall not model the constitution according to your will and the interests of the dominant party of the day."

We are prepared to resist your power unless you will be able to assure us and prove to us that the people by whom alone you exist, by whose mandate you hold power, sanctions this strange exercise of power, and we utterly repudiate the idea that in assuming that attitude we shall be misconstrued by our countrymen.

I am sure that they will feel that in this, as in so many other cases, liberty has had to fear chiefly from the hands of its professed friends. We have been maintaining the essential conditions on which popular government reposes, and we have been upholding the true and ancient principles of English liberty.

THE EGYPTIAN QUESTION

DELIVERED AT EDINBURGH IN NOVEMBER, 1882

WITH regard to the campaign, the first thing that strikes you when you look at it as a whole is wonder that Arabi Pasha, with his force and with his opportunities, should have defied as he did the power of such a country as Great Britain. How is that mystery to be solved? If any nation suffers itself to get into war with a weaker nation which is sufficiently civilized to know the great difference that exists between them, you may depend upon it that there is something in the conduct of that stronger nation which induces the weaker nation to believe that the larger country will never exert its strength.

We have heard a great deal about prestige. I detest the word. It does not really express what we mean. I should rather say "military credit." Military credit stands in precisely the same position as financial credit. The use of it is to represent a military power, and to effect the objects of a military power without the necessity of a recourse to arms. You know that the man possessed of great financial credit can perform great operations by the mere knowledge of the wealth of which he is master, and that it is not necessary to sell him up, and ascertain if he can pay twenty shillings in the pound, in order to have the benefit of all the wealth he can command.

It is the same with a military nation that is careful to preserve its military credit. If it does so, it may, without shedding one drop of blood or incurring one penny of expenditure, effect all the objects which, without that military credit, can only result in much waste of blood and treasure.

Now, we were in the position of a financial operator who had raised his own credit by doubtful and dangerous operations. We had squandered our military credit at Majuba Hill, where we took up the position of a power that was willing to submit to any insult that might be placed upon it. We had proclaimed to the world that we were not ready to fight for our military renown, and the tradition of our ancestors was lost to us.

It was a false proclamation, a proclamation that the ministry had no mandate from the nation to make, and which the nation at the first opportunity forced them to disavow. But the disavowal has cost blood and treasure which, if they had been more careful of the reputation of this country, need never have been expended. Three years ago those who maintained such doctrines and insisted on the necessity of the maintenance of your military credit as one of the most precious inheritances of the nation, were denounced as "Jingoes!"

But these Jingoes are justified now. They have her Majesty's government for converts. They have forced her Majesty's government to demonstrate by action that which is their principal contention, that if you suffer military credit to be obscured the fault must be wiped out in blood.

I feel how inadequate I am to deal with a question like this in a place such as this. I know it has been occupied by a much greater artist; and I feel that there has been a loss to the world of splendid specimens of political denunciation, because the misdeeds of the ministry of 1882 are, unfortunately, not subject to the criticism of the orator of

1880. What magnificent lessons, what splendid periods of eloquence we have lost!

Just think that if Mr. Gladstone, when the spirit of 1880 was upon him, could have had to deal with the case of a ministry professing the deepest respect for the concert of Europe, and the deepest anxiety to obey its will — a ministry which, with these professions on its lips, assembled a conference and kept it for months in vain debate, and, under cover of its discussions, prepared armaments, asked for leave to invade a country, and then, when a refusal was given and the armaments were ready, calmly showed the conference to the door, and took, in despite of Europe's will, the country which they had asked the leave of Europe to take — if the orator of 1880 had had such a theme to dwell upon, what would he have said of disingenuousness and subtlety?

Or, take another case: supposing that unequalled orator had had before him the case of a government who sent a large fleet into a port where they had no international right to go, and when that fleet was there had demanded that certain arrangements should be made on land which they had no international right to demand, and when these demands were not satisfied had forthwith enforced that by the bombardment of a great commercial port, would you not have heard about political brigandage? What sermons you would have had to listen to with respect to the equality of all nations, of the weakest and the strongest, before the law of Europe; what denunciations would you not have heard of those who could for the sake of British interests expose such a city to such a catastrophe, and carry fire and sword among a defenceless people!

That great artist drew a picture of Sir Frederick Roberts. I cannot help wishing that he had to draw a portrait of Sir

Beauchamp Seymour; but allow me to say in passing that, if my poor pencil could be employed, it would be drawn in nothing but the most flattering colors.

I think if we can imagine anything so impossible as the orator of 1880 having to describe and comment on the events of 1882, that he would have noticed one of the most remarkable coincidences which the history of this country furnishes. It is a very curious fact that we have only had one member of the Society of Friends — commonly called on the Statute-book "Quakers" — so that I may use the name without offence — in the Cabinet, we have only had one Quaker; and only once in the history of the world, so far at least as this hemisphere is concerned, if I am not mistaken, has a great commercial city of the first class been subject to bombardment.

It is a remarkable fact that when the order was given to bombard that commercial city that Quaker was in the Cabinet. At any rate, grave as these events have been, I think they will furnish some good fruit at least for the future. I hope we have taken a new departure in Liberal politics. I trust that for the future any minister who cares about British interests, and thinks it right to go to war in their defence, will not be subject to denunciation on the part of the Liberal party for doing so.

I am quite aware British interests were treated with scant respect in 1880. I am quite aware Mr. Gladstone denounced as monstrous the idea that we could claim to control a country simply because it lay on our route to India. But if ever there was a war — I do not know what to call it — I believe it was not a war; but if ever there were sanguinary operations undertaken for the sake of British interests, undoubtedly these recent operations in Egypt have deserved the character. . . .

After this precedent it will be impossible for any Liberal government to limit, as they have done in the past, the rights of national self-defence. With respect to the end of that war we have yet to wait. We do not know what the present negotiations may bring forth. We must suspend our judgment until we see what the result will be. I confess that I should be inclined to look on all these circumstances to which I have alluded with a very indulgent eye if the result of the negotiations which are pending should be to extend the strength, the power, and the predominant influence of Great Britain, for I am old-fashioned enough to believe in that empire and believe in its greatness.

I believe that wherever it has been extended it has conferred unnumbered benefits upon those who have been brought within its sway, and that the extension of the empire, so far from being the desire of selfishness or acquisitiveness, as it has been represented to be — deserving to be compared to acts of plunder in private life — is in reality a desire not only to extend the commerce and to strengthen the power of the government here at home, but to give to others those blessings of freedom and order which we have always prized among ourselves.

Let us therefore in the negotiations which are before us not be ashamed of our empire. We are now the predominant power in Egypt. The valor of our troops has made us so. Let us observe with rigid fidelity every engagement we have made with the amiable and respectable prince who rules in Egypt; but as regards the other powers of Europe, let us follow our position to its logical result. We are the predominant power. Why should we cease to be so? Why should we allow diplomacy to fritter away what the valor of our soldiers has won?

A BURNING QUESTION

DELIVERED DURING DEBATE ON THE QUEEN'S SPEECH IN THE HOUSE OF LORDS, FEBRUARY 15, 1883

We learn from the speech that her Majesty's government have suppressed with rapidity and completeness a formidable rebellion in Egypt. Then we are told that "the withdrawal of the British troops is proceeding as expeditiously as a prudent consideration of the circumstances will admit."

But the great anxiety of the world is to know whether the British troops are to be withdrawn altogether, and when; and upon neither of those questions does the speech give us the slightest hint as to the intentions of her Majesty's government. The government are able to say that they have submitted to the friendly consideration of the powers the mysterious arrangement by which the stability of the Khedive and the prosperity and happiness of the Egyptian people are to be secured. But we have not a hint that any one of those powers has expressed its approval of the arrangement proposed. . . . Hitherto we have spoken of the announcements of the Queen's speech. If the present practice is followed we shall have to drop the phrase and speak of the innuendoes of the Queen's speech. . . . The policy of dealing by innuendoes with unimportant measures might be passed over without remark; but with respect to the burning questions of the day, I cannot help thinking that it is singularly misplaced. First take Egypt.

With respect to that country we have undoubtedly, since Parliament met last year, witnessed a great transformation scene. For the first six months the policy of the government was instinct with the doctrines connected with the name of that distinguished gentleman, Mr. Bright, who has left the government. For the last six months they have returned to an earlier and a sounder model; but their repentance does not entirely wash away their sin.

It does not efface the effects of their temporary concession to the policy of weakness, vacillation, and self-effacement. The result of their action, or want of action at the proper time, has been that the mechanism has been destroyed by which the results they now look for should be attained. Had they interfered in time, the Khedive's government would have remained upright, and the future conduct of Egypt might not have been difficult. But all the powers that the Khedive's government possessed of itself have been swept away, and for the future all the power of Egypt must be derived from the protective influence of the British government. . . . But if we rightly understand the policy of her Majesty's government — at present we have it only from non-official sources — they intend to rely for the future predominance of England in Egypt only on the prestige derived from the success of the arms of my noble and gallant friend [Lord Wolseley].

I do not dispute the greatness of that prestige. I do not dispute that our army has dealt a good lesson to Egypt and the eastern world, but the recollection of the power of it will speedily fade away. Remember this, that you failed before in your endeavor to maintain the government of Egypt, whether by your own fault or not, though you had not only your own military prestige, proved in every quarter of the world, to sustain you, but the prestige of France as well. . . .

The time is come when it would be of great diplomatic

importance, and of great assistance to the conduct of England in the future, that her position with respect to Egypt should be fully and rigidly defined. We hear from one member of the government that the troops are not to stay in Egypt. We hear from another member that they are to stay until certain objects are achieved, which we know cannot be achieved at an early period. We hear from Mr. Chamberlain that, considering the interests it has, it is impossible for England to look with apathy on anarchy in Egypt; and from Mr. Courtney we hear an inspired panegyric on anarchy, which he appears to regard as the highest blessing that can be bestowed upon a nation. That seems to show that you have no definite policy; and those who look forward to the time when their own influence and power will be restored again, are encouraged to make their preparations for that period, and to keep alive every source of discontent and disturbance that may be at their command.

SPEECH ON THE ABANDONMENT OF GENERAL GORDON

DELIVERED FEBRUARY 26, 1885

[The words of Lord Salisbury's motion of censure were, "That this House, having taken into consideration the statements that have been made on behalf of her Majesty's government, is of opinion that the deplorable failure of the Soudan expedition to obtain its object has been due to the undecided councils of the government and to the culpable delay attending the commencement of operations; that the policy of abandoning the whole of the Soudan after the conclusion of military operations will be dangerous to Egypt and inconsistent with the interests of the empire."]

THE motion which I have the honor to lay before your lordships has a double aspect — it passes judgment on the past, and expresses an opinion with regard to the policy of the future. Some people receive with considerable impatience the idea that, at the present crisis of our country's destiny, we should examine into the past, and spend our time in judging of that which cannot be recalled.

But I think that such objections are unreasonable. We depend in one of the greatest crises through which our country has ever passed on the wisdom and decision of those who guide our counsels, and we can only judge of what dependence is rightly to be placed by examining their conduct in the past, and seeing whether what they have done justifies us in continuing that confidence in the difficulties which are to come.

Now, whatever else may be said of the conduct of her Majesty's government, I think those who examine it carefully will find that it follows a certain rule and system, and that in that sense, if in no other, it is consistent. Their conduct at the beginning of the Egyptian affair has been analogous to their conduct at the end; throughout there has been an unwillingness to come to any requisite decision till the last moment.

There has been an absolute terror of fixing upon any settled course, and the result has been that, when the time came that external pressure forced a decision on some definite course, the moment for satisfactory action had already passed, and the measures that were taken were taken in haste, with little preparation, and often with little fitness for the emergencies with which they had to cope. The conduct of the government has been an alternation of periods of slumber and periods of rush. The rush, however vehement, has been too unprepared and too unintelligent to repair the damage which the period of slumber has effected.

I do not wish to go far back into the Egyptian question, but it is necessary to point out the uniformity of the character and conduct of the government. The first commencement of our trouble was the height to which Arabi's rebellion was allowed to go. The government knew very well the danger of Arabi while he was yet a small man and had little influence. They were perfectly aware of the mischief he was brewing, but they not only declined to act themselves, but, unless they have been greatly maligned, they prevented the local authorities from acting. They also prevented Arabi from being removed, as he should have been, from the confines of Egypt, by which, had it been done, all the evil would have been averted.

While this enterprise was going on the government reposed in absolute security, and took no effective measure till the pressure of public opinion forced upon them the movement of the fleet into the harbor of Alexandria. That was a very fair illustration of the vice which characterized their policy. That movement was made suddenly, with no preparation, and forced us into what followed. The fleet was moved in; as a matter of course Arabi resisted, and the fleet, as was inevitable, suddenly replied; and then it was found that there were no forces to land and back up the action that was taken.

The result of that imprudence was that not only was the Khedive's throne shaken and the fidelity of his army utterly destroyed, but the town and fortifications of Alexandria were grievously injured, and that tremendous debt for the injury to Alexandria was incurred which still remains as a burden upon Egyptian finance, and a hindrance to all negotiations for the settlement of foreign claims. That was the first specimen of their period of slumber, followed by a sudden and unprepared rush.

Then came the question of the Soudan. It was no new question, for before the battle of Tel-el-Kebir the Mahdi was already in arms. It was a matter with which anybody who undertook to deal with the destiny of Egypt ought to have been familiar and ready with a decision. But none was at hand, and matters were allowed to drift. The government, plunged in absolute torpor, seemed to have but one care — that they should escape the nominal responsibility, though real responsibility must inevitably attach to their action. Their despatches, one after another, during that period, merely repeated the old burden, that the government had no responsibility.

The result was that the unhappy Hicks went into the Soudan wretchedly equipped, with an army beneath the number he ought to have had, and composed of men turned out as worthless from the Egyptian army. The inevitable result followed — a result at which her Majesty's government had no reason to be surprised, for they were warned of the danger by their own confidential agents, yet absolutely declined to interfere. They hoped by disclaiming responsibility to escape the consequences of their own neglect.

Hicks's army was totally destroyed, and not a man escaped to tell the tale, and then the government awoke from the period of slumber, and the period of rush began. They adopted two measures, both of them as inadequate and inapplicable to the circumstances as it was possible to conceive, and both big with future trouble.

In the first place they announced suddenly to the world and to Egypt that Egypt must abandon the Soudan. It was impossible to have conceived a more stupendous political blunder. It was a proclamation to our enemies that they should enjoy impunity, and to our friends that they would be handed over without mercy to those who claimed to overcome them. But that announcement was made, and from that moment the fate of the garrisons scattered over the Soudan was sealed. The fate of the garrison of Khartoum was brought home to them forcibly, but did they take any reasonable measures for its relief? Did they send any troops on which they could rely to defend the garrison?

No, they adopted the absurd and Quixotic plan of taking advantage of the chivalry and devotion of one of the noblest spirits our age has seen, by sending him forward on the impossible and hopeless errand of accomplishing by mere words and promises that which they had not the courage to do by force of arms. From that commencement, the abandonment of the Soudan to the mission of General Gordon, all our subsequent troubles arose.

But that was not all, for among those garrisons in the Soudan were those of Sinkat and Tokar, which, so far back as November, 1883, were severely pressed by the Mahdi's lieutenants, and their danger was announced to the government as extreme. But for three months they took no notice of that danger. They allowed the matter to be left to General Baker and a body of Egyptians, whose worthlessness was denounced in every page of the correspondence that was laid before them. Of course General Baker with such a force was inevitably defeated; but it was not until April or May — I think not till a vote of censure was announced — that the government determined on making an effort to do that which they ought to have done, and which, if they had not been asleep, they would have done, three months before — namely, to relieve the garrisons of Sinkat and Tokar. And when the resolution came at last — when the necessity dawned upon their minds — they plunged into it with their usual imprudence and want of plan. They sent men down to Suakim apparently with no idea as to what those men were to do, and before they could take effective measures Sinkat had fallen and the garrison of Tokar, giving up in despair, had surrendered themselves.

Then the aimlessness of the government was revealed. Having landed their forces they would not expose themselves to the ridicule of taking them away without doing anything, so they slaughtered 6,000 Arabs, and then came away absolutely without any result for the blood of their friends and their enemies shed. They came away guilty of all this bloodshed, because they had plunged into the enterprise without any definite view or any fixed plan by which they proposed to guide themselves.

Now, my lords, these three things, the case of the bombardment of Alexandria, the abandonment of the Soudan, and the mission of General Graham's force — they are all on the same plan, and they all show that remarkable characteristic of torpor during the time that action was needed, and of impulsive, hasty, and ill-considered action when the moment for action had passed by.

Their future conduct was modelled on their conduct in the past. So far was it modelled that we were able to put it to the test which establishes a scientific law. The proof of scientific law is when you can prophesy from previous experience what will happen in the future. It is exactly what took place in the present instance. We had had these three instances of the mode of working of her Majesty's government before us. We knew the laws that guided their action, as astronomers, observing the motions of a comet, can discover by their observations the future path which that comet is to travel; and we prophesied what would happen in the case of General Gordon.

My right honorable friend Sir Stafford Northcote prophesied it in the House of Commons, and was met by a burst of fury from the prime minister such as that assembly has seldom seen. He was told that Egypt was of much less importance than, I think, Sutherland or Caithness, that everything wrong was the result of deficits imputed to him in the finances of some ten years ago, and he was generally denounced because he interfered with the beneficent legislation on the subject of capable citizens, and so forth, by introducing the subject of Egypt as many as seventeen times. That did not prevent his prophecies being correct, and I ventured to repeat them in this House.

I do not like to quote my own words; it is egotistical; but as proof of what I call the accuracy of the scientific law, I should like to refer to what I said on the 4th of April, when we were discussing the prospect of the relief of General Gordon. The government were maintaining that he was perfectly safe, and that it was very unreasonable for us to raise the question in Parliament. What I said was this:

"Are these circumstances encouraging to us, when we are asked to trust to the inspiration of the moment, that when the danger comes the government will find some means of relieving General Gordon? I feel that the history of the past will be again repeated, and just again when it is too late the critical resolution will be taken. The same news will come that the position of Gordon is forlorn and helpless, and then some desperate resolution of sending an expedition will be formed too late to achieve its object."

I quote these words to show that we had ascertained the orbits of those eccentric comets who sit on the Treasury Bench. Now, the terrible responsibility and blame which rests upon them does so because they were warned in March and April of the danger of General Gordon; they had received every intimation which men could reasonably look for that his danger would be extreme, and delayed it from March and April right down to the 15th of August before they took a single measure.

What were they doing all that time? It is very difficult to conceive. Some people have said, but I think it is an unreasonable supposition, that the cause of the tardiness of her Majesty's government was the accession to the Cabinet of the noble earl the secretary for the colonies [Earl of Derby]. I have quoted, partly with the object of defending the noble lord from that charge, for I have quoted to show that the government were almost as bad before he joined them as they were after. What happened during these eventful months?

I suppose one day some memoirs will tell our grandchildren, but we shall never know. Some people think there were divisions in the Cabinet, and that, after division and division the decision was put off in order that the Cabinet should not be broken up. I am rather inclined to think that it was due to the peculiar position of the prime minister. He came in as the apostle of the Midlothian campaign, loaded with the doctrines and the follies of that pilgrimage. We have seen it on each occasion, after each one of these mishaps when the government has been forced by events and the common sense of the nation to take same more active steps. We have seen how his extreme supporters in that campaign have reproached him as he deserted their opinions and disappointed their ardent hopes. I think that he always felt the danger of that reproach, and the debt he had incurred to those supporters, and felt a dread lest they should break away and put off again and again till the last practical moment any action which might bring him into open conflict with the doctrines by which his present eminence was gained.

At all events, this is clear, that throughout those six months the government knew perfectly well the danger in which General Gordon was placed. It has been said that General Gordon did not ask for troops. Well, I am surprised at that defence. One of the characteristics of General Gordon was the extreme abnegation of his nature. It was not to be expected that he should send home a telegram to say, "I am in great danger, therefore send me troops." He would probably have cut off his right hand before he would have sent such a telegram. But he did send a telegram that the people of Khartoum were in danger, and that the Mahdi must win unless military succor was sent forward, and distinctly telling the government — and this is the main point — that unless they would consent to his views the supremacy of the Mahdi was assured.

This is what he said not later than the 29th of February, almost as soon as he first saw the nature of the problem with which he had been sent to deal. It is impossible that General Gordon could have spoken more clearly than he did, but Mr. Power, who was one of the three Englishmen in Khartoum, and who was sent down with Stewart on that ill-fated journey, on the 23rd of March sent a telegram saying, "We are daily expecting British troops; we cannot bring ourselves to believe that we are to be abandoned by the government. Our existence depends on England."

My lords, is it conceivable that after that — two months after that — in May, the prime minister should have said that the government were waiting to have reasonable proof that Gordon was in danger? By that time Khartoum was surrounded, and the governor of Berber had announced that his case was desperate, which was too surely proved by the massacre which took place in June.

And yet in May Mr. Gladstone was waiting for reasonable proof that they were in danger. Apparently he did not get that proof till August.

I may note in passing that I think the interpretation which the government have placed upon the language of their trusted officers has been exceedingly ungenerous. They told us that they did not think it necessary to send an expedition to relieve Sinkat and Tokar because they could quote some language of hope from the despatches of General Baker, and in the same way they could quote some language of hope from the despatches of General Gordon.

But a general sent forward on a dangerous expedition does not like to go whining for assistance, unless he is pressed by absolute peril. All those great qualities which go to make men heroes are such as are absolutely incompatible with such a course, and lead them to shrink as from a great disgrace from any unnecessary appeal for exertion for their protection. It was the business of the government not to interpret General Gordon's telegrams as if they had been statutory declarations, but to judge for themselves of the circumstances of the case, and to see that those who were surrounded, who were the only three Englishmen amongst this vast body of Mohammedans, who were already cut off from all communication with the civilized world by the occupation of every important town upon the river, were in real danger.

I cannot understand what blindness fell over the eyes of some members of the government. Lord Hartington, on the 13th of May, gave utterance to this expression: "I say it would be an indelible disgrace if we should neglect any means at the disposal of this country for saving General Gordon."

And after that announcement by the minister chiefly responsible, three months elapsed before any step was taken for doing that which he admitted the government were bound to do under the penalty of indelible disgrace. It has been said that Gordon was destroyed by treachery, and that treachery would have happened at any time when the British army came near Khartoum. What does that extraordinary theory mean?

It means that the Mahdi had agreed with Farag Bey that it was much more comfortable to go on besieging, and that until Lord Wolseley made it dangerous they would go on besieging. I think those who started that unreasonable theory could hardly have been aware of the straits to which the Mahdi had been put. His army was suffering from fever, from cholera, from smallpox; there was great danger of dealing with his men, who were constantly threatening mutiny and desertion. Never was a force more hardly put to it to maintain its position than was this; and depend upon it, if he could have shortened that period of trial by an hour he would certainly have done so. But, supposing it was true that treachery was certain to do its work, what does that prove? Does it not show that sending Gordon to Khartoum was an act of extreme folly?

I do not know any other instance in which a man has been sent to maintain such a position without a certain number of British troops. If the British troops had been there treachery would have been impossible, but sending Gordon by himself to rely on the fidelity of Africans and Egyptians was an act of extreme rashness, and if the government succeed in proving, which I do not think they can, that treachery was inevitable, they only pile up an additional reason for their condemnation. I confess it is very difficult to separate this question from the personal matters involved. It is very difficult to argue it on purely abstract grounds without turning for a moment to the character of the man who was engaged and the terrible position in which he was placed.

When we consider all that he underwent, all that he sacrificed in order to serve the government in a moment of extreme exigency, there is something infinitely pathetic in reflecting on his feelings, as day after day, week after week, month after month passed by — as he spared no exertions, no personal sacrifice, to perform the duties that were placed upon him — as he lengthened out the siege by inconceivable prodigies of ingenuity, of activity, of resource — and as, in spite of it all, in spite of the deep devotion to his country, which had prompted him to this great risk and undertaking, the conviction gradually grew upon him that his country had abandoned him.

It is terrible to think what he must have suffered when at last, as a desperate measure to save those he loved, he parted with the only two Englishmen with whom during those long months he had had any converse, and sent Stewart and Power down the river to escape from the fate which had become inevitable to himself. It is very painful to think of the reproaches to his country and to his country's government that must have passed through the mind of that devoted man during those months of unmerited desertion. In Gordon's letter of the 14th of December he said: "All is up. I expect a catastrophe in ten days' time; it would not have been so if our people had kept me better informed as to their intentions."

They had no intentions to inform him of. They were merely acting from hand to mouth to avert the parliamentary censure with which they were threatened. They had no plan, they had no intentions to carry out. If they could have known their intentions, a great hero would have been saved to the British army, a great disgrace would not have fallen on the English government.

Now, by the light of this sad history, what are the prospects for the future? Was there ever a time when clearness of plan and distinctness of policy were more required than they are now? I am not going to say that the policy of the government is bad. It would be paying them an extravagant compliment if I said so. They have no policy. My right honorable friend Mr. Gibson epigrammatically described their policy when he said, "They were going to Khartoum to please the Whigs, and were going to abandon Khartoum to please the Radicals."

Is there not something strange that at such a crisis of our country's fate, in both Houses of Parliament, in the press, in society, and everywhere you hear people asking what is their policy, and can get no answer? Here and there you get a distant echo of policy, something vague and ill-defined, like a distant sound to which you can attach no definite meaning. You sometimes for a moment see the phantom of a policy, but if you try to grasp it, it escapes you.

We used to think the policy of the government was the evacuation of the Soudan as soon as the military operations were over — a very bad policy — but even that does not seem to be their policy. They do not know whether they are going to evacuate the Soudan or not. They don't know who is to hold the Soudan — it may be the Italians, it may be the Turks, or the Chinese.

On one point only do they put down their foot, and that is, the Egyptians shall not keep it. We were told that they were going to smash the Mahdi, but now we are to make peace with the smashed Mahdi. If you smash the Mahdi thoroughly he will be of no use to you, and if you do not smash him thoroughly he may maintain at the bottom of his heart a certain resentment against the process of being smashed.

It is probable that the Mahdi, in fulfilment of the claims of the religious position he occupies, will decline to have any dealings with the infidel; and if you crush him so entirely by force of arms, he will have lost all his position in the minds of his countrymen; and you will in his assistance or support not find any solution of the terrible problem with which you have to deal.

In the same way with the railway. So far as I know, it is unprecedented to project a railway through an enemy's country, but it implies some views of policy. It appears that her Majesty's government are going to make a railway, and then leave it to the first comers to do what they like with it. Now, it appears to me that in this matter of our Egyptian policy, though I do not say we can lay down the precise steps by which our ends may be obtained — this must depend in a great measure on the judgment of the ministry — still, it is time when we should conceive to ourselves what the ends of our policy are to be, and clearly define it and follow it up with consistency and persistency.

Now, let us examine what are the interests of England in this matter. With Mediterranean politics as such we have no great interest to concern ourselves; but Egypt stands in a peculiar position. It is the road to India. The condition of Egypt can never be indifferent to us, and, more than that, we have a duty to insist — that our influence shall be predominant there. I do not care by what technical arrangements that result is to be obtained; but, with all due regard to the rights of the suzerain, the influence of England in Egypt must be supreme.

Now, the influence of England in Egypt is threatened from two sides. It is threatened from the north diplomatically. I do not think it is necessary that the powers should have taken up the position they have done, and I believe that with decent steering it might have been avoided; but, unfortunately, we have to face inchoate schemes which will demand the utmost jealousy and vigilance of Parliament. I do not know what arrangement the government has arrived at, but I greatly fear that it may include a multiple control, and to that I believe this country will be persistently and resolutely hostile.

But we have to face a danger of another kind. We have forces of fanatical barbarians let loose upon the south of Egypt, and owing to the blunders that have been committed this danger has reached a terrible height. Unless we intend to give over Egypt to barbarism and anarchy we must contrive to check this inroad of barbarian fanaticism, which is personified in the character and action of the Mahdi. General Gordon never said a truer thing than that you do this by simply drawing a military line. If the insurgent Mohammedans reach the north of Egypt it will not be so much by their military force, as by the moral power of their example. We have therefore to check this advance of the Mahdi's power.

Her Majesty's government in the glimpses of policy which they occasionally afford us have alluded to the possibility of setting up a good government in the Soudan. I quite agree that a good government is essential to us in the Soudan. It is the only dyke we can really erect to keep out this inundation of barbarism and fanatical forces.

But her Majesty's government speak as if a good government were a Christmas present, which you can give a country and then take away. A good government, like any other organization, must pass through the stages of infancy to maturity. There must be a long stage of infancy, during which that government is unable to defend itself, and it requires during that period protection and security, which it can only derive from the action of an external power. It is that protection and security which England must give. She must not desert her task in the Soudan until there is that government there which can protect Egypt, in which the interests of this country are vital. I do not say whether it should be done from the Nile or from Suakim.

I see a noble lord, one of the greatest ornaments of this House, who has conducted an expedition, not of 250 miles, but of 400 miles, and that with success, over the same burning country, and his opinion, given last year, was that Suakim and Berber are the roads by which we should advance. In that opinion I do not say I concur — that would be impertinent — but it is an opinion to which I humbly subscribe. I believe that by the Suakim and Berber route we may obtain a hold over that portion of the Soudan which may enable us to perform our primary duty — namely, to repress the forces of barbarism and fanaticism, to encourage that civilization which, if protected, will find such abundant root in that fertile country, and, above all, to restrain, check, and ultimately to destroy the slave trade, which has been the curse of Africa.

All those advantages can be obtained if England will lay down a definite policy and will adhere to it, but consistency of policy is absolutely necessary. We have to assure our friends that we shall stand by them; we have to assure our enemies that we are permanently to be feared. The blunders of the last three years have placed us in the presence of terrible problems and difficulties. We have great sacrifices to make. This railway will be an enormous benefit to Africa, but do not let us conceal from ourselves that it is a task of no small magnitude. If you are to carry this railway forward you will not only have to smash the Mahdi, but Osman Digma also.

All this will involve great sacrifices and the expenditure not only of much money, but of more of the English blood of which the noblest has already been poured forth. And we are not so strong as we were. At first all nations sympathized with us, but now they look on us coldly and even with hostility. Those who were our friends have become indifferent, those who were indifferent have become our adversaries; and if our misfortunes and disasters go on much longer we shall have Europe saying that they cannot trust us, that we are too weak, that our prestige is too low to justify us in undertaking this task.

My lords, those great dangers can only be faced by a consistent policy, which can only be conducted by a ministry capable of unity of counsel and decision of purpose. I have shown you that from this ministry we can expect no such results. They can only produce after their kind. They will only do what they have already done. You cannot look for unity of counsel from an administration that is hopelessly divided. You cannot expect a resolute policy from those whose purpose is hopelessly halting.

It is for this reason, my lords, that I ask you to record your opinion that from a ministry in whom the first of all — the quality of decision of purpose — is wanting, you can hope no good in this crisis of our country's fate. And if you continue to trust them, if for any party reasons Parliament continues to abandon to their care the affairs which they have hitherto so hopelessly mismanaged, you must expect to go on from bad to worse; you must expect to lose the little prestige which you retain; you must expect to find in other portions of the world the results of the lower consideration that you occupy in the eyes of mankind; you must expect to be drawn on, degree by degree, step by step, under the cover of plausible excuses, under the cover of highly philanthropic sentiments, to irreparable disasters, and to disgrace that it will be impossible to efface.

MURRAY

GEORGE MURRAY, Canadian educator and literarian, born in Regent Square, London, March 23, 1830, the only son of the late Jas. Murray, in his lifetime foreign editor of the London "Times." He received his early education at the school of Dr. J. G. Greig, Walthamstow, Essex, afterward matriculating at King's College, London, where he took the chaplain's two prizes for English verse—original and translated—the principal's prize for Latin verse, the senior classical scholarship, and was elected A.K.C., the highest honor that could be conferred by the college. Proceeding to Oxford, he obtained among other honors the Lusby scholarship and the Lucy exhibition. Before taking his degree he published "The Oxford ars Poetica; or, How to Write a Newdigate." In 1859, after spending some years on the continent, he came to Canada and was appointed shortly afterward senior classical master of the Montreal High School, a position which he held until 1892. He was a contributor to the press, and in 1891 he published his poems in a volume entitled "Verses and Versions," dedicated to "Sir Edwin Arnold, my dearest companion for many years." Among his journalistic enterprises were "Diogenes," a serio-comic weekly, and the "Free Lance," both published in Montreal, the last-named in conjunction with the late Geo. T. Lanigan. In 1882 he established "Notes and Queries" in the Montreal "Star" and of this department he has always been and still is the editor. He wrote also for the English "Notes and Queries" and for "Once a Week." As a classical scholar, the Ottawa "Journal" places him among the foremost on the American continent. On the formation of the Royal Society of Canada, in 1882, he was appointed by its founder, the Marquis of Lorne, to be one of the twenty original Fellows of the section of English literature, history, etc. He was secretary for some years of the old Montreal Literary Club, and on the death of the Hon. T. D. McGee, one of the Fellows of that society, was chosen, with two others, to edit the literary remains of the lamented poet-statesman.

PUBLIC SPEAKING

PARTS OF AN ADDRESS DELIVERED BEFORE THE ATHENÆUM CLUB OF MONTREAL IN 1880

THE question whether oratorical ability be on the whole a public benefit or a mischief, was frequently debated among the ancients; but in the present day it would be a waste of time to dilate upon the advantages of being a skilful speaker. The tongue, which is the sword of the orator, equals or surpasses in effect, at least for the time being, the pen of the ablest writer. If the true function of eloquence is to enlighten the understanding, to please the imagination, to stir the passions, or to influence the will; the accomplished orator who can attain these ends, and even the less effective speaker, in a minor degree, are possessed of a mighty power, either for good or evil. "The wise in heart," says Solomon, "shall be called prudent, but the sweetness of the lips increaseth learning."

Lord Chesterfield, a very superficial Solomon, but still a man of great worldly wisdom, constantly repeated to his son, that no man in his time could make a fortune or a figure in England without speaking, and speaking well, in public. "It does not surprise us," writes Emerson, "to learn from Plutarch what large sums were paid at Athens to the teachers of rhetoric, and if the pupils got what they paid for, the lessons were cheap."

Even a single triumphant speech has occasionally conferred a quasi-immortality. In the year 1755, when Lord Chatham was attacking the Newcastle administration, a member who voted with the ministry found their cause one evening in extreme danger. He accordingly rose, we are told, though he had never before addressed the House, and poured forth a speech, full of cogent argument and fervid emotion, with all the ease and confidence of a practised speaker. But the success of his maiden speech sealed his lips for the future. He was ever after getting ready, but never was ready for a second effort which should surpass his first; and the orator survives in the annals of fame under the sobriquet of "Single-Speech Hamilton."

Again, the loss to the world of speeches which were unrecorded at the time of their delivery has been vainly regretted by the most illustrious orators; and it is related by Lord Brougham of the younger Pitt that when the conversation turned on lost works, and some said they would prefer to recover the lost books of Livy, some those of Tacitus, and some a Latin tragedy, he at once decided for a speech of Bolingbroke. This was a noble tribute to the oratorical genius of the idol of Swift and of Pope, coming from one who in his own time, though accused by Mr. Windham of speaking in a "state-paper style," produced almost magical effects upon a refined and critical audience.

Let me here, before I forget to introduce it, quote the simple but eloquent panegyric penned by one of England's greatest poets on England's greatest philosopher:

"There happened," writes Ben Jonson, "in my time one noble speaker who was full of gravity in his speaking. No man ever spoke more neatly, more expressively, more weightily, or suffered less emptiness, less idleness in what he uttered. No member of his speech but consisted of its own graces. His hearers could not cough or look aside from him without loss. He commanded where he spoke, and had his judges angry or pleased at his devotion. The fear of every man that heard him was that he should make an end."

"No finer description," says Dugald Stewart, "of the perfection of this art is to be found in any author, ancient or modern."

The prince of Roman orators used the following language in his speech for Muræna: "*Magnus dicendi labor, magna res, magna dignitas, summa autem gratia,*" that is to say: "Great is the labor that qualifies speaking, great the art itself, great its dignity, and most great too, the influence connected with it." Apart from its professional value and advantages to the clergyman, the senator, and the lawyer, the art of public speaking is the surest means of gratifying that laudable ambition which prompts most men to take some part in the social and political life of their generation. Wherever self-government is recognized there must be gatherings of different kinds for the transactions of public business, and in these the ablest speaker will win the attention and arouse the sympathies of all who listen to his sentiments. Pericles, as we learn from Thucydides, once remarked that, "a man who forms a judgment on any point, and cannot explain his views clearly to the people, might as well have never thought on the subject." This assertion is perhaps too absolute, but, at any rate, it points out with emphasis that the value of a mental action is obviously depreciated when we cannot use the result of it orally for the benefit of others. Mankind seem to agree almost unanimously that no accomplishment gains consideration for its possessor so speedily as public speaking; and there is none for which there is so persistent a demand.

Let me again quote some words of Cicero, from one of his best rhetorical treatises:

"I cannot conceive anything more excellent than to be able, by language, to captivate the affections, to charm the understanding, and to impel or restrain the will of whole assemblies, at pleasure. Among every free people, especially in peaceful, settled governments, this single art has always eminently flourished, and always exercised the greatest sway. For what can be more surprising than that, amidst an infinite multitude, one man should appear who shall be almost the only one capable of doing what nature has put in every man's power? Or, can anything impart such exquisite pleasure to the ear and to the intellect as a speech in which the wisdom and dignity of the sentiments are heightened by the utmost force and beauty of expression? Is there anything so commanding, so grand, as that the eloquence of one man should direct the inclinations of the people, the consciences of judges and the majesty of senates? Nay, further, can aught be esteemed so great, so generous, so public-spirited, as to assist the suppliant, to rear the prostrate, to communicate happiness, to avert danger, and to maintain the rights of a fellow citizen? Can anything be so necessary as to keep those arms always in readiness, with which you may defend yourself, attack the profligate, and redress your own or your country's wrongs?"

Notwithstanding the truth of these eloquent observations, notwithstanding the acknowledged fact that public speaking as a rule is the passport to profit, to high station, and even to fame, it is certain that as an art, it is comparatively neglected; and the character of the oratory which we usually hear is far inferior to what we might expect from the ordinary culture and intellectual vigor of the present age.

What, then, is the cause of this strange state of things? I would suggest the two following reasons as accounting in a measure for the phenomenon: First, the majority of people seem hastily to have adopted the notion that the faculty of public speaking is simply and wholly a gift or instinct, peculiar to few, and unattainable by the many. They believe that, like Dogberry's reading and writing, oratory comes by nature — that the orator, in fact, as has been said of the poet, *nascitur non fit;* while the reverse of the case is nearer the truth — *orator fit, non nascitur.* I am far from denying that some men by nature are better fitted than others to become orators. Still less do I affirm that all men are capable of making themselves good speakers. But I firmly believe that all who are not tonguetied, or positively deficient in intellect can learn by diligent practice to express their thoughts publicly in intelligible and intelligent language, and in a manner which is not painful either to themselves or to their audience. "The speaker must learn his crafts as thoroughly as a painter, a sculptor, or a musician; although, like them also, he must have from nature some special aptitude for his vocation." Lord Chesterfield was, I think, guilty of exaggeration when he maintained that a good speaker is as much a mechanic as a good shoemaker, and that the two trades are equally to be learned by the same amount of application.

The second reason why public speaking as an art is neglected is, that even those who hold the same opinions that I have expressed are still unwilling to undergo the necessary labor to become good speakers. They did not, they say, begin the task early in life, as Henry Ward Beecher recommends in his "Lectures on Preaching," and a new study now appears tedious and irksome to them, or they have really not time for the requisite training, and have no pressing need for the accomplishment as no immediate emolument can be derived from it.

It would be wasting breath to argue against these frivolous objections. The best way to expose their futility, and at the same time to show how the art of public speaking may be acquired, is carefully to ascertain by what means the greater number of those who have succeeded as orators or debaters have attained their success. Those who endeavor to follow their example and adopt their methods may probably fail to gain their supreme mastery over the instrument of language; but, in the end, they will have profited largely by their self-discipline, and it is honorable to win by hard work even a low rank amid a crowd of competitors.

Some years ago, on the occasion of distributing the prizes at University College, London, the Earl of Derby delivered a speech, which no one, old or young, can read without profit or admiration. Part of it I shall quote as strictly applicable to the present subject. As the orator of old insisted on action, so Lord Derby insisted on industry, premising that his exhortations on this head must necessarily appear common-place. But a common-place well explained is no common-place in the ordinary sense of the term, and Lord Derby did not declare industry to be the grand secret of success in life without showing its necessity and its products. Capital, in whatever shape it may be accumulated, whether pecuniary or intellectual, is hoarded labor. The man who is ready now has constantly worked hard to be ready, and his present state of modest confidence is the result of unwearied drill. In the words of Lord Derby, "We have heard at the bar, or in Parliament, men whose instantaneous command of words, whose readiness of thought as well as of expression, seemed the effect of instinct rather than of training; but what is the secret of that readiness? Why, this — that the mind has previously been so exercised on similar subjects that not merely the necessary words, but the necessary arguments and combinations of thought, have become by practice as instinctive as those motions of the body by which we walk or speak, or do any habitual and familiar act.

"One man will pore and perplex himself over a difficult point, be it in law or science, or what you will; another will come in and see at a glance where the difficulty lies, and what is the solution. Does that necessarily prove that the latter has more genius? No, but it proves that his faculties have been sharpened by familiarity with such topics; and the ease with which he now does his work, so far from proving that he has always worked with ease, is a measure, so to speak, of the labor by which he has prepared himself for doing it."

These are wise and true words, well worthy of our attention. To the same effect is the testimony of Sydney Smith, who shows by indubitable proofs that the greatest poets, historians, and orators have labored as hard in their specialties as the makers of dictionaries and the compilers of indexes. No man, says Henry Ward Beecher, can preach well except out of an abundance of well-wrought material. Some sermons seem to start up suddenly, body and soul, but in fact they are the product of years of experience. Natural genius is but the soil, which let alone, runs to weeds. If it is to bear fruit and harvests worth reaping, no matter how good the soil is, it must be ploughed and tilled with incessant care.

"The heights by great men reached and kept
Were not attained by sudden flight;
But they, while their companions slept,
Were toiling upward in the night."

Lord Brougham, whose competency to instruct us on the subject of public speaking no one will be bold enough to deny, used the following language in 1820, and was apparently so satisfied with its truthfulness that he reproduced it forty years afterward in the address which he delivered at his installation as chancellor of the University of Edinburgh:

"I dwell upon the subject of what is called extempore speaking in order to illustrate the necessity of full preparation and of written composition of those who would attain real excellence in the rhetorical art. In truth, a certain proficiency in public speaking may be acquired by any one who chooses often to try it, and can harden himself against the pain of frequent failures. If he is a person of no capacity his speeches will of course be bad; but even though he be man of genius, they will not be eloquent.

"A sensible remark or a fine image may occur; but the loose and slovenly diction, the want of art, in combining and disposing his ideas, the inability to bring out many of his thoughts, and the incompetency to present any of them in the most efficient form, would reduce the speaker to the level of an ordinary talker. His diction is sure to be clumsy and incorrect — unlimited in quantity, but of no real value.

"Such a speaker is never in want of a word, and hardly ever has one that is worth hearing. '*Sine hac quidem conscientia*,' says Quintilian, speaking of the habit of written composition, '*illa ipsa extempore dicendi facultas inanem modo loquacitatem dabit, et verba in labris nascentia*.'[1] It is a common error to call this natural eloquence. It is the reverse: It is neither natural nor eloquent."

If public men in every grade would but take to heart this advice of Lord Brougham, the quantity would be reduced and the quality enhanced of what commonly passes by the name of eloquence. It is not that the age of oratory like that of chivalry has passed away, but that the necessity for study and the discipline it exacts is not sufficiently recognized.

"The untaught speaker [continues Lord Brougham] who utters according to the dictates of his feelings, may now and then achieve a success. But in these instances he would not be less successful if he had studied the art, while that study would enable him to succeed equally in all that he delivers. Herein, indeed, consists the value of the study: It enables a man to do at all times what nature teaches only on rare occasions."

We cannot value too highly these opinions of Lord Brougham. The eloquence of the untrained and uncultivated is elicited only by special occasions. It is not at command. The speaker does not master his powers, but is mastered by them. When wanted, they are not always at hand, and when drawn forth by emergencies, they often transport him beyond his mark. As Archbishop Whately once said, "he has but

---

[1] Without this consciousness that very power of extempore speaking will give merely an empty loquacity and words stringing forth from the lips.

the same 'command of language' that the rider has of a horse that has run away with him." But the eloquence of the trained and cultivated speaker is a power, though often dormant, yet always ready for use; when summoned it appears, though there be no favoring circumstances. It can speak even to reluctant ears, and compel an audience.

The story of Demosthenes, whose orations, according to Hume, present to us the models which approach the nearest to perfection, is well known to every schoolboy. How he was nick-named "ὁ Βαταλός" or "the stammerer;" how he cured his stuttering by speaking with pebbles in his mouth; how he strengthened his weak lungs by repeating verses of the poets as he ran up hill; how he declaimed on the seashore in stormy weather to accustom himself to the tumult of the Athenian popular assemblies; how his first oratorical effort was received with ridicule — these and other statements may, perhaps, not be literally true, but at any rate they attest the tradition of antiquity that he labored hard and successfully to overcome his natural deficiencies for public speaking. In spite of the severe discipline which he underwent to master the art of rhetoric, and notwithstanding the faculty of speech which he must have acquired by persistent practice, it is related of him that, like Pericles, whom he so greatly admired, he had an unconquerable aversion to extemporaneous addresses. He was unwilling to "trust his success to Fortune," that is, to the uncertain inspiration of the moment.

By a detailed examination of the repetitions that occur in some of his finest orations, Lord Brougham has enabled us to appreciate the progressive workmanship of many striking passages. We are thus, as it were, let into the secret of their composition, almost as if the rough draught had been preserved. As Moore has pointed out in his "Life of Sheridan" that many of his *soi-disant* spontaneous witticisms — the hoarded repartees and matured jests with which Pitt taunted him — had passed through numerous editions on paper before they charmed the social circle or electrified the House of Commons; so Lord Brougham shows that some of the most admired sentences of Demosthenes, when he wished to adapt them to new occasions, were invested with fresh beauty by happy variations in expression which had been suggested subsequently to their original delivery.

Passing over the incredible labors of Cicero, which he ha fully described in his various works on oratory, let us select some "modern instances," all tending to prove the value and necessity of incessant toil. When Woodfall, a tolerably good judge of public speaking, had heard Sheridan's maiden speech in Parliament, he said to him discouragingly: "I am sorry to say that I do not think this is your line; you had much better have stuck to your former pursuits."

"It is in me, however," said Sheridan, after a short pause, "and, by God, it shall come out."

This has been called a case of the intuitive consciousness of latent power; but, if Brougham is correct in his estimate, Sheridan's genius for oratory fell far short of his assiduity in cultivating it. Some defects, we are told, he never could eradicate. A thick and indistinct mode of delivery, and an inability to speak without the most careful preparation characterized him to the end; but by excessive labor he verified his own prediction, and as an orator eventually attained to excellence rarely equalled, and, if we are to judge by the verdict of his contemporaries, never, with all his faults, surpassed.

When Burke brought forward in the House of Commons the various accusations against Warren Hastings, the charge relating to the spoliation of the Begums was allotted to Sheridan. His speech was made on February 7, 1787, and occupied nearly six hours in delivery. When the orator sat down, the whole house as if fascinated with his eloquence burst into an involuntary tumult of applause. It was the first time, we are told, that any speech in Parliament had ever been received with cheers.

Burke declared it to be the most extraordinary effort he had ever witnessed; while Fox said, "all that he had ever heard, all that he had ever read, when compared with it, dwindled into nothing, and vanished like vapor before the sun."

Even Pitt, who had frequently satirized the dramatic turns and epigrammatic points of Sheridan, acknowledged "that it surpassed all the eloquence of ancient and modern times, and possessed everything that genius or art could furnish to agitate and control the human mind."

Twenty years afterward Windham asserted that "the speech deserved all its fame, and was, in spite of some faults of taste, such as were seldom wanting in the literary and parliamentary performances of Sheridan, the greatest that had been delivered within the memory of man."

It should not be forgotten that the debate was adjourned when the speech was concluded, in order that the House might have time to recover their calmness and collect their reason. As Lord Lytton describes the scene in his poem of "St. Stephen's:"

"He who had known the failure, felt the sneer,
Smit burning brows in muttering, 'It is here'—
He now, one hour the acknowledged lord of all,
Hears Pitt adjourn the agitated hall,
That brain may cool, and heart forget to swell,
And dawn relax the enchanter's midnight spell."

This effective oration, though written out in full, and committed accurately to memory, was never published. The author preferred trusting his fame to the tradition of its effects rather than to the production itself. In so doing he probably acted wisely. He never, says Moore, made a speech of any moment of which a sketch was not found among his papers, with the showy parts written two or three times over. His memoranda show the exact place where the involuntary exclamation, "Good God, Mr. Speaker," was to be introduced, and exhibited elaborate "burst of passion," into which it was his intention to be "hurried." Lord Brougham has thus recorded the means by which after a most unpromising beginning Sheridan finally attained his prodigious success: —

"What he wanted in acquired learning and natural quickness he made up by indefatigable industry. Within given limits toward a present object no labor could daunt him. No man could work for a season with more steady and unwearied application. By constant practice in small matters, or before private committees, by diligent attendance upon all debates, by habitual intercourse with all classes of dealers in political wares, he trained himself to a facility of speaking absolutely essential to all but first-rate genius, and all but necessary even to that. By these steps he rose to the rank of a first-rate speaker, and as great a debater as want of readiness and need for preparation would permit."

The case of Benjamin Disraeli bears some resemblance to that of Brinsley Sheridan. In 1837 he was elected member for Maidstone. On December the seventh of that year his maiden speech in the House was deservedly cut short by a burst of inextinguishable laughter, and he ended it with the memorable words: "I am not at all surprised at the reception which I have experienced. I have begun several times many things, and I have often succeeded at last. I will sit down now, but the time will come when you will hear me."

His prophecy, like Sheridan's, has also been verified, and by dint of the same indefatigable toil.

Chatham and Burke in like manner, Pitt and Fox, Grattan, Erskine, Curran and Shiel, Lord Brougham, Macaulay, and the finest orators of the present day, form no exception to the fixed law that genius, to succeed even in public speaking, cannot afford to dispense with labor, all it can do is to shorten the time of labor. Lord Chatham, at the age of eighteen, when he went to the University of Oxford, forthwith entered upon a severe course of rhetorical training. We are informed by his biographers that he adopted the practice of translating largely from the most famous orators and historians of antiquity. His model was Demosthenes, and by frequently writing translations of his finest orations, he insensibly acquired the habit of always using the right word in the right place. This practice of accurate translation he adopted from Cicero, who has recommended it in his treatise "De Oratore," and whose preface to his versions of both Demosthenes' and Æschines' "De Corona" is extant, though the translations themselves have perished. As another means of acquiring a *copia verborum,*[1] and a choice diction, he diligently studied the sermons of Barrow; and, with the same view went twice through Nathan Bailey's folio dictionary, examining the exact meaning and use of every word until he thoroughly appreciated the strength, beauty, and significance of the English language, and could enlist any part of it at will in the service of his oratory. He trained himself at the same time for the graces of public speaking by unwearied exercises in elocution. An imposing figure

---

[1] A sufficient vocabulary.

and an eagle eye aided him materially in the effects that he produced, but the amount of drudgery that he underwent is, in the case of so great a man, almost more wonderful than his eloquence I know of no more striking evidence that in the words of the Latin poet: "*Nil sine magno Vita labore dedit mortalibus.*"[1]

But to select an orator of a more argumentative class than Lord Chatham, how did Fox acquire his skill as a debater? "Those, indeed, notably err," writes one of his admirers, "who judging only by the desultory social habits and dissipated tastes of Mr. Fox, concluded that his faculties attained their strength without the necessary toil of resolute exertion."

The propensity to labor at excellence, even in his amusements, distinguished him through life; and we learn from his nephew, Lord Holland, that at every little diversion or employment, at chess, cards, or carving at dinner, he would exercise his faculties with wonderful assiduity till he had attained the required degree of perfection. Fox once remarked to a friend that he had literally gained his skill "at the expense of the House," for he had sometimes tasked himself during a whole session to speak on every question that came up, whether he was interested in it or not, as a means of training his ability for debate.

A debater has been aptly described as "one who goes out in all weathers." He must always be prepared for every emergency, and ready to grapple with his antagonist at a moment's notice. Spurred on by ambition, and untiring in his zeal, Fox rose, as Burke declared, "by slow degrees to be the most brilliant and accomplished debater the world ever saw."

Let us take the case of the last quoted orator and philoso-

[1] Life gives nothing to mortals without great labor.

pher. Burke says of himself in one of his letters: "I was not swaddled and dandled and rocked into a legislator. *Nitor in adversum*[1] is the motto for a man like me." His studies at the University of Dublin were severe. Leland, the translator of Demosthenes, used to speak of him as "a young man more anxious to acquire knowledge than to display it." Accordingly, when he had left college he had mastered most of the great writers of antiquity. Poets and historians, philosophers and orators — all had been laid under tribute to enrich the intellectual treasury of the future orator. Bacon, Shakespeare, and Milton were the great English triumvirate whom he daily studied, and his memory was a vast storehouse of all wisdom, ancient and modern, sacred and profane. Though often spoken to almost empty benches, Burke's speeches are probably the most eloquent ever delivered by any uninspired man. The very reasons which made them unpleasant to the parliamentary members of his own day are those which have rendered them invaluable to posterity. Burke's oratory was essentially didactic. His speeches were dissertations, or declaimed pamphlets, and while his hearers were absorbed in considering what they deemed the mere question of the hour he rose to grand generalizations until his arguments on particular topics assumed the dignity of universal propositions. To quote once more from Lord Lytton's poem:

> "But what the faults that could admirers chill,
> And then the benches plain Dundas could fill?
> Partly in matter—too intent to teach—
> Too filed as essay not to flag as speech;
> Too swift a fellowship with those around,
> Words too ornate, and reasonings too profound;
> All this a Chatham might have brought in vogue—
> Yes—but then Chatham did not speak in brogue!"

---

[1] I struggle against opposition.

Fox, in distinction to Burke, at once seized the strong points of a case and avoiding all circuitous processes and subtle exposition, struck at the very heart of a subject, and forced the attention of his audience. Nevertheless, in 1790 Fox stated in the House of Commons that "if he were to put all the political information which he had learned from books, all that he gained from science, and all that any knowledge of the world and its affairs had taught him, into one scale; and if the improvements which he had derived from his right honorable friend's instruction and conversation were placed in the other, he should be at a loss to decide to which to give the preference." "Burke's talk," said Dr. Johnson, "is the ebullition of his mind. He does not talk from a desire of distinction, but because his mind is full." On another occasion he declared: "Burke is the only man whose common conversation corresponds with the general fame which he has in the world. Take up whatever topic you please, he is ready to meet you." Again: "No man of sense can meet Mr. Burke by accident under a gateway, to avoid a shower, without being convinced that he is the first man in England."

We may rest assured that Burke did not become her greatest orator, the most instructive conversationalist, and the first man in England (according to Dr. Johnson) without having previously undergone almost superhuman labor. Nay, more, he boasted of his incessant toil, and, disclaiming superior abilities, attributed his success to his superior industry.

We are accustomed to read accounts which seem almost fabulous of the oratorical powers of Curran. He could command at will the laughter and the tears of his audience; and it has been said that while he poured forth his invective like a stream of lava he could inflame the minds of his countrymen almost to madness by a recital of their alleged wrongs. Lord Brougham, who, however, has given us no sketch of his life, calls him "the greatest orator, after Grattan and Plunket, that Ireland has produced, and, in every respect, worthy of being placed on a line with those great masters of speech." We might reasonably imagine that Curran if any one was a born orator; but what do we find stated if we turn to any of his biographies? We learn that his voice was bad, his articulation indistinct, and that he was nicknamed by his school fellows, "Stuttering Jack Curran."

Certainly a curious coincidence between his case and that of Demosthenes, to which I alluded before. Nor were the two men unlike in many other respects, though their style of oratory was wholly different. Curran's manner was awkward, and his general appearance ridiculous. The portrait of him prefixed to his life by Charles Phillips is one that can scarcely be forgotten. It was only by unremitting efforts that he conquered his innumerable faults, both of action and elocution. Keenly alive to his deficiencies he declaimed daily before a mirror (as Demosthenes had done two thousand years ago) and recited *ore rotundo* select passages from standard authors. His repeated failures at the London debating societies procured for him the title of "Orator Mum." But, as Sir Thomas Fowell Buxton has said: "The main difference between the great and the insignificant is energy, invincible determination, a purpose once fixed, and then — death or victory. That quality will do anything that can be done in the world." That quality Curran possessed, and with him the struggle ended not in death, but in victory. "He turned his shrill and stumbling brogue," writes one of his friends, "into a flexible, sustained, and finely modulated voice. His action became free and forcible; and he acquired a perfect readiness in thinking on his legs. His oratorical training was as severe as any Greek ever underwent."

In a letter which is dated March 10, 1823, and written to Zachary Macaulay, with reference to the oratorical education of his son, Thomas Babington, Lord Brougham has these words: "I composed the peroration of my speech for the Queen in the Lords after reading and repeating Demosthenes for three or four weeks. I composed it twenty times over at least, and it certainly succeeded in a very extraordinary degree, and as far above any merits of its own." This famous peroration is as follows. The climax in the opening sentence has been much admired:—

"Such, my lords, is the case now before you! Such is the evidence in support of this measure — evidence inadequate to prove a debt — impotent to deprive of a civil right — ridiculous to convict of the lowest offence — scandalous if brought forward to support a charge of the highest nature which the law knows — monstrous to ruin the honor, to blast the name of an English Queen! What shall I say, then, if this is the proof by which an act of legislation, a parliamentary sentence, an *ex post facto* law, is sought to be passed against this defenceless woman? My lords, I pray you to pause. I do earnestly beseech you to take heed! You are standing upon the brink of a precipice — then beware! It will go forth your judgment, if sentence shall go forth against the Queen. But it will be the only judgment you ever pronounced which, instead of reaching its object, will return and bound back on those who give it.

"Save the country, my lords, from the horrors of this catastrophe — save yourselves from this peril — rescue that country of which you are the ornaments, but in which you can flourish no longer when severed from the people than the blossom when cut off from the roots and stem of the tree. Save the country that you may continue to adorn it — save the crown, which is in jeopardy — the aristocracy, which is shaken — save the altar, which must stagger with the blow that rends its kindred throne!

"You have said, my lords, you have willed — the church and the King have willed — that the Queen should be deprived of its solemn service. She has, instead of that solemnity, the heartfelt prayers of the people. She wants no prayers of mine. But I do here pour forth my humble supplications at the Throne of Mercy that that mercy may be poured down upon the people in a larger measure than the merits of their rulers may deserve, and that your hearts may be turned to justice."

Undoubtedly this is powerful rhetoric, though by no means beyond the reach of criticism; but the following passage from Lord Brougham's speech in the House of Commons in 1830, on negro slavery, is, I think, more vigorous and impulsive:

"Tell me not of rights — talk not of the property of the planter in his slaves. I deny the right — I acknowledge not the property. The principles, the feelings of our common nature rise in rebellion against it. Be the appeal made to the understanding or the heart, the sentence is the same that rejects it. In vain you tell me of laws that sanction such a claim.

"There is a law above all the enactments of human codes — the same throughout the world, the same in all times — such as it was before the daring genius of Columbus pierced the night of ages, and opened to one world the sources of power, wealth, and knowledge — to another all unutterable woes. It is the law written in the heart of man by the finger of his Maker; and by that law, unchangeable and eternal, while men despise fraud, and loathe rapine, and abhor blood, they will reject the wild and guilty phantasy that man can hold property in man! In vain you appeal to treatises, to covenants between nations, the covenants of the Almighty, whether of the old covenant or the new, denounce such unholy pretensions."

As a contrast to the rushing vehemence of Brougham let me quote a brief passage of calm beauty from Daniel Webster's oration on Adams and Jefferson. To me it seems almost a perfect specimen of what the subtle grace of simple words can effect when they are combined by the hand of a master:

"Although no sculptured marble should rise to their memory, nor engraved stone bear record to their deeds, yet will their remembrance be as lasting as the land they honored. Marble columns may indeed molder into dust — time may erase all impress from the crumbling stone — but their fame remains, for with American liberty it rose, and with American liberty only can it perish. It was the last peal of yonder choir, 'Their bodies are buried in peace, but their name liveth evermore.' I catch the solemn song, I echo that lofty strain of funeral triumph, 'Their name liveth evermore.'"

The first of ancient critics asserted of the diction of Plato that it resembled a piece of sculpture or fine chasing rather than written composition. In like manner it can be shown, by innumerable quotations from the speeches of John Bright, that severe simplicity of style is in many cases the result of exquisite workmanship. I select two examples from parliamentary speeches delivered during the Russian war, to which, as indeed to all wars, Mr. Bright was strongly opposed.

"I am not, nor did I ever pretend to be a statesman; and that character is so tainted, and so equivocal in our day, that I am not sure that a pure and honorable ambition would aspire to it. I have not enjoyed for thirty years, like these noble lords, the honors and emoluments of office. I have not set my sails to every passing breeze. I am a plain and simple citizen, sent here by one of the foremost constituencies of the Empire, representing feebly, perhaps, but honestly, I dare aver, the opinions of very many and the true of all those who have sent me here. Let it not be said that I am alone in my condemnation of this war, and of this incapable and guilty administration.

"And even if I were alone, if mine were a solitary voice, raised amid the din of arms and the clamor of a venal press,

I should have the consolation I have to-night — and which I trust will be mine to the last moment of my existence — the priceless consolation that no word of mine has tended to promote the squandering of my country's treasure, or the spilling of one drop of my country's blood."

The second sample that I shall quote is equally simple and effective: —

"I cannot but notice that an uneasy feeling exists as to the news which may arrive by the very next mail from the East. I do not suppose that your troops are to be beaten in actual conflict with the foe, or that they will be driven into the sea; but I am certain that many homes in England in which there now exists a fond hope that the distant one may return — many such homes will be rendered desolate when the next mail shall arrive.

"The Angel of Death has been abroad throughout the land; you can almost hear the beating of his wings. There is no one, as when the first-born were slain of old, to sprinkle with blood the lintel and the two sideposts of our doors, that he may spare and pass on. He takes his victims from the castle of the noble, the mansion of the wealthy, and the cottage of the poor and lowly; and it is on behalf of all these classes that I now make this solemn appeal."

Though Mr. Bright is no classical scholar, he is obviously indebted to Horace for the wording of part of this passage. To prove, moreover, with what care he refines and elaborates his sentences, I may mention that in the first edition of his speeches the passage to which I refer read as follows: "But he calls at the castle of the noble and the mansion of the wealthy, equally as at the cottage of the humble." The alteration, no doubt, is slight, but the improvement is undeniable.

Equally simple in its diction is the peroration of Mr. Gladstone's speech in 1866 on Lord Grosvenor's amendment to the motion for the second reading of the Suffrage Extension Bill. I will read it to you as it is not long: —

"We stand or fall with this bill, as has been declared by my noble friend, Lord Russell. We stand with it now; we may fall with it a short time hence. If we do so fall, we, or others in our places, shall rise with it hereafter. I shall not attempt to measure with precision the forces that are to be arrayed against us in the coming issue. Perhaps the great division of to-night is not to be the last, but only the first of a series of divisions. At some point of the contest you may possibly succeed. You may drive us from our seats. You may slay, you may bury the measure we have introduced. But we will write upon its gravestone for an epitaph this line, with certain confidence in its fulfilment:

Exoriere aliquis nostris ex ossibus ultor.[1]

You cannot fight against the future. Time is on our side. The great social forces which move onward in their might and majesty, and which the tumult of these debates does not for a moment impede or disturb, those great forces are against you; they work with us — they are marshalled in our support. And the banner which we now carry in the fight, though perhaps at some moment of the struggle it may droop over our sinking heads, will yet float again in the eye of heaven, and will be borne by the firm hands of the united people of the three kingdoms, perhaps not to an easy, but to a certain and to a not distant victory."

I purposed when I began this address merely to offer some plain and practical hints on the subject of public speaking — hints drawn partly from a personal study of many of the best English speakers, and partly from wise counsels that I have at times received from competent instructors, but I have dwelt so long upon the patient and indispensable labor by which almost all famous orators have attained their renown, that I have left myself no space for my intended observations. This, however, I cannot regret, as the time has, I

---

[1] Some avenger shall arise from our ashes.

hope, been not unprofitably employed in dilating upon the necessity of industry, and in reading to you varied, though necessarily brief, specimens of the choicest eloquence.

For several years I enjoyed the honor and privilege of being intimately acquainted with the lamented D'Arcy McGee. The subject of oratory was one about which he delighted to converse, and on which he was well qualified to discourse with authority. Though a ready speaker himself, both from natural genius and from long practice he was like Demosthenes or Pericles of old, by no means an advocate of strictly extemporaneous oratory. He held, with a wise living critic, that the ease with which a half-formed idea, swimming on the mind's surface, is clothed in equivocal words and illustrated with vague images, is the "fatal facility" which produces mediocrity of thought. It was for this reason that never, if he could help it, did he deliver even a ten-minutes' speech in public without careful premeditation and the use of the pen. He deemed it a want of respect, or rather an insult to an intelligent audience, that any ordinary man, relying on mere fluent elocution, should presume to advise or instruct them without having maturely reflected on the topic of discussion, and shaped his thoughts into order and consistency.

Hence, his few remarks on the murder of President Lincoln, and his brief address on the ter-centenary of Shakespeare, are favorable specimens of thoughtful eloquence. It is no secret to many of us that, during the latter years of his life in Montreal, when he so frequently spoke in the evening at the gatherings of national societies, he invariably wrote beforehand a comprehensive abridgment of his intended speech, and sent it to one of the papers for publication next morning. This circumstance will account for the fact that the reports of the speeches to which I allude will be found, on comparison, to differ considerably in the versions of our two morning journals. The one recorded the substance, and often the very language of what actually was said: and the other printed an elaborate abstract of what the orator had designed to say. Mr. McGee told me more than once that he hoped some day to publish an annotated edition of all the speeches in Milton's "Paradise Lost," as he considered them almost faultless models of the rhetorical art. He regretted also the want of some cheap school book, which should contain select specimens of British oratory, with an introduction, and critical notes accompanying each extract.

But I must leave these recollections and hasten to a close. In his Inaugural Discourse delivered fifty years ago at the University of Glasgow, Lord Brougham seems to have said all that is essential on the subject of public speaking. "I should," says he, "lay it down as a rule admitting of no exception that a man will speak well in proportion as he has written much; and that, with equal talents, he will be the first extempore speaker who has prepared himself the most sedulously when he had an opportunity of delivering a premeditated speech. All the exceptions which I have heard cited to this principle are apparent ones only proving nothing more than that some few men of rare genius have become great speakers without preparation, but in nowise showing that with preparation they would not have reached a much higher pitch of excellence."

Few of us will refuse credit to these convictions of Lord Brougham, for, surely, we have all experienced that the tongue's most powerful auxiliary is the pen. "Nulla res," writes Cicero, "tantum ad disendum proficit quantum scriptio;" and again: "Caput est quod minime facimus:

est enim magni laboris quod fugimus, quam plurimum scribere." Once more: "Stylus optimus et præstantissimus dicendi effector et magister," that is to say, writing is the best and most excellent modeller and teacher of oratory; and to use his own beautiful simile, the habit of writing the higher passages in a speech will communicate force to the extemporaneous portions, as a boat retains her onward way from the impulse previously given, even when the strokes of the oar have ceased.

It is by no means advisable, in any case, that the whole of a speech should be committed to writing, and then committed to memory. Unless a man be an actor like Shiel — "the Kean of orators," as Lord Lytton called him — he will not be able to speak with real freedom, point or vigor, if he adopts the *memoriter* method. The strain upon the memory is apt to be too severe, and a collapse has not infrequently occurred from a speaker's having degraded himself to be the mere slave of his recollection.

Partial preparation is allowable — nay, advisable in the greatest orators. Exordiums and perorations, and the general sketch of the speech may well be arranged and shaped beforehand; but some scope should be left for the impulse of the moment. The greatest thoughts are often those struck out by the mind when at a glow, and in debate they are caught up by other minds in a congenial state. Had Macaulay not composed beforehand, and carefully committed to memory the whole of his speeches, he would probably have been considered the finest orator in the world. As it was, when he was called up suddenly, under circumstances which precluded the possibility of verbatim preparation, he produced more striking effects than usual, and attained that inspiring fervor which comes direct from the heart, and finds at once a kindred response. Such, at any rate, is the verdict of those who listened most often to his oratory.

Nevertheless, the habit of composition will suggest to the speaker at all times the best word and the best sentence, and, according to universal experience, will be of invaluable assistance when the necessity arises for unpremeditated reply. Familiarity with writing and practice in speaking act and react advantageously upon one another. On this point I cannot resist an apposite quotation from Quintilian (Book x, chap. 7): "Both exercises are reciprocally beneficial since it is found that by writing we speak with great accuracy, and by speaking we write with greater ease."

"Reading," said Bacon, "makes a full man; speaking, a ready man; and writing, a correct man. The perfection of public speaking consists in the union of the three qualities — fulness, readiness, and correctness."

VANCE

ZEBULON BAIRD VANCE, an American congressman, was born in Buncombe County, North Carolina, May 13, 1830, and educated in Washington College, Tennessee, and the University of North Carolina. After studying law and being admitted to the bar in 1853 he settled in Asheville, in his native State, and entered the North Carolina legislature the next year. He was elected to Congress in 1858, at which time he was opposed to the secession of his State, nevertheless after the outbreak of the Civil War he entered the Confederate army as a captain in 1861. He was elected governor of North Carolina in 1862 and re-elected in 1864. In 1863 he urged President Davis to undertake negotiations with the United States to bring about a cessation of hostilities, and did much to mitigate the discomforts of the Union soldiers imprisoned within his jurisdiction. After the occupation of North Carolina by the Federal troops he was imprisoned for some weeks in Washington. In 1870 he was elected to the United States Senate, but being refused admission resigned in 1872 and practised law at Charlotte till his election to the governorship of his State for the third time in 1876. His political disabilities having now been removed by Congress he was again chosen to the national Senate in 1879, of which he continued a member until his death at Washington, April 14, 1894. He was chairman of many congressional committees and was one of the most popular members of the Senate. Vance was an eloquent speaker and earnestly advocated the cause of free silver and of tariff reform.

THE SLAVERY QUESTION

FROM SPEECH DELIVERED IN THE HOUSE OF REPRESENTATIVES, MARCH 16, 1860

THE scheme of removing and colonizing four million people is so utterly absurd in practice that it needs only to be suggested to exhibit its entire impracticability. Amalgamation is so odious that even the mind of a fanatic recoils in disgust and loathing from the prospect of intermingling the quick and jealous blood of the European with the putrid stream of African barbarism.

What, then, is best and right to be done with our slaves? Plainly and unequivocally, common sense says, keep the slave where he is now — in servitude. The interest of the slave himself imperatively demands it. The interest of the master, of the United States, of the world, nay, of humanity itself, says, keep the slave in his bondage; treat him humanely, teach him Christianity, care for him in sickness and old age, and make his bondage light as may be; but above all, keep him a slave and in strict subordination; for that is his normal condition; the one in which alone he can promote the interest of himself or of his fellows.

If this is not the language of political philosophy and true philanthropy, if this is not right, then are my most ardent convictions and the most generous impulses of my heart but shallow and false delusions; and I pray to be enlightened, as one who would, if possible, rise above all the surroundings of prejudice and section to view this great question solely by the pure and unflickering light of truth.

Such being our circumstances, and such our convictions, it is time for the opponents of slavery to know, and to be warned, that it is something more than pecuniary interest that binds us to that institution. It is not, as we are often tauntingly told, a desire for gain, or an aversion to physical labor, that makes us jealous of any interference with slavery.

The principle is more deeply seated than this. The general welfare and prosperity of our country, the very foundation of our society, of our fortunes, and, to a greater or less extent, the personal safety of our people, combine to make us defend it to the last extremity. And neither considerations of the Federal Union, nor any other good, will allow us to permit any direct interference with our rights in this respect.

But we are to be lulled to sleep, and our fear quieted, as to the purposes of the Republican party, by the oft-repeated assertions of your leaders, that you do not intend to interfere with it in the States. You say, again and again, that you only intend to prevent its extension into the Territories; and you complain that southern men will unjustly continue to charge you with interference with it inside the States. Mr. Seward, in his recent opiate, says:

"3. That the capital States [by which he is supposed to mean slave States] do not practically distinguish between legitimate and constitutional resistance to the extension of slavery in the common Territories of the Union, and unconstitutional aggression against slavery established by local laws in the capital States."

And Mr. Wade has laid it down recently, as one of the grand principles of the Republican party, that there shall be no interference with slavery inside the States. I contend, sir, that to prohibit slavery in all the Territories, by an act of Congress, or to refuse to admit a new State because she recognizes slavery, would be a direct and unequivocal interference, about which common sense will admit of no sort of doubt.

In the first place, because it materially impairs the value of my property to restrain my power to remove it; and especially to make it no longer my property when I take it into what Mr. Seward himself acknowledges to be "the common territory." If your shoes and cotton fabrics were prohibited by Congress from entering the south, you would find their value impaired most woefully, and would justly regard it as an interference with the rights of trade.

In the second place, by surrounding the slave States with free territory, and building us in with an impassable wall, you would eventually force the abolition of slavery. Our population would become so dense, and our slaves so numerous, that we could not live; their value would depreciate to nothing, and we would not be able to keep them.

Do you not call this interference? If not, then what is it? A general desires to take a certain city; thinking it too strong to be won by storm, he sits down with his army before it, draws his lines of circumvallation, cuts off its supplies, and, shutting off all communication, waits patiently for famine and domestic insurrection to do their work. True, he says, "Don't be alarmed in there; I am not going to interfere with your internal affairs; I have no right to do that; in fact, one of the rules of war in my camp is, no interference with the internal affairs of this city; my only intention is that you shall not spread, as you are a very sinful people."

Yet that city, in spite of these protestations, would soon find itself subjugated and ruined. You are interfering with our rights in the most dangerous manner by thus seeking to violate one of the oldest and plainest principles of justice and reason — that you cannot do indirectly that which you are forbidden to do directly. The voice of the nation speaking through its representatives by a majority of four to one, North and South, affirmed this in 1838. In the twenty-fifth Congress, Mr. Atherton, of New Hampshire, moved a series of resolutions on this subject, the third of which sets forth —

"That Congress has no right to do that indirectly which it cannot do directly; and that the agitation of the subject of slavery in the District of Columbia or the Territories, as a means, and with the view of disturbing or overthrowing that institution in the several States is against the true spirit and meaning of the constitution, an infringement of the rights of the States affected, and a breach of the public faith upon which they entered into the Confederacy."

Upon this resolution the yeas were one hundred and sixty-four, and the nays forty. Well may you complain that the South will not distinguish between your resistance to the extension of slavery into the Territories and a direct interference with its existence in the States. The acutest minds can only see a different means of attaining the same result.

In the third place, your agitation and eternal harangues have a direct and inevitable tendency to excite our slaves to insurrection. I know that you deny not only an intention to do so, but the effect also.

But you speak in ignorance or disregard of history. It is unnatural to suppose that the noise of this great conflict will not reach the negro's ear, and that your violent professions of regard for his rights will not make him believe that those who shelter him when he runs away, will not also help him to cut his master's throat. The constant denunciation of his owners by your crazy fanatics will make him regard them as monsters, and will cause him to cherish the coals of rebellion until they burst forth into a consuming fire.

Wilberforce and Macaulay did not even intend to abolish slavery in the West Indies when they began their struggle for the rights of the negro — so they said — and they scouted the idea with horror that their agitation would lead to servile war And yet, when the shrieks of murdered men and outraged women went up through the hot roar of conflagration throughout those lovely islands, the raging demons of lust and brutality bore upon their standards the name of Wilberforce, the philanthropist, beneath the effigy of a white woman kneeling at the feet of a negro, and on which was inscribed, "Liberty and white wives!"

And so strongly do these facts press upon you, as the legal result of your abolition teachings, that we have witnessed the mortifying spectacle of gentlemen rising on this floor and solemnly declaring that they were not in favor of servile insurrection!

But all this injustice will you do, and all these dangers to our wives and children will you incur, rather than permit slavery to enter another Territory, or permit it to come into the Union as a slave State, even though the unanimous voice of the people thereof so desired it. And this Territory, which you mock us by calling "common," what do you intend to do with it?

Sir, there are some districts in the south, in which the widows of slain Mexican volunteers will outnumber the whole forces which some of your northern States had in the field during that war. And yet these widows and their orphans are not permitted to enter, with their property, upon these fair lands which their husbands purchased with their blood. They have not even the satisfaction of seeing them sold for the use of the public treasury. You thrust them aside; and, by what you call a "homestead bill," propose to give them away to those among you who cannot pay one shilling per acre for homes.

The advocates of this agrarian iniquity unblushingly avow that it will enable them to ship off the refuse scum and redundant villainy of the cities of the north. Your high-sounding catchwords of "homes for the homeless" and "lands for the landless" can deceive no one. Why not give also money to the moneyless, and shoes to the barefoot? Why not imitate Rome, when growing corrupt, and distribute largesses of money and provisions among the people?

It would be the same, with the difference that Rome robbed her provinces to feed her citizens, whilst you would rob your citizens to feed the provinces. Nay, you would feed the world; for every jail, workhouse, and penitentiary in Europe would be emptied in our Territories. The Atlantic Ocean would be bridged, and swarms would pour across to enter into this land, which is too good for southern slaveholders. The good would come no faster, and of the bad we have enough already. The old States lose their population fast enough as it is, and no one should desire to increase the depopulation. The true title of the bill, sir, should read: "A bill to encourage foreign and domestic vagabondism, by granting quarter sections of the public land to each actual vagabond that cannot pay twelve-and-a-half cents per acre for a home."

I would finally beg to say to these anti-slavery gentlemen, that for purposes of present advantage they take but a limited view of the future of this great question. A world in arms could not abolish slavery in the southern States to-day, or, if once abolished, a world in arms would rise up and demand its restoration to-morrow. Our slaves are this moment more firmly fixed in their bondage than at any previous moment in our history. Their labor has become an indispensable necessity, not only to ourselves, but to the civilized world; and statesmen, whether British or American, know it.

Our united people will defend it with their blood in the Union, and should your whole society, yielding to a mad fanaticism, so trespass upon our rights as to drive us from the Union, we would find ourselves able to defend it as an independent nation. In fact, we have all the capacities for a separate and independent existence that are calculated to make a great and prosperous State. We produce all the great items of raw material necessary for manufactures; the well-watered valleys of the mountain regions in Virginia, Kentucky, Tennessee, and North Carolina present the most desirable seats for manufactories in the world.

The beautiful, healthful, and magnificent mountain region

of western Carolina, which I am proud to represent on this floor, presents greater facilities itself for manufacturing than all New England put together. The coalfields of my State would feed the glowing furnace for ages to come; and the fertile plains of the northwestern States do not furnish a finer region for the production of the common articles of food, than the great States of Kentucky, Tennessee, and North Carolina.

In fact, we combine everything within ourselves that is necessary for a separate and independent existence. Norfolk, which I believe is in any event destined to become a rival of New York and Liverpool, would then become the great port of entry for the south; and the opening up of the great regions of the west by the Southern Pacific Railroad, and the mingling of the waters of the Ohio with those of the Chesapeake Bay, by canal, would make her to rival the magnificence of Tyre and Sidon. In all these mutations, whilst we could flourish, your prosperity would be stricken down to the dust, and your dependence upon raw material would still hold you our obsequious dependent.

You talk now of forbearing to interfere with slavery among us, because of the delicacy of the question and the interest it involves to us; but you know that your own prosperity is still more dependent upon its existence. It is a tender regard for the goose that lays for you the golden egg, that makes you profess to be unwilling to lay hands upon it. You know that slave labor has built all your cities and towns, has erected your great warehouses, freights your rich navies, and carries wealth and happiness throughout all the bleak and sterile hills of New England.

You know that the shirt you wear, when you stand up to denounce the slaveholder; that the sugar that sweetens your tea, when you sit down to the evening and morning meal — nay, the very paper on which you indite your senseless philippics against the south, are the products of slave labor. You not only thus grow rich upon what you call an iniquity, but you owe your positions in this Hall to the prejudice which you feed and pamper against slavery, and which alone constitutes your whole stock in trade.

Think not, therefore, that you can prevent the extension of slavery, or abolish it where it is. For should you succeed, as you threaten, in cooping us up and surrounding us by Wilmot provisoes, or by your homestead bills, in filling up the common Territories with northern and foreign squatters inimical to slavery, the time will come when the southern people, gathering up their households together, sword in hand, will force an outlet for it at the cannon's mouth.

Long years might intervene before this necessity came upon us, but come it certainly would, and we would then go forth and find other lands whose soil and climate were adapted to our institutions, from which you would not dare to attempt to expel us. But will you drive us to this course? Will the great conservative masses of the northern people, who are inheritors with us alike of the common glories of the past, and heirs-apparent of the unspeakable glories of our future, continue to urge this dire extremity upon their southern brethren?

Or will they not rather "be still, and behold how God will bring it to pass?" Will they not wait with patience for this great and all-absorbing problem to work itself out according to the immutable laws of climate, soil, and all the governing circumstances with which he has ever controlled the uprisings and the down-sittings of men?

In this way, and this only, as the waters of the great sea

purify themselves, will the good of both the African slave and his European master be accomplished; without violence, without bloodshed, and without a disruption of the bonds which bind together this blood-bought and blood-cemented Union, which our fathers founded in the agony of the greatest of human struggles, and builded with prayers to Heaven for its perpetuity.

This way alone will enable us to avoid that dread day of disunion, of which I have thought in the bitterness of my spirit that I could curse it even as Job cursed his nativity: "Let that day be darkness; let not God regard it from above, neither let the light shine upon it. Let it not be joined unto the days of the year; let it not come into the number of the months. Let the stars of the twilight thereof be dark; let it look for light, but have none; neither let it see the dawning of the day."

TELLER

HENRY MOORE TELLER, an American lawyer and politician, was born at Granger, New York, May 23, 1830. After graduating from Rushford Academy and Alfred University and teaching for a few years he was admitted to the bar in 1856, practising first in Illinois and then in Colorado. He was a major-general of the Colorado militia during the last two years of the Civil War, and in December, 1876, was United States senator. From April, 1882, until March, 1885, during President Arthur's administration, he was secretary of the interior, resigning to take his seat again in the Senate. In 1897 he was re-elected as an Independent Silver Republican with a term to expire in March, 1903.

ON PORTO RICO

[Speech delivered in the Senate, March 14, 1900, during the consideration of the bill temporarily to provide revenues for the relief of Porto Rico.]

MR. PRESIDENT,— Before we get through with this question of the power of the United States and what ought to be its policy there will be ample time, I know, for me to discuss it, and I will go directly to the bill, so that I may shorten my remarks within a proper time, in view of the fact that the senator from Washington has yielded the floor to me for a few moments.

In dealing with these new possessions my theory is that we may make them a part of the United States if we see fit. Now, if we conclude that we do not want to make them a part of the United States, I believe we have the same power to hold them, in a different relation, that Great Britain has. I have listened to all the discussion that has gone on here, and I can conceive of no reason why the sovereignty of the United States is limited to territory that they must make a part of the United States. They will be a part of the United States in one sense undoubtedly if we exercise a protectorate over them. They will be a dependency, and they will have a different relation to us from what the other Territories organized as incipient States have. If we choose, we can provide that the territory of Puerto Rico — I am speaking now of the geographical territory — shall be under the control and sovereignty of the United States, that the people of that island may make all the laws that we say they may make. We may give them absolute self-control, or, in my opinion, we may reserve the right to say to them, "There are certain things you cannot be allowed to do; and if you do certain things, we will intervene and nullify your action."

Mr. President, from my standpoint, then, there is no difficulty in dealing with these possessions, and it becomes simply a question of policy. In this I am speaking for myself only. I do not represent any political organization, and I am not bound by any caucus or by any influences of that character. So far as I am concerned, I do not want to make Puerto Rico nor do I want to make the Philippines an integral part of the United States; I do not want to make their people citizens of the United States, with all the rights that citizenship of the United States ought to carry with it.

The relation that I would establish for those people is absolutely consistent with every tradition of our government and our people from the time we organized the government of the United States up to the present hour. If I had time, I could show historically that the fathers of this Republic contemplated that we should some day have colonies. It may be that it is not good policy to have colonies. That is another question. It may be — although I do not believe it — that it would be wise for us to get rid of Puerto Rico and return it to Spain, or to give it to the people of the island themselves.

It may be that it would be wise for us to turn over the Philippine Islands to the anarchy and confusion which I believe would follow the withdrawal of the American troops from those islands at the present time. But I do not believe it.

I will admit that there will be some difficulties in dealing with those people. I foresaw that in the beginning, and I see it more clearly now than I did a year ago, as I believe everybody else does. But, as I said a long time since in this body, the American people will deal with this question in a spirit of fairness and in a spirit of courage. They are not going to be frightened by a contemplation of the fact that there are difficulties in front of them. If anybody can show a better way out of the difficulty than for us to hold those possessions, I am prepared to consider it. I am now considering, first, what is the duty that we owe, not to the Filipinos, not to the Puerto Ricans, but to the people of the United States? That is the paramount question. I believe we can deal with those people without doing any injustice to them or any injustice to ourselves. But we must have a policy; we must lay down a rule and follow it. What I complain of in the party in power is that it has not a policy, as it seems to me, on this question.

I do not know whether we are to have a colonial system or whether we are to make those people part and parcel of the United States. One or the other we must do. I regard the latter as infinitely more dangerous than the former. I would a great deal rather make Puerto Rico a colony than to make her a State; I would a great deal rather make the Philippine Islands a colony, a province, a dependency, or whatever you may choose to call it, than to make those islands into a State or to make their inhabitants citizens of the United States, with all the rights and privileges which follow, and which must ultimately mean, if they become citizens of the United States, that they shall stand before the law on an equality with all other citizens of the United States. If you make Puerto Rico a Territory, an incipient State, its people will have a right some day to expect to become a State of the Union; but if you hold them in tutelage and pupilage for an indefinite period as citizens of the United States, they will have a right to complain.

Mr. President, Puerto Rico is not a part of the United States to-day, neither are the Philippine Islands. In all the acquisitions of territorial property heretofore, we have had, before we acquired it, some relations established by treaty, or otherwise, with the people that we took under our control. When we took in Louisiana, we stipulated with France that we would make the people of that Territory citizens of the United States, entitled to all the rights, privileges, and immunities of citizens; when we took in Florida, we did the same with Spain; when we took in a portion of Mexico, we did the same with Mexico; and when we took in Alaska, we did the same with Russia. When we acquired our new possessions, the commission that went over to Paris very wisely said that their political status should be as Congress should determine.

In an early day, when Louisiana was taken in as a part of the United States, it was questioned in the House of Representatives, and even here, whether by the treaty-making power alone that could be done. In my judgment it could, because otherwise there would be a restriction upon the treaty-making power, which I think would be inconsistent with sovereignty. But here we have no question. The people in these possessions are not citizens to-day. The Filipinos are not citizens nor are the Puerto Ricans. The bill now pending before the Senate makes citizens of the inhabitants of Puerto Rico of the United States *ex industria*. That feature alone, if there were no other in it, would compel me to vote against the bill. I do not want those people made citizens of the United States. I want to extend to them all the privileges which are consistent with their relations to this government, save that of citizenship. I would extend to those territories all the privileges, all the blessings which the constitution of the United States is, by some, supposed to have conferred, but which I say are not conferred, but inherited, inhering in a free government. I would not establish a relationship which would enable them to participate with us in the election of a President and to have their representatives on this floor or in the other House.

I am told by some senators here that this bill does make citizens of the people of Puerto Rico, but does not make Puerto Rico a part and parcel of the United States. If it is possible by language in a statute to make Puerto Rico a part of the United States, it is so made by this bill. In the first place, the people there are made citizens, their ports are made ports of the United States, and the writs of their courts run in the name of the people of the United States; we extend the internal revenue laws over them, the postal laws, and almost all other laws over them, except simply the laws as to the collection of duty on imports. We provide that their products coming into our ports shall pay duty.

Mr. President, if those people are to be a part and parcel of the United States, as they will be if this bill shall be enacted into law as it now stands, and as they will be if a considerable part of it should be stricken out, as I hear vague rumors that it may be, they will have such a relation, in my judgment, to the people of the United States that some of the provisions of this act will be absolutely indefensible and cannot be maintained in any case.

Mr. President, I am not going to waste time in speaking about the provision which puts a duty upon goods going into Puerto Rico. I think that was pretty well exploded here the other day, and I understand that it is liable to be abandoned. But the other question presents itself whether we have a right to put a duty on goods coming from Puerto Rico into the United States. In my judgment that whole question must be solved by what is their relation to the people of the United States. If they are a part of the United States, if their people are citizens of the United States, you have no right to put a duty upon their goods. If they are not citizens of the United States, then it is a question of policy and not a question of justice; but what right have the Puerto Ricans to insist now that they shall have free trade with us if they are not part and parcel of the United States?

Mr. President, we are told that there is a great sugar interest and a great tobacco interest, or something of that kind, demanding that this duty shall be put on those people. I know nothing about that, and I do not care to consider it. It is not a question to be considered in determining this matter as to what influences are back of it. The question is, what is justice? If they are citizens, as they will be under this bill, you have not any right to impose duties upon them, and it would be an act of gross injustice and one which cannot be legally maintained. If they are not citizens, you have as much right to put a duty upon them as you have to put it on English subjects who send their goods here from London.

A great number of people now in Puerto Rico who are clamoring for free trade with us are not citizens of that country at all, and the large sugar interests there are held by people who are not connected by any ties of citizenship with that country. English capitalists and other foreign capitalists are the owners of the sugar plantations. If we should accept the newspaper accounts we might suppose that every man in Puerto Rico, poverty-stricken as many of them are, was engaged in shipping sugar and tobacco into the United States. There is not two per cent of the people of Puerto Rico who have any interest in shipping sugar here, and there is not two per cent of them who have any interest in shipping tobacco here. That is done by a few capitalists, and it is those who are interested in this subject. If you let them bring their sugar here at fifteen per cent of the regular tariff which the Cubans, for instance, must pay, the sugar and tobacco planters of Puerto Rico will make a great profit; and, with a two-years' accumulation of sugar in the hands of those rich people, they will be the ones who will be still more enriched and not the poverty-stricken people of that island. As suggested to me by the senator from Wisconsin [Mr. Spooner], the sugar people pay labor such wages as Americans would starve upon.

The great question to be considered all the time is, How can we treat these islands consistently with the traditions of the American people? How can we do justice to them and justice to ourselves at the same time? If we give to them practically self-government, they have no right to ask us for participation in the affairs of the general government; and anything that we may do for them, bad as this bill is — and I think it violates some of our traditions as it is — but, bad as it is, is it not better than anything that those people ever heretofore had or anything that they had any hope of having two years ago?

If we keep steadily in view the idea that if these people are capable of self-government, they shall have it — and I have no doubt of their ability to manage their own internal and domestic affairs practically without our supervision, although some senators say that is not the fact — if we yield that to them, we have not violated any principle of free government and of a free people; and all of this repeated newspaper clamor that we are about to do something extremely bad if we deny to those people full citizenship, it seems to me, is without any foundation whatever.

Mr. President, I had intended, as I said before, to go into very many phases of this case, and to touch upon even our relations with our Asiatic possessions; but I shall not do so now. I shall content myself with saying practically now what I have said — that this bill seems to me to be incongruous and unsatisfactory from any standpoint; I do not care whether it be from that of making Puerto Rico a part of the United States or making it a colony.

KNOTT

JAMES PROCTOR KNOTT, an American congressman, was born at Lebanon, Kentucky, August 29, 1830. At sixteen he began to study law and removing in 1850 to Memphis, Missouri, was licensed to practice there the following year. In 1858 he entered the State legislature and was made chairman of the judiciary committee. He became attorney-general of the State soon after, but refusing to take the test oath in 1861, regarding it as too stringent in its character, his office was declared vacant and he was disbarred. In 1862 he returned to his birthplace in Kentucky where he practised his profession till his election to Congress in 1866. After some adverse discussion he was permitted to take his seat in the House, where his first speech was directed against the constitutionality of the test oath and its application to members of Congress. He was re-elected in 1868 and served on various important committees, making on one occasion a humorous speech against a bill for the improvement of Pennsylvania avenue, which defeated the bill amid roars of laughter. In the same Congress his famous "Duluth" speech gave him a national reputation as a humorist. Knott was again a member of Congress, 1875-83, and was governor of Kentucky, 1883-87.

SPEECH ON "DULUTH"

DELIVERED IN THE HOUSE OF REPRESENTATIVES, JANUARY 21, 1871

MR. SPEAKER,—If I could be actuated by any conceivable inducement to betray the sacred trust reposed in me by those to whose generous confidence I am indebted for the honor of a seat on this floor; if I could be influenced by any possible consideration to become instrumental in giving away, in violation of their known wishes, any portion of their interest in the public domain, for the mere promotion of any railroad enterprise whatever, I should certainly feel a strong inclination to give this measure my most earnest and hearty support; for I am assured that its success would materially enhance the pecuniary prosperity of some of the most valued friends I have on earth; friends for whose accommodation I would be willing to make almost any sacrifice not involving my personal honor or my fidelity as the trustee of an express trust.

And that act of itself would be sufficient to countervail almost any objection I might entertain to the passage of this bill, not inspired by the imperative and inexorable sense of public duty.

But, independent of the seductive influences of private friendship, to which I admit I am, perhaps, as susceptible as any of the gentlemen I see around me, the intrinsic merits of the measure itself are of such an extraordinary character as to commend it most strongly to the favorable consideration of every member of this House, myself not excepted, notwithstanding my constituents, in whose behalf alone I am acting here, would not be benefited by its passage one particle more than they would be by a project to cultivate an orange grove on the bleakest summit of Greenland's icy mountains.

Now, sir, as to those great trunk lines of railways, spanning the continent from ocean to ocean, I confess my mind has never been fully made up. It is true they may afford some trifling advantages to local traffic, and they may even in time become the channels of a more extended commerce. Yet I have never been thoroughly satisfied either of the necessity or expediency of projects promising such meagre results to the great body of our people. But with regard to the transcendent merits of the gigantic enterprise contemplated in this bill, I have never entertained the shadow of a doubt

Years ago, when I first heard that there was somewhere in the vast *terra incognita*, somewhere in the bleak regions of the great northwest, a stream of water known to the nomadic inhabitants of the neighborhood as the river St. Croix, I became satisfied that the construction of a railroad from that raging torrent to some point in the civilized world was essential to the happiness and prosperity of the American people, if not absolutely indispensable to the perpetuity of republican institutions on this continent.

I felt, instinctively, that the boundless resources of that prolific region of sand and pine shrubbery would never be fully developed without a railroad constructed and equipped at the expense of the government, and perhaps not then. I had an abiding presentiment that, some day or other, the people of this whole country, irrespective of party affiliations, regardless of sectional prejudices, and "without distinction of race, color, or previous condition of servitude," would rise in their majesty and demand an outlet for the enormous agricultural productions of those vast and fertile pine barrens, drained in the rainy season by the surging waters of the turbid St. Croix.

These impressions, derived simply and solely from the "eternal fitness of things," were not only strengthened by the interesting and eloquent debate on this bill, to which I listened with so much pleasure the other day, but intensified, if possible, as I read over, this morning, the lively colloquy which took place on that occasion, as I find it reported in last Friday's "Globe." I will ask the indulgence of the House while I read a few short passages, which are sufficient, in my judgment, to place the merits of the great enterprise, contemplated in the measure now under discussion, beyond all possible controversy.

The honorable gentleman from Minnesota [Mr. Wilson] who, I believe, is managing this bill, in speaking of the character of the country through which this railroad is to pass says this:

"We want to have the timber brought to us as cheaply as possible. Now, if you tie up the lands in this way, so that no title can be obtained to them — for no settler will go on these lands, for he cannot make a living — you deprive us of the benefits of that timber."

Now, sir, I would not have it by any means inferred from this that the gentleman from Minnesota would insinuate that the people out in this section desire this timber merely for the purpose of fencing up their farms so that their stock may not wander off and die of starvation among the bleak hills of St. Croix. I read it for no such purpose, sir, and make no comment on it myself. In corroboration of this statement of the gentleman from Minnesota, I find this testimony given by the honorable gentleman from Wisconsin [Mr. Washburn]. Speaking of these same lands, he says:

"Under the bill, as amended by my friend from Minnesota, nine tenths of the land is open to actual settlers at $2.50 per acre; the remaining one tenth is pine-timbered land, that is not fit for settlement, and never will be settled upon; but the timber will be cut off. I admit that it is the most valuable portion of the grant, for most of the grant is not valuable. It is quite valueless; and if you put in this amendment of the gentleman from Indiana you may just as well kill the bill, for no man, and no company will take the grant and build the road."

I simply pause here to ask some gentleman better versed in the science of mathematics than I am, to tell me if the timbered lands are in fact the most valuable portion of that section of the country, and they would be entirely valueless without the timber that is on them, what the remainder of the land is worth which has no timber on them at all?

But, further on, I find a most entertaining and instructive interchange of views between the gentleman from Arkansas

[Mr. Rogers], the gentleman from Wisconsin [Mr. Washburn], and the gentleman from Maine [Mr. Peters], upon the subject of pine lands generally, which I will tax the patience of the House to read:

"Mr. Rogers — Will the gentleman allow me to ask him a question?"

"Mr. Washburn — Certainly."

"Mr. Rogers — Are these pine lands entirely worthless except for timber?"

"Mr. Washburn — They are generally worthless for any other purpose. I am personally familiar with that subject. These lands are not valuable for purposes of settlement."

"Mr. Farnsworth — They will be after the timber is taken off."

"Mr. Washburn — No, sir."

"Mr. Rogers — I want to know the character of these pine lands."

"Mr. Washburn — They are generally sandy, barren lands. My friend from the Green Bay district [Mr. Sawyer] is himself perfectly familiar with this question, and he will bear me out in what I say, that these timber lands are not adapted to settlement."

"Mr. Rogers — The pine lands to which I am accustomed are generally very good. What I want to know is, what is the difference between our pine lands and your pine lands?"

"Mr. Washburn — The pine timber of Wisconsin generally grows upon barren, sandy land. The gentleman from Maine [Mr. Peters] who is familiar with pine lands, will, I have no doubt, say that pine timber grows generally upon the most barren lands."

"Mr. Peters — As a general thing pine lands are not worth much for cultivation."

And further on I find this pregnant question, the joint production of the two gentlemen from Wisconsin.

"Mr. Paine — Does my friend from Indiana suppose that in any event settlers will occupy and cultivate these pine lands?"

"Mr. Washburn — Particularly without a railroad. Yes, sir, particularly without a railroad."

It will be asked after awhile, I am afraid, if settlers will go anywhere unless the government builds a railroad for them to go on.

I desire to call attention to only one more statement, which I think sufficient to settle the question. It is one made by the gentleman from Wisconsin [Mr. Paine] who says:

"These lands will be abandoned for the present. It may be that at some remote period there will spring up in that region a new kind of agriculture, which will cause a demand for these particular lands; and they may then come into use and be valuable for agricultural purposes. But I know, and I cannot help thinking, that my friend from Indiana understands that, for the present, and for many years to come, these pine lands can have no possible value other than that arising from the pine timber which stands on them."

Now, sir, after listening to this emphatic and unequivocal testimony of these intelligent, competent, and able-bodied witnesses, who that is not as incredulous as St. Thomas himself will doubt for a moment that the Goshen of America is to be found in the sandy valleys and upon the pine-clad hills of the St. Croix? Who will have the hardihood to rise in his seat on this floor and assert that, excepting the pine bushes, the entire region would not produce vegetation enough in ten years to fatten a grasshopper? Where is the patriot who is willing that his country shall incur the peril of remaining another day without the amplest railroad connection with such an inexhaustible mine of agricultural wealth? Who will answer for the consequences of abandoning a great and warlike people, in the possession of a country like that, to brood over the indifference and neglect of their government? How long would it be before they would take to studying the Declaration of Independence, and hatching out the damnable heresy of secession? How long before the grim demon of civil discord would rear again his horrid head in our midst, "gnash loud his iron fangs and shake his crest of bristling bayonets?"

Then, sir, think of the long and painful process of reconstruction that must follow, with its concomitant amendments to the constitution, the seventeenth, eighteenth, and nineteenth articles. The sixteenth, it is of course understood, is to be appropriated to those blushing damsels who are, day after day, beseeching us to let them vote, hold office, drink cocktails, ride a-straddle, and do everything else the men do. But, above all, sir, let me implore you to reflect for a single moment on the deplorable condition of our country in case of a foreign war, with all our ports blockaded, all our cities in a state of siege, the gaunt spectre of famine brooding like a hungry vulture over our starving land; our commissary stores all exhausted, and our famishing armies withering away in the field, a helpless prey to the insatiate demon of hunger; our navy rotting in the docks for want of provisions for our gallant seamen, and we without any railroad communication whatever with the prolific pine thickets of the St. Croix.

Ah, sir, I could very well understand why my amiable friends from Pennsylvania [Mr. Myers, Mr. Kelley, and Mr. O'Neill] should be so earnest in their support of this bill the other day; and, if their honorable colleague, my friend, Mr. Randall, will pardon the remark, I will say that I consider his criticism of their action on that occasion as not only unjust, but ungenerous. I knew they were looking forward with the far-reaching ken of enlightened statesmanship to the pitiable condition in which Philadelphia will be left unless speedily supplied with railroad connection in some way or other with this garden spot of the universe.

And besides, sir, this discussion has relieved my mind of a mystery that has weighed upon it like an incubus for years. I could never understand before why there was so much excitement during the last Congress over the acquisition of Alta Vela. I could never understand why it was that some of our ablest statesmen and most disinterested patriots should entertain such dark forebodings of the untold calamities that were to befall our beloved country unless we should take immediate possession of that desirable island. But I see now that they were laboring under the mistaken impression that the government would need the guano to manure the public lands on the St. Croix.

Now, sir, I repeat, I have been satisfied for years that, if there was any portion of the inhabited globe absolutely in a suffering condition for want of a railroad it was these teeming pine barrens of the St. Croix. At what particular point on that noble stream such a road should be commenced I knew was immaterial, and it seems so to have been considered by the draughtsman of this bill.

It might be up at the spring or down at the foot-log, or the water-gate, or the fish-dam, or anywhere along the bank, no matter where. But, in what direction should it run, or where it should terminate, were always to my mind questions of the most painful perplexity. I could conceive of no place on "God's green earth" in such straitened circumstances for railroad facilities as to be likely to desire or willing to accept such a connection.

I knew that neither Bayfield nor Superior City would have it, for they both indignantly spurned the munificence of the government when coupled with such ignominous conditions, and let this very same land grant die on their hands years and years ago, rather than submit to the degradation of a direct communication by railroad with the piney woods of the St. Croix; and I knew that what the enterprising inhabitants of those giant young cities would refuse to take, would have few charms for others, whatever their necessities or cupidity might be.

Hence, as I have said, sir, I was utterly at a loss to determine where the terminus of this great and indispensable road should be, until I accidentally overheard some gentleman the other day mention the name of "Duluth."

"Duluth!" The word fell upon my ear with a peculiar and indescribable charm, like the gentle murmur of a low fountain stealing forth in the midst of roses; or the soft, sweet accents of an angel's whisper in the bright joyous dream of sleeping innocence.

"Duluth!" 'Twas the name for which my soul had panted for years, as the hart panteth for the water-brooks.

But where was "Duluth?"

Never in all my limited reading, had my vision been gladdened by seeing the celestial word in print. And I felt a profound humiliation in my ignorance that its dulcet syllables had never before ravished my delighted ear. I was certain the draughtsman in this bill had never heard of it, or it would have been designated as one of the termini of this road. I asked my friends about it, but they knew nothing of it. I rushed to the library, and examined all the maps I could find. I discovered in one of them a delicate hair-like line, diverging from the Mississippi near a place marked Prescott, which, I supposed, was intended to represent the river St. Croix, but could nowhere find "Duluth."

Nevertheless, I was confident it existed somewhere, and that its discovery would constitute the crowning glory of the present century, if not of all modern times. I knew it was bound to exist in the very nature of things; that the symmetry and perfection of our planetary system would be incomplete without it. That the elements of maternal nature would since have resolved themselves back into original chaos, if there had been such a hiatus in creation as would have resulted from leaving out "Duluth!"

In fact, sir, I was overwhelmed with the conviction that "Duluth" not only existed somewhere, but that wherever it was it was a great and glorious place. I was convinced that the greatest calamity that ever befell the benighted nations of the ancient world was in their having passed away without a knowledge of the actual existence of "Duluth;" that their fabled Atlantis, never seen save by the hallowed vision of the inspired poesy, was in fact but another name for "Duluth;" that the golden orchard of the Hesperides was but a poetical synonym for the beer-gardens in the vicinity of "Duluth." I was certain that Herodotus had died a miserable death, because in all his travels and with all his geographical research he had never heard of "Duluth."

I knew that if the immortal spirit of Homer could look down from another heaven than that created by his own celestial genius upon the long lines of Pilgrims from every nation of the earth, to the gushing fountain of poesy, opened by the touch of his magic wand, if he could be permitted to behold the vast assemblage of grand and glorious productions of the lyric art, called into being by his own inspired strains, he would weep tears of bitter anguish, that, instead of lavishing all the stores of his mighty genius upon the fall of Ilion, it had not been his more blessed lot to crystallize in deathless song the rising glories of "Duluth."

Yes, sir, had it not been for this map, kindly furnished me by the legislature of Minnesota, I might have gone down to my obscure and humble grave in an agony of despair, because I could nowhere find "Duluth." Had such been my melancholy fate, I have no doubt that with the last feeble pulsation of my breaking heart, with the last faint exhalation of my fleeting breath, I should have whispered, "Where is 'Duluth'?"

But, thanks to the beneficence of that band of ministering angels who have their bright abodes in the far-off capitol of Minnesota, just as the agony of my anxiety was about to culminate in the frenzy of despair, this blessed map was placed in my hands; and, as I unfolded it, a resplendent scene of ineffable glory opened before me, such as I imagined burst upon the enraptured vision of the wandering peri through the opening gates of Paradise.

There, there, for the first time, my enchanted eye rested upon the ravishing word, "Duluth!" This map, sir, is intended, as it appears from its title, to illustrate the position of "Duluth" in the United States; but if the gentlemen will examine it I think they will concur with me in the opinion that it is far too modest in its pretensions. It not only illustrates the position of "Duluth" in the United States, but exhibits its relations with all created things. It even goes further than this. It hits the shadowy vale of futurity, and affords us a view of the golden prospects of "Duluth," far along the dim vista of ages yet to come.

If the gentlemen will examine it they will find "Duluth" not only in the centre of the map but represented in the centre of a series of concentric circles one hundred miles apart and some of them as much as four thousand miles in diameter, embracing alike in their tremendous sweep the fragrant savannas, the sunlit south, and the eternal solitudes of snow that mantle the icebound north. How these circles were produced is perhaps one of those primordial mysteries that the most skilled paleologist will never be able to explain. But the fact is, sir, "Duluth" is pre-eminently a central point, for I am told by gentlemen who have been so reckless of their own personal safety as to venture away into those awful regions where "Duluth" is supposed to be, that it is so exactly in the centre of the visible universe that the sky comes down at precisely the same distance all around it.

I find by reference to this map that "Duluth" is situated somewhere near the western end of Lake Superior, but as there is no dot or other mark indicating its exact location I am unable to say whether it is actually confined to any particular spot or whether "it is just lying around there loose."

I really cannot tell whether it is one of those ethereal creations of intellectual frostwork, more intangible than the rose-tinted clouds of a summer sunset; one of those airy exhalations of the speculator's brain which, I am told, are very fitting in the form of towns and cities along those lines of railroad, built with government subsidies, luring the unwary settler, as the mirage of the desert lures the famishing traveller on, until it fades away in the darkening horizon; or whether it is real *bona fide*, substantial city, all "staked off," with the lots marked with their owners' names, like that proud commercial metropolis recently discovered on the desirable shores of San Domingo. But however that may be I am satisfied "Duluth" is there, or thereabouts, for I see it stated here on the map that it is exactly thirty-nine hundred and ninety miles from Liverpool, though I have no doubt, for the sake of convenience, it will be moved back ten miles, so as to make the distance an even four thousand.

Then, sir, there is the climate of "Duluth," unquestionably the most salubrious and delightful to be found anywhere on the Lord's earth. Now I have always been under the impression, as I presume other gentlemen have, that in the region around Lake Superior it was cold enough for at least nine months of the year to freeze the smokestack off a locomotive.

But I see it represented on this map that "Duluth" is situated exactly half way between the latitudes of Paris and Venice, so that gentlemen who have inhaled the exhilarating air of the one or basked in the golden sunlight of the other may see at a glance that "Duluth" must be the place of untold delight, a terrestrial paradise, fanned by the balmy zephyrs of an eternal spring, clothed in the gorgeous sheen of ever-blooming flowers and vocal with the silvery melody of nature's choicest songsters.

In fact, sir, since I have seen this map I have no doubt that Byron was vainly endeavoring to convey some faint conception of the delicious charms of "Duluth" when his poetic soul gushed forth in the rippling strains of that beautiful rhapsody—

> "Know ye the land of the cedar and the vine,
> Whence the flowers ever blossom, the beams ever shine;
> Where the light wings of Zephyr, oppressed with perfume,
> Wax faint o'er the gardens of Gaul in her bloom;
> Where the citron and olive are fairest of fruit,
> And the voice of the nightingale never is mute;
> Where the tints of the earth and the hues of the sky,
> In color though varied, in beauty may vie?"

As to the commercial resources of "Duluth," sir, they are simply illimitable and inexhaustible, as is shown by this map.

I see it stated here that there is a vast scope of territory, embracing an area of over two millions of square miles, rich in every element of material wealth and commercial prosperity, all tributary to "Duluth."

Look at it, sir [pointing to the map]. Here are inexhaustible mines of gold, immeasurable veins of silver, impenetrable depths of boundless forest, vast coal measures, wide-extended plains of richest pasturage—all, all embraced in this vast territory—which must, in the very nature of things, empty the untold treasures of its commerce into the lap of "Duluth."

Look at it, sir [pointing to the map]; do you not see from these broad, brown lines drawn around this immense territory that the enterprising inhabitants of "Duluth" intend some day to inclose it all in one vast corral, so that its commerce will be bound to go there whether it would or not? And here, sir [still pointing to the map], I find within a convenient distance the Piegan Indians, which, of all the many accessories to the glory of "Duluth," I consider by far the most inestimable. For, sir, I have been told that when the smallpox breaks out among the women and children of the famous tribe, as it sometimes does, they afford the finest subjects in the world for the strategical experiments of any enterprising military hero who desires to improve himself in the noble art of war, especially for any valiant lieutenant-general whose

> "Trenchant blade, Toledo trusty,
> For want of fighting has grown rusty,
> And eats into itself for lack
> Of somebody to hew and hack."

Sir, the great conflict now raging in the Old World has presented a phenomenon of military science unprecedented in the annals of mankind, a phenomenon that has reversed all the traditions of the past, as it has disappointed all the expectations of the present. A great and warlike people, renowned alike for their skill and valor, have been swept away before the triumphant advance of an inferior foe like autumn stubble before a hurricane of fire.

For aught I know the next flash of electric fire that simmers along the ocean cable may tell us that Paris, with every fiber quivering with the agony of impotent despair, writhes beneath the conquering heel of her loathed invader. Ere another moon shall wax and wane the brightest star in the galaxy of nations may fall from the zenith of her glory never to rise again. Ere the modest violets of early spring shall ope their beauteous eyes the genius of civilization may chant the wailing requiem of the proudest nationality the world has ever seen, as she scatters her withered and tear-moistened lilies o'er the bloody tomb of butchered France.

But, sir, I wish to ask if you honestly and candidly believe that the Dutch would have overrun the French in that kind of style if General Sheridan had not gone over there and told King William and Von Moltke how he had managed to whip the Piegan Indians?

And here, sir, recurring to this map, I find in the immediate vicinity of the Piegans "vast herds of buffalo" and "immense fields of rich wheat lands."

[Here the hammer fell. Many cries, "Go on! Go on!"
The Speaker—Is there any objection to the gentleman from Kentucky continuing his remarks? The chair hears none. The gentleman will proceed. Mr. Knott continued:]

I was remarking, sir, upon these vast "wheat fields" represented on this map, in the immediate neighborhood of the buffaloes and Piegans, and was about to say that the idea of there being these immense wheat fields in the very heart of a wilderness, hundreds and hundreds of miles beyond the utmost verge of civilization, may appear to some gentlemen as rather incongruous, as rather too great a strain on the "blankets" of veracity.

But to my mind there is no difficulty in the matter whatever. The phenomenon is very easily accounted for. It is evident, sir, that the Piegans sowed that wheat there and plowed it in with buffalo bulls. Now, sir, this fortunate combination of buffaloes and Piegans, considering their relative positions to each other and to "Duluth," as they are arranged on this map, satisfies me that "Duluth" is destined to be the best market of the world. Here, you will observe [pointing to the map], are the buffaloes, directly between the Piegans and "Duluth;" and here, right on the road to "Duluth," are the Creeks. Now, sir, when the buffaloes are sufficiently fat from grazing on those immense wheat fields, you see it will be the easiest thing in the world for the Piegans to drive them on down, stay all night with their friends, the Creeks, and go into "Duluth" in the morning.

I think I see them now, sir, a vast herd of buffaloes, with their heads down, their eyes glaring, their nostrils dilated, their tongues out, and their tails curled over their backs, tearing along toward "Duluth," with about a thousand Piegans on their grass-bellied ponies yelling at their heels! On they come! And as they sweep past the Creeks they join in the chase, and away they all go, yelling, bellowing, ripping and tearing along amid clouds of dust until the last buffalo is safely penned in the stockyards at "Duluth."

Sir, I might stand here for hours and hours and expatiate with rapture upon the gorgeous prospects of "Duluth," as depicted upon this map. But human life is too short and the time of this House far too valuable to allow me to linger longer upon this delightful theme. I think every gentleman upon this floor is as well satisfied as I am that "Duluth" is destined to become the commercial metropolis of the universe, and that this road should be built at once. I am fully persuaded that no patriotic representative of the American people, who has a proper appreciation of the associated glories of "Duluth" and the St. Croix, will hesitate a moment, that every able-bodied female in the land, between the ages of eighteen and forty-five, who is in favor of "woman's rights," should be drafted and set to work upon this great work without delay. Nevertheless, sir, it grieves my very soul to be compelled to say that I cannot vote for the grant of lands provided for in this bill.

Ah, sir, you can have no conception of the poignancy of my anguish that I am deprived of that blessed privilege! There are two insuperable obstacles in the way. In the first place my constituents, for whom I am acting here, have no more interest in this road than they have in the great question of culinary taste now, perhaps, agitating the public mind of Dominica, as to whether the illustrious commissioners, who recently left this capital for that free and enlightened republic, would be better fricasseed, boiled or roasted, and, in the second place, these lands, which I am asked to give away, alas, are not mine to bestow! My relation to them is simply that of trustee to an express trust! And shall I ever betray that trust? Never, sir! Rather perish "Duluth!" Perish the paragon of cities! Rather let the freezing cyclones of the bleak northwest bury it forever beneath the eddying sands of the raging St. Croix.

DIAZ

PORFIRIO DIAZ, a distinguished Mexican soldier and statesman, president of the Mexican Republic, was born at Oaxaca, September 15, 1830. He was educated in the Institute of the State of Oaxaca and after beginning the study of law abandoned it to enter the national guards when the American army invaded Mexico. In 1854 he engaged in the rebellion against Santa Anna and for the next twenty years was incessantly active in the numerous revolts and insurrections against the successive governments of Mexico. He attained the rank of general in 1861 and took part in the defence of Puebla against the French in 1863. Upon its surrender he made his escape from a short imprisonment within the French lines and took command of the Mexican army. In spite of many obstacles and reverses he maintained the Republican cause through the period of the French rule under Maximilian, which was brought to an end by Diaz's capture of Puebla on April 21, 1867, and that of the city of Mexico two months later. In October of that year Diaz was an unsuccessful candidate for the presidency against Juarez, and for the next eight or nine years was usually in opposition to the government. He headed the revolt against the administration of President Lerdo in 1876, putting Lerdo's forces to rout in several engagements. In 1877 he was elected president for four years, but his administration was an unquiet one and he was principally occupied in putting down revolts. He secured the election of General Gonzalez as his successor in 1880, and on the expiration of Gonzalez's term of office in 1884 Diaz was elected president a second time. Through successive re-elections he has continued in office as chief magistrate of Mexico until the present time (1900). He is very popular throughout Mexico and in his administration of affairs has exhibited wisdom and executive ability. Under his government the trade and manufacture of Mexico have been greatly augmented, education has been advanced, the resources of the country have been developed and railroads and telegraphs have been extended.

PEACE ROOTED IN THE HEARTS OF ALL

SPEECH DELIVERED AT A BANQUET GIVEN IN HIS HONOR, DECEMBER 1, 1900

GENTLEMEN,—In responding to my distinguished and good friends, Governor Obregón and the honorable deputy Chavero, I begin with manifesting to them and to their respective constituents, in whose name they have honored me, my profound gratitude for the delicate and kindly expressions with which their eloquence enlarges upon the services rendered to the country by the personal direction of the administration over which I have the honor of presiding. If there may be any merit in the felicitous choice of its personnel, that would be mine.

The enthusiasm with which my fellow citizens celebrate the countersigning of my mandate honors me as amply as it does undeservedly, because, presuming that that enthusiasm signifies a vote of approval, it may be interpreted as a ratification of those which, in their legal capacity, they cast in my honor. I esteem their friendly manifestations at their full value, and I accept them with all the gratitude of which I am capable; but in so far as the eulogium lavished upon me declares me author of the peace that the Republic enjoys, notwithstanding that it bears the character of a delicate compliment inspired by the well wishes of my friends, I cannot excuse myself from subjecting it, with all respect, to an opportune rectification.

To restore peace to a people whose moral sense has been fed for more than a half century by frequent and sanguinary struggles of force against law, the action of one man does not suffice, whatever be his power and his prestige; it necessitates the positive and very vigilant labor of many men, armed with the powerful, intelligent, and enthusiastic will to harmonize the conformities and interests of society with the conformities and interests of all and each of its associates; and who are possessed with such abnegation that they can with serenity receive and pardon the most injurious and untruthful imputations while the masses are beginning to perceive that they are engaged in preparing a great benefaction.

The triumph of one of the parties is a propitious occasion to initiate a period of peace, if at the root of victory the bustle of a general industrial activity makes itself felt, giving work to many thousands of men, bread to as many families, and which, in obedience to a well-meditated system of reproductive improvements, promises to capital a safe and immediate theatre for undertakings so lucrative as to provoke the eager influx of foreign investments.

In the contrary case, when the defeated recover from their stupor they associate themselves with the growing phalanx of the deceived to fan the embers of revolution; unscrupulously aided by the press that, from self-interest, thirsts for everything sensational, whether it be true or doubtful, or even false.

Our last war, in its closing stages, offered us in their order the successive pictures of this natural evolution.

In the first days of relative peace, out of regard to the state of the treasury it was not possible to undertake public works of importance; and, as was to be expected, there surged up a new revolution which the government was able to suppress with energy scarcely sufficient to be efficacious. From that time on, the dissidents adopted an attitude as hostile as the tolerance of the governing power, which was not slight, would permit, occupying themselves with criticising pitilessly all the acts of the government and more than once carrying their fervor to the point of calumny.

The disaster of that attempted revolution prolonged the period of expectation, and, although painfully, the government was enabled to formulate its first contracts for public works and credit, proceeding immediately to the extension of various railways and telegraph lines; and it dedicated itself fundamentally, and accepting all kinds of responsibilities, to the complete extinction of brigandage, which threatened to take possession of the entire territory of the nation.

As soon as commerce could count upon security on the highways and upon facile locomotion there began to be felt the activity of capital, its corresponding and well-merited profit, and the vigorous and growing influx of foreign money. A new perspective so grateful in the country, and a horizon clear of revolutionary prognostications, caused the dissidents—who until then had remained hostile to the government and to the shelter of the barrier which in itself it provided for them through its respect for the rights of others, began to pour torrents into the seductive arena of business, then and there and unreservedly affiliating themselves with the lovers of peace, leaving their fortunes in action as substantial guarantee of their good faith.

The government, now freed from the necessity of keeping on its guard which had been imposed upon it by the spectre of revolution, its confidence in the future invigorated, summoned to the work of public administration all the ex-revolutionists whose honor, ability, talents, and prestige gave assurance that they could serve their country. It is a pleasure for me to declare here that all who were called have loyally performed their labors.

The government having once felt itself supported by all Mexicans, without distinction of parties and with equal confidence in the patriotism of all, put into execution its so often dreamed-of program that is condensed in these words: "Little politics, much administration."

Ever since then the net of railways has been rapidly extended in all directions, and throughout the whole national territory has been spread the telegraphic system, with nocturnal service, reduced tariffs, and connected with the inter-continental cables; fiscal and banking laws, far-reaching, like that which liberated commerce from internal tariffs, have been promulgated; and with all its energies the government proceeded to construct ports, lighthouses, and other great protective works, hygienic and commercial, which for future generations will furnish as many evidences of the present civilization; it perfected the postal service, giving cheap and daily communication for all cities, towns, and villages in the Republic, with letters, parcels, and money orders, and with representation in the International Postal Union of the civilized world; and it normalized fiscal credit with great mercantile benefits.

I have here sketched in large strokes the real concurrent factors, not of peace directly, but certainly of the harmony of interests which, in consideration of welfare of self, unified the will of all citizens in favor of peace and created this grateful ambient medium, this general well-being, in which we live, which induces the promotion of festivals like the present, and which, in the ultimate result, is nothing else than the manifestation that all legitimate ambitions are either satisfied or are in the normal and certain way of so becoming.

And here I have likewise the demonstration of my proposition: That genuine peace, the peace that is rooted in the hearts of all, that which is substantial and fruitful, is not, nor cannot be, the work of one man, nor of many men, but of all the active members of the societies that have the fortune to enjoy it; sufficient is the honor to be one of these.

In giving thanks once more to my personal friends and to the honorable governors for the much that they have given me and honored me, I urge them to join with me in thanking also the honorable diplomatic corps for their presence at our table, and to drink with them to the peace and prosperity of the nations which they so worthily and so sagaciously represent, and to the personal happiness and long life of their august sovereigns and worthy chiefs of state respectively; and to invite them to drink with us, because from our entrance upon the century whose gates we are touching, there stands pre-eminent at the head of all purposes of all Mexicans, that of making our country as great, as illustrious, and as rich as it is hospitable and sympathetic.

[Special translation by Sylvester Baxter.]

McCARTHY

JUSTIN McCARTHY, a noted Irish political leader, journalist and author, was born at Cork, November 22, 1830, and educated privately. He was a journalist in his native city, 1848-52, and in Liverpool, 1852-60. Going then to London he was on the staff of "The Morning Star," 1860-68, and during the next three years travelled and lectured in the United States and was for a time one of the editors of the New York "Independent." He returned to London in 1870 and joined the staff of the "Daily News" as a radical leader writer. In 1879 he entered Parliament and soon became a leader of the Home Rule party and after the fall of Parnell was chairman of the Irish parliamentarians. In 1886 he revisited the United States where he delivered a number of public addresses. He has achieved distinction both as a historian and as a novelist. His novels have attained considerable popularity. His works include "Prohibitory Legislation in the United States" (1872); "Modern Leaders" (1872); "History of Ireland from the Union," "History of Our Own Times," perhaps his ablest work (1880); "History of the Four Georges" (1889); "Ireland's Cause in England's Parliament" (1888); "Life of Sir Robert Peel" (1891); "Life of Pope Leo XIII" (1896); "The Story of Mr. Gladstone's Life" (1898); "Modern England" (1898); "Reminiscences" (1899); "The Story of the People of England in the Nineteenth Century" (1899).

IN DEFENCE OF HIS COLLEAGUES

[In the adjourned debate on the amendment proposed on the main question affecting Irish affairs in the Queen's speech, Mr. W. E. Forster charged Mr. Justin McCarthy and his colleagues with complicity in the recent outrages and crimes in Ireland. Mr. McCarthy replied in the following speech in the House of Commons, February 23, 1883:]

THE fate of the amendment now before the House gives me very little concern. Neither its fate, nor its purport, nor its wording is of much account to me, or to those with whom I have the honor to act. One thing is clear, that the amendment is directed not against the Irish members, but against her Majesty's ministers. I care not whether it is rejected or passed, and I do not propose to make my business either the arraignment or the defence of the government as regards its general policy.

I shall confine myself to two speeches delivered in the course of this debate — that of the right honorable gentleman the member for Bradford [Mr. Forster], and that of the right honorable gentleman the chief secretary for Ireland. Now the speech of the right honorable gentleman the member for Bradford was undoubtedly what writers in the newspapers sometimes call "a great effort." It was a tremendous effort. I always thought the right honorable gentleman had a good deal of theatrical talent, which he had not up to the present fully developed. Those who heard his remarkable speech will agree with me that it was mimetic as well as historic. It gave us that entertainment which is often described in the playbills of theatres and music halls as "imitations of popular performers." I wish I saw him in his place in the House at present. I am hardly mistaken in thinking that he favored the House with what he believed to be imitations of the voices and manners of some honorable members of the Irish party. I am content that he shall have all the favor which his familiar attacks upon some members of that party, and his erudition in American newspapers, can win him for a time from this House and the public.

I know, too, that his motive was not merely, although it was mainly, to discredit the Irish members. He had his mind fixed also upon discrediting and damaging the government from which he has been discarded; and I am convinced that there are members of that government—aye, members who are at this moment sitting on the Treasury Bench—whom he had in his mind with a wish to discredit my honorable friend the member for the City of Cork [Mr. Parnell]. Whatever his speech was made up from — from American newspapers, from reports of meetings in the country, from hints, and more than hints, in the passionate press of London — there was one quality of that speech which was all the right honorable gentleman's own, and that was its envenomed malignity.

I never heard in this House a speech more entirely inspired with the purpose of deliberate defamation. I believe it was the right honorable gentleman's intention to do all the damage he could to the characters of some members of the House by a process of systematic calumny. He accused some of my honorable friends, and with them of course myself, of conniving at outrage and assassination. He talked of offering us an alternative; but he gave none. He made it clear that his charge was nothing short of deliberate connivance with outrage and assassination. Here is the sort of alternative the right honorable gentleman offered us —

"I give the honorable member an alternative, that either he connived at outrages, or, when warned by facts and statements, he determined to remain in ignorance; that he took no trouble to test the truth of whether outrages had been committed or not, but that he was willing to gain the advantage of them."

I point out that this is no alternative; that men who are informed that outrage and assassination are going on, and who determine to remain in ignorance, and are willing to gain the benefit of outrage and assassination, are distinctly conniving at those crimes.

Therefore, I tell the right honorable gentleman that when he pretended to give us an alternative he did nothing of the kind; and that as he had made up his mind to charge us by implication with conniving at murder, he ought to have stood boldly up and said so. He ought to have said so in those plain words he sometimes is able to use, and ought not to have shielded himself behind the pretence of an alternative. I should have thought that the right honorable gentleman would be the member of this House least inclined, owing to certain memories he must have, to fling accusations of sympathy with murder recklessly at other men.

When charging us with these crimes, he must have recalled a time when a newspaper, then far more influential than it now is — the "Times"— charged him with sympathy with secret assassination. I do not charge the right honorable gentleman with having sympathy with crime; but for the reason I have stated he ought to have felt a sentiment which would have prevented him from recklessly hurling similar charges in the faces of men as honorable as himself, and who feel as little thirst for blood as he does.

On the 14th of March 1864, one who was then a member of this House, and is now high in her Majesty's colonial service — Sir John Pope Hennessy — brought forward certain statements in this House with regard to a right honorable friend of mine, for whom I have the highest respect, the member for Halifax [Mr. Stansfeld], and who was accused by certain newspapers of sympathy with assassination because he had harbored Mazzini and some of his friends.

This became the subject of debate in this House, and led to the right honorable gentleman the member for Halifax resigning his position in the government. The right honorable gentleman the member for Bradford stood up for his friend. I do not blame him for that — he believed him to be innocent. But what were the evidences given, and the assassination theory held, by the man for whom the right honorable gentleman the member for Bradford stood up in this House? Extracts were then read from Mazzini's letter, "The Theory of the Dagger." Such passages as these were read —

"Blessed be the knife of Palafox: blessed be in your hands every weapon that can destroy the enemy and set you free.

The weapon that slew Mincovich in the Arsenal initiated the insurrection in Venice. It was a weapon of irregular warfare like that which, three months before the Republic, destroyed the Minister Rossi in Rome. . . . Sacred be the stiletto that began the Sicilian Vespers."

The right honorable gentleman the member for Bradford rose and said —

"The honorable and learned gentleman has brought forward a charge against an absent man — Signor Mazzini — who, whatever his faults, was a man of high character."

Whatever his faults? What though he blessed the knife of one man and the dagger of another, and the system of "irregular warfare" which removed Count Rossi, the minister of the late Pope Pius IX, who was murdered on the steps of the capitol, he was "a man of high character!" The right honorable gentleman's leader of the present day did not agree with his estimate of Signor Mazzini. The present prime minister had written in a preface to a translation of Signor Farini's "Roman States" — "The Satellites of Mazzini make common cause with assassins." After those extracts had been read and four days had passed, during which the right honorable member for Bradford had time for reflection, the subject was again raised, and the right honorable gentleman said —

"I should not be ashamed of being the friend of Mazzini." [Irish cheers, and a cry of "The Dagger!"] "I am not ashamed of being his acquaintance."

Well, I think that that incident is not without its interest and moral. The Irish members who brought forward that question at the time did not charge the right honorable gentleman, or think of charging him, with sympathy with assassination. The charge was that he and his companions showed a levity which disregarded what a man might do, so long as that man was a foreign patriot.

The "Times" of March 15, 1864, had a leading article on the subject, which is not without its application to the present circumstances. The right honorable gentleman was not then in the flush and heyday of youth. He was able to judge whether Mazzini and his associates and satellites were what they were represented to be. The "Times" said —

"Who, then, is this M. Mazzini, to whose innocence this gentleman [Mr. Stansfeld] and Mr. W. E. Forster pledge themselves? Let any one read the passages quoted by Mr. Hennessy last night, and say whether the friends of M. Mazzini have any right to indulge in high-flown indignation when it is alleged that he might possibly be engaged in a conspiracy against a potentate's life."

I ask whether the right honorable member for Bradford was justified in seizing at the chance of high-flown indignation because the newspaper that accused him then of sympathy with assassination accuses some of us now of the same thing. I wonder that the memory of that episode in his career has not made him more generous — yes, I will say, more honest — toward men whom, in his heart, he no more believes to be guilty of that charge than honorable men then believed him to be.

I pass from that not uninstructive incident to the right honorable gentleman's attack on Irish members, and the grounds on which that attack was made. He had something to say about myself in connection with "United Ireland," a paper published in Dublin. He said much the same thing about a year ago. He then went over the story of some articles that he said appeared in that paper. I believe they were not articles, but headings of paragraphs; and he appealed to me, though I was not in my place at the time, to know whether I approved of all these various paragraphs and headings.

Now, the right honorable gentleman must have known — at all events he might have known — that I could not have seen that newspaper then. He knew that I had been out of England the whole of that recess, from the end of one session to the beginning of another. [An Irish member: "He did."]

He did, and he said so himself in this House, for he indulged in some more or less graceful satire at my expense, and complained that, instead of helping to keep order in Ireland, I had been enjoying myself among the monuments of ancient Greece.

But since I was so culpable as to be enjoying myself among the monuments of ancient Greece, and in countries much farther off, he might have known that it was not likely that a Dublin paper followed me in all my wanderings. He knew that at the time he was speaking — at the time he was so playfully chiding me for the amusement of the House — he must have known that that paper was prevented from coming into this country; and though I made strenuous efforts shortly after to get copies of it, and see if it contained the terrible things it was said to contain, I was unable to obtain a copy.

However, I allow that to pass. It would not much matter if the right honorable gentleman could have sustained his charge. If he had not returned to it, I should not have cared to raise it. But I am quite willing to tell him, if it affords him the slightest interest, the history of my connection with that paper. It was started to get rid of a notorious print, which appears lately to have lived by the levying of blackmail in Dublin. It was founded by a committee of gentlemen in whom I have the greatest trust; and the editorship was given to a man whom I regard and respect, and whom I know to be incapable of conducting a journal on the principles the right honorable gentleman described.

Under these conditions I felt content, having no control over the paper, to go abroad among the monuments of ancient Greece, and to leave the paper in the hands of the able editor who has already shown his ability in this House. I did not inquire in my absence how he conducted it. I know he conducted it honorably and well; and we have learned that the only things the right honorable gentleman objects to are the paragraphs and headings which got into the paper while he had the responsible editor under lock and key in one of his prisons.

I have said enough on that point. I do not believe that any investigation would convict that editor of publishing any articles which men of honor would be ashamed to sanction.

The right honorable gentleman went over many points with the object of associating me and others with plots and assassinations. For example, he spoke of a telegram sent by Mr. Brennan, who was the correspondent of the "Irish World," to that paper. The telegram is given variously in the different journals, but I would ask the right honorable gentleman, Is this which I am about to read the right version?

"All sorts of theories are afloat concerning this explosion"—that is the Salford dynamite explosion—"but the truly loyal one is that Fenianism did it."

What is the plain and evident meaning of that? Is it not that the fashionable and loyal theory, as a matter of course, is that the Fenians did it? I ask the right honorable gentleman, is not that the manifest meaning? [Mr. W. E. Forster.—"I would ask the honorable member to read the remainder of the telegram."] I quote the whole of the printed version I have. The right honorable gentleman charged me with deliberate avoidance of reading articles in order that I might be able to say I do not know of the incitement to assassination they contained. Then he said:

"I expect, or suspect"—probably suspect, it is more in his line—"I suspect the honorable member"—meaning myself—"has been careful not to read the articles to which I refer."

The charge is, perhaps, hardly parliamentary. There was a rude interruption last night, which we all regret, to an imputation which ought not to have been made; but the right honorable gentleman is allowed to say: "I suspect the honorable member has been careful not to read the articles to which I refer."

The whole theory and purpose of his declamation and defamation was to make members of this House responsible for every violent act done, and every violent word said, by any supposed follower of his in this country or America. I should like to know how that theory would apply to the right honorable gentleman.

The right honorable gentleman has not forgotten the riots which occurred in the Reform years, nor the men who got up those riots. He has not forgotten the riot which led to the breaking down of the Hyde Park railings, and the maiming and wounding of many of the mob and some policemen. The right honorable gentleman and his friends came back to power on that smash of the Hyde Park railings.

The right honorable gentleman was well acquainted with

the leader of the democratic movement—the late Mr. Beales. [Mr. W. E. Forster.—"I did not know him personally."] Neither do I know personally those who have uttered these violent words and done these violent acts in Ireland, for which I am sought to be made responsible. Mr. Beales is dead. Mr. Beales was a man of honor and courage. I knew him and I respected him. But he certainly got around him, and could not help getting around him, men of very odd character and very odd pretensions. Does the right honorable gentleman remember a certain Mr. Joseph Leicester, a famous glass-blower? [Mr. W. E. Forster.—"I do not remember him."]

He does not remember him? As a famous actress said on one occasion, "What a candor; but what a memory!" At the time Mr. Leicester's name used to appear in every London newspaper every morning. This distinguished supporter of the right honorable gentleman's party went to a great meeting one day—a great trades' demonstration, held, I think, in Trafalgar Square—and this was part of the speech of Joseph Leicester. There was then, as there has been more lately, a kind of rush and raid on the House of Commons to force them to pass a certain bill, and this was what this demagogue here said:

"The question is, were they to suffer those little-minded, decrepit, hump-backed, one-eyed scoundrels, who call themselves the House of Commons, to defraud them any longer of their rights?"

I was not a member of the House of Commons then and did not come in for any part of that lively personal description; but I ask the right honorable gentleman if some one as nearly connected with the honorable member for the city of Cork as Mr. Leicester was with the right honorable gentleman, had used words of that description to a meeting of Irishmen, what would he have said? The riots in Hyde Park took place and people were wounded. [" Question! "]

There was no cry of " Question " when the right honorable gentleman was defaming me and others, and went over land and sea and over years to find charges against us. It is quite to the question. I want to say to him and the House that it is impossible in any movement to hold the leaders responsible for every idle word and act said and done by their followers. Of this movement Mr. Beales was the leader, and when the right honorable gentleman and his friends came into power did they repudiate Mr. Beales? They made him a county court judge. Did they at any time, while these proceedings were going on, repudiate the language of any man? No.

There was a newspaper in London at the time, of which the right honorable gentleman sitting near him [Mr. John Bright] knew something, in which a writer, not now living, had once called on the people, if a certain thing were not done, to destroy the House of Lords, and to strew the Thames with the wreck of their painted chamber. I ask the right honorable gentleman, who took in that paper, whether he read it or not? [Cries of " Morning Star."]

Yes, the " Morning Star." [Mr. W. E. Forster.—" I was not a shareholder."] The matter was brought to the notice of this House by an honorable member, and I am not aware that the right honorable gentleman said one single word in condemnation of that language. And remember, Mr. Speaker, that the time of the Hyde Park riots was not a time of peace. We have heard, again and again, that things may be allowed in time of peace; but that was not a time of peace. Those were dangerous times. Troops were kept in readiness—the air was full of danger. During the whole of that time the right honorable gentleman never said, as far as I know, one word to dissociate himself or any of his friends from those acts or words.

I should like to ask the right honorable gentleman another question. Did he never hear at that time that a famous continental leader of revolution was over in London and was in negotiation with some of the men concerned in these affairs with the hope of assisting them in a democratic revolution? [Mr. W. E. Forster.—" No."]

He never heard of it? He never read any of the papers published at that time? He never read histories published since that time? Over and over again—in newspapers, magazines, and books—has the story of the foreign incendiary been told, and the right honorable gentleman never heard of it or read of it; and yet he supposes I read every copy of the " Irish World!"

I think I have sufficiently shown that the right honorable gentleman ought to be cautious how he makes charges against us of sympathy with assassination, or of having assisted or connived at crimes, and how he lays down the theory that a man is bound to know what is done by everybody else who is concerned with him in any popular movement. I will tell the right honorable gentleman and the House how outrages grew up in Ireland of late. The Land League was formed with the full and deliberate intent of drawing agitation above the surface.

That was its motive. Its purpose was to maintain public platforms on which agitation might go on openly and in the face of day, by which men would be withdrawn from that terrible system of conspiracy which has been the bane and curse of Ireland for so many years. That was the motive of the Land League. I saw that was its distinct purpose, and it was succeeding so manifestly in the purpose that I joined the

League. The right honorable gentleman expects that every one has read every letter written by every one else. I should ask him if he did me the favor of reading a letter of mine which was published in all the papers in England in reference to my joining the Land League? [Mr. W. E. Forster.—"No."]

He did not. He only reads the "Irish World," and I did not write to the "Irish World" to explain my intentions. In that letter I stated concisely and clearly my reasons for believing the Land League would do good, and why I thought it was the duty of every patriotic Irishman to join it. I believed it was doing good by helping to close the era of conspiracy. But there came upon Ireland one autumn and one winter three influences of evil together—famine, the House of Lords, and the right honorable gentleman. The country was miserably pinched with hunger. The House of Lords rejected the poor little Compensation for Disturbance bill, which might have stopped for a while the sufferings of the people; and then, to improve the situation, the right honorable gentleman got his law for the arrest of suspicious men, under which he flung the leaders of the people into prison. Then it was that outrages began to increase. After the arrest of the honorable member for the city of Cork the movement drifted leaderless and hopeless, dropped from the high point to which it had risen in publicity and on the platform, into the seething ferment of the sea of conspiracy. The leaders of the land movement had nearly succeeded in raising Ireland out of conspiracy. That is what I fully and firmly believe, and thus history hereafter will I am certain write it out.

The chief secretary to the lord-lieutenant made a serious mistake when he appealed to us to-night to justify all manner of executions simply on the ground that so many murders had been committed. It is not the theory of this country that for so many murders there shall be so many executions. That is the theory of certain eastern states; but that is happily not yet the theory even in Ireland. Were the murders ten times more in number than the men put on trial for them, I should be at liberty still, if I thought I had reason, to examine into the justice of each trial and the way in which it had been conducted; and if it could be shown that there was anything like systematic jury-packing in even one trial, no matter how many murders had been committed, I should denounce it.

The right honorable gentleman seemed a little hopeful toward the end of his speech when he spoke of the great decrease of outrages, and when there was drawn from him the statement that there was also a decrease of evictions. In searching for the causes which had led to this decrease of outrages, the fact of the decrease of evictions must not be overlooked. The right honorable gentleman then became a little more ominous in saying that he feared that lately evictions had been on the increase. Was it not possible that with the increase of evictions might come an increase of outrages? It must be remembered that there is now no such thing as the right of public meeting or free speech in Ireland. A man may make a speech if he likes at his own risk; but the right honorable gentleman tells us that if he thinks there is anything in the speech which might lead to inflame the feelings of any one, he will prevent or punish the making of such speeches, although he knows the speaker had no evil intention whatever.

There is no free platform in Ireland; no free press—no right to hold a public meeting. There is no way in which the sentiments and grievances of the people can be freely expressed. You are laboring in the dark. You are driving disaffection beneath the surface. You alone will be responsible for the consequences of the terrible and stringent measures you have adopted. As the honorable member for the city of Cork said, there is no longer any probability of the Irish leaders or Irish members of Parliament standing between you and the elements of conspiracy. I do not blame the right honorable gentleman the chief secretary so much for the change that has come about. The responsibility for that change I lay, as I have already said, on the shoulders of another man. I may say of him, as was said of another famous politician, that it has seldom been within the power of any human creature to do so much good as the right honorable gentleman for Bradford has prevented.

VEST

GEORGE GRAHAM VEST, an American congressman, was born at Frankfort, Kentucky, December 6, 1830, and educated at Centre College in that State. He subsequently studied law in the Transylvania Law School at Lexington, Kentucky, and in 1856 removed to Brownsville, Missouri. Four years later he entered the Missouri Legislature, but gave up his seat in 1861 to serve in the Confederate army. He was for two years a member of the Confederate Congress and after the close of the Civil War resumed the practice of his profession at Sedalia, Missouri. In 1878 he entered the United States Senate retaining his seat through successive re-elections until the present (1900). He has been prominent as a vigorous debater, and besides having spoken on most of the important measures before Congress in the past twenty years has been chairman of various congressional committees.

ON INDIAN SCHOOLS

SPEECH DELIVERED IN THE UNITED STATES SENATE, APRIL 7, 1900

MR. PRESIDENT,—I shall not take the time of the Senate in discussing this oft-debated question as to the contract schools. My opinions have been so emphatically and repeatedly expressed that it is hardly necessary for me now to give information on that subject to any one who has taken any interest in the matter.

There are people in this country, unfortunately, who believe that an Indian child had better die an utter unbeliever, an idolater even, than to be educated by the Society of Jesus or in the Catholic church. I am very glad to say that I have not the slightest sympathy with that sort of bigotry and fanaticism. I was raised a Protestant; I expect to die one; I was never in a Catholic church in my life, and I have not the slightest sympathy with many of its dogmas; but, above all, I have no respect for this insane fear that the Catholic church is about to overturn this government. I should be ashamed to call myself an American if I indulged in any such ignorant belief.

I look upon this as a man of the world, practical, I hope, in all things, and especially in legislation, where my sphere of duty now is. Unfortunately I am not connected with any religious organization. I have no such prejudice as would prevent me from doing what I believed to be my duty. I would give this question of the education of Indian children the same sort of consideration that I would if I were building a house or having any other mechanical or expert business carried on. I had infinitely rather see these Indians Catholics than to see them blanket Indians on the plains, ready to go on the warpath against civilization and Christianity.

I said a few minutes ago that I was a Protestant. I was reared in the old Scotch Presbyterian church; my father was an elder in it, and my earliest impressions were that the Jesuits had horns and hoofs and tails, and that there was a faint tinge of sulphur in the circumambient air whenever one crossed your path. Some years ago I was assigned by the Senate to duty upon the committee on Indian affairs, and I was assigned by the committee, of which Mr. Dawes was then the very zealous chairman, to examine the Indian schools in Wyoming and Montana. I did so under great difficulties and with labor which I could not now physically perform. I visited every one of them. I crossed that great buffalo expanse of country where you can now see only the wallows and trails of those extinct animals, and I went to all these schools. I wish to say now what I have said before in the Senate, and it is not the popular side of this question by any means, that I did not see in all my journey, which lasted for several weeks, a single school that was doing any educational work worthy the name of educational work unless it was under the control of the Jesuits. I did not see a single government school, especially these day schools, where there was any work done at all.

Something has been said here about the difference between enrollment and attendance. I found day schools with 1,500 Indian children enrolled and not ten in attendance, except on meat days, as they called it, when beeves were killed by the agent and distributed to the tribe. Then there was a full attendance. I found schools where there were old, broken-down preachers and politicians receiving $1,200 a year and a house to live in for the purpose of conducting these Indian day schools, and when I cross-examined them, as I did in every instance, I found that their actual attendance was about three to five in the hundred of the enrollment. I do not care what reports are made, for they generally come from interested parties. You cannot educate the children with the day schools.

In 1850 Father De Smet, a self-sacrificing Christian Jesuit, went, at the solicitation of the Flatheads, to their reservation in Montana. The Flatheads sent two runners, young men, to bring the black robes to educate them and teach them the religion of Christ. Both of these runners were killed by the Blackfeet and never reached St. Louis. They then sent two more. One of them was killed, and the other made his way down the Missouri River after incredible hardships and reached St. Louis. Father De Smet and two young associates went out to the Flathead reservation and established the mission of St. Mary in the Bitter Root and St. Ignatius on the Jocko reservation. The Blackfeet burned the St. Mary mission, killed two of the Jesuits and thought they had killed the other—Father Ravaille. I saw him when on this committee, lying in his cell at the St. Mary's mission, paralyzed from the waist down, but performing surgical operations, for he was an accomplished surgeon, and doing all that he possibly could do for humanity and religion. He had been fifty-two years in that tribe of Indians. Think of it! Fifty-two years. Not owning the robe on his back, not even having a name, for he was a number in the semi-military organization called the Company of Jesus; and if he received orders at midnight to go to Africa or Asia he went without question, because it was his duty to the cause of Christ and for no other consideration or reason.

Father De Smet established these two missions and undertook to teach the Indian children as we teach our children in the common schools by day's attendance. It was a miserable failure. The Jesuits tried it for years, supported by contributions from France, not a dollar from the government, and they had to abandon the whole system. They found that when the girls and boys went back to the tepee at night all the work of the day by the Jesuits was obliterated. They found that ridicule, the great weapon of the Indian in the tepee, was used to drive these children away from the educational institutions established by the Jesuits. When the girl went back to the tepee with a dress on like an American woman and attempted to speak the English language, and whom the nuns were attempting to teach how to sew and spin, and wash and cook, she was ridiculed as having white blood in her veins, and the result was that she became the worst and most abandoned of the tribe, because it was necessary in order to reinstate herself with her own people that she should prove the most complete apostate from the teachings of the Jesuits.

After nearly twenty years of this work by the Jesuits they abandoned it, and they established a different system, separating the boys and the girls, teaching them how to work, for that is the problem, not how to read or spell, nor the laws of arithmetic, but how to work and to get rid of this insane prejudice taught by the Indians from the beginning that nobody but a squaw should work, and that it degrades a man to do any sort of labor, or in fact to do anything except to hunt and go to war.

The hardest problem that can be proposed to the human race is how to make men self-dependent. There can be no self-respect without self-dependence. There can be no good government until a people are elevated up to the high plane of earning their bread in the sweat of their faces. When you come to educate negroes and Indians there is but one thing that will ever lift them out of the degradation in which long years of servitude and nomadic habits have placed them, and that is to teach them that the highest and greatest and most elevating thing in the human race is to learn how to work and to make themselves independent.

I take off my hat, metaphorically, whenever I think of this negro in Alabama—Booker Washington. He has solved that problem for his race, and he is the only man who has ever done it. Fred Douglass was a great politician, but he never discovered what was necessary for the negro race in this country. I have just returned from the south after a sojourn of five weeks upon the Gulf of Mexico.

The negro problem is the most terrible that ever confronted a civilized race upon the face of the earth. You cannot exterminate them; you cannot extradite them; you must make them citizens as they are and as they will continue to be. You must assimilate them. Exportation is a dream of the philanthropist, demonstrated to be such by the experiment in Liberia. Mr. Lincoln tried it, and took his contingent fund immediately after the war, shipped negroes to a colony in the West Indies, and those who were left from the fever after two years came back to the United States, and every dollar expended was thrown away. Washington, this negro in Alabama, has struck the keynote. It will take years to carry it out, and he has the prejudices of his own race and the prejudices of the ignorant whites against him; but he deserves the commendation of all the people, not only of the United States, but those of the civilized world.

Mr. President, the Jesuits have elevated the Indian where-ever they have been allowed to do so without interference of bigotry and fanaticism and the cowardice of insectivorous politicians who are afraid of the A. P. A. and the votes that can be cast against them in their district and States. They have made him a Christian, and above even that have made him a workman able to support himself and those dependent upon him. Go to the Flathead reservation, in Montana, and look from the cars of the Northern Pacific Railroad, and you will see the result of what Father De Smet and his associates began and what was carried on successfully until the A. P. A. and the cowards who are afraid of it struck down the appropriation. There are now four hundred Indian children upon that reservation without one dollar to give them an hour's instruction of any kind. That is the teaching of many professors of the religion of Christ in the Protestant churches. I repudiate it. I would be ashamed of myself if I did not do it, and if it were the last accent I ever uttered in public life it would be to denounce that narrow-minded and unworthy policy based upon religious bigotry.

This A. P. A. did me the greatest honor in my life during their last session in this city, two years ago. They passed a resolution unanimously demanding that I should be impeached because I said what I am saying now. Mr. President, the knowledge of the constitution of this country developed by that organization in demanding the impeachment of a United States senator for uttering his honest opinion in this chamber puts them beyond criticism. It would be cowardly and inhuman to say one word about ignorance so dense as that.

Mr. President, as I said, go through this reservation and look at the work of the Jesuits, and what is seen? You find comfortable dwellings, herds of cattle and horses, intelligent, self-respecting Indians. I have been to their houses and found that under the system adopted by the Jesuits, the new system, as I may call it, after the failure of that which was attempted for twenty years, to which I have alluded, after they had educated these boys and girls and they had intermarried, the Jesuits would go out and break up a piece of land and build them a house, and that couple became the nucleus of civilization in the neighborhood. They had been educated under the system which prevented them from going back to the tepee after a day's tuition. The Jesuits found that in order to accomplish their purpose of teaching them how to work and to depend upon themselves it was necessary to keep them in school, a boarding school, by day and night, and to allow even the parents to see them only in the presence of the brothers or the nuns.

I undertake to say now—and every senator here who has passed through that reservation will corroborate my statement—that there is not in this whole country an object lesson more striking than that to be seen from the cars of the Northern Pacific Railroad, the fact that these Jesuits alone have solved the problem of rescuing the Indians from the degradation in which they were found.

Mr. President, these Jesuits are not there, as one of them

told me, for the love of the Indian. Old Father Ravaille told me, lying upon his back in that narrow cell, with the crucifix above him, "I am here not for the love of the Indian, but for the love of Christ," without pay except the approval of his own conscience. If you send one of our people, a clergyman, a politician even, to perform this work among the Indians, he looks back to the fleshpots of Egypt. He has a family, perchance, that he cannot take with him on the salary he receives. He is divided between the habits and customs and luxuries of civilized life and the self-sacrificing duties that devolve upon him in this work of teaching the Indians.

The Jesuit has no family. He has no ambition. He has no idea except to do his duty as God has given him to see it; and I am not afraid to say this, because I speak from personal observation, and no man ever went among these Indians with more intense prejudice against the Jesuits than I had when I left the city of Washington to perform that duty. I made my report to the secretary of the interior, Senator Teller, now on this floor, and I said in that report what I say here and what I would say anywhere and be glad of the opportunity to say it.

Mr. President, every dollar you give these day schools might as well be thrown into the Potomac River under a ton of lead. You will make no more impression upon the Indian children than if you should take that money and burn it and expect its smoke by some mystic process to bring them from idolatry and degradation to Christianity and civilization. If you can have the same system of boarding schools supported by the government that the Jesuits have adopted after long years of trial and deprivation, I grant that there might be something done in the way of elevating this race.

The old Indians are gone, hopelessly gone, so far as civilization and Christianity are concerned. They look upon all work as a degradation and that a squaw should bear the burden of life. The young Indian can be saved. There are 3,000 of them to-day in the Dakotas—in South Dakota, I believe—who are voters, exercising intelligently, as far as I know, the right of suffrage. Go to the Indian Territory, where there are the Five Civilized Tribes, and you will see what can be done by intelligent effort, not with day schools, but with schools based upon the idea of taking the children and removing them from the injurious influence of the old Indians and teaching them the arts of civilization and of peace.

If I have ever done anything in my whole career in this chamber of which I am sincerely proud it is that upon one occasion I obtained an appropriation of $10,000 for an industrial school at St. Ignatius, in Montana. A few years afterward, in passing through to the Pacific coast, I stopped over to see that school. They heard I was coming and met me at the depot with a brass band, the instruments in the hands of Indian boys, and they played without discrimination Hail Columbia and Dixie. They had been taught by a young French nobleman whom I had met two years before at the mission, who had squandered the principal portion of his fortune in reckless dissipation in the salons of Paris and had suddenly left that sort of life and joined the company of Jesus and dedicated himself to the American missions. He was an accomplished musician, and he taught those boys how to play upon the instruments.

I went up to the mission and found there these Indian boys making hats and caps and boots and shoes and running a blacksmith shop and carrying on a mill and herding horses and cattle. The girls and boys when they graduated, intermarrying, became heads of families as reputable and well-behaved and devoted to Christianity as any we can find in our own States. They were Catholics. That is a crime with some people in this country.

Mr. President, are we to be told that a secret political organization in this country shall dictate to us what we ought to do for this much-injured race whom we have despoiled of their lands and homes and whom God has put upon us as an inheritance to be cared for? I accuse no senator here of any other motive than a desire to do his public duty. I shall do mine, and I should gladly vote for an amendment to this bill infinitely stronger than that of the senator from Arkansas. I would put this work, imperative upon us, in the hands of those who could best accomplish it, as I would give the building of my house to the best mechanic, who would put up a structure that suited me and met the ends I desired. If the Catholics can do it better than anybody else, let them do it. If the Presbyterian, the Methodist, the Congregationalist, or any other denomination can do it, give the work to them; but to every man who comes to me and says this is a union of church and state, I answer him, "Your statement is false upon the very face of it." Instead of teaching the Indian children that they must be Catholics in order to be good citizens, they are simply taught that work is ennobling, and with the sense of self-dependence and not of dependence upon others will come civilization and Christianity. These are my feelings, Mr. President, and I would be glad if I could put them upon the statute books.

CAPRIVI DE CAPRERA

DE MONTE CUCCULI, GEORGE LEO VON CAPRIVI DE CAPRERA, a distinguished German statesman and soldier, the son of a high legal Prussian functionary, was born at Charlottenburg February 24, 1831. Entering the army in 1849 he was rapidly promoted, and served with honor in the campaigns of 1864 and 1866, and in the Franco-Prussian war was chief of staff of the Tenth Corps. In 1883 he was advanced to the rank of lieutenant-general and the next year was transferred to the headship of the admiralty on the retirement of Von Stosch. Caprivi exhibited extraordinary vigor in his new position, as well as a thorough comprehension of naval methods, and not long after the accession of William II had completely reorganized the navy. In recognition of his eminent services he was transferred back to the army and given command of the Tenth or Hanoverian Army Corps, a highly prized position. On March 19, 1890, he succeeded Bismarck as chancellor and president of the Prussian council, and in 1891 received from the emperor the title of count. In March, 1892, he resigned his position as Prussian prime minister, but retained his chancellorship till his resignation of that office also, October 26, 1894. In the last-named year appeared his "Reden im deutschen Reichstage," with biography.

ON COLONIAL POSSESSIONS

[First speech as chancellor in the Reichstag, delivered on May 12, 1890, in answer to Dr. von Bamberger's speech on the relinquishment of all colonial possessions.]

GENTLEMEN,—The gentleman who has just spoken has turned his attention from the question before the House to the important subject of our colonial policy. I wish to state with pleasure that he has expressed his approval of the fact that the government has carried out the intentions of the Reichstag. Such is indeed the fact, and I need not enumerate the long series of resolutions through which this House has acknowledged its willingness to support the measures of the federal government. I am convinced, therefore, like my predecessor,[1] that a colonial

[1] Bismarck.

policy is desirable only in as far as it is approved and supported by the will and—with due respect to Mr. Bamberger—by the feeling of the nation.

The honorable gentleman has intimated that possibly through my entrance into office a change of policy might be effected. That I most emphatically deny. I believe it is very generally known among those who have had the opportunity of an earlier acquaintance with me that I have not been an advocate of the colonial policy. For various reasons I looked upon the introduction of a colonial policy at that time as extremely dangerous. Now however I am convinced, that in view of the situation to-day, we cannot withdraw without stain upon our honor and financial loss; we cannot even stand still; nay, we must push forward.

Mr. Bamberger has declared that if the government would make known its purpose, and if the demands were not exorbitant, both he and his party might give their support. I infer, therefore, with a feeling of satisfaction that even among his associates there will not be found a Hannibal Fischer[1] for the German colonies.

G

If, however, he expects me to set forth a definite program, or to state on the spot: We shall take so many millions and spend them; and then to say we have reached a position where it is possible to dispense with the support of the empire and leave the colonies to themselves,—if, I repeat, he expects this—he is doomed to disappointment. In matters subjected to so many casualities and sealed, as it were, against penetrating into their inner nature as the beginning of colonies in foreign lands,—territory not only unknown to our-

[1] Hannibal Fischer sold by order of the Federal Diet in 1852 the German fleet lying in Bremerhaven, and thereby aroused the indignation of the German people.

selves but to all other nations as well,—it is simply impossible to predict that twelve months hence such events will happen or we shall need so much money. I can only emphasize—and the fact perhaps will give me more weight with Mr. Bamberger's partisans—that I am not a colonial enthusiast, that even to-day I look upon the matter with perfectly cool judgment, and that with my advice matters will only go as far as the honor and the interests of Germany demand.

The honorable gentleman looks upon the colonial policy as a money question and says: a colonial policy is an economic policy, and in a certain sense he is right, although he draws the line a little too closely. Therefore he has described the economic policy hitherto pursued by the federal government toward the colonies in a light not altogether favorable; he has named sums much too large in my estimation for expenses incurred so far. I have a natural aversion to enter into details with a shrewd financier, but I can state as a fact that he has counted into the expenses quoted by him: subsidies for steamships, appropriations for the maintenance of war-vessels, for salaries of officials, expenses pertaining in a certain measure to other purposes also, and which would have been necessary, even if we had decided upon no colonial policy. According to documents before me the sum hitherto expended by the empire for colonial purposes amounts to not quite 5,500,000 marks, and the money invested by companies—as far as I am able to ascertain—to somewhat less than 15,000,000 marks.

I admit that with the appearance of the colonial policy a great many misconceptions crept in. There was a belief for instance that we had but to stretch out our hands to find in one colony a nugget of gold, in another manufactured cigars, errors easily refuted by those who had seriously studied the question. The territory left for German colonies was decidedly not of that kind; on the contrary it became clearer day by day that profits could be realized only with great labor and after a considerable lapse of time.

Mr. Bamberger presents to us the example of the English. "Their companies," he says, "colonize without the assistance of the government." We would gladly follow their example, and we admit it to be our aim some day to reach a point where our government will cease to make appropriations and the companies will take upon themselves all responsibility and expense and thereby guarantee a profit to those engaged in the enterprise. But we are absolutely unable to carry out this English system immediately. In the short time that I have been in office I have learned how difficult it is to find a competent man for a comparatively subordinate position in the colonies, to say nothing of a man qualified both by natural ability and experience to fill a high position. But there is another point in which we differ from England. History tells us that English private capital has a tendency to turn to such enterprises; German capital, on the other hand, prefers investment in the doubtful securities of doubtful foreign states.

The reasons for this are well known, and the honorable and experienced gentleman undoubtedly knows them much better than I do.

The federal government cannot—as proved by the measure submitted to us here—state on the first of April of the present year how much they will have spent next year. This is where we would have the nation and the Reichstag believe that we will go no further than is absolutely necessary. We wish to be so far trusted as not to be open to suspicion in case we should spend 4,000,000 instead of 2,500,000; such increased expenditure is sometimes unavoidable. The colonial policy cannot be awarded to the lowest bidder; it must be given to those who are willing to undertake the matter.

In the debate to-day we are principally thinking of East Africa, and this is only natural. But if we wish to draw conclusions for the future from the past, as far as the financial side is concerned, East Africa offers a singularly unfavorable field: first, it is an unbounded territory; secondly, existing conditions are heterogeneous; and thirdly, the insurrection there has interrupted the natural development. Yet, leaving out the expenses of the navy and the officials, I can state that the Protectorates of Togo and Kamerun are self-supporting. We do not therefore—thanks to an able administration—show a deficit everywhere. This happy state of affairs will probably not be brought about so rapidly in East Africa; it will take years, but I have faith and hope that we shall achieve it some day; and in colonial affairs some faith and trust are necessary.

Let us consider the origin of the colonial policy and ask ourselves: What induced the imperial government to enter into what the gentleman is pleased to term "an ill-considered policy"? It is obvious that besides the expectation of financial gain other motives must have co-operated, else so many prudent and sensible men as the members of this House would hardly have embarked on this ship.

The honorable member has touched upon the humane and religious question of anti-slavery! Whatever importance may be attached to it here, I will leave undecided, but I believe it must be admitted even by those who are not inclined to favor this movement that flourishing industry and trade, nay, even well-conducted farming, is impossible without giving the natives some moral and intellectual education.

If we wish to bring them to this condition, we have, in my judgment, the obligation—even for the sake of our own pecuniary interests—to support the missions and to promote the civilization of these people.

It is a well-known fact that the Centre[1] gave its consent to the colonial policy influenced by religious motives and the anti-slavery movement. But as far as I have been able to follow the stenographic reports, the Centre did not object, if incidentally German national interests might be advanced thereby.

Others emphasize the national economic interests, yet accept with gratitude any advance toward christianization and German civilization made through this initiative. Each one must decide for himself how important he considers these matters, but through the Congo acts we are under international obligations to do something toward the advancement of civilization, and shall be still more strongly bound through the conference of Brussels now in session.

It is my opinion that only through the establishment of an organization, approaching to what in Europe we term a state, shall we be enabled effectually to resist slavery. But this is still in the dim future. First of all we must establish stations in the interior from which the missionary, as well as the merchant, may extend the field of their activities; to attain the result desired by the Centre, gun and Bible must work side by side, for without killing the slave-traders we can never put an end to slavery.

But there is one reason which the honorable member considers unimportant, and therefore puts aside—the national feeling! I am convinced, and I know whereof I am speaking, that one of the factors which led us to launch into the

[1] Catholic party.

colonial policy was the endeavor to maintain a tide of national feeling. After the war of 1870 there came a period of inertia in which the national spirit seemed to be paralyzed. It had no particular object to turn to; idealism, so necessary to the German mind, had lost its faculty of manifesting itself in the intellectual sphere. The war had provided it with practical aims, yet there remained an overflow of energy seeking an outlet. Then came the colonial policy, and the feeling for national honor and greatness with all its intensity—in many instances blindness—threw itself into this field.

You know, gentlemen, that the German nature, leaning as it does, strongly toward particularism, needs idealism if it is to be usefully employed. To concentrate itself this idealism needs a focal point; such a focus was found in the colonial policy, and was, as far as I know, gratefully received by the nation. Mr. Bamberger calls this a "romantic" feeling and considers it of little importance. I should like to ask him if he thinks the German Reichstag would be sitting here to-day but for this "romantic" feeling of the people?

I think not. I attach great importance to this national instinct, the "unconscious" in the soul of the people; moreover, should I find evidences of the smoldering of such a fire I should deem it my duty to search for it, foster it, and lead it into useful channels.

I concur however with Mr. Bamberger in his belief that this enthusiasm alone is of little value, since it is difficult to convert it into hard cash, German colonial enthusiasm in particular, which proverbially tightens the purse-strings. Nevertheless I am of the opinion that after the pacification of the natives and the establishment of a well-regulated government, East Africa will offer special inducements for the investment of private capital. I sincerely hope that whatever is left of colonial enthusiasm may overcome this obstacle and manifest itself in the form of ringing coin.

With many people the national question was synonymous with power, and I must confess this question of power in the colonial policy was treated by the majority with a surprising display of ignorance. It was believed we had only to buy colonies, paint the map of Africa the German color and proclaim to all the world: We are a great people!

But not so; in its inception, a colonial policy, as far as power is concerned, operates negatively; its success can be secured only by great sacrifices both of men and money. If it is a policy of faith and hope from the financial and ethical point of view, it is equally so with regard to power, and perhaps in this direction the necessity of faith is even more urgent. I can assure the honorable member that as far as I am concerned not a man shall be sacrificed or a mark spent more than is absolutely necessary to maintain and develop what is ours. I should never consent to send large sums of money or numbers of men to East Africa merely to gratify a desire to display power.

Mr. Bamberger has also touched upon the question of war, saying that in such a calamity colonies are dangerous possessions. I am willing to admit that they are doubtful ones, yet as an old soldier I know that the decision at the principal seat of war is always decisive of the fate of the dependencies. If war should break out in Europe—which heaven forbid—and we be victorious here, it would be immaterial whether some colony or other should find itself in an evil plight, the peace stipulations would fully reinstate us.

Looking into the future, I do not deem it impossible that the progress and development of the world at large will force Germany to enter into closer—and let us hope peaceful relations—with trans-oceanic states. The Phæacian existence of a small European state must cease, we shall have to deal with powers across the ocean, which are masters of enormous treasures in people and money, unknown to us; and if we realize that the time will come when German spirit and German power must manifest themselves more vigorously than heretofore, we must reach the conclusion that a navy is necessary. It was my aim during the years that I had the honor of being chief of the admiralty to labor for the development of the navy, that we might the better maintain our prestige in the event of our enlarging the sphere of our activities.

If we admit the possibility of our being placed in such a position as to need the display of a naval force in peace and war in foreign waters, we must necessarily ask ourselves: Where shall it take its supplies, the substance without which it is able neither to move nor to fight? Should we now become engaged in a war with a foreign power, we have some few but inadequate means of providing our vessels with coal. On the whole we should have to depend upon the friendliness of neutral powers; yet those who believe in the great future of the navy cannot tolerate such conditions for any length of time. We must therefore gain possession of a few places where German coal may be supplied to German ships by German authorities. The existence of coaling-stations is therefore the prime condition for naval activity in the future wars; and if we are called upon at this moment to vote some insignificant sums for our colonies, I am sanguine that this capital is a good investment and that we shall reap a manifold return.

To sum up then: We shall endeavor to advance step by step (if the Reichstag will support us); we shall not launch out into any risky enterprise; we shall strive to bring the companies to where they originally stood—that is, make them as independent as possible, although I am not able to state to-day to what extent these companies will feel inclined to work independently. At this time we have in East Africa, created by the Wissmann laws, a body of soldiers belonging to no one knows whom. I do not deem it improbable that in after years, when the dictatorship and state of war shall have ceased, these troops, recruited by Wissmann in the old lansquenet[1] style, may be changed into imperial troops, thus achieving more than now, when we recruit by contract.

It shall be our endeavor to respect foreign rights everywhere, as amplified by the secretary of state, and to protect the German empire. I firmly believe the federal government able to conduct the colonial policy in such a way as not to endanger the German universal policy and not to offend the legitimate development of German national feeling.

[Translated by Helena Nordhoff Gargan.]

[1] From the German "Landsknecht,"—soldier of fortune.

FARRAR

FREDERICK WILLIAM FARRAR, a distinguished English church dignitary and preacher, the son of an Anglican clergyman, was born in Bombay, India, August 7, 1831. He was educated at King William's College, Isle of Man, King's College, London, and Trinity College, Cambridge University, ordained deacon in the English church in 1854 and advanced to the priesthood in 1857. He was an assistant master at Harrow, 1855-71, and headmaster of Marlborough College, 1871-76. In the latter year he was appointed canon in Westminster Abbey and rector of St. Margaret's Church, and archdeacon of Westminster in 1883, becoming dean of Canterbury in 1895. He has several times been select preacher at each of the universities, delivering the Hulsean lectures at Cambridge in 1870, and the Bampton lectures at Oxford in 1885. From 1869 to 1873 he was honorary chaplain to the Queen and subsequently one of her chaplains-in-ordinary. He has taken an active part in the cause of temperance and other reforms, but is especially noted for his liberal utterances on the subject of eternal punishment. His religious works, which have been widely popular in England and America and have in some cases been translated into a number of languages, include "Seekers After God" (1869); "The Witnesses of History to Christ" (1871); "In the Days of Thy Youth" (1877); "The Life of Christ," a work which has had a wide reading (1874); "Life of St. Paul" (1879); "Early Days of Christianity" (1882); "Eternal Hope" (1880); "Darkness and Dawn," "The Lord's Prayer," "Life of Christ in Art," "The Voice of Sinai," "The Young Man, Master of Himself" (1897); "The Bible, Its Meaning and Supremacy" (1897); "The Herods" (1897); "The Life of Lives" (1899); "Texts Explained" (1899). Farrar has also written three popular books for boys, "Eric" (1858); "Julian Home" (1859); "St. Winifred's, or the World of School" (1863). Still other works by him are "The Origin of Language" (1860); "Chapters on Language" (1865); "Greek Syntax" (1866); "Families of Speech" (1870); "Language and Languages" (1878); "Temperance Reform" (1899).

EULOGY OF GENERAL GRANT

[The following eloquent address was delivered by Archdeacon Farrar at the impressive memorial service, held in Westminster Abbey August 4, 1885, as an expression of England's sympathy for the loss sustained by the United States in the death of General Grant.]

EIGHT years have not passed since the Dean of Westminster, whom Americans so much loved and honored, was walking round this Abbey with General Grant and explaining to him its wealth of great memorials.

Neither of them had attained the allotted span of human life, and for both we might have hoped that many years would elapse before they went down to the grave full of years and honors. But this is already the fourth summer since the Dean "fell on sleep," and to-day we are assembled for the obsequies of the great soldier whose sun has set while it yet was day, and at whose funeral service in America tens of thousands are assembled at this moment to mourn with his weeping family and friends.

Life at the best is but as a vapor that passeth away.

> "The glories of our birth and state
> Are shadows, not substantial things."

When death comes, what nobler epitaph can any man have than this — that "having served his generation, by the will of God he fell on sleep!"

Little can the living do for the dead. The voices of praise cannot delight the closed ear, nor the violence of censure vex it. I would desire to speak simply and directly, and, if with generous appreciation, yet with no idle flattery, of him whose death has made a nation mourn. His private life, the faults and failings of his character, whatever they may have been, belong in no sense to the world. We touch only on his public actions and services — the record of his strength, his magnanimity, his self-control, his generous deeds.

His life falls into four marked divisions, of which each has its own lesson for us. He touched on them himself in part when he said, "Bury me either at West Point, where I was trained as a youth; or in Illinois, which gave me my first commission; or at New York, which sympathized with me in my misfortunes."

His wish has been respected, and on the bluff overlooking

the Hudson his monument will stand to recall to the memory of future generations those dark pages of a nation's history which he did so much to close. First came the long early years of growth and training, of poverty and obscurity, of struggle and self-denial. Poor and humbly born, he had to make his own way in the world. God's unseen providence, which men nickname chance, directed his boyhood. A cadetship was given him at the military academy at West Point, and after a brief period of service in the Mexican war, in which he was three times mentioned in despatches, seeing no opening for a soldier in what seemed likely to be days of unbroken peace, he settled down to humble trades in provincial districts. Citizens of St. Louis still remember the rough backwoodsman who sold cord-wood from door to door. He afterward entered the leather trade in the obscure town of Galena.

Men who knew him in those days have said that if any one had predicted that the silent, unprosperous, unambitious man, whose chief aim was to get a plank road from his shop to the railway depot, would become twice President of the United States and one of the foremost men of his day, the prophecy would have seemed extravagantly ridiculous.

But such careers are the glory of the American continent. They show that the people have a sovereign insight into intrinsic force. If Rome told with pride how her dictators came from the plough-tail, America too may record the answer of the President, who, on being asked what would be his coat of arms, answered, proudly mindful of his early struggles, "A pair of shirt sleeves."

The answer showed a noble sense of the dignity of labor, a noble superiority to the vanities of feudalism, a strong conviction that men are to be honored simply as men, not for the prizes of accident and birth. You have of late years had two martyr Presidents. Both were sons of the people. One was the homely man who at the age of seven was a farm-lad, at nineteen a rail-splitter, at twenty a boatman on the Mississippi, and who in manhood proved to be one of the strongest, most honest, and most God-fearing of modern rulers. The other grew up from a shoeless child in a log hut on the prairies, round which the wolves howled in the winter snow, to be a humble teacher in Hiram Institute. With these Presidents America need not blush to name also the leather-seller of Galena.

Every true man derives his patent of nobleness direct from God. Did not God choose David from the sheepfolds to make him ruler of his people Israel? Was not the "Lord of life and all the worlds" for thirty years a carpenter at Nazareth? Do not such careers illustrate the prophecy of Solomon, "Seest thou the man diligent in his business? he shall stand before kings." When Abraham Lincoln sat, book in hand, day after day, under the tree, moving round it as the shadow moved, absorbed in mastering his task; when James Garfield rang the bell at Hiram Institute, day after day, on the very stroke of the hour, and swept the school-room as faithfully as he mastered the Greek lesson; when Ulysses Grant, sent with his team to meet some men who were to load the cart with logs, and finding no men there, loaded the cart with his own boy strength — they showed in conscientious duty and thoroughness the qualities which were to raise them to rule the destinies of men.

But the youth was not destined to die in that deep valley of obscurity and toil in which it is the lot — perhaps the happy lot — of many of us to spend our little lives. The hour came; the man was needed.

In 1861 there broke out the most terrible war of modern days. Grant received a commission as colonel of volunteers, and in four years the struggling toiler had risen to the chief command of a vaster army than has ever been handled by any mortal man. Who could have imagined that four years could make that stupendous difference? But it is often so. The great men needed for some tremendous crisis have often stepped as it were through a door in the wall which no one had noticed, and unannounced, unheralded, without prestige, have made their way silently and single-handed to the front.

And there was no luck in it. He rose, it has been said, by the upward gravitation of natural fitness. It was the work of inflexible faithfulness, of indomitable resolution, of sleepless energy, of iron purpose, of persistent tenacity. In battle after battle, in siege after siege, whatever Grant had to do he did it with his might. He undertook, as General Sherman said, what no one else would have adventured, till his very soldiers began to reflect some of his own indomitable determination. With a patience which nothing could tire, with a firmness which no obstacle could daunt, with a military genius which embraced the vastest plans, yet attended to the smallest minutiæ, he defeated one after another every great general of the Confederates except General Stonewall Jackson.

Grant had not only to defeat armies, but to "annihilate resources"— to leave no choice but destruction or submission. He saw that the brief ravage of the hurricane is infinitely less ruinous than the interminable malignity of the pestilence, and that in that colossal struggle victory — swift, decisive, overwhelming, at all costs — was the truest mercy. In silence, in determination, in clearness of insight, he was your Washington and our Wellington. He was like them also in this, that the word "can't" did not exist in his soldier's dictionary, and that all that he achieved was accomplished without bluster and without parade.

After the surrender at Appomattox, the war of the Secession was over. It was a mighty work, and Grant had done it mightily. Surely the light of God, which manifests all things in the slow history of their ripening, has shown that for the future destinies of a mighty nation it was a necessary and a blessed work. The Church hurls her most indignant anathema at unrighteous war, but she has never refused to honor the faithful soldier who fights in the cause of his country and his God. The gentlest and most Christian of poets has used the tremendous words that —

> "God's most dreaded instrument,
> In working out a pure intent,
> Is man—arrayed for mutual slaughter;
> Yea, carnage is his daughter."

We shudder even as we quote the words; but yet the cause for which Grant fought — the unity of a great people, the freedom of a whole race of mankind — was as great and noble as that when at Lexington the embattled farmers fired the shot which was heard round the world. The South has accepted that desperate and bloody arbitrament. Two of the Southern generals will bear General Grant's funeral pall. The rancor and the fury of the past are buried in oblivion. True friends have been made out of brave foemen, and the pure glory and virtue of Lee and of Stonewall Jackson will be part of the common national heritage with the fame of Garfield and of Grant.

As Wellington became Prime Minister of England, and was hooted in the streets of London, so Grant, more than half against his will, became President, and for a time lost much of his popularity. He foresaw it all; but it is for a man not to choose, rather to accept his destiny. What verdict history will pronounce on him as a politician I know not; but here and now the voice of censure, deserved and undeserved, is silent. When the great Duke of Marlborough died, and one began to speak of his avarice, "He was so great a man," said Bolingbroke, "that I had forgotten he had that fault."

It was a fine and delicate rebuke; and ours at any rate need not be the "feeble hands iniquitously just" which rake up a man's faults and errors. Let us write his virtues "on brass for man's example; let his faults, whatever they may have been, be written in water." The satirist has said how well it would have been for Marius if he had died as he stepped from the chariot of his Cimbric victory; for Pompeius, if he had died after his Mithridatic war. And some may think how much happier it would have been for General Grant had he died in 1865, when steeples clashed and cities were illuminated, and congregations rose in his honor. Many and dark clouds overshadowed the evening of his days — the blow of financial ruin, the dread of a tarnished reputation, the terrible agony of an incurable disease.

To bear that sudden ruin and that speechless agony required a courage nobler and greater than that of the battlefield, and human courage rose to the height of human calamity. In ruin, in sorrow, on the lingering deathbed, Grant showed himself every inch a hero, bearing his agonies and trials without a murmur, with rugged stoicism, and unflinching fortitude, and we believe with a Christian prayer and peace. Which of us can tell whether those hours of torture and misery may not have been blessings in disguise?

We are gathered here to do honor to his memory. Could

CHAUNCEY M. DEPEW

Orations—Volume twenty-two

we be gathered in a more fitting place? We do not lack here memorials to recall the history of your country. There is the grave of André; there is the monument raised by grateful Massachusetts to the gallant Howe; there is the temporary resting-place of George Peabody; there is the bust of Longfellow; over the Dean's grave there is the faint semblance of Boston harbor.

We add another memory to-day. Whatever there be between the two nations to forget and to forgive, it is forgotten and it is forgiven. "I will not speak of them as two peoples," said General Grant in 1877, "because in fact we are one people with a common destiny, and that destiny will be brilliant in proportion to the friendship and co-operation of the brethren dwelling on each side of the Atlantic."

If the two peoples which are one people be true to their duty, true to their God, who can doubt that in their hands are the destinies of the world? Can anything short of utter dementation ever thwart a destiny so manifest? Your founders were our sons. It was from our past that your present grew. The monument of Sir Walter Raleigh is not that nameless grave in St. Margaret's; it is the State of Virginia. Yours alike and ours are the memories of Captain John Smith and Pocahontas, of the Pilgrim Fathers, of General Oglethorpe's strong benevolence of soul, of the mission labors of Eliot and Brainerd, of the apostolic holiness of Berkeley, and the burning zeal of Wesley and Whitefield. Yours alike and ours are the plays of Shakespeare and the poems of Milton; ours alike and yours all that you have accomplished in literature or in history — the wisdom of Franklin and Adams, the eloquence of Webster, the song of Longfellow and Bryant, the genius of Hawthorne and Irving, the fame of Washington, Lee, and Grant.

But great memories imply great responsibilities. It was not for nothing that God has made England what she is; not for nothing that the "free individualism of a busy multitude, the humble traders of a fugitive people," snatched the New World from feudalism and from bigotry — from Philip II and Louis XIV; from Menendez and Montcalm; from the Jesuit and the Inquisition; from Torquemada and from Richelieu — to make it the land of the Reformation and the Republic, of prosperity and of peace. "Let us auspicate all our proceedings on America," said Edmund Burke, "with the old Church cry, *sursum corda.*" It is for America to live up to the spirit of such words. We have heard of

> "New times, new climes, new lands, new men; but still
> The same old tears, old crimes, and oldest ill."

It is for America to falsify the cynical foreboding. Let her take her place side by side with England in the very van of freedom and of progress. United by a common language, by common blood, by common memories, by a common history, by common interests, by common hopes, united by the common glory of great men, of which this temple of silence and reconciliation is the richest shrine, be it the steadfast purpose of the two peoples who are one people to show to all the world not only the magnificent spectacle of human happiness, but the still more magnificent spectacle of two peoples who are one people loving righteousness and hating iniquity, inflexibly faithful to the principles of eternal justice, which are the unchanging law of God.

GOSCHEN

GEORGE JOACHIM GOSCHEN, a distinguished English statesman, was born in London, of German parentage, August 10, 1831, and educated at Rugby and Oriel colleges, Oxford. After leaving the university in 1853 he engaged at once in mercantile life, giving especial attention to financial questions and becoming vice-president of the board of trade and a director of the Bank of England. In 1863 he entered Parliament as a Liberal member for London, and was very active in agitation for opening the universities to dissenters, and the abolition of religious tests. He was a privy councillor in 1865, chancellor of the Duchy of Lancaster in 1866, president of the poor law board, 1868-71, and first lord of the admiralty, 1871-74. In 1876 Goschen and Joubert were sent to Cairo as delegates of English and French holders of Egyptian bonds to arrange plans for the conversion of these debts, and in 1880, while ambassador extraordinary to Constantinople, he secured the cession of certain territory from Turkey to Greece. On the formation of the Liberal-Unionist party in 1887 Goschen seceded from the Liberal ranks and ceased to act with Gladstone. He became chancellor of the exchequer in Lord Salisbury's administration in 1887, and in 1889 secured the success of the scheme for reduction of the interest on the national debt. In 1895 he was again appointed first lord of the admiralty. He was elected lord rector of the University of Aberdeen in 1874 and 1888, and lord rector of the University of Edinburgh, 1890. For many years he has been considered the highest living authority on finance. Among his speeches may be named "Address on Education and Economic Subjects" (1885), and speeches on the "Oxford University Tests Abolition Bill," and on "Bankruptcy Legislation." He has published "The Theory of Foreign Exchanges" (1863), which has passed into many editions; "Probable Result of an Increase in the Purchasing Power of Gold" (1883).

ON THE CULTIVATION OF THE IMAGINATION

FROM ADDRESS DELIVERED AT THE LIVERPOOL INSTITUTE, LIVERPOOL, NOVEMBER 29, 1877

I ADDRESS these words in favor of the cultivation of the imagination to the poorest and most humble in the same way that I address them to the wealthiest and those who have the best prospects in life. I will try not to make the mistake which doctors commit when they recommend patients in receipt of two pounds a week to have recourse to champagne and a short residence at the seaside.

In what sense, then, do I use the word imagination? Johnson's dictionary shall answer. I wish you particularly to note the answer Johnson gives as regards the meaning of "imagination." He defines it as "the power of forming ideal pictures;" "the power of representing absent things to ourselves and to others."

Such is the power which I am going to ask you, confidently, to cultivate in your schools, by your libraries at home, by every influence which I can gain for the cause; and I hope I shall be able to carry you with me and show you why you should cultivate that power. I repeat it is the power of forming ideal pictures and of representing absent things to yourselves and to others. That is the sense in which I shall use the word imagination in the course of my address.

Now follow out this thought and I think I can make my meaning clear. Absent things! Take history. History deals with the things of the past. They are absent in a sense, from your minds—that is to say you cannot see them; but the study of history qualifies you and strengthens your capacity for understanding things that are not present to you, and thus I wish to recommend history to you as a most desirable course of study.

Then again take foreign countries—travels. Here again you have matters which are absent, in the physical sense, from you; but the study of travels will enable you to realize things that are absent to your own minds. And as for the power of forming ideal pictures, there I refer you to poets, dramatists, and imaginative writers, to the great literature of all times and of all countries Such studies as these will enable you to live, and to move, and to think, in a world different from the narrow world by which you are surrounded. These studies will open up to you sources of amusement which, I think I may say, will often rise into happiness.

I wish you, by the aid of the training which I recommend, to be able to look beyond your own lives and have pleasure in surroundings different from those in which you move. I want you to be able—and mark this point—to sympathize with other times, to be able to understand the men and women of other countries, and to have the intense enjoyment—an enjoyment which I am sure you would all appreciate—of mental change of scene. I do not only want you to know dry facts; I am not only looking to a knowledge of facts, nor chiefly to that knowledge. I want the heart to be stirred as well as the intellect. I want you to feel more and live more than you can do if you only know what surrounds yourselves. I want the action of the imagination, the sympathetic study of history and travels, the broad teaching of the poets, and, indeed, of the best writers of other times and other countries, to neutralize and check the dwarfing influences of necessarily narrow careers and necessarily stunted lives. That is the point which you will see I mean when I ask you to cultivate the imagination. I want to introduce you to other, wider, and nobler fields of thought, and to open up vistas of other worlds, whence refreshing and bracing breezes will stream upon your minds and souls. . . .

And do not believe for a moment—I am rather anxious on this point—that the cultivation of this faculty will disgust you or disqualify you for your daily tasks. I hold a very contrary view. I spoke just now of mental change of scene; and as the body is better for a change of scene and a change of air, so I believe that the mind is also better for occasional changes of mental atmosphere. I do not believe that it is good either for men or women always to be breathing the atmosphere of the business in which they are themselves engaged.

You know how a visit to the seaside sometimes brings color to the cheeks and braces the limbs. Well, so I believe that a mental change of scene which I recommend will bring color into your minds, will brace you to greater activity, and will in every way strengthen both your intellectual and your moral faculties. I want you—if I may use the phrase—to breathe the bracing ozone of the imagination.

And over what worlds will not fancy enable you to roam?—the world of the past, ideal worlds, and other worlds beyond your sight, probably brighter worlds, possibly more interesting worlds than the narrow world in which most of us are compelled to live; at all events, different worlds and worlds that give us change. . . .

I am an enthusiast for the study of history and I entreat you to give it as much attention as you can at this place. You will see that my whole argument tends to the study of history and of general literature, not for the sake of the facts alone, not for mere knowledge, but for their influence on the mind. History may be dry and technical if you confine yourself to the chronological order of facts—if you study only to know what actually took place at certain dates.

I am sure we have all suffered from the infliction of skeleton histories—excellent tests of patience, but I am afraid as little exciting to the imagination as any other study in which any one can possibly engage. What I am looking to is rather the coloring of history—the familiarity with times gone by, with the characters, the passions, the thoughts and aspirations of men who have gone before us. History with that life and color—and many historians of the present day write histories which fulfil these conditions—history with that life and color cultivates the imagination as much and better than many of the best romances.

When thus written and when once the reader is fairly launched into it history is as absorbing as a novel and more amusing and interesting than many a tale.

I will be quite candid with you. I am something of a novel reader myself. I admit that I like reading a novel occasionally. The fact is there is one difference between a novel and a history which is in favor of the former at the first start. In a history the first fifty pages are often intolerably dull, and it is the opening which, to use a familiar expression, chokes off half the readers. You generally have some preliminary description—of the state of Europe, for instance, or of the state of India, or the state of France, or some other country at a given time. You don't come to the main point—you don't come to what interests you at first sight; and thus many persons are frightened off before they thoroughly get into the book, and they throw aside a history and characterize it as being very dull. Now, in a novel you very often begin to enjoy yourself at the very first page.

Still, when I have taken up some interesting history—for instance, lately I have been reading "Kaye's History of the Sepoy War"—and when I have got over the first few introductory pages, which are a little heavy, I say to myself, How is it possible that a man of sense can spend his time on reading novels when there are histories of this absorbing interest which are so vastly more entertaining, so vastly more instructive, and so much better for the mind than any novel? Believe me an intelligent and a systematic study of history contains a vast resource of interest and amusement to all those who will embark in it.

Let me explain a little more. Histories, if you only deal with chronological details, you may possibly find to be exceedingly like "Bradshaw's Railway Guide"—very confusing, very uninteresting in themselves, only useful sometimes in enabling you to know how to go from one period to another—to make an historical journey.

Or you might compare these general surveys of history of which I was speaking to a skeleton map of a country of which you know very little. You see the towns noted down. They are but uninteresting spots on the map. They convey nothing to you; they don't interest you. But if you have travelled in that country, if you know the towns mentioned on the map, then you pore over the map with a very different interest. It gives you real personal pleasure; your mind and imagination recall the country itself. So you will find that the grand secret to enjoy history is to get beyond the outlines, to be thoroughly familiar with a particular period, to saturate yourselves with the facts, the events, the circumstances, and the personages which belong to a certain time in history.

When you have done this, the men and women of that period become your personal friends; you take an intense delight in their society, and you experience a sense of pleasure equivalent to what is given by any novel. I heard yesterday an anecdote of a lady who had lived a great deal in political circles. She had received from a friend a book about Sir Thomas More. When she had read it she wrote back and thanked the sender of the book, telling him with what delight she had perused it, and adding, "Sir Thomas More and Erasmus are particularly intimate friends of mine." She was so well acquainted with that period that all that was written about it came home to her heart—she knew it, she had lived in it, and it had a living interest for her. That is the mode and manner in which I would recommend you to study history.

Let me be more precise. I would not gallop through histories any more than I would through a country if I wanted to explore it. I would take a particular period and read every book bearing on that particular period which my library supplied me, and which I had time to read. Then I would read the poets who had written in the same period. I should read the dramas relating to that period, and thus I should saturate myself with everything which was connected with it, and by that means I would acquire that power which I value, which I want you to have individually and which I should like every English man and woman to have as far as they could, namely, the power of being able to live in other times and sympathize with other times, and to sympathize with persons and races and influences different from those amongst which we move.

And do not think that in such studies you lose your time. Are there fathers and mothers here who hold that it is a dangerous doctrine which I preach? If so, I hope I may be able to reassure them; for I hold that in all spheres and all classes culture of this kind is of the highest value and that it does not disqualify, but the reverse, for business life. Amongst the wealthier classes of business men I rejoice to think that prejudice against culture as being dangerous to business is rapidly dying out, and that a university education is no longer regarded with suspicion.

"What do men learn at Oxford and Cambridge that will fit them for business?" was formerly often asked; but I do not think this question is put quite so often now. I will tell you what once occurred to myself in regard to this point. Some eight years ago I met a distinguished modern poet, calling at the same house where I was calling, and he asked, "What becomes of all the senior wranglers and of all the Oxford first class men? One does not hear of them in after life." I ventured very modestly to say in reply that, not being a Cambridge man, I could not speak on behalf of Cambridge men; but as to Oxford I was able to inform him that eight of her first class men were at that moment in her Majesty's cabinet.

But you may say, "This is all very well for the greater affairs of life, but as regards the general rough-and-tumble of business life, why should you have this cultivation? Is it not dangerous and does it not rather hamper a young man when he goes into business life?"

Let me give you another instance on this point and you will forgive me if it is somewhat of a personal character; but it may come home to some of the young men here more forcibly than the most eloquent generalization. My own father came over to England as a very young man, with one friend as young as himself, and with very little more money in his pocket than a great many of the students here, I dare say, possess; and he has told me, half in joke and half in earnest, that he was obliged to found a firm because he wrote such a bad hand that no one would take him for a clerk. But he was steeped to the lips in intellectual culture. In his father's[1] house, as a boy, he had met all the great literary men of the best period of German literature. He had heard Schiller read his own plays. He had listened to the conversation of great thinkers and great poets. He was a good historian, an acute critic, well versed in literature, and a very good musician to boot. But did this stand in his way as a young man coming over to London with a view to found a business? Has

---

[1] **Georg Joachim Göschen (1752-1828), the famous Leipzig bookseller.**

it stood in his way of founding a firm of which I, as his son, am very proud? It did not stand in his way. On the contrary it aided his success; and, with this before me, I hope you will say that I am able to speak with affectionate conviction of the fact that culture will not interfere with the due discharge of the duties of business men in any sphere of business life.

I will not add to what I have said about the great increase of happiness and amusement to be gained for your own leisure in after-life if you follow the studies I have named. It is most certainly for your happiness and advantage; but you may remember that I used much stronger language than this. I said it was not only of advantage for the young themselves, but for the national advantage, that imaginative culture should be considered as one of the aims of education.

I have still got to make this point good. Consider what are the duties of this country in which we live. Let me now take you away from Liverpool—away even from England—and ask you to look at our imperial duties—at our colonies, at our vast empire, at our foreign relations—and then I want you to ask yourselves whether it is important or not that Englishmen shall be able to realize to themselves what is not immediately around them, that they shall be able to transport themselves in imagination to other countries over which they rule. It is not sufficient for Englishmen to think only of their own surroundings.

There was a time when the destinies of England used to be wielded by a few individual men, or by small coteries of trained statesmen. India was governed for years externally to the influence of public opinion. But that is past now. Public opinion is now stepping in; and if public opinion steps in I wish that public opinion to be properly trained. Why, even ministers for foreign affairs now declare that they wait the behests of the public, their employers, before they take any decided step. If public opinion assumes these responsibilities, again I say, "Let us look to the formation of that public opinion, and see that the young generation of Englishmen are trained properly for the discharge of these functions."

Parliament is more and more sharing with the executive government of the country the duties of administration, and the press and the public are more and more sharing this duty with Parliament. Therefore you will understand the importance I attach to the training of the coming generation, not only in useful knowledge, but in all that they ought to know and ought to be able to feel and think when they are discharging imperial duties.

And, I ask, by what power can this result be better obtained than by the intelligent study of history and of modes of thought which lie beyond our own immediate range? It is no easy thing for democracies to rule wisely and satisfactorily self-governing colonies or subject races. Imagination, in its highest and broadest sense, is necessary for the noble discharge of imperial duties.

DONNELLY

IGNATIUS DONNELLY, an American editor, humorist, and orator, was born in Philadelphia November 3, 1831, where he was educated at the Central High School. In 1852 he was admitted to the bar and four years later emigrated to Minnesota, where he rapidly rose to notice and was elected successively lieutenant-governor and governor. In 1863 he was sent to Congress and served six years. He was president of the State Farmers' Alliance of Minnesota and was chairman of the National Anti-monopoly convention that nominated Peter Cooper for president in 1872. He engaged actively in newspaper work and was several times a member of the Minnesota legislature. In 1898 he was nominated for vice-president of the United States on the ticket of People's party. Among his best known publications are "The Great Cryptogram," in which he claimed to have discovered an arithmetical word-cypher in the works of Shakespeare, proving the author of those plays to have been Lord Bacon; "Atlantis, the Ante-Diluvian World," "Ragnarök," "Cæsar's Column," and "The Golden Bottle." He died in 1901.

RECONSTRUCTION

IN THE HOUSE OF REPRESENTATIVES, JANUARY 18, 1866

[The House having under consideration House bill No. 543, to provide for restoring to the States lately in insurrection their full political rights, Mr. Donnelly said:]

MR. SPEAKER,—I desire to express myself in favor of the main purposes of the bill now under consideration. [To provide for restoring to the States lately in insurrection their full political rights.]

Through the clouds of a great war and the confusion of a vast mass of uncertain legislation we are at length reaching something tangible; we have passed the "Serbonian bog," and are approaching good dry land.

This is the logical conclusion of the war. The war was simply the expression of the determination of the nation to subordinate the almost unanimous will of the white people of the rebellious States to the unity and prosperity of the whole country. Having gone thus far we cannot pause. We must still subordinate their wishes to our welfare.

This bill proposes to commence at the very foundation and build upward.

We have the assurance of President Johnson that "the rebellion has in its revolutionary progress deprived the rebellious States of all civil government," and that their State institutions have been "prostrated and paid out upon the ground."

In such a state of anarchy and disorganization the very foundations of society are laid bare; and we reach, as it were, the primary rocks, the everlasting granite of justice and right which underlies all human government.

In the language of the great Edmund Burke:

"When men break up the original compact or agreement which gives its corporate form and capacity to a State they are no longer a people; they have no longer a corporate existence; they have no longer a legal coactive force to bind within nor a claim to be recognized abroad. They are a number of vague, loose individuals, and nothing more; with them all is to begin again. Alas! they little know how many a weary step is to be taken before they can form themselves into a mass which has a true political personality."[1]

I shall not stop to consider the objection made to the second section of the bill by the gentleman from Wisconsin [Mr. Paine]. With the purpose and intent of his remarks I thoroughly concur. I conclude, howe er, that the object of the gentleman from Pennsylvania [Mr. Stevens], in providing for such a partial and temporary recognition of the rebel governments, was to protect society from the evils of a total abrogation of all law and order. But it seems to me that whatever

[1] Burke's Works, vol. iii, p. 82.

binding force those governments can have, founded as they are upon revolution and by the hands of revolutionary agents, is to be derived solely from such recognition as Congress may give them. It may be possible in this and other particulars to perfect the bill. I desire to speak rather to its general scope and purpose.

Government having, by the acknowledgment of the President, ceased to exist, law being swept aside, and chaos having come again in those rebellious States, by what principle shall the law-making power of the nation—the Congress—govern itself? Shall it bend its energies to renew old injustice? Shall it receive to its fraternal embrace only that portion of the population which circumstance or accident or century-old oppression may have brought to the surface? Shall it—having broken up the armies and crushed the hopes of the rebels—pander to their bigotries and cringe to their prejudices? Shall it hesitate to do it right out of deference to the sentiments of those who but a short time since were mowed down at the mouth of its cannon?

It is to my mind most clear that slavery having ceased to exist the slaves became citizens; being citizens they are a part of the people; and being a part of the people no organization deserves a moment's consideration at our hands which attempts to ignore them. If they were white people whom it was thus sought to disfranchise and outlaw not a man in the nation would dare to say nay to this proposition; every impulse of our hearts would rise up in indignant remonstrance against their oppressors. But it has pleased Almighty God, who takes counsel of no man, not even of the founders of the rebellion, to paint them of a different complexion, and that variation in the *pigmentum mucum* is to rise up as a perpetual barrier in our pathway toward equal justice and equal rights.

For one, with the help of God, I propose to do what I know to be right in the face of all prejudices and all obstructions; and so long as I have a seat in this body I shall never vote to reconstruct any rebellious State on any such basis of cruelty and injustice as that proposed by the Opposition here.

Take the case of South Carolina. She has 300,000 whites and 400,000 blacks; and we are asked to hand over the 400,000 blacks to the unrestrained custody and control of the 300,000 whites. We are to know no one but the whites; to communicate with no one but the whites; this floor is to recognize no one but white representatives of the whites. The whites are to make the laws, execute the laws, interpret the laws, and write the history of their own deeds; but below them, under them, there is to be a vast population—a majority of the whole people—seething and writhing in a condition of suffering, darkness, and wretchedness unparalleled in the world.

And this is to be an American State! This is to be a component part of the great, humane, Christian Republic of the world. This is to be the protection the mighty Republic is to deal out to its poor black friends who were faithful to it in its hour of trial; this is the punishment it is to inflict upon its perfidious enemies.

No, sir, no sophistry, no special pleading, can lead the American people to this result. Through us or over us it will reconstruct those States on a basis of impartial and eternal justice. Such a mongrel, patchwork, bastard reconstruction as some gentlemen propose, even if put into shape, would not hold together a twelvemonth. Four million human beings consigned to the uncontrolled brutality of 7,000,000 of human beings! The very thought is monstrous. The instinct of justice which God has implanted in every soul revolts at it. The voice of lamentation would swell up from that wretched land and fill the ears of mankind. Leaders and avengers would spring up on every hilltop of the north. The intellect, the morality, the soul of the age would fight in behalf of the oppressed, and the structure of so-called reconstruction would go down in blood.

Does any man think that it is in the American people, who rose at the cry of the slave under the lash of his master, to abide in quiet the carnival of arson, rapine, and murder now raging over the south? Sir, a government which would perpetuate such a state of things would be a monstrous barbarism; the legislative body which would seek to weave such things into the warp and woof of the national life would deserve the vengeance of Almighty God.

A senator from Pennsylvania [Mr. Cowan] the other day in the United States Senate said:

"I have no doubt but there are large numbers of the American people who are exceedingly anxious to compel negro suffrage through the southern States. But has any one of them ever made an argument to show that the southern States would be better governed; that there would be more peace and more quiet in consequence of it? I have never heard those arguments if they have been made, and I do not know how anybody could make them."

I will give the honorable senator an argument most potent and convincing as to the kind of "peace and quiet" which now reign in the south without negro suffrage and which will reign there so long as negro suffrage is denied. General Ord has just made a report upon the condition of things in Arkansas. He sums up matters as follows:

"Outrages, assaults, and murders committed on the persons of freed men and women are being continually reported from all sections of the State, and a decided want of disposition to punish offenders apparently exists with the local civil officers and in the minds of the people. There have been reported fifty-two murders of freed persons by white men in this State in the past three or four months, and no reports have been received that the murderers have been imprisoned or punished. In some parts of the State, particularly in the southwest and southeast, freedmen's lives are threatened if they report their wrongs to the agent of the bureau, and in many instances the parties making reports are missed and never heard of afterward. "It is believed that the number of murders reported is not half the number committed during the time mentioned."

Or if this is not sufficient, I would answer the distinguished senator still further by quoting from the report of the officers of the Freedmen's Bureau as to the state of affairs in Tennessee as a further testimony to the condition of southern society without impartial suffrage:

"Captain Kendrick reports in substance that having proceeded to Union City, he conversed with many of the citizens, who told him that but few freedmen were left about there, as they were driving them away as rapidly as possible. There seems to be a fixed determination that the freedmen shall not reside there, and the citizens force them to fly by ravishing the females, shooting, beating, whipping, and cheating them. The superintendent of the bureau there, while investigating a case of assault upon a negro, was compelled to desist by threats upon his life. The magistrate of the town states that he is powerless to administer justice, owing to the feeling in the community.

"Captain Kendrick mentions the case of a freedwoman named Emeline, living in Union City, who, during the absence of her husband, was brutally violated by a party of whites. She appealed to the justice of the peace, who informed her that nothing could be done for her on account of the feeling in the town. The next day two men, named Goodlow and Avons, of Union City, took her into a field and whipped her. A freedman named Callum was whipped by a man named

Stanley for saying that he had fought in the Union army. A Mr. Roscol, county trustee, has been persistently persecuted by a gang of desperadoes because he was prominent in defending the Union, and has been shot at several times while sitting in his house. About a dozen bullet holes may be seen in his door. At Troy the freedmen are getting on prosperously and have no complaints to make. The feeling of hostility toward northern men at this place, the captain reports, is more bitter even than at Union City. Loyal citizens are waylaid and shot and the ruffians escape punishment.

"A man named Hancock was called out of church, where he had just experienced religion, by a Dr. Marshall, who told him two persons outside wished to see him. When he had gone a short distance two men named Carruthers attacked and severely beat him with clubs because Hancock wore a federal uniform coat. Several other cases of outrage of an aggravated character and even murder are reported by Captain Kendrick, and those who are thus maltreated dare not utter a word of complaint through fear of the desperadoes. He recommends that a detachment of troops be permanently stationed in this county, and says that matters will grow worse instead of better until it is done."

I find in the morning papers the following letter, which explains itself:

HEADQUARTERS, DEPARTMENT OF THE SOUTH,
CHARLESTON, S. C., *Jan.* 10, 1867.

GENERAL,—According to an article in the Charleston "Daily News" of this morning, it appears that the jail at Kingstree, South Carolina, has been destroyed by fire, and twenty-two colored prisoners smothered or burned to death, while the only white prisoner was permitted to escape. The article states that the jailer, who had the keys, refused to open the doors without the authority of the sheriff, and the sheriff refused to act without the orders of the lieutenant commanding the troops at Kingstree. This statement presents a degree of barbarity that would appear incredible except in a community where no value is placed upon the lives of colored citizens. The general commanding directs that you cause an immediate and thorough investigation of this affair; that in the meantime you arrest the sheriff and jailer, and if the facts prove to be as stated, that you hold them in military confinement under the charge of murder until the civil authorities shall be ready and willing to try them.

Very respectfully, your obedient servant,

J. W. CLOUS,
Brev. Capt. and First Lieut. Sixth Infantry,
A.A.A.G.

Brev. Maj. Gen. H. K. SCOTT,
Com. Mil. Com., S. C.

I might fill pages with similar testimony, but it is not required.

It is too evident that when you strip a man of all means of self-defence, either through the courts or the laws, deprive him of education and leave him to the mercy of his fellow men, he must suffer all the pangs which our unworthy human nature is capable of inflicting. Who is there believes that man can safely intrust himself solely and alone to the mercy of his fellow man? Let such a one step forward and select his master! Let him in the wide circle of the world choose out that man—pure, just, and humane—upon whose vast, all-embracing charity he can throw the burden of his life. Alas! there is no such man.

Life is a perpetual struggle even under the most favorable circumstances; an unending fight of man against man,

"For some slight plank whose weight will bear but one."

And occasionally how monstrous and horrible are the giant selfishnesses which start up under our feet like ghouls and affrights!

History is the record of the gradual amelioration of deep-rooted, ancient injustice. What a hard, long, bloody, terrible fight it has been! But for the fact that our national organization rests upon a basis of new colonizations we would not possess the large measure of liberty we now enjoy; we would be as are the old lands of the world, still weighed down by the burdens of feudality and barbarism. But being peopled by the overflowings of the poor laboring people of Europe, who left the errors and prejudices of the Old World in mid-ocean, we have started upon our career of national greatness on the grand basis of the perfect political equality of all men.

We cannot fail to recognize the all-fashioning hand of God as clearly in this sublime declaration as in the geologic eras, the configuration of the continents, or the creation of man himself. What a world of growth has already budded and flowered and borne fruit from this seed! What an incalculable world of growth is to arise from it in the future!

Now, then, comes the question to each of us, by what rule shall we reconstruct these prostrated and well nigh desolated States? Shall it be by the august rule of the Declaration of Independence; or shall we bend our energies to perpetuate injustice, cruelty, and oppression; and make of this fair government a monstrosity, with golden words of promise upon its banners, a fair seeming upon its surface, but a hideous and inhuman despotism within it; the Christianity and civilization of the nineteenth century crystallized into a nation with Dahomey and Timbuctoo in its bowels! A living lie, a rotten pretense, a mockery, and a sham, with death in its heart.

There are but two forms of government in the world; injustice, armed and powerful and taking to itself the shape of king or aristocracy; and, on the other hand, absolute human justice, resting upon the broad and enduring basis of equal rights to all. Give this and give intelligence and education to understand it and you have a structure which will stand while the world stands. Anything else than this is mere repression, the piling of rocks into the mouth of the volcano, which sooner or later will fling them to the skies.

What is this equality of rights? Is it the prescribing of a limit to human selfishness. It is the hospital measure which gives so many feet of breathing space to each man in the struggle for life. I must not intrude upon my neighbor's limit nor he upon mine. It is universal selfishness regulated by a sentiment of universal justice; fair play recognized as a common necessity. Break down this barrier and the great waves sweep in and all is anarchy. Hear Motley's description of society in the ancient time, ere this principle arose "to curb the great and raise the lowly:"

"The sword is the only symbol of the law, the cross is a weapon of offence, the bishop a consecrated pirate, and every petty baron a burglar; while the people alternately the prey of duke, prelate, and seignior, shorn and butchered like sheep, esteem it happiness to sell themselves into slavery or to huddle beneath the castle walls of some little potentate for the sake of his wolfish protection."[1]

Sir, all history teaches us that man would be safer in the claws of wild beasts than in the uncontrolled custody of his fellow men. And can any man doubt that he who lives in a community and has no share in the making of the laws which govern him is in the uncontrolled custody of those who make the laws? The courts simply interpret the laws, and what will it avail a man to appeal to the courts if the laws under every interpretation are against him?

Set a man down in the midst of a community, place the mark of Cain upon his brow, declare him an outlaw, take from him every protection, and you at once invite everything base, sordid, and abominable in human nature to rise up and assail

[1] Rise of the Dutch Republic, p. 14.

him. Is there any man within the sound of my voice who thinks so highly of our common humanity that he would dare trust himself in such a position for a day or for an hour?

But if to this you superadd the fact that the poor wretch so stripped of all protection was but the other day a bondman, and was forcibly wrested from the hands of his master, and that to the common sordidness of our nature must be added the inflamed feelings growing out of a long civil war and the wrath and bitterness begotten of disappointed cupidity, you have a condition of things at which the very soul shudders.

But this is not all; you must go a step farther and remember that the poor wretch who thus stands helpless, chained, and naked in the midst of his mortal foes was our true, loyal, and faithful friend in the day of our darkness and calamity; and that those who now flock around him like vultures gathering to the carnage were but the other day our deadly enemies and sought our destruction and degradation by bloody and terrible means.

Sir, I say to you that if, in the face of every prompting of self-interest and self-protection, and humanity and gratitude, and Christianity and statesmanship, we abandon these poor wretches to their fate the wrath of an offended God cannot fail to fall upon the nation.

There never was in the history of the world an instance wherein right and wrong met so squarely face to face and looked each other so squarely in the eyes as in this matter. Never did truth array herself in such shining and glorious habiliments; never did the dark face of error look so hideous and forbidding as in this hour. And yet in the minds of some we find hesitation and doubt.

I cannot but recur to a famous parallel in history.

On the 22d of January, 1689, the English Parliament assembled to decide upon the most momentous question ever submitted to that body. The king, James II, had fled the realm; the great seal of royalty had been thrown into the Thames; William had landed; the nation was revolutionized.

The great debate commenced. On the one side was the party of human liberty striving to cast down forever a dynasty strangely devoted to tyranny and absolutism; striving to make plainer the doctrine that the king reigned by virtue of the consent of his subjects. On the other hand were arrayed all the evil forces of the time and all the restraints of conservatism.

In precisely the same temper in which it is now argued that a State can do no wrong and that under no circumstances can it cease to be a State, it was then argued that, although the king had fled the land and was at the court of France, nevertheless the magistrate was still present, that the throne, by the maxim of English law, could not be vacant for a moment; and that any government organized to act during the king's absence must act in the king's name.

It was most plain that the liberty, the prosperity of England could only be secured by the deposition of James; and yet those who sought by direct measures to reach that end were encountered at every step by a mass of technical objections. The musty precedents of the law, a thousand years old, were raked up; and texts of the Holy Book were called into the defence of royalty as liberally as we have seen them in our own day paraded in defence of slavery. St. Paul's injunction to the Romans to obey the civil power played as important a part in those debates as the texts of Ham and Onesimus have played upon the floor of this House.

Either the liberty of England must have perished, encumbered in this mass of precedents and technicalities, or the common sense of England must reach its own safety over the whole mass of rubbish. The common sense of England triumphed. James having fled, he was declared to have abdicated the throne, and the throne being vacant, Parliament asserted the right to fill it.

Now, in like manner at this day the resolute common sense of the American people must find its way out of the entanglements that surround it and go straight forward to its own safety.

The purpose of government is the happiness of the people, therefore of the whole people. A government cannot be half a republic and half a despotism—a republic just and equable to one class of its citizens, a depotism cruel and destructive to another class; it must become either all despotism or all republic.

If you make it all republic the future is plain. All evils will correct themselves. Temporary disorders will subside, the path will lie wide open before every man and every step and every hour will take him farther away from error and darkness. Give the right to vote and you give the right to aid in making the laws; the laws being made by all will be for the benefit of all; the improvement and advancement of each member of the community will be the improvement and advancement of the whole community.

Dealing with men, with all the attributes of men, with the souls, hearts, and minds of men, it is contemptible to attempt to turn justice aside by appeals to the color of the skin. At what precise point of the mingling of complexions shall these statesmen drive the stake and say, Thus far is man and beyond is brute; here human rights begin and there they terminate! What chemist shall analyze the mixture of man and beast and tell us what fraction of an immortal soul is possessed by such a one? Or how many mulattoes go as component parts to make up one soul in heaven?

Sir, such a doctrine is too monstrous for consideration! The earth is God's and all the children of God have an equal right upon its surface; and human legislation which would seek to subvert this truth merely legislates injustice into law; and he who believes that injustice conserves the peace, order, or welfare of society has read history to little purpose.

Let us then go straight forward to our duty, taking heed of nothing but the right. In this wise shall we build a work in accord with the will of him who is daily fashioning the world to a higher destiny; a work resting at no point upon wrong or injustice, but everywhere reposing upon truth and justice; a work which all mankind will be interested in preserving in every age, since it will insure the increasing glory and well-being of mankind through all ages.

GARFIELD

JAMES ABRAM GARFIELD, the twentieth President of the United States, was born at Orange, Ohio, November 19, 1831. He had few advantages in early youth, and as he grew to manhood he worked on a farm, and learned the carpenter's trade. After obtaining an education at Hiram College, Ohio, and at Williams College, he became president of the first named institution in 1857, studied law and having become well known in northwestern Ohio as a public speaker was sent to the Ohio senate in 1859. He entered the Federal army as lieutenant-colonel of an Ohio regiment in 1861 and after serving with distinction in many engagements received a major-general's commission in 1863. In that year he was elected to Congress as representative from his native State and took his seat in December. He served on a number of important congressional committees and was an acknowledged leader of the Republicans in the House. In 1880 he was elected to the Senate and receiving the Republican nomination for the Presidency was elected in the following autumn. After becoming President he sent in his nominations to the Senate for confirmation; in making these he had insisted on exercising the independence of the executive and thus caused the New York senators, Conkling and Platt, to resign their seats. On July 2, 1881, while waiting for a train in a railway station at Washington the President was shot by a disappointed office seeker named Guiteau, and after lingering many weeks died from the effect of the wound on September 19, 1881, at Elberon, New Jersey. In addition to a very brief but memorable address made to an excited throng in New York on the receipt of the news of Lincoln's assassination, among Garfield's most noted addresses may be included a speech "On Enrolling the National Forces" (1864); "Currency and the Public Faith" (1874); "The Democratic Party and the South" (1876); "Treason at the Polls" (1879). His "Collected Works" in two volumes were issued in 1883. See "Lives" by Bundy (1880), Coffin (1880), Conwell (1881).

INAUGURAL ADDRESS

DELIVERED MARCH 4, 1881

FELLOW CITIZENS,—We stand to-day upon an eminence which overlooks a hundred years of national life — a century crowded with perils, but crowned with the triumphs of liberty and love. Before continuing our onward march, let us pause on this height for a moment, to strengthen our faith and renew our hope, by a glance at the pathway along which our people have travelled. It is now three days more than one hundred years since the adoption of the first written constitution of the United States, the articles of confederation and of perpetual union. The new Republic was then beset with danger on every hand. It had not conquered a place in the family of nations. The decisive battle of the war for independence, whose centennial anniversary will soon be gratefully celebrated at Yorktown, had not yet been fought. The colonists were struggling, not only against the armies of Great Britain, but against the settled opinions of mankind, for the world did not believe that the supreme authority of government could be safely intrusted to the guardianship of the people themselves. We cannot overestimate the fervent love of liberty, the intelligent courage, and saving common sense, with which our fathers made the great experiment of self-government. When they found, after a short time, that the confederacy of States was too weak to meet the necessities of a vigorous and expanding Republic, they boldly set it aside, and, in its stead, established a national Union, founded directly upon the will of the people, and endowed it with future powers of self-preservation, and with ample authority for the accomplishments of its great objects. Under this constitution the boundaries of freedom have been enlarged, the foundations of order and peace have been strengthened, and the growth, in all the better elements of national life, has vindicated the wisdom of the founders, and given new hope to their descendants. Under this constitution our people long ago made themselves safe against danger from without, and secured for their marines and flag an equality of rights on all the seas. Under the constitution twenty-five States have been added to the

Union, with constitutions and laws, framed and enforced by their own citizens, to secure the manifold blessings of local and self-government. The jurisdiction of this constitution now covers an area fifty times greater than that of the original thirteen States, and a population twenty times greater than that of 1870. The supreme trial of the constitution came at last, under the tremendous pressure of civil war. We, ourselves, are witnesses that the Union emerged from the blood and fire of that conflict purified and made stronger for all the beneficent purposes of good government, and now, at the close of this first century of growth, with inspirations of its history in their hearts, our people have lately reviewed the condition of the nation, passed judgment upon the conduct and opinions of the political parties, and have registered their will concerning the future administration of government. To interpret and execute that will, in accordance with the constitution, is the paramount duty of the Executive.

Even from this brief review, it is manifest that the nation is resolutely facing to the front, resolved to employ its best energies in developing the great possibilities of the future. Sacredly preserving whatever has been gained to liberty and good government during the century, our people are determined to leave behind them all those bitter controversies concerning things which have been irrevocably settled, and the further discussion of which can only stir up strife and delay the onward march. The supremacy of the nation and its laws should be no longer a subject of debate. That discussion, which for half a century threatened the existence of the Union, was closed at last in the high court of war, by a decree from which there is no appeal, that the constitution and laws made in pursuance thereof shall continue to be the supreme law of the land, binding alike upon the States and upon the people. This decree does not disturb the autonomy of the States, nor interfere with any of their necessary rules of local self-government, but it does fix and establish the permanent supremacy of the Union. The will of the nation, speaking with the voice of battle, and through the amended constitution, has fulfilled the great promise of 1776, by proclaiming, "Liberty throughout the land to all the inhabitants thereof."

The elevation of the negro race from slavery to the full rights of citizenship is the most important political change we have known since the adoption of the constitution of 1787. No thoughtful man can fail to appreciate its beneficent effect upon our institutions and people. It has freed us from the perpetual danger of war and dissolution. It has added immensely to the moral and industrial forces of our people. It has liberated the master as well as the slave from the relation which wronged and enfeebled both. It has surrendered to their own guardianship the manhood of more than 5,000,000 people, and has opened to each one of them a career of freedom and usefulness; it has given new inspiration to the power of self-help in both races, by making labor more honorable to one, and more necessary to the other. The influence of this force will grow greater and bear richer fruit with coming years. No doubt the great change has caused serious disturbance to our southern community. This is to be deplored, though it was unavoidable; but those who resisted the change should remember that, under our institutions, there was no middle ground for the negro race between slavery and equal citizenship. There can be no permanent disfranchised peasantry in the United States. Freedom can never yield its fulness of blessings as long as law, or its administration, places the smallest obstacle in the pathway of any virtuous citizen. The emancipated race has already made remarkable progress. With unquestioning devotion to the Union, with a patience and gentleness not born of fear, they have "followed the light as God gave them to see the light." They are rapidly laying the material foundations for self-support, widening the circle of intelligence, and beginning to enjoy the blessings that gather around the homes of the industrious poor. They deserve the generous encouragement of all good men. So far as my authority can lawfully extend, they shall enjoy the full and equal protection of the constitution and laws.

The free enjoyment of equal suffrage is still in question, and a frank statement of the issue may aid its solution. It is alleged that in many communities negro citizens are practically denied the freedom of the ballot. In so far as the truth of this allegation is admitted, it is answered that in many places honest local government is impossible, if the mass of uneducated negroes are allowed to vote. These are grave allegations. So far as the latter is true, it is the only palliation that can be offered for opposing the freedom of the ballot. A bad local government is certainly a great evil which ought to be prevented, but to violate the freedom and sanctity of suffrage is more than an evil; it is a crime, which, if persisted in, will destroy the government itself. Suicide is not a remedy. If in other lands it be high treason to compass the death of the king, it should be counted no less a crime here to strangle our sovereign power and stifle its voice. It has been said that unsettled questions have no pity for the repose of nations; it should be said, with the utmost emphasis, that this question of suffrage will never give repose or safety to the States or to the nation until each, within its own jurisdiction, makes and keeps the ballot free and pure by the strong sanctions of law.

But the danger which arises from ignorance in the voter cannot be denied. It covers a field far wider than that of negro suffrage, and the present condition of that race. It is a danger that lurks and hides in the courses and fountains of power in every State. We have no standard by which to measure the disaster that may be brought upon us by ignorance and vice in citizens when joined to corruption and fraud in suffrage. The voters of the Union, who make and unmake constitutions, and upon whose will hangs the destiny of our governments, can transmit their supreme authority to no successor, save the coming generation of voters, who are sole heirs of our sovereign powers. If that generation comes to its inheritance blinded by ignorance and corrupted by vice, the fall of the Republic will be certain and remediless. The census has already sounded the alarm in appalling figures, which mark how dangerously high the tide of illiteracy has risen among our voters and their children. To the south the question is of supreme importance, but the responsibility for the existence of slavery did not rest on the south alone. The nation itself is responsible for the extension of suffrage, and is under special obligations to aid in removing the illiteracy which it has added to the voting population of the north and south alike. There is but one remedy. All the constitutional power of the nation and of the States and all the volunteer forces of the people should be summoned to meet this danger by the saving influence of universal education.

It is a high privilege and sacred duty of those now living to educate their successors, and fit them by intelligence and virtue for the inheritance which awaits them in this beneficent work. Sections and races should be forgotten, and partisanship should be unknown. Let our people find a new meaning in the divine oracle which declares that "a little child shall lead them." For our little children will soon control the destinies of the Republic.

My countrymen, we do not now differ in our judgment concerning the controversies of past generations, and fifty years hence our children will not be divided in their opinions concerning our controversies. They will surely bless their fathers and their fathers' God that the Union was preserved, that slavery was overthrown, and that both races were made equal before the law. We may hasten or we may retard, but we cannot prevent the final reconciliation. Is it not possible for us now to make a truce with time, by anticipating and accepting its inevitable verdicts? Enterprises of the highest importance to our moral and material well-being invite us, and offer ample scope for the employment of our best powers. Let all our people, leaving behind them the battle-fields of dead issues, move forward, and, in the strength of liberty and a restored Union, win the grander victories of peace.

The prosperity which now prevails is without parallel in our history. Fruitful seasons have done much to secure it, but they have not done all.

The preservation of the public credit, and the resumption of specie payments, so successfully attained by the administration of my predecessors, has enabled our people to secure the blessings which the seasons brought. By the experience of commercial nations in all ages, it has been found that gold and silver afford the only safe foundation for a monetary system. Confusion has recently been created by variations in the relative value of the two metals, but I confidently believe that arrangements can be made between the leading commercial nations which will secure the general use of both metals. Congress should provide that compulsory coinage of silver now required by law may not disturb our monetary system by driving either metal out of circulation. If possible, such adjustment should be made that the purchasing power of every coined dollar will be exactly equal to its debt-paying power in the markets of the world. The chief duty of the national government, in connection with the currency of the country, is to coin and declare its value. Grave doubts have been entertained whether Congress is authorized, by the constitution, to make any form of paper money legal tender. The present issue of United States notes has been sustained by the necessities of war, but such paper should depend for its value and currency upon its convenience in use and its prompt redemption in coin at the will of a holder, and not upon its compulsory circulation. These notes are not money, but promises to pay money. If holders demand it, the promise should be kept.

The refunding of the national debt, at a lower rate of interest, should be accomplished without compelling the withdrawal of the national bank notes, and thus disturbing the business of the country. I venture to refer to the position I have occupied on financial questions, during my long service in Congress, and to say that time and experience have strengthened the opinions I have so often expressed on these subjects. The finances of the government shall suffer no detriment which it may be possible for my administration to prevent.

The interests of agriculture deserve more attention from the government than they have yet received. The farms of the United States afford homes and employment for more than one half the people, and furnish much the largest part of all our exports. As the government lights our coasts for the protection of mariners and for the benefit of commerce, so it should give to the tillers of the soil the lights of practical science and experience.

Our manufactures are rapidly making us industrially independent, and are opening to capital and labor new and profitable fields of employment. This steady and healthy growth should still be maintained.

Our facilities for transportation should be promoted by the continued improvement of our harbors and great interior water-ways, and by the increase of our tonnage on the ocean. The development of the world's commerce has led to an urgent demand for shortening the great sea voyage around Cape Horn, by constructing ship canals or railways across the isthmus which unites the two continents. Various plans to this end have been suggested, but none of them have been sufficiently matured to warrant the United States extending pecuniary aid. The subject is one which will immediately engage the attention of the government, with a view to thorough protection to American interests. We will urge no narrow policy, nor seek peculiar or exclusive privileges in any commercial route; but, in the language of my predecessors, I believe it is to be "the right and duty of the United States to assert and maintain such supervision and authority over any inter-oceanic canal across the isthmus that connects North and South America as will protect our national interests."

The constitution guarantees absolute religious freedom. Congress is also prohibited from making any law respecting the establishment of religion or prohibiting the free exercise thereof. The Territories of the United States are subject to the direct legislative authority of Congress, and hence the general government is responsible for any violation of the constitution in any of them. It is, therefore, a reproach to the government that in the most populous of the Territories the constitutional guarantee is not enjoyed by the people, and the authority of Congress is set at naught. The Mormon church not only offends the moral sense of mankind by sanctioning polygamy, but prevents the administration of justice through the ordinary instrumentalities of law. In my judgment it is the duty of Congress, while respecting to the utmost the conscientious convictions and religious scruples of every citizen, to prohibit, within its jurisdiction, all criminal practices, especially of that class which destroy family relations and endanger social order; nor can any ecclesiastical organization be safely permitted to usurp in the smallest degree the functions and powers of the national government.

The civil service can never be placed on a satisfactory basis until it is regulated by law. For the good of the service itself, for the protection of those who are intrusted with the appointing power, against the waste of time and the obstruction to public business caused by inordinate pressure for place, and for the protection of incumbents against intrigue and wrong, I shall, at the proper time, ask Congress to fix the tenure of minor offices of the several executive departments, and prescribe the grounds upon which removals shall be made during the terms for which the incumbents have been appointed.

Finally, acting always within the authority and limitations of the constitution, invading neither the rights of States nor the reserved rights of the people, it will be the purpose of my administration to maintain authority, and in all places within its jurisdiction to enforce obedience to all the laws of the Union; in the interest of the people, to demand a rigid economy in all the expenditures of the government, and to require honest and faithful services of all the executive officers, remembering that offices were created not for the benefit of incumbents or their supporters but for the service of the government.

And, now, fellow citizens, I am about to assume the great trust which you have committed to my hands. I appeal to you for that earnest and thoughtful support which makes this government—in fact as it is in law—a government of the people. I shall greatly rely upon the wisdom and patriotism of Congress, and of those who may share with me the responsibilities and duties of the administration; and, above all, upon our efforts to promote the welfare of this great people and their government I reverently invoke the support and blessing of Almighty God.

TALMAGE

THOMAS DE WITT TALMAGE, a popular American preacher and lecturer, was born at Bound Brook, New Jersey, January 7, 1832, and educated at the University of the City of New York. He studied theology at the Theological Seminary at New Brunswick, New Jersey, and was pastor of a Reformed Dutch church at Belleville in his native State, 1856-59, and of a church at Syracuse, New York, 1859-62. For the next seven years he was in charge of a Presbyterian church in Philadelphia, being already widely known as a preacher and lecturer. He was called to the Brooklyn Tabernacle in 1870, remaining there until 1894, when he took charge of the Lincoln Memorial Church in Washington city. He has been an incessant contributor to the religious press, and for many years his sermons have been issued weekly. Among his many published books are "The Almond Tree in Blossom" (1870); "Targets," "Crumbs Swept Up" (1870); "Sermons" (1872-75); "Abominations of Modern Society" (1872); "The Battle for Bread," "Old Wells Dug Out" (1874); "Sports that Kill" (1875); "Everyday Religion" (1875); "Night Sides of City Life" (1878); "The Mask Torn Off" (1879); "The Marriage Ring" (1886); "Social Dynamite" (1887); "The Pathway of Life," "From the Pyramids to the Acropolis" (1892); "From Manger to Throne" (1894); "The Earth Girdled" (1896).

CHANT AT THE CORNER-STONE

"Who laid the corner-stone thereof, when the morning stars sang together?"—Job xxxviii, 6, 7.

WE have all seen the ceremony at the laying of the corner-stone of church, asylum or Masonic temple. Into the hollow of the stone were placed scrolls of history and important documents, to be suggestive if, one or two hundred years after, the building should be destroyed by fire or torn down. We remember the silver trowel or iron hammer that smote the square piece of granite into sanctity. We remember some venerable man who presided, wielding the trowel or hammer. We remember also the music as the choir stood on the scattered stones and timber of the building about to be constructed. The leaves of the notebooks fluttered in the wind and were turned over with a great rustling, and we remember how the bass, baritone, tenor, contralto, and soprano voices commingled. They had for many days been rehearsing the special program that it might be worthy of the corner-stone laying. The music at the laying of corner-stones is always impressive.

In my text God, addressing the poet of Uz, calls us to a grander ceremony—the laying of the foundation of this great temple of a world. The corner-stone was a block of light and the trowel was of celestial crystal. All about and on the embankments of cloud stood the angelic choristers unrolling their librettos of overture, and other worlds clapped shining cymbals while the ceremony went on, and God, the architect, by stroke of light after stroke of light, dedicated this great cathedral of a world, with mountains for pillars, and sky for frescoed ceiling, and flowering fields for floor, and sunrise and midnight aurora for upholstery. "Who laid the corner-stone thereof, when the morning stars sang together?"

The fact is that the whole universe was a complete cadence, an unbroken dithyramb, a musical portfolio. The great sheet of immensity had been spread out and written on it were the stars, the smaller of them minims, the larger of them sustained notes. The meteors marked the staccato passages, the whole heavens a gamut with all sounds, intonations and modulations; the space between the worlds a musical interval, trembling of stellar light a quaver, the thunder a base clef, the wind among trees a treble clef. That is the way God made all things a perfect harmony.

But one day a harp-string snapped in the great orchestra. One day a voice sounded out of tune. One day a discord, harsh and terrific, grated upon the glorious antiphone. It was sin that made the dissonance, and that harsh discord has been sounding through the centuries. All the work of Christians and philanthropists and reformers of all ages is to stop that discord and get all things back into the perfect harmony which was heard at the laying of the corner-stone when the morning stars sang together.

Before I get through, if I am divinely helped, I will make it plain that sin is discord and righteousness is harmony. That things in general are out of tune is as plain as to a musician's ear is the unhappy clash of clarionet and bassoon in an orchestral rendering. The world's health out of tune; weak lung and the atmosphere in collision, disordered eye and noonday light in quarrel, rheumatic limb and damp weather in struggle, neuralgias and pneumonias and consumptions and epilepsies in flocks swoop upon neighborhoods and cities. Where you find one person with sound throat and keen eyesight and alert ear and easy respiration and regular pulsation and supple limb and prime digestion and steady nerves, you find a hundred who have to be very careful because this or that or the other physical function is disordered.

The human intellect out of tune; the judgment wrongly swerved, or the memory leaky, or the will weak, or the temper inflammable, and the well-balanced mind exceptional.

Domestic life out of tune; only here and there a conjugal outbreak of incompatibility of temper through the divorce courts, or a filial outbreak about a father's will through the surrogate's court, or a case of wife-beating or husband-poisoning through the criminal courts, but thousands of families with June outside and January within.

Society out of tune; labor and capital, their hands on each other's throats. Spirit of caste keeping those down in the social scale in a struggle to get up, and putting those who are up in anxiety lest they have to come down. No wonder the old pianoforte of society is all out of tune when hypocrisy and lying and subterfuge and double-dealing and sycophancy and charlatanism and revenge have all through the ages been banging away at the keys and stamping the pedals.

On all sides there is a perpetual shipwreck of harmonies. Nations in discord without realizing it, so antipathetic is the feeling of nation for nation, that symbols chosen are fierce and destructive. In this country, where our skies are full of robins and doves and morning larks, we have for our national symbol the fierce and filthy eagle, as immoral a bird as can be found in all the ornithological catalogues. In Great Britain, where they have lambs and fallow deer, their symbol is the merciless lion. In Russia, where from between her frozen north and blooming south all kindly beasts dwell, they chose the growling bear; and in the world's heraldry a favorite figure is the dragon, which is a winged serpent, ferocious and dreadful.

And so fond is the world of contention that we climb out through the heavens and baptize one of the other planets with the spirit of battle and call it Mars, after the god of war, and we give to the eighth sign of the zodiac the name of the scorpion, a creature which is chiefly celebrated for its deadly sting. But, after all, these symbols are expressive of the way nation feels toward nation. Discord wide as the continent and bridging the seas.

I suppose you have noticed how warmly in love drygoods stores are with other drygoods stores, and how highly grocerymen think of the sugars of the grocerymen on the same block. And in what a eulogistic way allopathic and homeopathic doctors speak of each other, and how ministers will sometimes put ministers on that beautiful cooking instrument which the English call a spit, an iron roller with spikes on it, and turned by a crank before a hot fire, and then if the minister who is being roasted cries out against it, the men who are turning him say: "Hush, brother, we are turning this spit for the glory of God and the good of your soul, and you must be quiet, while we close the service with:

> 'Blest be the tie that binds
> Our hearts in Christian love.'"

The earth is diametred and circumferenced with discord, and the music that was rendered at the laying of the world's corner-stone when the morning stars sang together is not heard now; and though here and there, from this and that part of society, and from this and that part of the earth, there comes up a thrilling solo of love, or a warble of worship, or a sweet duet of patience, they are drowned out by a discord that shakes the earth.

Paul says, "The whole creation groaneth," and while the nightingale and the woodlark and the canary and the plover sometimes sing so sweetly that their notes have been written out in musical notation, and it is found that the cuckoo sings in the key of D, and that the cormorant is a basso in the winged choir, yet sportsmen's gun and the autumnal blast often leave them ruffled and bleeding or dead in meadow or forest. Paul was right, for the groan in nature drowns out the prima donnas of the sky.

Tartini, the great musical composer, dreamed one night that he made a contract with Satan, the latter to be ever in the composer's service. He thought in his dream that he handed to Satan a violin, on which Diabolus played such sweet music that the composer was awakened by the emotion and tried to reproduce the sounds, and therefrom was written Tartini's most famous piece, "The Devil's Sonata;" a dream, ingenious but faulty, for all melody descends from heaven and only discords ascend from hell. All hatreds, feuds, controversies, backbitings, and revenges are the devil's sonata, are diabolic fugue, are demoniac phantasy, are grand march of doom, are allegro of perdition.

But if in this world things in general are out of tune to our frail ear, how much more so to ears angelic and deific. It takes a skilled artist fully to appreciate disagreement of sound. Many have no capacity to detect a defect of musical execution and, though there were in one bar as many offences against harmony as could crowd in between the low F of the bass and the high G of the soprano, it would give them no discomfort; while on the forehead of the educated artist beads of perspiration would stand out as a result of the harrowing dissonance. While an amateur was performing on a piano and had just struck the wrong chord, John Sebastian Bach, the immortal composer, entered the room, and the amateur rose in embarrassment, and Bach rushed past the host who stepped forward to greet him, and before the strings had stopped vibrating put his adroit hands upon the keys and changed the painful inharmony into glorious cadence. Then Bach turned and gave salutation to the host who had invited him.

But worst of all is moral discord. If society and the world are painfully discordant to imperfect man, what must they be to a perfect God. People try to define what sin is. It seems to me that sin is getting out of harmony with God, a disagreement with his holiness, with his purity, with his love, with his commands; our will clashing with his will, the finite dashing against the infinite, the frail against the puissant, the created against the Creator.

If a thousand musicians, with flute and cornet-a-piston and trumpet and violincello and hautboy and trombone and all the wind and stringed instruments that ever gathered in a Düsseldorf jubilee should resolve that they would play out of tune, and put concord on the rack, and make the place wild with shrieking and grating and rasping sounds, they could not make such a pandemonium as that which a sinful soul produces in the ears of God when he listens to the play of its thoughts, passions and emotions—discord, lifelong discord, maddening discord!

The world pays more for discord than it does for consonance. High prices have been paid for music. One man gave two hundred and twenty-five dollars to hear the Swedish songstress in New York, and another six hundred and twenty-five dollars to hear her in Boston, and another six hundred and fifty dollars to hear her in Providence. Fabulous prices have been paid for sweet sounds, but far more has been paid for discord.

The Crimean war cost one billion seven hundred million dollars, and our American civil war over nine and a half billion dollars, and our war with Spain cost us about three hundred million dollars, and the war debts of professed Christian nations are about fifteen billion dollars. The world pays for this red ticket, which admits it to the saturnalia of broken bones and death agonies and destroyed cities and ploughed graves and crushed hearts, any amount of money Satan asks. Discord! Discord!

But I have to tell you that the song that the morning stars sang together at the laying of the world's corner-stone is to be resumed. Mozart's greatest overture was composed one night when he was several times overpowered with sleep, and artists say they can tell the places in the music where he was falling asleep and the places where he awakened. So the overture of the morning stars, spoken of in my text, has been asleep, but it will awaken and be more grandly rendered by the evening stars of the world's existence than by the morning stars, and the vespers will be sweeter than the matins. The work of all good men and women and of all good churches and all reform associations is to bring the race back to the original harmony. The rebellious heart to be attuned, social life to be attuned, commercial ethics to be attuned, internationality to be attuned, hemispheres to be attuned.

In olden times the choristers had a tuning fork with two prongs and they would strike it on the back of pew or music rack and put it to the ear and then start the tune, and all the other voices would join. In modern orchestra the leader has a perfect instrument, rightly attuned, and he sounds that, and all the other performers tune the keys of their instruments to make them correspond, and sound the bow over the string and listen, and sound it out over again, until all the keys are screwed to concert pitch, and the discord melts into one great symphony, and the curtain hoists, and the baton taps, and audiences are raptured with Schumann's "Paradise and the Peri," or Rossini's "Stabat Mater," or Bach's "Magnificat" in D or Gounod's "Redemption."

Now our world can never be attuned by an imperfect instrument. Even a Cremona would not do. Heaven has ordained the only instrument, and it is made out of the wood of the cross and the voices that accompany it are imported voices, cantatrices of the first Christmas night, when heaven serenaded the earth with "Glory to God in the highest and on earth peace, good will to men."

Lest we start too far off and get lost in generalities, we had better begin with ourselves, get our own hearts and lives in harmony with the eternal Christ. Oh, for his almighty Spirit to attune us, to chord our will and his will, to modulate our life with his life, and bring us into unison with all that is pure and self-sacrificing and heavenly. The strings of our nature are all broken and twisted and the bow is so slack it cannot evoke anything mellifluous. The instrument made for heaven to play on has been roughly twanged and struck by influences worldly and demoniac. Oh, master-hand of Christ, restore this split and fractured and despoiled and unstrung nature until first it shall wail out for our sin and then trill with divine pardon.

The whole world must also be attuned by the same power. A few days ago I was in the Fairbanks weighing scale manufactory of Vermont. Six hundred hands, and they have never made a strike. Complete harmony between labor and capital, the operatives of scores of years in their beautiful homes near by the mansions of the manufacturers, whose invention and Christian behavior made the great enterprise. So, all the world over, labor and capital will be brought into euphony.

You may have heard what is called the "Anvil Chorus," composed by Verdi, a tune played by hammers, great and small, now with mighty stroke and now with heavy stroke, beating a great iron anvil. That is what the world must come to—anvil chorus, yard-stick chorus, shuttle chorus, trowel chorus, crowbar chorus, pick-axe chorus, gold-mine chorus, rail-track chorus, locomotive chorus. It can be done and it will be done. So all social life will be attuned by the gospel harp.

There will be as many classes in society as now, but the classes will not be regulated by birth or wealth or accident, but by the scale of virtue and benevolence, and people will be assigned to their places as good or very good or most excellent. So also commercial life will be attuned and there will be twelve in every dozen and sixteen ounces in every pound and apples at the bottom of the barrel will be as sound as those on the top and silk goods will not be cotton, and sellers will not have to charge honest people more than the right price because others will not pay, and goods will come to you corresponding with the sample by which you purchased them, and coffee will not be chickoried, and sugar will not be sanded, and milk will not be chalked, and adulteration of food will be a State-prison offense.

Aye, all things shall be attuned. Elections in England and the United States will no more be a grand carnival of defamation and scurrility, but the elevation of righteous men in a righteous way.

In the sixteenth century the singers called the Fischer Brothers reached the lowest bass ever recorded, and the highest note ever trilled was by La Bastardella, and Catalini's voice had a compass of three and a half octaves; but Christianity is more wonderful; for it runs all up and down the greatest heights and the deepest depths of the world's necessity, and it will compass everything and bring it in accord with the song which the morning stars sang at the laying of the world's corner-stone. All the sacred music in homes, concert halls, and churches tends toward this consummation. Make it more and more hearty. Sing in your families. Sing in your places of business. •If we with proper spirit use these faculties we are rehearsing for the skies.

Heaven is to have a new song, an entirely new song, but I should not wonder if as sometimes on earth a tune is fashioned out of many tunes, or it is one tune with the variations, so some of the songs of the glorified of heaven may have playing through them the songs of earth; and how thrilling, as coming through the great anthem of the saved, accompanied by the harpers with their harps and trumpeters with their trumpets, if we should hear some of the strains of Antioch and Mount Pisgah and Coronation and Lenox and St. Martin's and Fountain and Ariel and Old Hundred. How they would bring to mind the praying circles and communion days and the Christmas festivals and the church worship in which on earth we mingled! I have no idea that when we bid farewell to earth we are to bid farewell to all these grand old gospel hymns, which melted and raptured our souls for so many years.

Now, my friends, if sin is discord and righteousness is harmony, let us get out of the one and enter the other. After our dreadful Civil War was over and in the summer of 1869 a great National Peace Jubilee was held in Boston, and as an elder of this church had been honored by the selection of some of his music, to be rendered on that occasion, I accompanied him to the jubilee. Forty thousand people sat and stood in the great coliseum erected for that purpose. Thousands of wind and stringed instruments. Twelve thousand trained voices. The masterpieces of all ages rendered, hour after hour, and day after day—Handel's "Judas Maccabæus," Sphor's "Last Judgment," Beethoven's "Mount of Olives," Haydn's "Creation," Mendelssohn's "Elijah," Meyerbeer's "Coronation March," rolling on and up in surges that billowed against the heavens.

The mighty cadences within were accompanied on the outside by the ringing of the bells of the city, and cannon on the commons, discharged by electricity, in exact time with the music, thundering their awful bars of a harmony that astounded all nations. Sometimes I bowed my head and wept. At other times I stood up in the enchantment, and there were moments when the effect was so overpowering I felt I could not endure it.

When all the voices were in full chorus and all the batons in full wave and all the orchestra in full triumph, and a hundred anvils under mighty hammers were in full clang, and all the towers of the city rolling in their majestic sweetness, and the whole building quaked with the boom of thirty cannon, Parepa Rosa, with a voice that will never again be equalled on earth until the archangelic voice proclaims that time shall be no longer, rose above all other sounds in her rendering of our national air, the "Star Spangled Banner." It was too much for a mortal and quite enough for an immortal to hear, and while some fainted, one womanly spirit, released under its power, sped away to be with God.

O Lord, our God, quickly usher in the whole world's peace jubilee, and all islands of the sea join the five continents, and all the voices and musical instruments of all nations combine, and all the organs that ever sounded requiem of sorrow sound only a grand march of joy, and all the bells that tolled for burial ring for resurrection, and all the cannon that ever hurled death across the nations sound to eternal victory, and over all the acclaim of earth and minstrelsy of heaven there will be heard one voice sweeter and mightier than any human or angelic voice, a voice once full of tears, but then full of triumph, the voice of Christ saying, "I am Alpha and Omega, the beginning and the end, the first and the last." Then, at the laying of the top-stone of the world's history, the same voices shall be heard as when at the laying of the world's corner-stone "the morning stars sang together."

CHOATE

JOSEPH HODGES CHOATE, an eminent American lawyer and diplomatist, was born at Salem, Massachusetts, January 24, 1832, and educated at Harvard University. He studied law at the Harvard Law School and was admitted to the bar in 1855. In the following year he removed to New York city, where he rapidly rose to eminence in his profession and was connected with many of the most important cases tried in that city. During the political campaign of 1856 Choate made many speeches in support of Frémont, the Free-Soil candidate for the Presidency, and after that time belonged to the Republican party, although strongly opposed to machine management. In 1898, as president of the American Bar Association, he made a memorable address before it in defence of trial by jury. He was president of the New York State constitutional convention in 1894, but until 1898 had held no political office. At the close of that year he succeeded John Hay as ambassador to England, in which capacity he was exceedingly popular both in England and at home.

ORATION ON RUFUS CHOATE

DELIVERED AT THE UNVEILING OF THE STATUE OF RUFUS CHOATE IN THE COURT HOUSE OF BOSTON, OCTOBER 15, 1898

MANY a noted orator, many a great lawyer, has been lost in oblivion in forty years after the grave closed over him, but I venture to believe that the bar of Suffolk, aye, the whole bar of America, and the people of Massachusetts, have kept the memory of no other man alive and green so long, so vividly and so lovingly, as that of Rufus Choate. Many of his characteristic utterances have become proverbial and the flashes of his wit, the play of his fancy, and the gorgeous pictures of his imagination are the constant themes of reminiscence wherever American lawyers assemble for social converse. What Mr. Dana so well said over his bier is still true to-day: "When as lawyers we meet together in tedious hours and seek to entertain ourselves, we find we do better with anecdotes of Mr. Choate than on our own original resources." The admirable biography of Professor Brown and his arguments, so far as they have been preserved, are text-books in the profession—and so the influence of his genius, character, and conduct is still potent and far-reaching in the land.

You will not expect me, upon such an occasion, to enter upon any narrative of his illustrious career, so familiar to you all, or to undertake any analysis of those remarkable powers which made it possible. All that has been done already by many appreciative admirers and has become a part of American literature. I can only attempt, in a most imperfect manner, to present a few of the leading traits of that marvellous personality which we hope that this striking statue will help to transmit to the students, lawyers and citizens who, in the coming years, shall throng these portals.

How it was that such an exotic nature, so ardent and tropical in all its manifestations, so truly southern and Italian in its impulses, and at the same time so robust and sturdy in its strength, could have been produced upon the bleak and barren soil of our northern cape and nurtured under the chilling blasts of its east winds is a mystery insoluble. Truly "this is the Lord's doing, and it is marvellous in our eyes."

In one of his speeches in the Senate he draws the distinction between "the cool and slow New England men and the mercurial children of the sun who sat down side by side in the presence of Washington to form our more perfect union."

If ever there was a mercurial child of the sun, it was himself most happily described. I am one of those who believe that the stuff that a man is made of has more to do with his career than any education or environment. The greatness that is achieved, or is thrust upon some men, dwindles before that of him who is born great. His horoscope was propitious. The stars in their courses fought for him. The birthmark of genius, distinct and ineffaceable, was on his brow. He came of a long line of pious and devout ancestors, whose living was as plain as their thinking was high. It was from father and mother that he derived the flame of intellect, the glow of spirit, and the beauty of temperament that were so unique.

And his nurture to manhood was worthy of the child. It was "the nurture and admonition of the Lord." From that rough pine cradle, which is still preserved in the room where he was born, to his premature grave at the age of fifty-nine, it was one long course of training and discipline of mind and character, without pause or rest. It began with that well-thumbed and dog's-eared Bible from Hog Island, its leaves actually worn away by the pious hands that had turned them, read daily in the family from January to December, in at Genesis and out at Revelations every two years; and when a new child was born in the household the only celebration, the only festivity, was to turn back to the first chapter and read once more how "in the beginning God created the heaven and the earth" and all that in them is.

This book, so early absorbed and never forgotten, saturated his mind and spirit more than any other, more than all other books combined. It was at his tongue's end, at his fingers' ends—always close at hand until those last languid hours at Halifax, when it solaced his dying meditations. You can hardly find speech, argument or lecture of his, from first to last, that is not sprinkled and studded with biblical ideas and pictures and biblical words and phrases. To him the book of Job was a sublime poem. He knew the Psalms by heart and dearly loved the prophets, and above all Isaiah, upon whose gorgeous imagery he made copious drafts. He pondered every word, read with most subtle keenness, and applied with happiest effect. One day, coming into the Crawford House, cold and shivering—and you remember how he could shiver—he caught sight of the blaze in the great fireplace and was instantly warm before the rays could reach him, exclaiming "Do you remember that verse in Isaiah, 'Aha! I am warm. I have seen the fire?'" and so his daily conversation was marked.

And upon this solid rock of the Scriptures he built a magnificent structure of knowledge and acquirement, to which few men in America have ever attained. History, philosophy, poetry, fiction, all came as grist to his mental mill. But with him time was too precious to read any trash; he could winnow the wheat from the chaff at sight, almost by touch. He sought knowledge, ideas, for their own sake and for the language in which they were conveyed.

I have heard a most learned jurist gloat over the purchase of the last sensational novel, and have seen a most distinguished bishop greedily devouring the stories of Gaboriau one after another, but Mr. Choate seemed to need no such counter-irritant or blister to draw the pain from his hurt mind. Business, company, family, sickness—nothing could rob him of his one hour each day in the company of illustrious writers of all ages. How his whole course of thought was tinged and embellished with the reflected light of the great Greek orators, historians and poets; how Roman history, fresh in the mind as the events of yesterday, supplied him with illustrations and supports for his own glowing thoughts and arguments, all of you who have either heard him or read him know.

But it was to the great domain of English literature that he daily turned for fireside companions and really kindred spirits. As he said in a letter to Sumner, with whom his literary fraternity was at one time very close: "Mind that Burke is the fourth Englishman,—Shakespeare, Bacon, Milton, Burke;" and then in one of those dashing outbursts of playful extravagance which were so characteristic of him, fearing that Sumner in his proposed review might fail to do full justice to the great ideal of both, he adds: "Out of Burke might be cut 50 Mackintoshes, 175 Macaulays, 40 Jeffreys, and 250 Sir Robert Peels, and leave him greater than Pitt and Fox together."

In the constant company of these great thinkers and writers he revelled and made their thoughts his own; and his insatiable memory seemed to store up all things committed to it, as the books not in daily use are stacked away in your public library, so that at that moment, with notice or without, he could lay his hand straightway upon them. What was once imbedded in the gray matter of his brain did not lie buried there, as with most of us, but grew and flourished and bore fruit. What he once read he seemed never to forget.

This love of study became a ruling passion in his earliest youth. To it he sacrificed all that the youth of our day—even the best of them—consider indispensable, and especially the culture and training of the body; and when we recall his pale face, worn and lined as it was in his later years, one of his most pathetic utterances is found in a letter to his son at school: "I hope that you are well and studious and among the best scholars. If this is so, I am willing you should play every day till the blood is ready to burst from your cheeks. Love the studies that will make you wise, useful, and happy when there shall be no blood at all to be seen in your cheeks or lips."

He never rested from his delightful labors—and that is the pity of it—he took no vacations. Except for one short trip to Europe, when warned of a possible breakdown in 1850, an occasional day at Essex, a three days' journey to the White Mountains, was all that he allowed himself. Returning from such an outing in the summer of 1854, on which it was my great privilege to accompany him, he said, "That is my entire holiday for this year."

So that when he told Judge Warren so playfully that "The lawyer's vacation is the space between the question put to a witness and his answer," it was of himself almost literally true. Would that he had realized his constant dream of an ideal cottage in the old walnut grove in Essex, where he might spend whole summers with his books, his children, and his thoughts.

His splendid and blazing intellect, fed and enriched by constant study of the best thoughts of the great minds of the race; his all-persuasive eloquence, his teeming and radiant imagination, whirling his hearers along with it and sometimes overpowering himself, his brilliant and sportive fancy, lighting up the most arid subjects with the glow of sunrise, his prodigious and never-failing memory, and his playful wit, always bursting forth with irresistible impulse, have been the subject of scores of essays and criticisms, all struggling with the vain effort to describe and crystallize the fascinating and magical charm of his speech and his influence.

And now, in conclusion, let me speak of his patriotism. I have always believed that Mr. Webster, more than any other man, was entitled to the credit of that grand and universal outburst of devotion with which the whole north sprang to arms in defence of the constitution and the Union many years after his death, when the first shot at Fort Sumter, like a fire-bell in the night, roused them from their slumber and convinced them that the great citadel of their liberties was in actual danger.

Differ as we may and must as to his final course in his declining years, the one great fact can never be blotted out, that the great work of his grand and noble life was the defence of the constitution—so that he came to be known of all men as its one defender—that for thirty years he preached to the listening nation the crusade of nationality and fired New England and the whole north with its spirit. He inspired them to believe that to uphold and preserve the Union against every foe was the first duty of the citizen; that if the Union was saved, all was saved; that if that was lost, all was lost. He molded better even than he knew. It was his great brain that designed, his flaming heart that forged, his sublime eloquence that welded the sword which was at last, when he was dust, to consummate his life's work and make liberty and union one and inseparable forever.

And so, in large measure, it was with Mr. Choate. His glowing heart went out to his country with the passionate ardor of a lover. He believed that the first duty of the lawyer, orator, scholar was to her. His best thoughts, his noblest words were always for her. Seven of the best years of his life, in the Senate and House of Representatives, at the greatest personal sacrifice he gave absolutely to her service.

On every important question that arose he made, with infinite study and research, one of the great speeches of the debate. He commanded the affectionate regard of his fellows and of the watchful and listening nation. He was a profound and constant student of her history and revelled in tracing her growth and progress from Plymouth Rock and Salem Harbor until she filled the continent from sea to sea. He loved to trace the advance of the Puritan spirit, with which he was himself deeply imbued, from Winthrop and Endicott, and Carver and Standish, through all the heroic periods and events of colonial and revolutionary and national life, until in his own last years it dominated and guided all of free America.

He knew full well and displayed in his many splendid speeches and addresses that one unerring purpose of freedom and of union ran through her whole history; that there was no accident in it all; that all the generations, from the "Mayflower" down, marched to one measure and followed one flag; that all the struggles, all the self-sacrifice, all the prayers and the tears, all the fear of God, all the soul-trials, all the yearnings for national life, of more than two centuries, had contributed to make the country that he served and loved. He, too, preached, in season and out of season, the gospel of Nationality.

He was the faithful disciple of Webster while that great master lived, and after his death he bore aloft the same standard and maintained the same cause. Mr. Everett spoke nothing more than the truth when he said in Faneuil Hall, while all the bells were tolling, at the moment when the vessel bringing home the dead body of his life-long friend cast anchor in Boston harbor: "If ever there was a truly disinterested patriot, Rufus Choate was that man. In his political career there was no shade of selfishness. Had he been willing to purchase advancement at the price often paid for it, there was never a moment from the time he first made himself felt and known that he could not have commanded anything that any party had to bestow. But he desired none of the rewards or honors of success."

He foresaw clearly that the division of the country into geographical parties must end in civil war. What he could not see was, that there was no other way—that only by cutting out slavery by the sword could America secure liberty and union too; but to the last drop of his blood and the last fibre of his being he prayed and pleaded for the life of the nation, according to his light. Neither of these great patriots lived to see the fearful spectacle which they had so eloquently deprecated.

But when at last the dread day came, and our young heroes marched forth to bleed and die for their country—their own sons among the foremost—they carried in their hearts the lessons which both had taught; and all Massachusetts, all New England, from the beginning, marched behind them, "carrying the flag and keeping step to the music of the Union," as he had bade them; and so, I say, let us award to them both their due share of the glory.

Thus to-day we consign this noble statue to the keeping of posterity, to remind them of "the patriot, jurist, orator, scholar, citizen, and nd," whom we are proud to have known and loved.

EMILIO CASTELAR

EMILIO CASTELAR was born in Cadiz, September 8, 1832, and while still young, made several ventures in literature. At the age of twenty-four he became Professor of History and Philosophy in the University of Madrid, and delivered lectures which attracted a great deal of attention. Eight years later, however, he was deprived of his professorship on account of his editorial association with a newspaper which opposed the party in power and advocated republican ideas. In 1866 not only was the newspaper suppressed, but he himself was sentenced to death, and had to remain in exile until the flight of Isabella II. enabled him in 1868 to return to Madrid and resume his professorship. Elected to the Cortes in the following year, he took a memorable part in debate, and, in the provisional republic which succeeded the short-lived monarchy of Amadeus, he became Minister of Foreign Affairs, and, ultimately, chief of the executive power. Constrained to resign his office in 1874, he remained for a good many years the leader of the Moderate Republicans, and universally acknowledged the greatest of Spanish orators, but in 1893 he announced his retirement from politics, expressing a regret that he had not supported the limited monarchy of 1869. He died May 25, 1899.

A PLEA FOR REPUBLICAN INSTITUTIONS

IN THE SPANISH ASSEMBLY, DEC. 18, 1869

BEFORE replying to Minister Sagasta's speech of last Saturday, I desire to say that my public life forbids me to defend myself against personal attacks such as the gentleman seems to delight in. The Minister of Government was extremely kind in speaking of my address as a brilliant one and extremely severe when he declared that it was wanting in truth. Neither criticism was just. Gentlemen, I would not have to defend my own speeches if they had the resplendency and the beauty attributed to them by Mr. Sagasta. I would be content to let them shine, confident, with the most eloquent and greatest of ancient philosophers, that "Beauty is the resplendency of Truth." After all, if there is any grand quality in this Assembly it is eloquence, the expressing of grand sentiments and sublime ideas in fervent language. I have heard such speeches come from every side of the Assembly and I would like to hear one, in the language of moderation, from the government. Discussions carried on in that manner, with eloquence and good judgment, give us hope for the future, for the laws of history do not permit a dictatorship to fasten itself upon a people whose faces are lighted by the fires of eloquence—a sure sign of grand apostolic work in social life.

I have said this, not being able to proceed without repelling a calumnious imputation directed against me by the Minister of Government. To a question of Mr. Oria relative to an attack on property, the gentleman replied that it was the work of the Federalists. In what article, in what proclamation, in what programme, in what bulletin, in what periodical, in what speech of a Federalist has the gentleman discovered that we attack property? Against the robbers are the courts and the judges, and it is an imposition on the Assembly and a calumny on our social conditions to charge us with such crimes and to seek to spatter this minority with the mud that bespatters all of you. This is not just.

Now, I must answer with calmness another slanderous imputation. The Minister of Government says that the Federal Republican party desired the dismemberment, the dissolution, the breaking up of this country. A party that aspires to a European confederation, a party that desires to see the abominable word "war" abolished, a party that desires to unite disunited people cannot seek the dismemberment of a country bound together by tradition and law. We desire that from Barcelona to Lisbon, from Irun to Cadiz, there shall be but one flag—a flag, however, under whose folds the citizen may have freedom, the municipality autonomy, and the province rights that belong to the whole country.

The accusation of the gentleman reminds me of the one concerning decentralization made by the Moderate party against the Progressive party, and the claim of the Moderates that with decentralization national unity was impossible. Notwithstanding this claim, it is generally believed to-day that people who suffer most in their independence have a centralized government, because it is enough to aim a blow at their head, like the blow aimed by the allied powers in Paris in 1815. The belief is general that those nations that have great internal dissensions are centralized nations, because they have an apoplectic head on a weak, stiff body. And so I say that, as centralization is believed in to-day, federation will be to-morrow—a federation the belief in which will result sooner or later in the organization of the United States of Spain within the United States of Europe.

Mr. Sagasta began to defend the dictatorship, and in defending it he drew an awful picture of our social condition, talking of crimes and criminals, and telling you that our education in the past was very bad, and that the corruption of to-day is very great. And what have the Republicans to see from that? For three centuries, yes, more than three centuries, our Church has been as an enemy to the human conscience. For many centuries it has been inimical to the national will. Consequently, if there is anything very bad or vicious here to-day, it is owing to institutions with which we have nothing to do. And more, this evil, this viciousness, owe their existence to a lack of respect among the people for the law. And this lack of respect for the law is born of the systematic abuse of power by our arbitrary government. Judges nominated by a party and appointed to revise the electoral lists; schools, so-called, for filling convents and military barracks; the jury outlawed; public life closed to the democracy; political corruption extending from above down in all directions—this is the product, and these the products, of the sore and wounded people painted by Mr. Sagasta; people who are the natural offspring of a long heredity of crime and error. It is impossible to cure the people if the system is not changed. . . .

Well, deputies, what form of government has come to Spain since the September revolution? The republican form has come and is still here. It so happens that you have not been able yet to implant monarchical institutions in its place. After having been fifteen days in power you declared yourselves for the monarchy. Did the monarchy come? After the elections you declared yourselves monarchists and us outlaws. Did you create the monarchy in the primaries? When the Assembly convened, the monarchy was proposed; there we have had great battles. Has the monarchy been established? The Conservatives, although they have not said so, have, I believe, agreed upon a candidate; the Radicals, more loquacious, have told us theirs; but have you, separated or united, produced a monarchy?

The Conservatives have a candidate who really represents the latest privilege granted the middle classes. Why is it that they do not bring him here? Because they know that this is a democratic monarchy, based, as it is supposably, on universal suffrage, and because the candidate has not, never had, and never will have, the votes, the indorsement, the backing of the people. And you? You want a monarchy to keep up appearances, a monarchy in order that Europe may say, "See how prudent, how God-fearing, how wise, how intelligent are the Spaniards; they have a disguised republic!" After a provisional government and a provisional regency you want a provisional monarchy also. You do not expect or want to be strong in the right, in liberty, in the will of the people or in national sovereignty. All you want is a king who shall represent the predominance and the egotism of a party. You ought to know that as the candidate of the Conservatives cannot come here without the consent of the people your candidate cannot come without the consent of the Conservatives. Do you believe that your candidate will last if all the Conservative forces do not support him? Notwithstanding all that the Conservatives have declared to their representatives here, not one of them has said that he renounces his dynastic faith. Therefore, deputies, you cannot establish the monarchy.

On Saturday I pictured to you, in colors more or less vivid, the prestige which monarchical institutions have enjoyed in our country, and for this the Minister of State upbraided me without understanding my arguments. I ask you to concentrate your attention for a moment upon the parallel which I am going to present and which may be called a summary of this speech. I said the other afternoon, that to establish monarchical institutions it was necessary to possess monarchical faith and sentiment. One must have the poetry and the traditions of monarchy. I said this because I know that, although the Assembly and the official authorities can make laws, they cannot decree ideas or sentiments, those real and solid foundations of institutions. Formerly, in other times, kings were representative of the national dignity, and now from those same benches we have heard that they sold their native soil to a foreigner and even prostrated themselves at his feet, the people in the meantime answering the enemy with the second of May and the siege of Saragossa. Formerly poetry, addressing the throne, exclaimed:

"Oh! what a profound abyss
Of iniquity and malice
The mighty of the world
Have made of your justice!"

Formerly art sketched the apotheosis of Charles V. with Titian's brush, or the ladies-in-waiting of Philip VI. with the brush of Velasquez; now it sketches the image of the communists, of the victims of Charles V., or the ship in which the Puritans took the republic to the bosom of virgin America. Formerly, the gala days of the people were the birthdays of kings and the anniversaries of the beginning of their reigns. Now, the great days of celebration are the tenth of August, the thirtieth of July, the twenty-fourth of February, and the twenty-ninth of September, days marking the expulsion of kings. Formerly, when a navigator landed in America, or an explorer went into the interior of a new country, the purest piece of gold, the largest pearl, the clearest diamond was reserved for the king. Now, your Minister of the Treasury claims from the king even the clasp which holds the royal mantle about his shoulders. I will not continue this parallel, as the Chamber clearly sees the application.

What does this mean? What does it signify? If the throne has fallen, if the throne is broken, if the throne is dishonored, if the throne cannot be restored, Conservatives, Unionists, Progressists, Democrats, repeat with the poet:

> "Mankind, weep;
> All of you laid your hands on him."

As there is no possibility of establishing the monarchy, as no candidate acceptable to all can be found, it is necessary, it is indispensable to get rid of the suspense, and I say that we should establish a republic. Have you not said that the forms of government are accidental? Gentlemen, you know the republic I want. It is a federal republic. I shall always defend the federal republic. I am a Federal, but, deputies, understand one thing, the republic is a form of government which admits many conditions, and which has many grades. From the republic of Venice to that of Switzerland there is an immense scale. Adjoining Mexico, where Church and State are separated, there is Guatemala, where the clergy have great power. Close to the decentralized and federal Argentine Republic is the Chilian Republic, another decentralized country enjoying great prosperity, its paper money being quoted in all the markets of Europe as high as that of England. Consequently, deputies, amid this great affliction and this great trouble and this unstable equilibrium, which surrounds you, you can establish a form of government which is of the people and for the people, a form of government in harmony with the institutions you have proclaimed, and with the sentiment which all of you guard in the bottom of your hearts.

Have you not seen in history the inability of an assembly or any power to establish a form of government in conflict with great ideas? Remember the eighteenth century. Never had a monarchy attained more power, never was absolutism so strong, never was the destruction of obstacles in the way of kings more complete. Philosophy ascended the throne with them, ascended with Charles III. and Aranda and Tombal. It ascended with Joseph I., with Frederick the Great, with Leopold of Tuscany. All seemed to conspire to establish the same idea, the idea of a philosophy and a liberalism. And did they succeed? No, they were the Baptists of the Revolution. They repented late, and the philosophy they had thrown at the feet of the thrones came to naught. And what happened? Some were sentenced by the Assembly. The crowns of divine right were melted into cannon balls by the soldiers of the Revolution. What does this signify? That great powers cannot place absolutism above philosophy any more than you can build monarchical institutions on individual rights. Therefore, I beseech you to establish the republic. You are assured of our patriotism, our great interest in the country, our abnegation. Cato committed suicide because he found a Cæsar. Radicals of Spain, do not commit suicide because you cannot find a monarch. I have spoken.

IN THE CAMPO SANTO OF PISA

AN EXAMPLE OF CASTELAR'S PROSE STYLE

DO YOU believe that death is the end of our being? I have never thought so. If it be, then the universe is created solely for destruction; and God is a child who has formed the world like a castle of cards, for the pleasure of overturning them.

The vegetable consumes the earth, the ox and the sheep graze upon the vegetable; we eat the ox and the sheep, and invisible agents which we call death or nothingness consume us. In the scale of existence some creatures serve only to destroy other creatures, and the universe is like an enormous polypus with a capacious stomach, or, if you desire a more classic image, a catafalque upon which burns a funeral torch, and is created the statue of fatal law. Some are patient because they have been born lymphatic; many are heroic because they have much blood; others are thinkers because they are bilious; more are poets because their nerves are sensitive; but all die of their own characteristics, and all live while their stomachs endure, while their hearts, their brains, their spines are sound. What we call virtues or vices are tendencies of organism; what we name faith is but a few drops less blood in the veins, or some irritation of the liver, or some atoms of phosphorus in the bones, and what we term immortality is but an illusion. Death alone is real and certain, and human history is a procession of shadows passing like bats between day and night, all to drop, one behind the other, into that obscure, unfathomable abyss which is called nothing, the unique atmosphere of the universe.

Oh! No! no! I cannot believe it! Human wickedness can never so much affect me as to obscure divine truths in my soul. As I can distinguish good from evil, so can I separate death from immortality. I believe in the Almighty, and in a vision of the Almighty in another and better world.

I leave my body as armor which fatigues me by its weight, to continue my infinite ascension to the heaven of heavens, bathed in light eternal.

It is true that death exists, but true also that there is a soul; against Realism that would enshroud me with its leaden mantle I have the glow and fire of thought; and against Fatalism, that would confine me by its chain, I have the power and force of liberty.

History is a resurrection. Barbarians buried the ancient Grecian statues, but they live again here in this cemetery, producing immortal generations of artists with kisses from their cold lips of marble. Italy was as dead as Juliet. Each generation flung a handful of earth upon her corpse, and placed a flower in her mortuary crown; yet Italy is alive again!

To-day tyrants sing the "Dies Iræ" on the field where unhappy Poland was divided. Yet soon humanity will approach, collect the bones, picked clean by the vultures of the Neva, and Poland will be reborn, standing like a statue of faith, with the cross in her arms and on her ancient altars.

I have always been impressed with the thought of immortality in cemeteries. But I felt it more than commonly in the Campo Santo of Pisa, filled with so much life; peopled by so many beings that give inspiration and consequently immortality, as the trunks of the trees distil honey when the bees have inhabited them. Insensibly the night falls. The grave-digger finishes his work, the noise of the shovel ceases, and I am asked to retire. But I prayed to remain another hour, in the bosom of night and of the shadows. I wish to submerge myself in the melancholy of nothingness, to anticipate my being in that place of silence and external repose, by long contemplation of the dust of the departed here where so many generations sleep forgotten.

There I remained leaning against a tomb, resting my forehead upon the marble, my eyes fixed on the picture of death and on the monsters of the Universal Judgment, illuminated by the last splendors of the expiring day, awaiting the greater sadness which the darkness of night would bring upon me.

But no! the fresh breeze of the sea comes to awaken me from my melancholy dreams; the sweet flowers of May raised their blossom before drooping; from the heat, a penetrating and intoxicating aroma, full of life and fragrance, diffused itself in the air; the winged glowworms began to hover between the shades of the cloister and the lines of the tombs like wandering stars, while the full moon rose above the horizon, floating majestically in ether, with her pale blue rays lighting up the faces of the funereal statues; and a nightingale, hidden in the thick branches of the highest cypress, chanted his song of love as a serenade to the dead and a supplication to the living.

SPEECH ON THE POLITICAL OATH

DELIVERED APRIL 7, 1883

GENTLEMEN,—The political oath is dead throughout Europe. Nominally it is still enforced. Custom preserves a worn-out institution of which the spirit has long since expired. Just as we still see the light of far distant suns long after they have been extinguished.

It is undeniable that if the political oath was a great and worthy institution it would merit the fate of all great and worthy institutions and be as immortal as compassion, charity, and beneficence.

There is a proper place for the oath; it belongs solely to the great and solemn functions of life, so let it not be contaminated by the strife of party politics.

Witness the stress laid upon oaths in every secret society; the more idolatrous a religion is, the more complicated its system of oaths, the greater the mystery, the more frequent the invocation to the supernatural; you see this in all secret societies, because there injustice and mystery are the rule; but you do not see it in public societies, because there law and order prevail.

Compare the mysteries of Eleusis and those for admission to the temple of the goddess Isis; compare any of the pagan liturgies with the command not to take the name of God in vain, and tell me, as Catholics, as believers in the Bible, as Christians, that it is not necessary to abolish the oath.

The modern social order is an evolution of natural law, and the natural law has as its characteristic note liberty of conscience, and liberty of conscience rejects the useless multiplication of oaths. Why then should you civil and political legislators exact irrational formulas? Be satisfied with external obedience and respect for the law, which is the only thing you can demand by reason of the authority which the nation has given you and the only thing that we, as free and true citizens, can promise.

But you will reply that we have abolished the oath that confirms a promise. And here let me say a few words regarding this absurd concession.

Laws are not made for imaginary people, but for those that really exist. The idealist suggests that we content ourselves with pure law, but in truth we must derive our inspiration from reality.

Now, gentlemen, there is a contrast, a deep contrast between the expression of external respect for the official religion and the profound indifference that there is in most souls and in the majority of consciences.

Go to the house of a sceptic, a freethinker, of any kind of a rationalist, go to that house and you will see expression of outward respect. The unbeliever scoffs at the efficacy of baptism, but although he disbelieves, he will have all his children baptized with due form and ceremony. At the table, where the soup and fish are steaming, he will ridicule the lenten discipline and criticise the proclamation of the Bull, but he will take good care to join his family in refraining from meat on Friday, through love for his wife, through consideration for his daughter, through respect for his mother, and even through fear of his mother-in-law; he will not communicate at Easter, oh, no, because he is secretly afraid of committing a profanation; but he will secretly bribe the priest or the sacristan of the parish to obtain the certificate that he has received his Easter communion, so that he may place it in the family prayer-book or present it to the pastor on his Easter visit.

He will work here in the Congress and in the cabinet that education may be freed from priestly influence, that marriage may be merely a civil ceremony, that the cemetery ought to be under the control of the laity; but nevertheless in his last will and testament he will request that he be buried in the shadow of the cross, under which rest his ancestors; for although he has really given up his faith and his religion, he has breathed it in from the very air; he has become so accustomed to it that it has permeated his whole being, and he wishes to die in that faith whose *dies iræs* and *misereres* have taught him the terrors of death and whose prayers and psalms have given him assurance of immortality.

Well, gentlemen, do you wish some one to make promises. No one shall promise anything, I least of all. So then, instead of abolishing the oath, you have made it more burdensome.

Gentlemen, I am going now to differ from my friend the Marquis de Pédal. Do you think that any people could be more interested in the improvement of the moral conscience and even the religious conscience than the Republican party?

I have said a thousand times that as soon as material ties are broken moral ones become more binding. If this is true is it necessary to strengthen them either in Congress, in the committees, or in our public ceremonies, jubilees, and festivals in which all unite in their supplications to one God, whom they implore to guard them and to protect their rights.

And here, gentlemen, I call your attention—the attention

of all Liberals—to the fact that I have the same regret my friend the Marquis de Pédal has for the religious crisis, for the philosophical crisis through which the human mind is passing, for that cloud of sophism and error which at this very moment threatens all that we have loved and adored on the face of this planet. I also, gentlemen, protest against that philosophy which proclaims mere materialism and which worships blind force.

I cannot endure the thought that the immensity of space is only a funeral shroud, under the gloomy folds of which humanity lies as inert and soulless as stone.

I cannot endure the thought that time is only an eternal river, without beginning and without end, on the surface of which we behold human beings idly drifting toward a bottomless abyss, in which they are at last to be swallowed up.

I cannot bear to think of dwelling in a universe without ideals, without law and order, governed by chance and bounded by oblivion, that ogre which devours human souls and consigns them to nothingness.

Gentlemen, I abhor these errors, and lifting my arms toward heaven, I implore God to enlighten these blinded people who ask him nothing less than the proof of his existence; as if fundamental truth could be demonstrated and as if mathematical axioms were not undemonstrable postulates, without which other demonstrable truths would not exist.

God is seen in the light, is felt in the heat; we are conscious of him throughout our whole being; and the more weak and sinful we are, the more we deserve his mercy; the more wretched and miserable this world is, the more we need the aid of his divine Providence.

Gentlemen, now that I have protested against these doctrines which declare that the human being is but a collection of atoms, conscience and the mind merely an association of ideas; now that I have protested, I say that we must avoid another form of materialism. I mean that ecclesiastical materialism which converts the ministers of Christ into Carlists, which makes Mount Esquinza an altar, and which blesses the infamous gems of the Curate of Santa Cruz.

Yet, on the other hand, it is most necessary that sincere belief should have its foundation in the intellect, for we may be sure that if the soul is left free it will seek God as its centre of gravity.

Gentlemen, do you know what are the faults of Catholicism? That is to say, the faults of the practice of Catholicism (it would be a profanation to say that Catholicism in itself has faults). Do you know wherein it fails? In its form and ritual. For men go to Mass without understanding the prayers that are said, and to the Communion without realizing why they participate. They worship with their lips but not with their hearts.

Gentlemen, the longer we live the more we become convinced that there are no new revelations. The longer we live the more we are convinced that no new religious ideas are necessary; but what we do need is that the people of the Latin race should spiritualize the old ones. We find ourselves in a position analogous to that which characterized the sixteenth century. We of the nineteenth century need an ideal as they needed it then, when Martin Luther kindled the fires of the glorious Reformation; that great and extraordinary man, the successor of Armenius, educated, as he was, in a monastery, and so prone to mysticism that he saw angelic visions and imagined that the devil himself came to tempt him, this great man, I say, believed that as an antidote to ecclesiastical materialism it was needful to read but one book, necessary only to follow the inspiration of conscience.

Luther recoiled from the marble cloisters surrounded with luxurious gardens, from incongruous groups of virgins and fawns, from elegant Ciceronians speaking classic Latin, which they were so anxious to retain that instead of praying to God they invoked the heathen deities of Rome.

Thus Luther brought forth that religious idea which in Germany has substituted the leadership of Protestant Prussia for the leadership of Catholic Austria, which has given to the world, instead of the Spanish colonial empire, the British colonial empire. And this new religion penetrates to the very heart of the people, and has made them more orthodox, because it has given them free thought and has proclaimed the great principle of the sacredness, the individuality, and the spirituality of conscience.

We need Christian unison; well, let us seek for it in our hearts. Do not demand a formal and liturgical oath; but instead take for an example the spontaneous prayer of gratitude which you offer God every day in return for his gracious gift of life.

I do not rise with a spirit of antagonism, gentlemen, but with a spirit of conciliation. I have no objection as long as they do not humiliate my conscience, my life, my traditions.

Why should I have any objections to using the name of God, gentlemen of the Congress? I see him in the realm of nature; I listen to him in the harmony of the spheres. I feel him in the beauty of art. I know him as the supreme immortal being. I proclaim him as the absolute truth in religion and in conscience.

I have no objection whatsoever to swearing by the holy

gospels, because, after having read the greatest books, I have found none more sublime than these. I have studied the greatest orators and have listened to their words, but I know of no oration so sublime, so divine as that which declares "blessed are they that mourn," "blessed are they that are persecuted." I know of nothing equal to our Lord's Sermon on the Mount.

I have seen the great places of the world—the Capitol which was called the head of the earth; the Parthenon, which was the spring of art; and I believe that there is no loftier height than the Cross, because its arms reach the heavens.

If you wish, I swear by God and the holy gospels, in the name of all we have respected on the face of this earth, with my hand upon my heart I swear fidelity by him alone who is eternal. I swear by him whose power has placed us upon earth; I swear by him, gentlemen, an eternal and inviolable fidelity to my country. But I will never take any other oath.

[Special translation.]

WHITE

ANDREW DICKSON WHITE, a distinguished American educator and diplomat, was born at Homer, New York, November 7, 1832. He received his early education in the public schools of Syracuse and graduated at Yale College in 1853. He afterward studied at the College of France and the University of Berlin. In 1857, after serving as attaché to the United States legation at St. Petersburg, he was appointed professor of history at the University of Michigan, where he taught for seven years. In 1863 he was elected a member of the New York Senate, and sat in that body until he became president of Cornell University in 1867. In 1871 he was sent to the republic of Santo Domingo as a special commissioner, and in 1878 was appointed special commissioner to the Paris exposition. In 1879 he went to Germany as United States minister and remained there three years. In 1885 he resigned the presidency of the University, and for a time was engaged in no public capacity, but in 1892 he became ambassador to Russia. In 1897, after having rendered signal services as a member of the Venezuela commission, he was again sent as ambassador to the Court of Berlin. He was a member of the Peace commission which met at The Hague in 1899. He was regent of the Smithsonian Institute and an officer of the Legion of Honor of the French Republic. Besides many contributions to the serious magazine literature of the day, he published "A History of the Warfare of Science with Theology;" "Lectures on Mediæval and Modern History;" "The New Germany;" "Studies in General History;" "History of the Doctrine of Comets;" "Paper Money Inflation in France," and many other books.

"THE APOSTLE OF PEACE AMONG THE NATIONS"

SPEECH DELIVERED AT THE PEACE CONFERENCE AT THE HAGUE

YOUR EXCELLENCIES, Mr. Burgomaster, Gentlemen of the University Faculties, My Honored Colleagues of the Peace Conference, Ladies and Gentlemen,—The Commission of the United States comes here this day to discharge a special duty. We are instructed to acknowledge, on behalf of our country, one of its many great debts to the Netherlands.

This debt is that which, in common with the whole world, we owe to one of whom all civilized lands are justly proud,—the poet, the scholar, the historian, the statesman, the diplomatist, the jurist, the author of the treatise "De Jure Belli ac Pacis."

Of all works not claiming divine inspiration, that book, written by a man proscribed and hated both for his politics and his religion, has proved the greatest blessing to humanity. More than any other it has prevented unmerited suffering, misery, and sorrow; more than any other it has ennobled the military profession; more than any other it has promoted the blessings of peace and diminished the horrors of war.

On this tomb, then, before which we now stand, the delegates of the United States are instructed to lay a simple tribute to him whose mortal remains rest beneath it—Hugo de Groot, revered and regarded with gratitude by thinking men throughout the world as "Grotius."

Naturally we have asked you to join us in this simple ceremony. For his name has become too great to be celebrated by his native country alone; too great to be celebrated by Europe alone: it can be fitly celebrated only in the presence of representatives from the whole world.

For the first time in human history there are now assembled delegates with a common purpose from all the nations, and they are fully represented here. I feel empowered to speak words of gratitude, not only from my own country, but from each of these. I feel that my own country, though one of the youngest in the great sisterhood of nations, utters at this shrine to-day, not only her own gratitude, but that of every part of Europe, of all the great Powers of Asia, and of the sister republics of North and South America.

From nations now civilized, but which Grotius knew only as barbarous; from nations which in his time were yet unborn; from every land where there are men who admire genius, who reverence virtue, who respect patriotism, who are grateful to those who have given their lives to toil, hardship, disappointment, and sacrifice, for humanity,—from all these come thanks and greetings heartily mingled with our own.

The time and place are well suited to the acknowledgment of such a debt. As to time, as far as the world at large is concerned, I remind you, not only that this is the first conference of the entire world, but that it has, as its sole purpose, a further evolution of the principles which Grotius first, of all men, developed thoroughly and stated effectively. So far as the United States is concerned, it is the time of our most sacred national festival—the anniversary of our national independence. What more fitting period, then, in the history of the world and of our own country, for a tribute to one who has done so much, not only for our sister nations, but for ourselves.

And as to the place. This is the ancient and honored city of Delft. From its Haven, not distant, sailed the "Mayflower"—bearing the Pilgrim Fathers, who, in a time of obstinate and bitter persecution, brought to the American continent the germs of that toleration which had been especially developed among them during their stay in the Netherlands, and of which Grotius was an apostle. In this town Grotius was born; in this temple he worshipped; this pavement he trod when a child; often were these scenes revisited by him in his boyhood; at his death his mortal body was placed in this hallowed ground. Time and place, then, would both seem to make this tribute fitting.

In the vast debt which all nations owe to Grotius, the United States acknowledges its part gladly. Perhaps in no other country has his thought penetrated more deeply and influenced more strongly the great mass of the people. It was the remark of Alexis de Tocqueville, the most philosophic among all students of American institutions, that one of the most striking and salutary things in American life is the widespread study of law. De Tocqueville was undoubtedly right. In all parts of our country the law of nations is especially studied by large bodies of young men in colleges and universities; studied, not professionally merely, but from the point of view of men eager to understand the fundamental principles of international rights and duties.

The works of our compatriots, Wheaton, Kent, Field, Woolsey, Dana, Lawrence, and others, in developing more and more the ideas to which Grotius first gave life and strength, show that our country has not cultivated in vain this great field which Grotius opened.

As to the bloom and fruitage evolved by these writers out of the germ ideas of Grotius I might give many examples, but I will mention merely three:

The first example shall be the act of Abraham Lincoln. Amid all the fury of civil war he recognized the necessity of a more humane code for the conduct of our armies in the field; and he entrusted its preparation to Francis Lieber, honorably known to jurists throughout the world, and at that time Grotius's leading American disciple.

My second example shall be the act of General Ulysses Grant. When called to receive the surrender of his great opponent, General Lee, after a long and bitter contest, he declined to take from the vanquished general the sword which he had so long and so bravely worn; imposed no terms upon the conquered armies save that they should return to their homes; allowed no reprisals; but simply said, "Let us have peace."

My third example shall be the act of the whole people of the United States. At the close of that most bitter contest, which desolated thousands of homes, and which cost nearly a million of lives, no revenge was taken by the triumphant Union on any of the separatist statesmen who had brought on the great struggle, or on any of the soldiers who had conducted it; and, from that day to this, north and south, once every year, on Decoration Day, the graves of those who fell wearing the blue of the North and the gray of the South are alike strewn with flowers. Surely I may claim for my countrymen that, whatever other shortcomings and faults may be imputed to them, they have shown themselves influenced by those feelings of mercy and humanity which Grotius, more than any other, brought into the modern world.

In the presence of this great body of eminent jurists from the courts, the cabinets, and the universities of all nations, I will not presume to attempt any full development of the principles of Grotius or to estimate his work; but I will briefly present a few considerations regarding his life and work which occur to one who has contemplated them from another and distant country.

There are, of course, vast advantages in the study of so great a man from the nearest point of view; from his own land, and by those who from their actual experience must best know his environment. But a more distant point of view is not without its uses. Those who cultivate the slopes of some vast mountain know it best; yet those who view it from a distance may sometimes see it brought into new relations and invested with new glories.

Separated thus from the native land of Grotius by the Atlantic, and perhaps by a yet broader ocean of customary thinking; unbiassed by any of that patriotism so excusable and indeed so laudable in the land where he was born; an American jurist naturally sees, first, the relations of Grotius to the writers who preceded him. He sees other and lesser mountain peaks of thought emerging from the clouds of earlier history, and he acknowledges a debt to such men as Isidore of Seville, Suarez, Ayala, and Gentilis. But when all this is acknowledged he clearly sees Grotius, while standing among these men, grandly towering above them. He sees in Grotius the first man who brought the main principles of those earlier thinkers to bear upon modern times,—increasing them from his own creative mind, strengthening them from the vast stores of his knowledge, enriching them from his imagination, glorifying them with his genius.

His great mind brooded over that earlier chaos of opinion, and from his heart and brain, more than from those of any other, came a revelation to the modern world of new and better paths toward mercy and peace. But his agency was more than that. His coming was like the rising of the sun out of the primeval abyss: his work was both creative and illuminative. We may reverently insist that in the domain of international law, Grotius said "Let there be light," and there was light.

The light he thus gave has blessed the earth for these three centuries past, and it will go on through many centuries to come, illuminating them ever more and more.

I need hardly remind you that it was mainly unheeded at first. Catholics and Protestants alike failed to recognize it.

"The light shone in the darkness, and the darkness comprehended it not."

By Calvinists in Holland and France, and by Lutherans in Germany, his great work was disregarded if not opposed; and at Rome it was placed on the Index of books forbidden to be read by Christians.

The book, as you know, was published amid the horrors of the Thirty Years' War; the great Gustavus is said to have carried it with him always, and he evidently at all times bore its principles in his heart. But he alone, among all the great commanders of his time, stood for mercy. All the cogent arguments of Grotius could not prevent the fearful destruction of Magdeburg, or diminish, so far as we can now see, any of the atrocities of that fearful period.

Grotius himself may well have been discouraged; he may well have repeated the words attributed to the great Swedish chancellor whose ambassador he afterward became, "Go forth, my son, and see with how little wisdom the world is governed." He may well have despaired as he reflected that throughout his whole life he had never known his native land save in perpetual, heartrending war; nay, he may well have been excused for thinking that all his work for humanity had been in vain when there came to his deathbed no sign of any ending of the terrible war of thirty years.

For not until three years after he was laid in this tomb did the plenipotentiaries sign the Treaty of Münster. All this disappointment and sorrow and lifelong martyrdom invests him, in the minds of Americans, as doubtless in your minds, with an atmosphere of sympathy, veneration, and love.

Yet we see that the great light streaming from his heart and mind continued to shine; that it developed and fructified human thought; that it warmed into life new and glorious growths of right reason as to international relations; and we recognize the fact that, from his day to ours, the progress of reason in theory and of mercy in practice has been constant on both sides of the Atlantic.

It may be objected that this good growth, so far as theory was concerned, was sometimes anarchic, and that many of its developments were very different from any that Grotius intended or would have welcomed. For if Puffendorff swerved much from the teachings of his great master in one direction, others swerved even more in other directions, and all created systems more or less antagonistic. Yet we can now see that all these contributed to a most beneficent result,—to the growth of a practice ever improving, ever deepening, ever widening, ever diminishing bad faith in time of peace and cruelty in time of war.

It has also been urged that the system which Grotius gave to the world has been utterly left behind as the world has gone on; that the great writers on international law in the present day do not accept it; that Grotius developed everything out of an idea of natural law which was merely the creation of his own mind, and based everything on an origin of jural rights and duties which never had any real being; that he deduced his principles from a divinely planted instinct which many thinkers are now persuaded never existed, acting in a way contrary to everything revealed by modern discoveries in the realm of history.

It is at the same time insisted against Grotius that he did not give sufficient recognition to the main basis of the work of modern international jurists; to positive law, slowly built on the principles and practice of various nations in accordance with their definite agreements and adjustments.

In these charges there is certainly truth; but I trust that you will allow one from a distant country to venture an opinion that, so far from being to the discredit of Grotius, this fact is to his eternal honor.

For there was not, and there could not be at that period, anything like a body of positive international law adequate to the new time. The spirit which most thoroughly permeated the whole world, whether in war or peace, when Grotius wrote, was the spirit of Machiavelli,—unmoral, immoral. It has been dominant for more than a hundred years. To measure the service rendered by the theory of Grotius, we have only to compare Machiavelli's "Prince" with Grotius's "De Jure Belli ac Pacis." Grant that Grotius's basis of international law was, in the main, a theory of natural law which is no longer held: grant that he made no sufficient recognition of positive law; we must nevertheless acknowledge that his system, at the time he presented it, was the only one which could ennoble men's theories or reform their practice.

From his own conception of the attitude of the Divine Mind toward all the falsities of his time grew a theory of international morals which supplanted the principles of Machiavelli: from his conception of the attitude of the Divine Mind toward all the cruelties which he had himself known in the Seventy Years' War of the Netherlands, and toward all those of which tidings were constantly coming from the German Thirty Years' War, came inspiration to promote a better practice in war.

To one, then, looking at Grotius from afar, as doubtless to many among yourselves, the theory which Grotius adopted seems the only one which, in his time, could bring any results for good to mankind.

I am also aware that one of the most deservedly eminent historians and publicists of the Netherlands during our own time has censured Grotius as the main source of the doctrine which founds human rights upon an early social compact, and, therefore, as one who proposed the doctrines which have borne fruit in the writings of Rousseau and in various modern revolutions.

I might take issue with this statement; or I might fall back upon the claim that Grotius's theory has proved, at least, a serviceable provisional hypothesis; but this is neither the time nor the place to go fully into so great a question. Yet I may at least say that it would ill become me, as a representative of the United States, to impute to Grotius, as a fault, a theory out of which sprang the nationality of my country: a doctrine embodied in that Declaration of Independence which is this day read to thousands on thousands of assemblies in all parts of the United States, from the Atlantic to the Pacific, and from the Great Lakes to the Gulf of Mexico.

But, however the Old World may differ from the New on this subject, may we not all agree that, whatever Grotius's responsibility for this doctrine may be, its evils would have been infinitely reduced could the men who developed it have caught his spirit,—his spirit of broad toleration, of wide sympathy, of wise moderation, of contempt for "the folly of extremes," of search for the great principles which unite men rather than for the petty differences which separate them?

It has also been urged against Grotius that his interpretation of the words *jus gentium*[1] was a mistake, and that other

[1] The right of nations, in other words, international law.

mistakes have flowed from this. Grant it; yet we, at a distance, believe that we see in it one of the happiest mistakes ever made; a mistake comparable in its fortunate results to that made by Columbus when he interpreted a statement in our sacred books, regarding the extent of the sea as compared with the land, to indicate that the western continent could not be far from Spain,—a mistake which probably more than anything else encouraged him to sail for the New World.

It is also not infrequently urged by eminent European writers that Grotius dwelt too little on what international law really was, and too much on what, in his opinion, it ought to be. This is but another form of an argument against him already stated. But is it certain, after all, that Grotius was so far wrong in this as some excellent jurists have thought him? May it not be that, in the not distant future, international law, while mainly basing its doctrines upon what nations have slowly developed in practice, may also draw inspiration more and more from "that Power in the Universe, not ourselves, which makes for righteousness."

An American, recalling that greatest of all arbitrations yet known, the Geneva Arbitration of 1872, naturally attributes force to the reasoning of Grotius. The heavy damages which the United States asked at that time, and which Great Britain honorably paid, were justified mainly, if not wholly, not on the practice of nations then existing, but upon what it was claimed ought to be the practice; not upon positive law, but upon natural justice: and that decision forms one of the happiest landmarks in modern times; it ended all quarrel between the two nations concerned, and bound them together more firmly than ever.

But while there may be things in the life and work of Grotius which reveal themselves differently to those who study him from a near point of view and to those who behold him from afar, there are thoughts on which we may all unite, lessons which we may learn alike, and encouragements which may strengthen us all for the duties of this present hour.

For, as we now stand before these monuments, there come to us, not only glimpses of the irony of history, but a full view of the rewards of history. Resounding under these arches and echoing among these columns, prayer and praise have been heard for five hundred years. Hither came, in hours of defeat and hours of victory, that mighty hero whose remains rest in yonder shrine and whose fame is part of the world's fairest heritage. But when, just after William the Silent had been laid in the vaults beneath our feet, Hugo de Groot, as a child, gazed with wonder on this grave of the father of his country, and when, in his boyhood, he here joined in prayer and praise and caught inspiration from the mighty dead, no man knew that in this beautiful boy, opening his eyes upon these scenes which we now behold, not only the Netherlands, but the whole human race, had cause for the greatest of thanksgivings.

And when, in perhaps the darkest hour of modern Europe, in 1625, his great book was born, yonder organ might well have pealed forth a most triumphant Te Deum; but no man recognized the blessing which in that hour had been vouchsafed to mankind: no voice of thanksgiving was heard.

But if the dead, as we fondly hope, live beyond the grave; if, undisturbed by earthly distractions, they are all the more observant of human affairs; if, freed from earthly trammels, their view of life in our lower world is illumined by that infinite light which streams from the source of all that is true and beautiful and good,—may we not piously believe that the mighty and beneficent shade of William of Orange recognized with joy the birth-hour of Grotius as that of a compatriot who was to give the Netherlands a lasting glory? May not that great and glorious spirit have also looked lovingly upon Grotius as a boy lingering on this spot where we now stand, and recognized him as one whose work was to go on adding in every age new glory to the nation which the mighty Prince of the House of Orange had, by the blessing of God, founded and saved; may not, indeed, that great mind have foreseen in that divine light, another glory not then known to mortal ken? Who shall say that in the effluence of divine knowledge he may not have beheld Grotius, in his full manhood, penning the pregnant words of the "De Jure Belli ac Pacis," and that he may not have foreseen—as largely resulting from it—what we behold to-day, as an honor of the august Monarch who convoked it, to the Netherlands who have given it splendid hospitality, and to all modern states here represented,—the first conference of the entire world ever held, and that conference assembled to increase the securities for peace and to diminish the horrors of war.

For, my honored colleagues of the Peace Conference, the germ of this work in which we are all so earnestly engaged lies in a single sentence of Grotius's great book. Others, indeed, had proposed plans for the peaceful settlement of differences between nations, and the world remembers them with honor: to all of them, from Henry IV, and Kant, and St. Pierre, and Penn, and Bentham, down to the humblest writer in favor of peace, we may well feel grateful; but the germ of arbitration was planted in modern thought when Grotius, urging arbitration and mediation as preventing war, wrote these solemn words in the "De Jure Belli ac Pacis": "Maxime autem christiani reges et civitates tenentur hanc inire viam ad arma vitanda."[1]

My honored colleagues and friends, more than once I have come as a pilgrim to this sacred shrine. In my young manhood, more than thirty years ago, and at various times since, I have sat here and reflected upon what these mighty men here entombed have done for the world, and what, though dead, they yet speak to mankind. I seem to hear them still.

From this tomb of William the Silent comes, in this hour, a voice bidding the Peace Conference be brave, and true, and trustful in that Power in the Universe which works for righteousness.

From this tomb of Grotius I seem to hear a voice which says to us, as the delegates of the nations: "Go on with your mighty work: avoid, as you would avoid the germs of pestilence, those exhalations of international hatred which take shape in monstrous fallacies and morbid fictions regarding alleged antagonistic interests. Guard well the treasures of civilization with which each of you is entrusted; but bear in mind that you hold a mandate from humanity. Go on with your work. Pseudo-philosophers will prophesy malignantly against you; pessimists will laugh you to scorn; cynics will sneer at you; zealots will abuse you for what you have not done; sublimely unpractical thinkers will revile you for what you have done; ephemeral critics will ridicule you as dupes; enthusiasts, blind to the difficulties in your path and to everything outside their little circumscribed fields, will denounce you as traitors to humanity. Heed them not,—go on with your work. Heed not the clamor of zealots, or cynics, or pessimists, or pseudo-philosophers, or enthusiasts,

[1] "But above all, Christian kings and states are bound to take this way of avoiding recourse to arms."

or fault-finders. Go on with the work of strengthening peace and humanizing war; give greater scope and strength to provisions which will make war less cruel; perfect those laws of war which diminish the unmerited sufferings of populations; and, above all, give to the world at least a beginning of an effective, practicable scheme of arbitration."

These are the words which an American seems to hear issuing from this shrine to-day; and I seem also to hear from it a prophecy. I seem to hear Grotius saying to us: "Fear neither opposition nor detraction. As my own book, which grew out of the horrors of the Wars of Seventy and the Thirty Years' War, contained the germ from which your great Conference has grown, so your work, which is demanded by a world bent almost to breaking under the weight of ever-increasing armaments, shall be a germ from which future Conferences shall evolve plans ever fuller, better, and nobler."

And I also seem to hear a message from him to the jurists of the great universities who honor us with their presence to-day, including especially that renowned University of Leyden which gave to Grotius his first knowledge of the law; and that eminent University of Königsberg which gave him his most philosophical disciple: to all of these I seem to hear him say: "Go on in your labor to search out the facts and to develop the principles which shall enable future Conferences to build more and more broadly, more and more loftily for peace."

And now, your excellencies, Mr. Burgomaster, and honored deans of the various universities of the Netherlands, a simple duty remains to me. In accordance with instructions from the President and on behalf of the people of the United States of America, the American Commission at the Peace

Conference, by my hand, lays on the tomb of Grotius this simple tribute. It combines the oak, symbolical of civic virtue, with the laurel, symbolical of victory. It bears the following inscription:

"TO THE MEMORY OF HUGO GROTIUS
IN REVERENCE AND GRATITUDE
FROM THE UNITED STATES OF AMERICA
ON THE OCCASION OF THE INTERNATIONAL PEACE CONFERENCE
AT THE HAGUE
JULY 4, 1899"

—and it encloses two shields, one bearing the arms of the House of Orange and of the Netherlands, the other bearing the arms of the United States of America; and both these shields are bound firmly together. They represent the gratitude of our country, one of the youngest among the nations of the earth, to this old and honored Commonwealth,—gratitude for great services in days gone by, gratitude for recent courtesies and kindnesses; and above all they represent to all time a union of hearts and minds in both lands for peace between the nations.

BJORNSON

BJORNSTJERNE BJORNSON, a celebrated Norwegian dramatist, novelist, and orator, was born at Krikne, in northwestern Norway, December 8, 1832. He was the son of a Lutheran clergyman, and, after studying at the Latin school at Molde, was sent to the University of Christiania. His attention was early given to literature, and his first book, "Solbakken," a novel of Norwegian peasant life, appeared in 1857. It was almost immediately popular and was followed within the next ten years by the novels "Arne" (1858); "En Glad Gut" ("A Happy Boy") (1859); "Fiskerjenten" ("The Fisher Lass") (1868). During this period he was engaged also in producing dramas, which did not so quickly win their way to favor, the first of them being a tragedy, "Halte-Hulda" (1858). To this succeeded "Kong Sverre" (1861); "Sigurd Slembe" (1862), a masterly trilogy which showed him at his best; "De Nygifte" ("The Newly Married") (1865), a comedy; "Maria Stuart" (1867), a tragedy. After 1870, Björnson devoted himself assiduously to the study of foreign thought and literature, with the result that by 1874 he came into prominence as an advocate of republican ideas, and free thought in religion. Besides declaring his new views in various pamphlets and addresses, he gave utterance to them in a notable series of dramas bearing upon the problems of the time, such as "Redakteren" ("The Editor") (1874); "En Fallit" ("Bankruptcy") (1875); "Det ny System" ("The New System") (1875); "Kongen" ("The King") (1879); "Leonarda" (1879); "En Hanske" ("A Glove") (1883); "Over Evne" ("Overstrained") (1883). Among other works of his are: "Magnhild" (1877); "Kaptejn Mansana" (1879); "Arnljot Gelline" (1892); "Johanne" (1898). Björnson was for many years the most popular as well as the greatest Norwegian orator, and his influence as a political leader was as marked a feature of his career as his literary success.

EXTRACT FROM ADDRESS AT THE GRAVE OF OLE BULL

OLE BULL was loved,—that has been shown at his grave to-day. Ole Bull was honored; but it is more to be loved than to be honored. If we wish to understand the origin of this deep affection for Ole Bull—to understand Ole Bull himself, what he was, and what he now is for us—we must go back to the time when he first came before the public.

We were a poor and diminutive people with a great past behind us and ambitions for the future which we were unable to fulfil; so we were looked upon with scorn. We were thought incapable of intellectual independence; even the so-called best among us thought the same. A Norwegian literature was thought an impossibility, even with its then rich beginnings; the idea of an independent Norwegian school of history was something to laugh at; our language was rough and unrefined, and not to be listened to unless spoken with the Danish accent; the development of Norwegian dramatic art was something too absurd to be thought of.

In politics it was the same. We had been newly bought and sold; and the freedom which we dared to take and which we had dared both to hold and to extend, even that gave us no security. We dared not show even "official" gladness, as it could be made uncomfortable for us in high places. . . .

Then a new generation came up, bred in those first years of our national life, which had not shared the burden of its elders nor sympathized with their forbearance and silence. On the contrary, it was inspired by a feeling of resentment; it was aggressive and restless as the sea. It revelled in the morning feeling of freedom; and just at this time Ole Bull's music came as the first gleams of the sun on the mountain's summit.

Our folk melodies were just beginning to be recognized as music; the democratic element was slowly leavening the aristocracy; a national feeling was being born.

When we talk with old people of the time when Ole Bull suddenly came before the world, of how he stood before emperors and kings; of how the great opera houses of Europe were thronged to listen to his music; how he played with a wild and mysterious power, a power peculiar to himself, which was heartfelt, was Norwegian; when they read to us how his violin sang the Norwegian folk melodies while his audiences laughed and cried, and behind all rose visions of our people and our magnificent country,—one can understand the promise, the feeling of self-dependence, of strength, of pride he awakened—he first—in Norwegian hearts.

When he came home from his first tour abroad, only to see him was a feast; when he played the old airs which had lain hidden in the hearts of the people, but which had been listened to with delight by kings and princes, then young Norway felt itself lifted to the supremest height of existence. To his immortal honor, he gave us the gift which at that time we most needed—self-confidence.

It may be asked how did it happen that Ole Bull was the one set apart to accomplish this work. He came of a musical race, but that would have availed little had it not been for his burning patriotism. He was a child in the time of our war for independence, and his young voice mingled with the first hurrah for our new freedom. When he was a lad his violin sang in jubilant tones our first national songs at the student quarters of Henrik Wergeland. Patriotism was the creative power in his life. When he established the Norwegian theatre; when he supported and encouraged Norwegian art; when he gave his help to the National museum; when he played for every patriotic object; when he stretched out a helping hand, wherever he went, to his countrymen in need,—it was not so much for the person or object as for Norway. He always in all places and under all conditions felt himself our representative.

There was something näive, something jealous about his patriotism, born of the peculiar conditions of the time. But it was something for us that our "finest" man, fresh from the courts and intellectual circles of Europe, could and would go arm-in-arm with our poor beginnings which were even less "fine" than now. It was this steadfast devotion to the things in which he believed that made Ole Bull dear to the people.

When he talked about his art he used to say, that he learned to play from the Italians. That was in a measure true. The outward form, the technique, was learned in Italy, but that in his playing which touched the heart and brought smiles and tears was born in his own soul, and its direct messenger was the folk song, tinged and permeated with the love of the fatherland.

[Special translation by Charles E. Hurd.]

MACVEAGH

WAYNE MACVEAGH, a distinguished Pennsylvania lawyer and politician, was born at Phœnixville, Pennsylvania, April 19, 1833, and graduated at Yale College in the class of 1853. Three years later he was admitted to the bar, and from 1859 until 1864 he was district attorney of Chester County. During the war, when the Confederate forces threatened to invade Pennsylvania, he served as captain of infantry. In 1863 he was chairman of the Pennsylvania Republican State Committee. In 1870-71 he was minister to Turkey, and on his return served as a member of the Pennsylvania Constitutional Convention for two years. In 1877 he was head of the so-called MacVeagh Commission sent to Louisiana to adjust party troubles in that State. During the presidency of Rutherford B. Hayes he was United States attorney-general, but in 1881 he resigned and resumed the practice of his profession in Philadelphia, supporting Grover Cleveland for the presidency the following year. From 1893 until 1897 he was ambassador to Italy, and on his return settled in Washington. He was prominent in reform movements, having been chairman of the Civil Service Reform Association of Philadelphia, and also of the Indian Rights Association of that city.

IDEALS IN AMERICAN POLITICS

DELIVERED BEFORE THE PHI BETA KAPPA SOCIETY AT CAMBRIDGE MASSACHUSETTS, JUNE 27, 1901

THE yearly observance of academic festivals in America has always seemed to me to be one of the most gracious and the most useful of the time-honored customs of our national life. They bring us together in the full beauty of our midsummer, with its wealth of fragrance and of bloom; and, while persuading us to lay aside the anxious cares, the absorbing pursuits, the engrossing ambitions which so easily beset us and fill far too large a part of our daily lives, they enable us to breathe a purer and serener air, to refresh ourselves with unaccustomed joys and a nobler reach of vision, and to live through these days of June less in the spirit of the age and more in the spirit of the ages.

Such an occasion is inspiring alike to the older alumni and to the younger. It is inspiring to those of us who in serenity of spirit bring hither a long retrospect of a life of labor passed in fairly good ways and in works which, if not filled with benediction, have been at least reasonably free from harm to our fellow men.

It is inspiring also to the ardent graduates of yesterday, who are just crossing the threshold which divides youth from manhood, and have before them a long prospect of days yet to be passed, let us hope, in ways and works at least equally free from blame—a prospect now seen through

> "Magic casements opening on the foam
> Of perilous seas in faëry lands."

And such a festival at the seat of this ancient and honored university is necessarily fraught with the buoyant and generous hopefulness born of her splendid history. In the grateful shade of these old elms, surrounded by these noble halls dedicated to the culture alike of character and of intelligence, the history of Harvard unrolls itself as on a golden page as we follow the slow procession of the fruitful years from its small beginnings to its present measure of renown and usefulness.

It is indeed impossible to measure the measureless bounty of this seat of liberal learning in that long interval to America. We cannot even recount the names of her illustrious dead, the priests and the poets, the scholars and the statesmen, the jurists and the soldiers, who received here for the first time the sign of the cross upon their foreheads, consecrating them as servants of mankind unto their life's end.

This uplifting work for the nation has gone steadily on,

with ever-widening influence, to its present yearly contribution of great numbers of young men of generous training and a high sense of duty, fitted to teach by precept and by example a nobler standard of life to their less fortunate brothers; for four years spent here at that period of life when the mind is most open to elevating impressions cannot fail to imbue them with unfaltering loyalty to their alma mater, and with a noble pride in what she has been and what she has done,—in her lasting contributions to scholarship, and to literature, her generous culture, her catholic toleration of all seekers after truth, and her ineffable charm for all her sons.

It seems to me there is no better work to be done at present by an American university than to again unseal those fountains of idealism where the human spirit has so often refreshed itself when weary of a too material age, to reawaken that enthusiasm for the moral law which we have all somehow lost, and to impress upon a people essentially noble, but now too deeply absorbed in the pursuit of wealth for wealth's sake, the advantages which the cherishing of ethical ideals may bring to all of us, even to those who pride themselves, above all things, upon being practical. It is for that reason that I venture to ask you to consider, during the time at our disposal, the value of such ideals in American politics.

While we must, of course, always insist upon the one vital distinction between true and false American patriotism, recognizing only as true that which possesses the ethical spirit, and rejecting as false that which does not possess it, we must also recognize that such a subject can be properly discussed only with that liberal and catholic feeling which makes the amplest allowances for difference of opinion; and upon an academic occasion like the present all discussion should be in a spirit even more liberal and more catholic than might otherwise be necessary, crediting all others with the same patriotism we claim for ourselves, and displaying a charity satisfying the apostolic definition, which vaunteth not itself, is not easily provoked, thinketh no evil, and yet rejoiceth in the truth.

It is assuredly the part of wisdom to recognize an existing situation with equal frankness whether it happens to meet our approval or our disapproval. Among the many wise sayings of Bishop Butler none was wiser than his declaring that "things are what they are, and the consequences of them will be what they will be"; and his question, like that of Pilate, has never been answered, "Why, then, should we, as rational creatures, seek to deceive ourselves?"

There is therefore no reason why we should not cheerfully admit that the controlling consideration in the immediate present is that of money, and that the controlling aspiration of the vast majority of men who have received more or less of intellectual training is to follow Iago's advice and put money in their purses. In thus frankly confronting existing conditions it is not at all necessary to be depressed by them or to acquire "a moping melancholy."

There is, indeed, a sheer delusion cherished by unintelligent people, of which it is desirable that they should free their minds. They stupidly imagine that whoever finds fault with existing conditions in American society must necessarily think the past age better than the present; but the exact contrary is the truth. It is because we know, and are glad to know, that there has been a steady progress, alike in spiritual and material blessings, since men first lived in civilized society together, that we so earnestly desire such progress to continue.

We appreciate with cheerful thankfulness that the vast majority of mankind are now living in far happier conditions, possess far better guarantees of liberty and peace, and are more fully enjoying the indispensable conditions of any life worth living than ever before; but this conviction only makes us the more ardently desire that that progress should not now be stayed, but rather should be continued and with ever-accelerated speed, and our discontent is only with the unnecessary obstacles to such continuance and acceleration.

The men who desire the world to be better than it is contemplate with abundant pleasure the promise of the new century, opening, in spite of all its serious drawbacks, upon a brighter prospect for that religion of humanity which preceded it, and it is because they know that each succeeding century of the Christian era has been better than its predecessor that they are impatient of any apparent relaxation of that progress, and they are quite as often amused as annoyed by the very stupid apologies offered them for such relaxation.

The human spirit has in different ages and in different countries devoted itself to varying aims and objects: to religion, as in Palestine; to art and letters, as in Greece; to arms and law, as in Rome; to the aggrandizement of the Church, as in Italy in the Middle Ages; to maintaining the Protestant religion, as in Germany after the revolt of Luther; and in America to the doctrine of liberty and equality among men, ever since the landing at Jamestown; and it has been found entirely compatible with the divine order in the education of the world, and not at all disastrous to the welfare of the race, that different nations should cherish such wholly different aspirations, for the pursuit of each object has in almost every case been found to furnish a basis for further progress in good directions.

The fact, therefore, that this age is devoted to the making of money as its chief ambition need not disturb us, for it is not at all certain that any better ambition could have been found at this time for the class of men engaged in practical business. It may, indeed, well happen that their labors are laying enduring foundations for far nobler standards of conduct, of effort, and of life than we are now enjoying; and, while it is true that so far these results have not been apparent, it is equally true that it is far too soon to expect them. In saying this I do not forget that Cicero declared that a general desire of gain would ruin any wealthy and flourishing nation, but I do not forget either that Mr. Burke, a far safer guide in the philosophy of politics than Cicero, declared that the love of gain is a grand cause of prosperity to all States.

Assuming, therefore, that we must deal with conditions as they exist, and present considerations likely to be acceptable to those to whom they are addressed, I have thought it might be useful to call the attention of our men of business to the commercial value of ethical ideas in American politics. If it is possible to satisfy them that the cherishing of such ideals may be of pecuniary advantage—may be, in truth, treated as a commercial asset—they may appreciate the wisdom of ceasing their efforts to destroy them, and may be persuaded to help in the good work of maintaining them and of extending their beneficent influence.

It would, of course, be foolish to undervalue the animosity men of practical business and men of practical politics now cherish toward such ideals. They insist—and I have no reason to doubt they honestly believe—that neither the business of the world nor its politics can now be successfully carried on if any respect is to be paid to such ideals.

A prosperous man is said to have recently declared that he had a great dislike for pessimists, and when asked what kind of people they were, he replied: "The people who are always talking of the Ten Commandments and the Sermon on the Mount, when everybody of sense knows you cannot conduct business or politics with reference to them." "Anyhow," he added, "my pastor assures me they were only addressed to Jews."

It is a part of the creed of such men that the substitution of money for morals is the only wise course for practical men to pursue in these days of ardent competition and of strenuous efforts by each man to get rich faster than his fellows and at their expense; but this belief is probably in great part founded upon a total misapprehension of the character of the idealism which it is desired to recommend to their favorable consideration. They have persuaded themselves that we wish to insist upon the immediate practical application of the standards of conduct of a far-distant and imagined perfection,—that if a person invades your household and takes your coat you shall now follow him upon the highway and beg him to accept your cloak also; and if a reckless assailant smites you upon one cheek you must now offer him the other for a like blow; while if you insist upon the wickedness of unnecessary or aggressive warfare you are supposed to imply that righteous warfare, animated by a noble purpose and struggling to attain a noble end, is unjustifiable.

What we ask is nothing impracticable or unreasonable. It is only that we shall return to the ancient ways of the fathers and again enjoy the elevation of spirit which was part of their daily lives. They were, as we ought to be, far from being blind to material advantages and far enough from being willing to live as idle enthusiasts. "Give me neither property nor riches" was their prayer, with an emphasis upon "poverty." They sought, as we do, to acquire property. They meant, as we mean, to get what comfort and enjoyment they could out of the possession of the world in which they worked and worshipped, and they felt themselves, as we ought to feel ourselves, co-workers with God when "the orchard was planted and the wild vine tamed, when the English fruits had been domesticated under the shadow of savage forests, and the maize lifted its shining ranks upon the fields which had been barren."

Surely there can be nothing impracticable, nothing un-American in striving to persuade ourselves again to cherish the lofty, inspiring, transforming, ethical ideals which prevailed at the birth of our country and have illumined, as with celestial light, the fiery ridges of every battle in which her sons have died for liberty.

Unhappily there is no immediate danger even of the most distant approach to a realization of such ideals—no alarming prospect that the noble conditions of human life such ideals encourage will too soon brighten the earth. They will probably always remain unattainable; but they are none the less always worth striving for and hoping for, and it is as certain as anything can be that to keep such ethical ideals constantly before the minds of the plain people born in America, as well as before the minds of the hordes of untaught immigrants who are flocking to our shores from every quarter of the globe, will have a tendency to soften their asperities, to lessen their animosities, and to encourage them to bear with greater patience the bitter and ever-growing contrast between the lives of idleness and luxury which we and those dear to us are privileged to lead, and the lives of labor and poverty which they and those equally dear to them are condemned to endure; for there is now no longer any pathway open by which many men who live upon the labor of their own hands can hope to pass into the class of those who live upon the labor of other men's hands.

The stock certificate and the corporate bond, in return for their many conveniences, have destroyed that possibility, as well as wrought other serious evils to society in divorcing the possession of wealth not only from all moral responsibility for the ways in which it is created, but even from all knowledge of the men and women whose toil creates it.

It is not difficult to understand why the free government under which we are privileged to live especially needs the influence of ethical ideals in the conduct of life, or why we may possibly incur danger if we are without the protecting and conservative influence of such ideals in that not-distant future when we may find them indispensable; for the essential difference which separates American democracy from the governments which have preceded it, as well as from those which are contemporary with it, is in the last analysis an ethical difference.

The three hundred Greeks who on that long summer day held the pass by the sea against the Persian invader were seeking to hold it for Greece alone. The splendid valor of the Roman soldiers who encompassed Cæsar as with triple lines of steel on the day he overcame the Nervii was a valor displayed for Rome alone. Even the long, heroic struggle of the Netherlands against the despotism of Philip, perhaps the most heroic struggle in history, was primarily a struggle for their own liberties.

The same absence of any ethical ideal runs through all the aggressions of the great Powers of Europe. In the seizure of India by the agency of Clive and Hastings, and the cynical acceptance of the unutterable infamies they perpetrated, as well as in exploiting that unhappy country to-day, though decimated by famine and desolated by the plague, there is no inconsistency with any standard Great Britain has proclaimed.

The same absence of inconsistency is observable in the forcible partition of Poland under the auspices of what was blasphemously called the Holy Alliance; in the annexation of Nice and Savoy by France; in the annexation by Germany of a part of Denmark and of two great provinces of France; in the steady and vast territorial aggrandizements of Russia; in the partition of Africa which has just been accomplished; or in the partition of China, which is in process of accomplishment.

Nothing can fairly be said to have been done, in any one of these conquests, incompatible with the avowed doctrines of those great predatory governments, for they never proclaimed an evangel of the rights of man, they never incurred any obligations to use the power they possessed for the advancement of the welfare or the promotion of the liberties of mankind.

It was permitted to each, without furnishing any basis for the charge of inconsistency, to rob any weaker people of its territory, to impose its own absolute and arbitrary will upon any weaker race upon which it possessed the physical power to impose it, and to take whatever such a people had of value for themselves.

But it would be very unwise for us to forget that American democracy has had a wholly different history. Not only was its inspiring and directing force the greatest ethical movement in the history of the human race, the struggle for civil and religious freedom, but it may be said without exaggeration to owe its very existence to it.

Lord Bacon, in the true marshalling of the sovereign

degrees of honor, assigns the first place to the founders of empires; and of all such founders none deserve more generous praise than those who came hither as from the fires of civil and religious persecution in the Old World to lay broad and deeper foundations of civil and religious freedom in the world just then offered to them for their new and far-reaching experiment.

From almost every civilized nation some of its best citizens sought safety in exile from their old homes in the wilderness of the New World, where they were free to strive at least for the realization of their belief in a common brotherhood of man on earth and a common fatherhood of God in heaven. No doubt with this ennobling creed there was mingled something of the dross of the weakness of human nature, but this was but as an atom in the great mass and had no shaping influence upon the fortune or the destiny of America; for the vast multitudes who come hither were actuated by the desire to secure for all other men the same measure of liberty they sought for themselves, the liberty conferred by equality of membership in a free church and equality of citizenship in a free State.

It is not at all necessary to take an alarmist view of the problems awaiting solution here in order to insist upon the practical and commercial value of the ethical ideals which have heretofore stood the nation in such good stead. Macaulay was not a profound student of comparative politics, and his well-known prophecy of the evil days which await the republic need not greatly disquiet us, although part of his prophecy has already been verified by the result. But Mr. Webster was a wise statesman, perhaps our wisest, and a profound student of our system of government, and he has left for our instruction this grave and weighty warning:

"The freest government would not be long acceptable if the tendency of the laws was to create a rapid accumulation of property in few hands, and to render the great mass of the population dependent and penniless. . . . In the nature of things, those who have not property and see their neighbors possess much more than they think them to need cannot be favorable to laws made for the protection of property. When this class becomes numerous it grows clamorous. It looks upon property as its prey and plunder, and is naturally ready at all times for violence and revolution."

Now, it is at least quite possible that in the not-distant future American politics may transform Mr. Webster's warning into history, for our electorate is already beginning to be divided, and must, in obedience to the law of social evolution, continue more and more to be divided, by that sharp cleavage which separates those who are contented with their lot from those who are discontented with their lot.

Under whatever disguises, called by whatever names, inheriting or seizing whatever partisan organizations, the alignment of the two great political divisions of American voters, who will sooner or later struggle against each other for the possession of the government, will inevitably be upon the basis I have named. The party of the contented will be ranged under one banner, and the party of the discontented will be ranged under the other, and that alignment will steadily develop increasing sharpness of division until the party of the discontented, being the majority, has obtained the control of the government to which, under our system, they are entitled; and then they will be sure to remodel the present system for the distribution of wealth, unless we have previously done so, upon bases wiser and more equitable than those now existing.

The one party will be, under whatever name, the party

of capital; and the other party will be, under whatever name, the party of labor. If any doubt had existed upon this subject among men accustomed seriously to reflect upon political problems, it ought to have disappeared in view of the developments of the last two presidential elections and of the present growing tendency alike of capital more and more to consolidate itself in great masses as in preparation for the coming struggle, and of the brotherhood of American labor more and more to consolidate itself in one organization in like preparation.

Ominous signs are indeed almost daily discernable that those leaders of confederated labor who are really loyal to it and are not purchasable by the party of capital have discerned that the true remedy for what seems to them the present unjust inequality in the distribution of wealth is through legislation.

If yesterday they foolishly resorted to attempts to overawe the nominees of the party of capital, sitting as legislators, by a display of force and threats of violence, by to-morrow they will probably have learned that the ballot in America, while not so noisy, is far more peremptory than the dynamite bomb. It does not explode, but it controls; and its control will be as resistless as fate if the party of labor decides to clothe all its demands, as it has already clothed many, in acts of legislation, for then will occur what the Duke of Wellington foresaw, "a revolution under the forms of law."

My purpose, therefore, is to point out, without the slightest bitterness, to the members of the contented class, the commercial value of ethical ideals as the safest source of the political aspirations of the majority of our people and the most conservative influence in our national life, and also to point out to them the grave dangers, from a business standpoint, in these days of possible conflict between capital and labor, of continuing to substitute money for morals as the permanent and controlling force in American politics.

In pointing out these dangers I accept to the fullest extent the proposition that this is an age of business, and I am quite willing to admit that the moral law is difficult of application to existing conditions. It is very apparent that difficulty is increased by the conduct of other nations which are now controlled by a consideration only of their material interests, the securing by force of new markets, the expansion of trade by war, the subjection of weaker peoples to the will of the stronger, and the ultimate partition, by blood and iron, of the whole habitable globe.

For us to enter upon a like course of expansion seems to many devout clergymen, to many successful politicians, and to many true patriots, our wisest policy. The gravity and the suddenness of our change of views in these matters is fitly illustrated by the recent voyage of capitalists of New York to England to indulge in expressions of sympathy and promises of alliance with a government which is now maintaining in the Transvaal camps of concentration as brutal and as inexcusable as those of Weyler in Cuba, the detestation of whose horrors only three years ago greatly helped to drive us headlong into war with Spain.

I am not aware that history offers another example of so grave a change of opinion in so short a time; but I cannot help believing that the destruction and denial of ethical ideals, so far as regards American democracy, is very poor religion, very poor business, and very poor politics.

The first ethical ideal which it seems to me it would be wise for us, even from the point of view of the stock exchange, to guard most zealously just now, is the ideal condition of society with which President McKinley closed his congratulations upon the opening of the exposition at Buffalo,—that of peace on earth and good will to men; for it may well happen that the safety of our institutions requires that the masses of our people shall continue to cherish the ethical ideals of Christianity, and that whoever lessens respect for them inevitably weakens the reverence of the majority of voters for the principles upon which our government is founded.

I observe with especial sorrow that many Protestant clergymen mistakenly suppose that they can safely substitute at this day and in our country the teaching of Mohammed for the teaching of Christ. We all know the temptations to which such clergymen are exposed.

It is so much more comfortable to "swim with the tide," and it is so much more certain that the incomes on which themselves and their families are dependent for the comforts and luxuries of life will share in the commercial prosperity of the country if the doctrines preached by them and advocated in their religious journals recognize that the making of money is the first duty of man in the new century, and that keeping one's self unspotted from the world, so far from being, as was formerly supposed, true religion and undefiled, is a foolish and sentimental expression, incapable of application in the rough world in which we live, where each man's duty is to take care of himself.

Knowing the despotism the practical men in the pews exercise over the pulpit in such matters, we ought to think with great charity, not only of the clergymen who fail to preach Christianity and who substitute Mohammedanism in its place, but also of the missionaries who, in distant lands and surrounded by traders and soldiers, have persuaded themselves that the robbery and murder of weaker peoples, with their attendant horrors, cannot really be helped in an age so practical as ours and so determined to pursue only practical ends, and that therefore such crimes are no longer to be unsparingly condemned; but, after making all the allowance the most abundant charity can suggest, it will still remain a grave and menacing peril to American respect for the moral law if clergymen are permitted without rebuke to preach the righteousness of unnecessary or aggressive warfare, the killing of weaker peoples in order to reduce them to subjection, and the robbing them of their possessions.

Indeed, our silence in presence of the appalling and even unnamable atrocities recently perpetrated in China by the nations calling themselves Christian is a terrible blow dealt to the faith of common men in a religion whose professors thus allow its fundamental principles to be trampled under foot without a word of protest or reprobation; and if the faith of our laboring people in the ethical ideals of Christianity is once destroyed by its professors here, as its professors destroyed it among the laboring people of France a hundred years ago, there will be lost one of the most valuable and conservative influences we possess,—an influence which it is not too much to say may yet prove to be absolutely indispensable to the preservation of that respect for law and order upon which, in the last resort, American society must depend for its peace.

Let us therefore ardently hope that the true American ideal of peace on earth and good will to men will again take possession of our hearts, and enable us, clergymen and laymen alike, to believe that it is not robbery, or conquest, or slaughter, or expansion, or even wealth, but righteousness only, which exalteth a nation; for if, in a free state like ours, you substitute the Mohammedan ideal, which is now so popular, of war on earth and the subjection of the weak to the strong, you help to undermine the very ground upon which respect for private property, when gathered in great masses in few hands and often displayed in vulgar and offensive forms, must ultimately rest.

If fighting and killing are to be encouraged; if those who indulge in them are to be especially honored, and if oppression of the weak is to be cherished, it will be difficult to prevent the class of the discontented from familiarizing themselves too thoroughly with fighting and killing, and from learning to cherish in their hearts a desire to oppress their weaker but more wealthy fellow citizens.

It seems to me quite too plain for dispute that no single member of a weaker race can be killed; no hut of such a race, however humble, can be burned; no one can be selected for special honor for his part in such pitiful warfare,—without its helping to light the torch which starts the fire by which some hapless negro is to be burned at the stake in our own country, not only in defiance but in contempt of law, and all such acts must be surely followed by greater insecurity for the surplus wealth which the contented class possesses.

We all read the other day that in a community almost within sight of Wall Street, where the cruel plot for the killing of the king of Italy was hatched, plots as cruel are now hatching for the killing of more crowned heads of the Old World; and I beg you to believe that that insensate rage against the sense of inequality and of pretended superiority to their fellows which these maddened members of the working classes attribute to crowned heads to-day may easily be transferred to-morrow to those of our citizens whose distinction rests upon the possession of too abundant riches; and for that reason, while the Mohammedan ideal of war on earth and the subjection of the weak to the strong must always lessen the security of private property in America, the Christian ideal of peace on earth and good will to men will always increase it.

It is quite possible there may also be great commercial value for us at the present time in the ethical ideal that all men are born equal, and equally entitled to life, liberty, and the pursuit of happiness. I fully recognize the present unpopularity of this ideal. I know that to declare one's belief in it is to expose oneself to the dreadful charge of disloyalty; but as in matters of religion American democracy rested at its birth upon the message of the herald angels, so in politics it rested at its birth upon the doctrine of the equality of men.

It is true that doctrine was not formulated in words until the necessity arose for binding the scattered colonies together in their effort to assert their right to be an independent nation; but it was an essential part of the very atmosphere which the first settlers breathed when they landed on these shores. There never was a single step taken of any enduring character toward civil government in the colonies which was not, consciously or unconsciously, based upon it.

From Massachusetts Bay to Georgia many theories of government found expression, and there were "many men of many minds" engaged in the work of settling the continent; but through all instinctively ran one great underlying ethical doctrine—that of equality of political rights.

Subsequently, no doubt, the importation of slaves from Africa, and to a much greater degree the inventions which made slave labor profitable, colored the judgments of many

Southern men and induced them to believe that that doctrine was inapplicable to a weaker people of a different color and from a different clime, and that they and their descendants, even if born here, might be rightly held in slavery forever.

Indeed, many of the statements we now read of the necessity of the strong and wise governing the weak and ignorant are almost literal reproductions of the arguments advanced by the slaveholders of the South in defence of slavery just preceding the outbreak of the Civil War. That divergence from our original ideal produced the pregnant sayings of Mr. Lincoln, "A house divided against itself cannot stand," and its corollary, "This nation cannot permanently endure half slave and half free." He saw clearly that American democracy must rest, if it continues to exist, upon the ethical ideal which presided over its birth—that of the absolute equality of all men in political rights.

I am well aware that it is supposed that exigencies now exist which require us to disavow that ideal, and to abandon the doctrine of equality we inherited, and to which Mr. Lincoln so frequently expressed his devotion. We are asked to take a new departure, to turn our backs upon the old doctrine, and to declare that our fathers were mistaken when they brought forth a nation conceived in liberty and dedicated to such an impracticable proposition as the equality of all men before the law. We are told that the exigencies of modern business and modern trade require a wholly different ideal to be set before the new century; that our present duty is to conquer any weaker people whose territory we covet, and to subject them to such government as in our opinion will best promote our profit and their welfare.

Of course many of the Southern people, brought up in the

belief that the subjection of the weak to the will of the strong was a divine institution, eagerly welcome our apparent conversion to their creed; and while I do not question the excellence of the motives of these new guides in American patriotism, I venture to warn you that if you follow them you abandon your best heritage,—that of being a beacon light and a blessing to all the oppressed of the earth.

Great popularity no doubt just now attaches to money, and great unpopularity to morals, on the ground that money is modern and practical, while morals are antiquated and impracticable; and, as conclusive arguments, they tell us that England has destroyed two republics in the interests of the capitalists who own the gold and diamond mines of South Africa; that Germany has seized a vast territory in China; that France has appropriated Madagascar; that Russia is benevolently assimilating Finland and absorbing Manchuria; and that Japan is casting longing eyes upon Korea; and they insist that, unless we bestir ourselves to like measures, we will be found to be laggards in the race of to-day, which is a race for new markets won by war, for the exploiting of weaker peoples, for larger armies, for ever-increasing navies, for expanding trade, and for greater wealth.

I confess I should have thought the growth of our own beloved country in material wealth and prosperity in the last thirty years of unbroken peace and of amity with all mankind had more than satisfied any avarice which could have found a place even in the dreams of civilized men. The marvellous story of that material progress is still dazzling the imaginations of all serious economists, and it is literally true of it, "State the figures however high, while the dispute exists the exaggeration ends."

The results of the thirty years from 1870 to 1900 prove beyond all question, and even beyond all cavil, that in order far to excel, not only all nations of the past, but also all nations of the present, in growth of agriculture, of manufactures, of commerce, of exports and of imports, and, above all, in population, it is not necessary to step beyond our own great, rich, and powerful country to subdue any weaker people, of whatever color, in any quarter of the globe; so that we are urged to betray the loftiest and noblest traditions of our history without even the poor excuse of needing the money we hope to make by such betrayal of the inspiring doctrine which Jefferson formulated and for which Washington fought. Those thirty years demonstrated that in order to be a world Power we need not be a robber nation.

There is still another ethical ideal which may soon prove to be of very great commercial value in American politics—the ideal of the citizen, whether in or out of office, exhibiting moral courage in dealing with important public questions. However much we may differ on other subjects, I cannot doubt we all recognize and regret that we are just now exhibiting a very pitiful moral cowardice in shirking such questions,—a cowardice which may be fraught with great evils, for it is still true that unsettled questions have no pity for the repose of nations.

It is somewhat trying to the patience of the most patient to listen to the noisy and senseless rhetoric which seeks to hide our lack of moral courage by extolling that mere physical courage which all men of the fighting races and many brutes possess, and which flamed just as high in the breasts of the conscript youth of France, fighting to subdue other kingdoms to be trodden under foot by their imperial master, as it flamed in the breasts of their fathers, rushing to fling themselves upon embattled Europe in defence of the liberties of France. The physical courage in both cases was just the same, and will never be excelled.

The only difference was an ethical difference: the fathers were fighting in a just cause, and the sons were fighting in an unjust cause. The truth is that physical courage has always been the most commonplace of virtues, and could aways be bought at a very cheap price, so that it has become an unfailing proof of decadence for any people to become hysterical over exhibitions of animal courage without regard to the moral quality of the service in which it was displayed or of the comparative weakness of the adversary.

Just the contrary is true of moral courage. It is among the rarest of virtues, and its services are of far greater value in the democratic ages than ever before. Indeed, the days may not be distant when the existence of law and order in America may depend upon it, for it may be found that it, and it alone, can protect us from the dangers which Mr. Webster believed would follow our present condition, "a rapid accumulation of property in few hands."

For that reason the commercial value of such courage in a government by the majority can hardly be over-estimated; and surely, if we are to find it a bulwark of defence in our day of need, we ought to be now commending it by our example, showing how really brave men face grave problems of government and set themselves, as brave men should, to finding the best possible solution of them.

It is perhaps inevitable, but it is none the less to be regretted, that a distinct lowering of moral standards should follow a state of war, inducing us to cherish the delusion that if we talk loudly enough and boast foolishly enough of our physical prowess by sea and land, and give our time and thought only to warlike actions and preparations, as we have been doing for the last three years, all serious moral and domestic questions will somehow settle themselves.

Such a delusion is equally childish and cowardly, and it is only necessary to glance at such questions to discover that instead of settling themselves they are daily growing in gravity, and how unwise it is, instead of facing them, to be actually running away from them. It is certainly in no spirit of criticism, and with no feeling of censoriousness, that I thus call your attention to the corroding influence of war and commercialism upon moral courage, but simply because a recrudescence of moral courage in dealing with these problems closely concerns the present peace and the future welfare of our beloved country.

As one example, take our attitude toward the corrupt use of money in our elections and in our representative bodies. Even the dullest intelligence must see that if we continue to destroy, as for some time past we have been destroying, the belief of the majority of our fellow citizens that elections are honestly conducted and laws are honestly made, we are destroying the best possible basis for the security of private property; for there can be no reverence for law where laws and law makers are bought with money, and I fear we are rapidly destroying the possibility of such reverence in the minds of the masses of our countrymen.

We ought never to forget that in democratic governments the black flag of corruption is very likely to be followed by the red flag of anarchy. Yet we close our eyes in sheer cowardice to this evil and the danger it is creating, and we gravely pretend to each other that it does not exist, while we all well know that it does exist. Representatives of vast accumulations of property, guardians of great trusts, individuals profiting by the opportunity offered here for suddenly acquiring colossal fortunes, and even those of us who have no fortunes, have not hesitated to give whatever money is needed to be applied to the purchase of the electorate and, when necessary, of the representative bodies elected by them.

Our municipal governments have long been a by-word of hissing and of shame, and they have been so because we decided we could make money by corrupting them. We have given freely to assist in electing persons known to be ready at the first opportunity to betray the sacred trust of the people committed to their keeping, in order to put the spoils of such betrayal in our own pockets. Many State legislatures have become equally objects of contempt and derision for the same reason. Then these corrupting influences have not hesitated to advance a step farther and lay their hand upon members of both branches of the national legislature until at last, so callous have we become upon the subject, that, if the case I am about to imagine occurred, I venture to assert that no earnest protest would be made by men of our class against its consummation.

Suppose an ambitious man, desiring to obtain the only success now deemed important in American life, should set himself to the work of making a large sum of money, and, having in any one of the ways now open to such efforts, succeeded beyond his hopes, he looked around to see what other distinction was open to him wherein he could use a portion of his gains so as bring to himself the most gratification; and that he should deside that he would give himself most pleasure by debauching the electorate of a State and thereby securing for himself a seat in the Senate of the United States.

Suppose, also, that he had so far imbibed the present American spirit as to feel quite sure that there was no need for secrecy in these operations, but that they were rather a subject of legitimate pride; and that in the course of time he had so far succeeded that only a minority of citizens and legislators of his own party stood between him and the realization of his desire, but that the members of that minority proved to be incorruptible, either by the baser temptation of money or in the more plausible form of public office, and that, continuing bravely to stand for the purity of American politics and the honor of their native State, they succeeded in defeating the success of such debauchery,—would their conduct be received with the applause it deserved?

If not, I venture to say that it is very poor politics for the party of capital thus openly and cynically to notify the party of labor that no respect is due to law or to the makers of law; that it is wholly a question of money and not at all a question of morals; that the right to make laws is now as legitimate a subject of bargain and sale as that of any merchandise, and that therefore nobody ought to pay any respect to law except where it happens to comport with his pecuniary advantage to do so.

I may be needlessly concerned about the matter, but I confess, in spite of my ardent Americanism and my confidence in the law-abiding spirit of my countrymen, I am disturbed when I see what I regard as one of the best protections of the future thus openly undermined and destroyed, while the moral cowardice of those of us who do not ourselves corrupt anybody prevents our uttering a word of protest against it.

Upon the ground of expediency alone, regarding it only as an element in our commercial expansion, in our growth of trade, in our increase of wealth, in the prosperity of our stock exchanges—even from this standpoint it is assuredly great practical folly to destroy the ethical ideal of law, as we are striving so earnestly to do.

There is another very grave problem which we are also refusing to consider, and by which refusal the ethical ideal of law is also being destroyed. It is the problem presented by our negro population, now approaching ten millions of souls. We gave them the suffrage, and we have allowed some of them to be killed for possessing it. We appointed some of them to office, and have stood meekly by when they were shot for having our commission in their hands. They are being burnt before our eyes without even a pretence of trial. We are allowing State after State openly, even contemptuously, to nulify a solemn amendment of the constitution enacted for their protection, to secure which we poured out our treasure without limit and shed the blood of our sons like water.

All of us, whether in public office or in private station, now concur in trying to ignore the existence of any such problem at our doors, while, laughing like the Roman augurs in each other's faces, we indulge in self-congratulations about the blessings we are carrying to another ten millions of dark-skinned races in far-distant lands.

I fully appreciate the difficulty in finding the best solution of this awful problem, but I do insist that our evasion of it is utterly unworthy of American manhood. It is not fair to the men and women of the South to leave them to settle it as they please, so long as we have duties connected with it; and it is useless to suppose that a problem involving ten millions of people is being solved by a few industrial schools fitting an inconsiderable fraction of the youth of both sexes for occupations most of which they will not be allowed to follow, and thereby unfitting them for the only occupations in which they will be at liberty to earn their bread; and it is equally useless for us to pretend that by making contributions to such institutions we have done our whole duty in meeting the test this problem presents of our courage alike as citizens and as men.

We ought in the North as in the South to face our responsibilities toward these descendants of a people we brought here against their will and solely for our own profit, and we ought seriously to discuss and determine, in Congress and out of it, what is the best possible relation to be established between them and us; and then we ought to have the courage to give that relation the sanction of law and to see that such law is respected and obeyed.

Such treatment of this problem would be a far greater security for our future peace than many new regiments and many new ships of war. At present the condition of the whole subject is lawlessness, and such a condition is disgraceful to us all and is fraught with the serious dangers which lawlessness always brings in its train—as the exact opposite of the ethical ideal of law.

Indeed, the ethical ideal of the legislator and the citizen, as men zealous to know their public duty and brave enough to do it, is also rapidly being destroyed by our failing even to attempt to deal seriously and adequately with many other problems now imperatively demanding our attention. Among these problems are the reform of our present shameless and corrupt pension legislation, costing us over $150,000,000 a year, although a quarter of a century ago it was demonstrated by the tables of mortality that $35,000,000 was the maximum sum which could properly be expended for legitimate pensions; the reform of much other equally shameless and corrupt legislation, of which a fair specimen is that known as the river and harbor bill; the courageous maintenance and extension of the merit system in appointments to subordinate positions under the government; the reform of the present system of taxation, so as to make wealth bear its proper share of the cost of government; the subjecting of the great monopolies which now control so much of the business of the country and so many of the necessaries of life to inspection and control by public authority; the devising of some just system of preventing the rapidly increasing conflicts between employers and employed; and the establishing of just and proper qualifications alike for immigrants and for electors.

It certainly would tend to make private property far more secure in America if the less fortunate majority of our population saw us of the more fortunate minority giving courage and time and thought to efforts to solve these problems and others like them, and thereby to lessen some of the evils which in many cases bear so heavily and so unjustly upon the poor.

Indeed, the influence of ethical ideals upon American democracy ought to be considered of value if only because the cultivation of such ideals will inevitably tend to make more really patriotic all classes of our countrymen, for such ideals lift us all above the unsatified standards of public duty with which we are vainly trying to content ourselves.

They bring us into the air of a higher and purer love of country, and they set us face to face with the early American spirit in its best estate. In such communion a sordid and selfish public opinion, with low methods to mean ends, tends to disappear, and a cowardly and corrupt public life becomes less possible.

You may not agree with me, but I am sure you will pardon

me for speaking of what seem to me to be the grave evils of the present tendencies of our national life and the serious dangers which, because of them, threaten the future of this government of ours, which our fathers sought to rest upon the enduring basis of liberty regulated by law,—a government which has the devotion of all our hearts to such degree that to keep it strong and pure and free we would all gladly lay down our lives; and while we must never despair of the republic, we must never cease our efforts to make it more worthy of the greatness of the opportunity offered it,—that of the leadership of the nations toward a civilization more peaceful, more serene, and more humane than the world has ever known.

Meanwhile it is consoling to know that, notwithstanding our failure to discharge our civic duties, many of the currents of our national life flow smoothly on, for the daily and obscure labors of the vast majority of our fellow citizens continue year after year in all the different phases of our national existence, and the laborers themselves have been sowing and reaping, working steadily at the tasks appointed them, taking the sunshine and the rain, mutely enduring the sufferings and the burdens given them to bear, and quitting themselves worthily as good men and women ought to do; and that daily confronting of the daily task, and doing it with patience, contentment, and courage, is as true to-day as ever; while it is also true that the recompense of such deserving labors, while less proportionately, is actually far greater in all measures, material and spiritual, than ever before, so that after all abatement we may regard the past with abundant gratitude and the future with absolute confidence, while on the threshold of the new century it is still true that the happiest of political fortunes is to be an American citizen, and that fortune is sure to grow happier "with the process of the suns."

The present paralysis of our moral courage; our present cowardly tolerance of loathsome corruption and its kindred evils, which seem seriously to threaten our peace; our present animal lust for blood; and the general degradation of the national spirit we are here considering,—will prove to be only temporary evils and will soon pass away, for the American conscience is not dead, but sleepeth, and even if we do not, our children will return to the old ways and the old faith.

Let me repeat once more for your encouragement and my own those inspired words of the first great American: "The nation shall under God have a new birth of freedom, and government of the people by the people and for the people shall not perish from the earth."

I am very grateful to this learned society for the repeated expression of its desire that I should address it. This year your invitation overtook me in the South, where—

"By the beached margent of the sea"

—I had just been reading a tale, the scene of which was laid in Italy, and cherishing the illusion that I was again standing for a moment on "the parapet of an old villa built on the Alban hills." Below I seem to see—

—"olive vineyards and pine plantations sink slope after slope, fold after fold, to the Campagna, and beyond the Campagna, along the whole shining land of the west, the sea met the sunset, while to the north a dim and scattered whiteness, rising from the plain, was—Rome."

And then, turning the leaves in the hope of finding another familiar scene, I was surprised to read these words:

"There are symbols and symbols. That dome of St. Peter's yonder makes my heart beat, because it speaks so much—half the history of our race. But I remember another symbol, those tablets in Memorial Hall to the Harvard men that fell in the war—that wall, those names, that youth and death, they remain as the symbol of the other great majesty in the world—one is religion and the other is country."

Reading those words, I seemed to hear again the illustrious laureate of your illustrious dead, who gave their youth for liberty, and standing here they seem indeed to—

—" come transfigured back,
Secure from change in the high-hearted ways,
Beautiful evermore, and with the rays
Of morn on their white shields of expectation."

In the spirit of their great sacrifice let us all cherish, in cheerfulness and in hopefulness an abiding devotion to both symbols,—that of religion and that of country; and let us labor together to the end that all the elevating influences which wait upon civilization may be more widely and generally diffused among all classes of our countrymen, and that we may all more ardently cherish the ethical idealism which seeks after peace and liberty, after equality and fraternity, and after respect and reverence for law.

In these ways, and in others we know not of, our American system of social and political life, by far the best ever yet enjoyed upon earth, may be placed upon the broad and enduring basis of true religion and true patriotism, and then at last the nation long foretold may appear, whose foundations are laid in fair colors and whose borders are of pleasant stones, and to it the promise of the prophet may be redeemed: " All their children shall be taught of the Lord, and great shall be the peace of their children."

DAWSON

SAMUEL EDWARD DAWSON, a prominent Canadian printer and author, was born in Halifax, June 1, 1833, and was educated at McCulloch's school in that city—commencing his business of bookseller and stationer at Montreal in partnership with his father. He was one of the founders of the "Dominion Bank Company," 1879, and one of the promoters of the "Montreal News Company," 1880. Appointed a member of the Board of Protestant School Commissioners, Montreal, 1878, he became also a member of the Board of Arts and Manufactures of the Province of Quebec, and was subsequently for some years president of that body, and likewise secretary to the Art Association. Dr. Dawson was one of the earliest contributors to the "Canadian Monthly Magazine," and has written many essays and articles on literary and historic subjects for the Athenæum Club, the Montreal "Gazette," the Montreal "Star," the Toronto "Week," and other well-known journals. Of separate works from his pen, the most important is "A Study of Lord Tennyson's Poem 'The Princess,'" (1882; 2d ed., 1884), which has been pronounced "the best and most appreciative study of the poem that has anywhere appeared." The preface to the last edition contains a long and interesting letter from the veteran Laureate, which "throws some light upon some important literary questions regarding the manner and method of the poet's working," and repudiates the charge of conscious imitation or plagiarism. Lord Tennyson truthfully described the "Study" as "an able and thoughtful essay." Dr. Dawson has also written two able monographs on the voyages of the Cabots and the land-fall of 1497, which were read before the Royal Society of Canada, of which honorable body he was elected a Fellow in 1893. In 1890 he received the degree of Litt. D. from Laval University, and was appointed "Queen's Printer, and Controller of Stationery of Canada" on November 7, 1891. He still fills the office as "King's Printer." It may be added that in 1881 he was appointed a delegate to Washington on the subject of "International Copyright."

THE PROSE WRITERS OF CANADA

[Address prepared for the American Library Association and delivered at Montreal, June 11, 1900. The fact that it was written for the librarians of America will account for the line of thought running through the address; because, outside of a few great institutions, few Canadian books are found in the libraries of the United States.]

IT is not possible in the compass of one lecture to give an adequate account of the prose-writers of Canada. In the first place there is the difficulty of dealing with a bi-lingual literature, and then there is the difficulty of separating

MARK TWAIN

that which deserves mention from the current mass of printed communication. When one is called upon—in this age of newspapers and magazines—to decide as to what is and what is not prose literature, the difficulty is enhanced by the fact that some of our best prose-writers have never published a single detached volume.

In a general review such as this it will be profitable to inquire into the circumstances under which Canadian literature originated and by which it was directed into its actual channels, when we will at once perceive that, with reference to the history of the other nations of America, Canada is both young and old. Jamestown, the first English settlement on this continent, was founded in 1607. It has been desolate for two hundred years, but Quebec—founded in 1608, only one year later—is still flourishing.

Besides being brave soldiers and skilful seamen, both Samuel de Champlain and Captain John Smith were authors and led the way in English and French prose-writing in America; but there was a break in the continuity of development in the north, while in the south the colony of Massachusetts became the centre of an intellectual life which, though it flowed in a narrow channel, was intense and uninterrupted.

Canadian literature and Canadian history open with the works of Samuel de Champlain. Champlain was an author in the fullest sense of the word; for he even illustrated his own works and drew excellent maps which he published with them. His works include not only his voyages in Acadia and Canada, but his previous voyage to the West Indies and his description of Mexico. He wrote also short treatises on navigation and map-making which are still useful to explain early cartography. The edition of his works published at

Quebec in 1870, under the auspices of Laval University, is a monument of the scholarship of the Abbé Laverdière, its editor, and of the generosity of its publisher. A librarian need no longer spend money upon original editions, for this is the most complete of all, and it is, besides, the most creditable specimen of the printer's art ever published in Canada.

From the time of Champlain down to the conquest in 1759 learned and cultivated men, ecclesiastics for the most part, wrote in and about Canada; but their books were published in Europe. Marc Lescarbot, a companion of Champlain in Acadia, wrote, in French, a history of New France and enticed "Les Muses de la Nouvelle France" to sing beside the rushing tides of the Bay of Fundy.

Then came the long series of Jesuit Relations, the books of Father Le Clercq, the Latin history of Du Creux, the learned work of Father Lafiteau, the letters of Marie Guyart, the Huron Dictionary and the History of Father Sagard, the Travels of Hennepin, the general treatise of Bacqueville de La Potherie, and the works of Father Charlevoix, still the great resource of writers on Canadian subjects.

There were many others. There was De Tonti—never since Jonathan was there friendship so devoted as his was to La Salle. There was Denys—the capable and enterprising governor of Cape Breton; and Boucher—the plain colonist from the frontier post of Three Rivers (then beset with savage Iroquois) who stood up before the Great King and pleaded the cause of the despairing colony; and then, lest we become too serious, we have that frivolous young officer, the Baron de Lahontan, who paid off the pious priests of Montreal for tearing leaves out of his naughty pagan books by telling slanderous stories of all the good people of Canada.

But this literature, while considerable in extent, was not

indigenous to the soil, although in quality it was, perhaps, superior to that of the English colonies. There were educational institutions and teaching orders and cultivated people; but education did not reach the mass. A printing-press was set up at Cambridge, Massachusetts, in the year 1639, but one hundred and twenty years later, when Canada passed under British rule, there was not one printing-press in the whole of New France. Even the card money was hand-written, and the Ordonnances—a sort of government debentures passing current as money—were printed in France. There was in New France a polite and cultivated society; but the literature which existed was a reflex of the culture of Old France—of the France of the Bourbon kings. This jealousy of the press in Canada is very remarkable, because there was at least one printing-press in Mexico in 1539, and in Peru in 1586.

Upon a people thus socially organized the English conquest fell with great force, for, at the peace in 1763, when New France was definitely ceded, a large number of the educated laymen emigrated to France and left the people without their natural leaders.

I am aware that this has been recently disputed; but I am loath to believe that Bibaud, Garneau, and above all the conscientious and judicious Abbé Ferland, can be in error. The truth lies probably between the two extremes, and it will be safer to say that those who had any concern with the French government or army, or who had any claims upon or connection with the French court, emigrated. Now, when we consider that the government was despotic, and that there was no semblance of free institutions to afford an outlet for independent energy or ambition, we will recognize the effect of such an emigration. It is to the honor of the clergy that they did not abandon their charge. Bowing to circumstances beyond their control, they severed their connection with their motherland; and, if French literature in Canada now breathes with a life all its own, it is due to the Church which sustained it in its time of sore discouragement.

Literature could not flourish under such conditions; moreover, French and English Canadians both had yet to undergo many trials and many political and military experiences. These they shared in common; for in those days intermarriages were frequent, and the two races understood each other better than they do now. Was it because the age of newspapers had not come?

The English who first came to Canada did not come in pursuit of literature; and, besides, the air was charged with electricity; for the treaty of peace had scarcely been ratified when the Stamp Act was passed. In the ensuing struggle, after some hesitation, the new subjects of England sided with her; for, in the much maligned Quebec Act, she had dealt justly, and even kindly, with them, and they rallied to her support. The war swept to the walls of Quebec, and yet the commissioners of the Continental Congress could not sweep the province into the continental union. Even the astute Franklin, in whose hands Oswald, and Hartley, and Lord Shelburne were as wax, and who was able to outwit even a a statesman like Vergennes, was foiled at Montreal by the polite but inflexible resolution of the French-Canadian clergy and gentry.

The tide of invasion receded, and peace came at last—but not repose; for with peace came the sorrowful procession of proscribed refugees who laid the foundations of English Canada. United Empire Loyalists they were called, and United Empire Loyalists are their descendants to the present day. Well is it for us they were educated men; for the institutions their fathers had helped to found had to be left behind; and they set their faces to the unbroken wilderness where the forest came down to the water's edge, where the only roads were Indian trails or paths made by wild animals through the thickets. The time for literature had not come; for there were farms to be cleared, and roads and bridges and churches and schoolhouses to be built. All these lay behind them in the homes from which they had been driven. Clearly, then, if we want original Canadian works for our libraries, we must pass over these years.

But not yet was this people to find repose, for our grandparents had scant time to organize themselves into civil communities when war broke out again and once more they took up arms for the principles they held dear. The struggle was exhausting, for they had to fight almost alone. The mother country could give very little assistance, because she was engaged in a life-and-death conflict with a world in arms. In that "splendid isolation" which has more than once been the destiny of England, the little half-French, half-English dependency stood firm; but her frontiers were again swept by invasion.

The destruction of war and subsequent recovery from its effects postponed again the era of literature; for our land was all border land and felt the scourge of war in its whole extent. At last came peace, and the Canadian people could settle down to the normal development of their own institutions; but long, long years had been lost, and it was not until 1825 or 1830 that any interest in the pursuit of literature began to be felt.

And now that I have endeavored to make plain the circumstances which retarded the development of Canadian literature, I will pass on to a short and necessarily imperfect survey of the books of which it is composed, and you will find, as might have been supposed, that our prose literature has naturally followed up those directions which had special reference to practical life.

No one, I think, but Rich, had been devoting himself to the bibliography of American books when Faribault published in 1837, at Quebec, in French, his "Catalogue of works on the history of America with special reference to those relating to Canada, Acadia, and Louisiana." He had served in the war; but when the Literary and Historical Society was founded he became one of its most active members. He was president and then perpetual secretary, and in his time were published those reprints of scarce works which are now so rare. He had been chief adviser in collecting the "Americana" in the Parliamentary library which was burned in 1849, and he was then sent to Europe to make purchases to replace the loss. Faribault's catalogue contains valuable notes, both original and extracted. It is now very scarce—a copy in the Menzies sale brought $8.

Morgan's "Bibliotheca Canadensis" is the next in order. It is a work of great industry and covers the whole period from the conquest down to the time of its appearance in 1867. The same writer's "Canadian Men and Women of the Time," published in 1898, practically continues the first work; for, although it contains notices of a vast number of people who are not in the remotest way connected with letters, yet all the *littérateurs* are there—"all," I said somewhat inadvertently, for there are a few important names omitted.

In 1886 the late Dr. Kingsford published a book called "Canadian Archæology," dealing with early printed Canadian books, and he supplemented it, in 1892, by another—the "Early Bibliography of Ontario"—for the first had been written too hurriedly to be accurate. Sir John Bourinot also has done excellent work in this field in his "Intellectual Development of the Canadian People" (Toronto, 1881), and in a monograph for the Royal Society of Canada, "Canada's Intellectual Strength and Weakness" (1893).

A work of great importance on Canadian bibliography is by Phileas Gagnon—"Essai de Bibliographie Canadienne"—a handsome octavo of 722 pages, published by the author at Quebec in 1895. It contains valuable notes and facsimile reprints of rare title-pages. Besides these there is an exhaustive annotated bibliography, by Macfarlane, of books printed in New Brunswick (St. John, 1895); Lareau's "Histoire de la Littérature Canadienne" (Montreal, 1874); and Haight's "Catalogue of Canadian Books" (Toronto, 1896). I can mention only these few: there are besides innumerable monographs in French and English, separate and in magazines, for the subject is a favorite one with Canadians. The catalogues of the parliamentary library at Ottawa and of the public library at Toronto are also very useful to collectors and students.

The English kings entertained no jealousy of the printing-press. William Caxton had a good position at the court of Margaret Plantagenet, Duchess of Burgundy, and her brother, King Edward IV, received him into high favor. In 1503 two of his apprentices were made "King's Printers," and since that time there has always existed by patent a royal printer ("Regius Impressor") through whom alone the orders and proclamations of the government were issued.

The office of king's printer became thereafter an important factor in English administration, and it was introduced into all the colonies. No sooner, therefore, was Canada definitely ceded in 1763 than a printing-office became a government necessity at Quebec, and in 1767 Brown & Gilmore published, by authority, a folio volume of Ordinances. William Brown continued to print for the Crown; but the first imprint which appears to indicate the existence of a formal royal patent direct from the Crown is that of William Vondenvelden in 1797. John Bennett was king's printer in Upper Canada in 1801. Christopher Sower was king's printer in New Brunswick in 1785, and John Bushell was king's printer in Nova Scotia as early as 1752. In 1756 we find his name affixed to a proclamation offering £25 for every Micmac scalp. Settlers on the outskirts of Halifax had been losing scalps; for the Micmacs made their collection a labor of love, and the Abbé le Loutre, who controlled the Micmacs, could buy eighteen British scalps for only 1,800 livres. Naturally they had to bid higher at Halifax. All this did not invite to literary pursuits; but the volumes of statutes and official documents were well printed, and if literature did not flourish it was not for want of a printing-office. These volumes were books, but not literature and cannot be noticed here.

It will be of interest to say a few words about the first books—the Canadian "incunabula" so precious to bibliophiles. The first book printed at Quebec was "Le Catéchisme du Diocèse de Sens" (Brown & Gilmore, 1764—one year after the cession). Only one copy is now known. Then followed, in 1767, an "Abridgment of Christian Doctrine," in Montagnais, by Father Labrosse. Then Cugnet's "Traité de la Loi des Fiefs"—and other branches of the old French law (for it was in four parts) (William Brown, 1775). Cugnet was a very able civil lawyer. He became clerk to the Council and assisted the English government by advising them upon the old laws of Canada.

The first book printed at Montreal was "Le Réglement de la Confrèrie de l'Adoration Perpétuelle du Saint Sacrement" (Mesplet & Berger, 1776). Then we have "Le Juge a Paix," a translation of a portion of Burn's "Justice of the Peace," by J. F. Perrault, a volume of 560 pages, octavo, printed by Mesplets in 1789. Religion and law are the two organizing factors of society, and this practical people were chiefly concerned with conduct in this world, not forgetting regard to the next, in which everybody fully believed. Later on, in 1810, we find the imprint of Nathan Mower on a reprint of Bishop Porteous's "Evidences." In 1812 appeared Blyth's "Narrative of the Death of Louis XVI," and in 1816 a volume of Roman Catholic prayers in Iroquois. These are not all the books printed in those years, but the titles indicate the tendencies of the people.

We have in Huston's "Répertoire National" (the first edition of which is very scarce, but which was reprinted in four volumes at Montreal in 1893) a collection of extracts, —in fact a cyclopædia of native French-Canadian literature from the earliest times down to 1848. One piece alone (a poem) bears date prior to the English period. It is dated 1734. From 1778 to 1802 there are only twelve articles. It was not until 1832 that the French national spirit became thoroughly awake, and from that year the extracts became increasingly numerous.

The first books in general literature began to appear in 1830 and 1831, and in 1832 the Legislative Assembly passed the first Copyright Act. That year would then be a convenient date from which to reckon the revival of literature in Canada. Do not suppose that the Canadian people were uncultivated in those days. Although they were too busy to become writers they were great readers, and there were more book-stores in proportion to the population than now.

The first book in general literature published in Upper Canada was a novel, "St. Ursula's Convent; or, The Nun of Canada," printed at Kingston in 1824. There was also a press at Niagara (on the Lake) which did some reprinting; for we find that in 1831 Southey's "Life of Nelson" and Galt's "Life of Byron" were printed there. The same press issued in 1832 an original work by David Thompson, a "History of the War of 1812," and in 1836 was printed at Toronto a book of 152 pages in octavo, "The Discovery of America by Christopher Columbus, and the Origin of the North American Indians." This book was reprinted in the United States.

I cannot pretend, in a paper like this, to give more than a general indication of the extent of publication in those days. There were books and pamphlets I shall not have space to mention; but there were very few books published in Lower Canada before 1833, and in Upper Canada before 1841. During all that period, however, there were many prose-writers; for the newspaper press was very active, and in the times before telegraphs, when news came by letter, the newspapers contained more original matter, compared with advertisements, than they do now. Newspapers did not contain so many contradictory statements, for there was more time to secure accuracy. They were diligently read, and editorials were more valued than now. Dare I say they were more carefully written?

The political circumstances of Canada are so exceptional that almost every problem which can arise in the domain of politics has been, at some time or other, encountered by our statesmen. Questions of race, of language, of religion, of education—questions of local government, of provincial autonomy, of federative union—of the relative obligations between an imperial central power and self-governing colonies—have all been, of necessity, threshed out in the Dominion of Canada. Their underlying principles have not only been laid bare, but legislation has built firm social and political structures upon them.

For this reason there has always been a great deal of political pamphleteering in Canada, and of solid thinking also, which in later days and in larger communities would have been expanded into books. I have a great respect for a pamphlet upon a serious subject, because I feel sure the author did not write it for money, but because he had something to say. Pamphlets come hot from the brain of a man who cannot help writing. Great revolutions have been wrought by pamphlets falling, like burning coals, upon inflammable materials. Many of the pamphlets relate to the union of the colonies. Many of them look forward to the organization of the Empire, but, able though many of them were, the times were not ripe. The people of England were then, as they still are, in political thought far behind the colonists.

For the reasons cited above, the number of our prose-writers who have devoted their labors to constitutional and parliamentary history and law is large. Two, however, stand out before the others and have won high reputation throughout Britain and her colonies. Dr. Alpheus Todd and Sir John Bourinot are known wherever parliamentary institutions are studied. Dr. Todd's chief work, "Parliamentary Government in England," is one of the great standard authorities. It has passed through two editions, and a condensed edition has been published by a leading English writer. It has also been translated into German and Italian. He wrote also a work, indispensable to the self-governing colonies of the Empire, "Parliamentary Government in the British Colonies," in which is set forth in clear detail and with abounding references the mode of adaptation of the British parliamentary system to all the diverse colonies of the Empire.

The name of Sir John Bourinot, the Clerk of the House of Commons, must frequently be mentioned in any account of Canadian literature. His literary work is large in extent and is valued throughout all English-speaking communities. His "Parliamentary Procedure" is the accepted authority of our Parliament. His "Constitutional History of Canada" is the best manual on the subject. His two series of "Lectures on Federal Government in Canada" and "Local Government in Canada" have been published in the Johns Hopkins "University Studies," and his "Comparative Study of the Political Systems of Canada and the United States," read before Harvard University and the Johns Hopkins School of Political Science, has been published in the "Annals of the American Academy of Political Science." On these and kindred subjects he has contributed largely, not only to the periodicals of his native country, but to reviews in England and in the United States.

Although I have specially mentioned these two writers there are many others who have done important work in this field; as, for instance, Prof. Ashley, now of Harvard, whose "Lectures on the Earlier Constitutional History of Canada" are highly esteemed, and William H. Clement, whose volume on "Canadian Constitutional Law" is the text-book at Toronto University. The field was very wide, and from the first the problems to be solved after the cession were complex and difficult. A people, alien in race, religion, and language, and immensely superior in numbers, were to be governed, not as serfs, but as freemen and equals. It was a civilization and a system of law equal to their own with which the English had to reckon; and with a religion which penetrated to the very foundation of society as deeply as did their own national churches. The subject is profoundly interesting, and there is a mass of literature relating to it.

A few English immigrants who came in from the southern colonies immediately after the conquest thought to govern the country without reference to the institutions of the conquered people, and the early English governors, General Murray and Lord Dorchester, were to the French Canadians a wall of defence. The period may be studied in the works of Baron Masères, a man of great ability who was attorney-general of the Province and afterward baron of the exchequer court in England. He was of Huguenot stock and had strong anti-Roman prejudices, though personally very amiable. He could not see why the French should not prefer the English civil and ecclesiastical laws, and he wrote a number of books to persuade them to do so. He utterly failed to comprehend the French Canadians, though he was French in race and spoke and wrote French like a native. Later on came the discussions which led to the division of the Province and the separation of Upper from Lower Canada. Then followed the agitations of Papineau in the Lower, and of Gourlay and Mackenzie in the Upper Province, with an abundant crop of pamphlets leading up to the re-union.

But while these were sometimes merely party pamphlets of no real value, there was also much writing by such men as the Howes, Sewells, Stuarts, Robinsons, Haliburtons, and others of refugee stock. These men were exponents of views concerning the destiny of the English race and the importance of an organization of the Empire which had been held by Shirley, Hutchinson, Dickinson, and even by Franklin himself in 1754 and down to a short time previous to the Revolution. The Loyalists had been, and these men were, as jealous of constitutional freedom as the leaders of the popular party.

Their successors in our days, Col. Denison, Dr. Parkin, O. W. Howland, and the Imperial Federation League, as well as our youth who have so recently fought in South Africa, are the heirs and representatives of the men who dreamed that great dream which Thomas Pownall (governor of the colonies of South Carolina, New York, and Massachusetts from 1753 to 1768) printed in capital letters in his "Administration of the Colonies," namely, that "Great Britain might no more be considered as the kingdom of this isle only, with many appendages of provinces, colonies, settlements, and other extraneous parts, but as a great marine dominion consisting of our possessions in the Atlantic and in America united into a one Empire in a one centre, where the seat of government is."

The dream was shut up for many days—and even many years; for the times of the "Little Englanders" were to come; but it may be that in the latter days, if not a *pax Britannica* a *pax Anglicana* may reach round the world—a peace of justice, of freedom, of equality before the law—and who can tell where the centre of the English-speaking world may then be?

The history of Canada and of its separate provinces has been the favorite theme of our writers of prose. The histories written during the French régime were published in

France; but soon after the cession a new movement toward the study of Canadian history commenced. Heriot—Deputy Postmaster-General of Canada—wrote, in 1804, a "History of Canada," of which only one volume appeared, but it was published in London and had no original merit.

The first really Canadian history was published by Neilson at Quebec in 1815. It is in two octavo volumes and is very fairly printed. The author, William Smith, was clerk to the Legislative Assembly, and besides Charlevoix (of whose labors he made free use) he had the records of government at his service. Nevertheless the work is not of much historical value. It is very scarce and a good copy will bring about $40. Robert Christie—a Nova Scotian by birth—is the next in order of date, and his literary work extends over a long life. He wrote a volume on the "Administrations of Craig and Prevost," which was published in 1818, and the same year a "Review of the Political State of Canada under Sir Gordon Drummond and Sir John Sherbrooke." He wrote also a "History of Lower Canada from 1791 to 1841," defective in literary form, but valuable as a mine of documents and extracts.

Michel Bibaud's volume of "Epîtres, Chansons, Satires, et Epigrammes," published in 1830, marked the commencement of modern French-Canadian literature. He wrote also a "History of Canada" in two volumes, published in 1837 and 1844, now very scarce and little referred to. Garneau is the first French-Canadian historian worthy of the name, both for literary style and for original research. His history is a work of great merit and in many respects has not been surpassed. Garneau's "History" was written in French, and the four octavo volumes of which it consists appeared between 1845 and 1852, a period of storm and stress in Canadian politics; hence it is animated by strong prejudice against his English compatriots. There have been several editions in French, and there is an English translation by Bell with corrective anti-Gallic foot-notes, after the manner of some of the orthodox annotated editions of Gibbon's History.

Very different is the "Histoire du Canada" of the Abbé Ferland, published from 1861 to 1865 at Quebec. It consists of a course of lectures which, as a professor of history, the author delivered at Laval University. The work, unfortunately extends only as far as the cession in 1763. It is the result of great labor and research and is written with impartiality. The same period is covered in English by a carefully written summary by Dr. H. H. Miles. This was published in 1881, and is a very convenient manual of the history of the French domination.

Benjamin Sulte's "Histoire des Canadiens-français," published in 1882-1884 in eight quarto parts, is a very valuable history, and, if it had been published in a more convenient form, would be known as widely as it deserves to be. The author's minute acquaintance with the inner life of the French-Canadian people makes his work necessary for reference. Mr. Sulte is one of our most prolific writers on historical subjects. His style is happy and his information accurate.

Dr. William Kingsford's "History," in ten volumes octavo, is the most important historical work which has hitherto been produced in Canada, and it extends from the discovery of the country down to the union of Upper and Lower Canada in 1841 He wrote with great independence of judgment, and he is the first of our writers to make extensive use of the precious collection of original papers collected by Dr. Brymner, the Dominion Archivist. His industry was indefatigable. His work is enduring, but his reward was inadequate, and the last years of his life were spent in labor which is now only—after he is dead—commencing to be appreciated.

A notice of the prose-writers of Canada is incomplete without mention of the Rev. Dr. Withrow, who has published a work on the Catacombs or Rome which passed through several editions and met with favor among the reviewers of the United Kingdom. He has written on the "Romance of Missions" and on the "Early History of the Methodist Church," and a list of his works would be too long to give here. A "History of Canada" by him, published in 1880, is highly esteemed. Mr. Charles G. D. Roberts, better known for his poetry, wrote a small popular "History of Canada" for the Appletons; but the most convenient manual of the history of Canada is that written by Sir John Bourinot for the "Story of the Nations" series and published in London and New York. An essential volume of reference for the student is Houston's volume of "Documents Illustrative of the Canadian Constitution, with Notes and Appendixes." It contains the foundation documents of the English period.

The war of 1812-14 is the subject of a number of narratives; but no connected work of special merit or research has appeared. One of the first volumes printed in Upper Canada was David Thompson's "History of the War of 1812," published at Niagara in 1832. It is now very rare. There is also a book on that war by Major Richardson, published at Brockville in 1842, and now scarce, and one by Auchinleck, published in Toronto in 1855. Colonel Coffin commenced to write, but his work did not reach a second volume. McMullan's "History of Canada," the first edition of which was printed at Brockville in 1855, contained the best Canadian history of the war until Dr. Kingsford's large work appeared. There are, however, innumerable pamphlets and articles treating of episodes of this war published by local historical societies or in magazines.

I come now to more specialized histories—and what shall I say? for the roll is long and the time is fleeting. There are George Stewart's "Life and Times of Frontenac" in Winsor's great work; Gerald Hart's "Fall of New France;" the Abbé Verreau's collection of "Memoirs on the Invasion of 1775;" the Abbé Casgrain's works on "Montcalm and Levis." There is the great work of the Abbé Faillon on the foundation of Montreal, published by the Gentlemen of the Seminary, and there are also a series of histories, bringing down to the present day the narratives of the general histories, such as Bedard's "Histoire de Cinquante Ans, 1791-1841;" Turcotte's "Canada sous l'Union, 1841-1867," and David's "L'Union des Deux Canadas." In Ontario there are a large number of corresponding works, such as Dent's "Last Forty Years," and his "Story of the Upper Canada Rebellion." Such books are rich material for the future historian when the calm comes after the heat of political struggle has been dissipated.

Then there are the histories of the separate Provinces. Commencing, where so much commences, with the Province by the sea, there is Haliburton's "History of Nova Scotia," in two volumes octavo, published as early as 1829. It is a history based on original research and a work of literature in every sense. Murdoch's "History," in three volumes octavo, is arranged more as annals, and is an important work as a quarry for succeeding writers. Dr. Akins has published valuable extracts from the archives of the Province, and Sir

John Bourinot's "Builders of Nova Scotia" (written last year for the Royal Society of Canada, but also published separately) will give the reader, not only in the letterpress, but by the numerous illustrations, a vivid picture of the early days of the colony. Cape Breton, now a part of Nova Scotia —an island interesting from its connection with the discovery of the continent and the eventful episode of Louisbourg —has its histories. Robert Brown wrote a scholarly history of the island, and Sir John Bourinot's monograph in the Transactions of the Royal Society has left nothing to be desired.

The first New Brunswick historian was the Rev. Robert Cooney, who wrote a history of that Province, printed at Halifax in 1832. There is also a volume by Alexander Munro; but the "History of Acadia" by James Hannay is the most important work of this class emanating from New Brunswick.

And then there is the Northwest with its wild and romantic annals and its literature of exploration, adventure, and daring courage. For this you must consult Masson's "Bourgeois de la Compagnie du Nordouest," Joseph Tassé's "Les Canadiens de l'Ouest," Beckles Willson's "History of the Hudson's Bay Company," and Dr. Bryce's recent work on the same subject. Manitoba has a group of writers. Professor Bryce's work on Manitoba and his "Short History of the Canadian people" were published in England and are much esteemed. Alexander Begg's "History of the Northwest," in three volumes, is an important work published in Toronto in 1894. Another writer of the same name has published a "History of British Columbia"—a well-written and useful work. These works (although there are many others I might name) cover the whole area of the continent west of

Ontario—to the green slopes of the western ocean and the ice-bound margin of the sluggish polar sea.

A leading American author in one of his early books, writing at Niagara and standing on his own side of the river, says with compassionate sententiousness, "I look across the cataract to a country without a history." He was looking into the emptiness of his own mind; for at that very time his countryman, Parkman, had commenced the brilliant series of histories of this country which have won for him an enduring name.

History! What country of the new world can unroll a record so varied and so vivid with notable deeds? From this very town went the men who opened out the continent to its inmost heart before the English had crossed the Alleghany Mountains. The streets of the old city have been thronged with painted warriors of the far unknown West, with boisterous *voyageurs*, with the white-coated soldiers of the French king, and with the scarlet uniforms of the troops of the English crown. For Montreal, from the earliest times, has been the vortex of the conflicting currents of our national life.

Few vestiges remain of the old town. The hand of the Philistine has been heavy. It is not so very long since I used to wander with Francis Parkman about the older streets; but landmark after landmark is gone or has suffered the last indignity of restoration. I remember taking Dean Stanley into the older part of the Seminary with a half-apology for its being little more than two hundred years old; while his own abbey reached back for nearly a thousand.

"I have learned," he replied, "to look upon two hundred years in America as equivalent to a thousand in Europe. They both reach back to the origins of things."

He had just come from Chicago, and they had shown him thousands of hogs marching to their doom; but the gentle scholar would not stay to hear an exposition of the amazing economies in the disposal of those hogs, rendered possible by the advance of science, but started for the east by the next train.

It is the mind which apprehends; for many have eyes and see not; but to men like Francis Parkman, Oliver Wendell Holmes, and Dean Stanley every vestige of the quaint old town brought back memories of a picturesque and adventurous life which had thronged the narrow streets. Narrow—yes, they were narrow, but just as passable after a snow-storm and just as clean.

But I have lost my way in the old town with companions of former years. They talked so well that I forgot—I only wanted to explain to my American friend across Niagara that this land has a history and we have matters of surpassing interest to relate. There is the story of the Acadian exile—Longfellow told it without ever visiting the locality or knowing much of the matter. If you wish to have the responsibility for the action brought home to the doors of the New England colonies, read Richard's "Acadia" and the series of monographs by the Abbé Casgrain; but if, on the other hand, you wish to know of the provocations the English suffered, you will learn them from Dr. Akins and Lieutenant-Governor Archibald. The controversy is keen, and from the conflicting writers the true motive (if you are clever) may be gathered.

Many of the local histories are full of interest,—histories of Annapolis, Yarmouth, Pictou, and Queen's counties in Nova Scotia; of St. John, New Brunswick; of Huntingdon and the Eastern Townships in Quebec; of Peterborough,

Dundas, Welland, and Wentworth in Ontario. Interesting also is the mass of historical and legendary lore collected in numerous volumes by Sir J. M. Lemoine about Quebec and the lower St. Lawrence. Hawkins's "Picture of Quebec," and Bosworth's "Hochelaga Depicta; or, Picture of Montreal," are scholarly works now become very scarce; and Dr. Scadding, the learned annalist of Toronto, has written much upon that city and its surroundings. John Ross Robertson's "Landmarks of Toronto," and Graeme Mercer Adam's Centennial volume, "Toronto New and Old," are continuous pictures of the growing life of the Queen City of the Canadian West. Even in the wilderness of Muskoka, to the north of Toronto, is a history written in blood; for there the forest has grown over the sites of the Huron towns and obliterated the traces of a war ruthless and horrible, but redeemed by the martyrdom of the saintly missionaries expiring under tortures with words of blessing and exhortation on their lips.

All these things have exercised the pens of the prose-writers of Canada; but how can I attempt to enumerate the books in which they are recorded? Time is passing, and you will soon be weary of my theme, so I must hurry on and turn a deaf ear to those voices of the past.

Much good prose-writing exists in Canada under the kindred heading of Biography. The political history of the last sixty years may be found in such works as Lindsay's "Life of William Lyon Mackenzie," in Mackenzie's "Life of George Brown," in Pope's "Life of Sir John A. Macdonald," in Sir Francis Hincks's "Autobiography," and in Buckingham and Ross's "Life of Alexander Mackenzie." The stir of the political arena runs through these; but there are others, such as Read's "Lives of the Judges," his "Life and Times of General Simcoe" and of "Sir Isaac Brock," which are freer from politics. There is also much matter of historical interest interwoven in such biographies as Bethune's "Life of Bishop Strachan," Hodgins's "Life of the Rev. Dr. Ryerson," Patterson's "Life of the Rev. Dr. McGregor."

No—I repeat it—our writers had not to cross the ocean for their inspiration. They had subjects for song and story full of heart-break and tears which they have not yet exhausted, and which some United States writers, notably Lorenzo Sabine of Maine, and Prof. Tyler of Cornell, have treated with generous sympathy. What could be more tragic than the exile of the United Empire Loyalists? There had been nothing like it for many centuries; there was nothing like it in Alsace or as a sequel to the late Civil War in the United States. Whoever were rebels, these were not; for they sided with the established existing government. There are not many books devoted specially to this subject, but there is a wilderness of detached monographs, and the "Transactions" of the literary societies are full of interesting reading-matter concerning it. Canniff's "History of the Settlements Round the Bay of Quinté" relates the fortunes of the earliest group of refugees in Ontario. The principal work is, however, Dr. Egerton Ryerson's "Loyalists of America and their Times," published at Toronto in 1880. Dr. Ryerson was a strong writer, but deficient in literary skill, and his work is rather materials for history than a finished historical treatise.

Much valuable prose-writing will be found in the "Transactions" of the learned Societies of Canada: such as the Literary and Historical Society of Quebec, the oldest of all, founded in 1824; the Historical Societies of Montreal, of

Nova Scotia, of Manitoba; of the Canadian Institute of Toronto, and of the smaller societies.

Then there is the "Canadian Magazine," established in Toronto in 1893—an illustrated magazine of the latest type. The larger universities have periodicals of their own, and, in French, among others, is the "Revue Canadienne," published in Montreal since 1864, and containing the best writings of French-Canadian *littérateurs*. The University of Toronto prints an "Annual Review" of all literature relating specially to Canada, extending its survey to works treating of the discovery of the Western World. It is made up of contributions by specialists upon the subjects of the books reviewed, and, being edited by the librarian and professor of history in the University, is an exceedingly interesting series. Last, but not least, is the Royal Society of Canada, whose "Annual Transactions," now in their seventeenth year, contain monographs by leading writers of Canada upon the history, literature, and natural history of the country. Of the invaluable services of Dr. Brymner, the Dominion Archivist, I need not speak. Every librarian in America knows the value of his "Annual Reports" and the research and accuracy of his copious annotations.

It would naturally follow, from what I have told you of the practical character of the Canadian people, that the literature of law is very extensive. This I cannot even touch upon, but would only remark that the variety which distinguishes the Dominion in other matters extends even to this branch of knowledge. While the English law prevails in Ontario and westward and in the provinces by the sea, the Roman Civil Law rules the Province of Quebec.

Law-books, however, are, of necessity, limited in scope to our own country, but the military instincts of the people, arising perhaps from the constant alarm in which they have grown up, have given us a writer on military history whose reputation extends over Europe. Colonel Denison, of Toronto, wrote in 1868 a work on "Modern Cavalry"; and, in 1877 he published a "History of Cavalry" which won the first prize in a competition instituted by the Emperor of Russia for the best work on that subject. It has been translated into Russan, German, and Hungarian, and is being translated into Japanese. Colonel Denison was the first to recognize that in the school of the American Civil War new principles of cavalry service had arisen which were destined to sweep away all the maxims of the European schools. It would have been well if the British Staff College had studied this work—even though it was written by a colonel of colonial militia; for the principles he laid down are those by which Roberts and Kitchener recently mobilized the army in South Africa.

Among the first books published in Montreal was the "Travels" of Gabriel Franchère—a native of this city, who was one of the founders of Astoria on the Columbia. The volume in its original French form is now exceedingly scarce, but it was translated and printed in New York in 1853. This leads to the remark that the exploration and discovery of the north and west of this continent has been mainly done by Canadians and Hudson's Bay *voyageurs;* although the books have generally been printed out of Canada. Sir Alexander Mackenzie was the first to reach the Pacific and Arctic oceans across the continent by land. His work has been printed in different editions. He was a partner in the Northwest Company of Montreal. Henry, whose adventures were published in New York in 1809, was a merchant of this city, and Harmon, whose "Travels" were published at Andover in 1820, was also a member of the Northwest Company. The travels of Ross Cox, Maclean, Ogden, Long, and other officers of the great fur companies, belong to our literature, though published in England. It was Dease and Simpson, and Rae and Hearne who traced out most of the Arctic coast of America. The work of these men is still being carried on by Tyrrell, McConnell, Low, Bell, and George Dawson. The writings of these last, and of many more whom I cannot stop to name, whether published elsewhere or embodied in reports or contributed to foreign periodicals and learned societies, are yet the works of Canadian prose-writers.

Canadian writers have also done good work in the archæology and languages of the Indian tribes. I have already said that among the "incunabula" of Canada are catechisms in Montagnais and Iroquois. Among the chief workers in this field was Dr. Silas Rand. He wrote upon the "History, Manners, and Language of the Micmac Tribe," and translated the Gospels and Epistles into Micmac. His Dictionary, English and Micmac, was published at the cost of the government; and the other half, Micmac into English, is in manuscript at Ottawa. A vote has been passed for money to print it. He wrote also a book on the "Legends of the Micmacs" which was published in New York and London in 1894. Canon O'Meara published the Common Prayer Book, the New Testament, the Pentateuch and a hymn book in Ojibway. Bishop Baraga is the author of an Ojibway dictionary, and Father Lacombe of one of the Cree language.

Father Petitot, for more than twenty years a missionary in the farthest north, has written much upon the Chippewayan tribes and the Esquimaux people. His works are published for the most part in France, and are better known there than here.

The Abbé Cuoq has published a dictionary of Iroquois, and grammars of both Iroquois and Algonquin, besides his "Etudes Philologiques" on both these languages. The Abbé Maurault wrote a "History of the Abenakis," the Rev. Peter Jones (an Ojibway by birth) wrote a history of his people, and a Wyandot, Peter Dooyentate Clarke, wrote a small volume on the "Origin and Traditional History of the Wyandots."

We cannot count the late Horatio Hale as a Canadian writer, although he lived in Canada for the latter years of his life and contributed to the "Transactions of the Royal Society," but we have in the Rev. Dr. Maclean a writer who has both the literary training and the actual experience to make anything from his hand upon Indian life valuable. His work, "Canadian Savage Folk—the Native Tribes of Canada," published in 1896 at Toronto, is one of much interest. He is, besides, a frequent contributor to periodical literature on ethnological subjects.

Sir Daniel Wilson, late Principal of the University of Toronto, although some of his works were written before he came to Canada, must be enrolled among Canadian prose-writers, for he was a frequent contributor to the "Canadian Journal" and to the Royal Society on his favorite subjects, archæology and ethnology. Some very important works—notably his "Prehistoric Man; or, Researches into the Origin of Civilization in the Old and New World"—were written in Canada.

Sir William Dawson also wrote much on kindred subjects, and in his book "Fossil Man," he employed the results of a long study of the Indians of Canada to illustrate the character and condition of the prehistoric men of Europe. His son, Dr. George M. Dawson, has not only written papers of value upon the races and languages of the Pacific coast, but he has assisted in the publication of many excellent monographs by missionaries resident among the western tribes.

I must not close without mention of the Rev. Prof. Campbell. His large work on the Hittites is well known. His contributions on Phœnician, Egyptian, Mexican, and Indian ethnology and philology will be found in many Canadian transactions and periodicals.

I ought not to speak of Canadian literature without mention of Dr. Goldwin Smith. He is not a product of our society. He does not think as we do; but neither does he think as anybody else does. He is *sui generis*—a product of the severest Oxford University culture mitigated by a quarter of a century's residence in Canada. It is not from Canadian springs that he draws the pure, pellucid English that reflects his thought like the still water of a forest lake. It is not from us that he derives that condensation of style —terse without obscurity—revealing great stretches of historic landscape in a few vivid phrases. These are not our gifts—but he could never have written his incomparable "History of the United States" had it not been for the constant attrition of twenty-five years of Canadian society. No unmitigated Oxford professor could have, or rather would have, understood the subject; and so we may claim some little share in that almost faultless history, which, if any man read, it will make him well and truly informed upon a subject above all others overlaid with falsehood and bombast. For edification and reproof has Dr. Smith been sent to us by a happy fortune, and though we hit back at times we must be grateful to a man who, in addition to the benefit we have derived from his literary labors, has out of his own private resources stimulated Canadian letters by the establishment or support of such publications as the "Nation," the "Week," the "Canadian Monthly," and the "Bystander."

You will scarcely be surprised if I say that the soil of Canada has not proved productive of writers upon metaphysics and logic. I can remember only two,—Prof. J. Clark Murray, of McGill, and Prof. Watson, of Queen's University. Their works have been published in England and in the United States, and their contributions to leading reviews in those countries, as well as to Canadian periodicals of the higher class, have been frequent. Dr. Murray has written an "Exposition of Sir William Hamilton's Philosophy," published in Boston, and a "Handbook of Psychology," published in London, and he has translated from the German "The Autobiography of Solomon Maimon"—a pessimistic philosopher who preceded Schopenhauer by more than one hundred years. Prof. Watson has written "Kant and his English Critics" (Glasgow, 1881); an "Exposition of Schelling" (Chicago, 1882); and the "Philosophy of Kant" (Glasgow and New York, 1892). Why commercial cities like Chicago, St. Louis, and Glasgow should be centres of philosophical speculation, and Montreal and Toronto be impervious to metaphysics, is a question worth consideration.

While no very remarkable work in mathematics and physics has yet been done among us, in the natural sciences Canadian writers are known and esteemed all over the world. Every standard book on geology, in America or in Europe, will be found to contain frequent references to Canadian writers and illustrations reproduced from their drawings. McGill University and the Geological Survey were the two centres of this strong eddy toward the study of natural history, and the dominant personalities of the principal of one, Sir William Dawson, and the first director of the other, Sir William Logan, were the chief moving springs. Sir William Logan was not a writer of books, beyond his reports, although he was a contributor to learned transactions and reviews; but Sir William Dawson, during all his lifetime, was a most industrious writer of books, monographs, and occasional articles. His writings cover the whole area of geology, botany, and zoology and, beyond these, the relations between natural science and religion were constantly the subject of his ready pen. I cannot begin to give you the names, even, of his works; but I have counted 107 important contributions to transactions of learned societies and reviews, and twenty separate volumes of notes. These are but a portion of the total mass of his writings, and his accurate and extensive knowledge and easy style made his works popular throughout the English-speaking world. The results of his laborious and self-sacrificing life are around you. Where-ever you turn you will see them—and his influence for all that is wise and good and noble will endure in Canada for generations to come.

Other workers in this field are not to be forgotten. The pioneer, Abraham Gesner, of Nova Scotia, published a volume on the geology of that Province as early as 1836. Prof. Henry Youle Hind published, in 1860, the scientific results of the expedition of 1857 sent to find a practicable immigrant route from Canada to Fort Garry, now Winnipeg, on the Red River. Three years later he published two volumes of "Explorations in Labrador." He has been a very frequent contributor to the "Canadian Journal," and to other scientific reviews here and in Europe. Nor should Elkanah Billings be forgotten, whose labors in palæontology are met with in every text-book; nor G. F. Matthew, of St. John, nor Prof. Bailey, of Fredericton. The officers of the Geological Survey are among our leading prose-writers—the present director, Dr. George M. Dawson, is known throughout Europe and America as the writer of important works on the geography, geology, and natural history of the Dominion, and he, as well as Dr. Robert Bell, Dr. Whiteaves, Prof. Macoun, and others, have enriched Canadian literature by numerous contributions to scientific publications.

The set toward the study of the natural sciences was not so dominant in the other cities of Canada, but Prof. Chapman and Dr. Coleman, of Toronto, are among our writers on chemistry and geology, and Dr. James Douglas, now of New York, is a writer of authority on all questions of metallurgy and mining. We must count among our writers, though now connected with Harvard University, Dr. Montagu Chamberlain, a New Brunswicker who has written extensively on the ornithology of Canada and on the Abenaqui and Malicete Indians of his native Province; and Ernest Seton Thompson, born in Toronto, but now residing in New York, who has written for the government of Manitoba upon the ornithology and mammalia of that Province. Sir James Lemoine and C. E. Dionne have published studies of the ornithology of Quebec; and the late A. N. Montpetit's work, "Les Poissons d'Eau Douce," is an illustrated octavo volume of ichthyology of the same Province.

Any notice of the prose-writers of Canada would be very imperfect without mention of Dr. Sterry Hunt, who was not only a chemist, geologist, and mineralogist of wide reputation, but a graceful and accurate master of English style. His contributions to these sciences extend over the transactions of learned societies in Europe and America, and many of them were translated into French, German, and Italian. He was born in Connecticut, and the last few years of his life were spent in New York, but all the strength of his manhood was spent in Canada and devoted to Canadian subjects. His chief works are "Mineral Physiology and Physiography," "Mineralogy According to a Natural System," "A New Basis for Chemistry," and a volume of "Chemical and Geological Essays." His life-work is stamped with rare originality and has left its impress on the sciences he followed.

Almost while I write, a Canadian well known for his contributions to scientific periodicals and as the leader in the movement for the appraisal of literature has stepped into the front rank of popular expositors of science. The handsome volume, "Flame, Electricity, and the Camera," by George Iles, is not merely a vivid exposition—it is an original explanation of the *rationale* of the rapid progress of science during the last years of the century, and of the causes of the accelerating speed of its advance.

I had hoped to say a few words about some of those strong prose-writers who in the greater newspapers wield more influence over the Canadian mind than most of the writers of books; but time will not permit. Not all our newspapers have succumbed to the scrappiness of newsiness. Thoughtful and finished editorials in dignified style may yet be found in number sufficient to send a note of sweeter reason through the din of political strife. It is in Canada as elsewhere; the sands are strewn with the wreck of ventures of purely "literary papers free from the ties of party or sect." Such were the "Week" and the "Nation," and many others; but, although it is abundantly clear that literature alone cannot support a newspaper, the greater newspapers have departments, sacred from intrusion, where reviews are faithfully given and questions of pure literature are discussed.

And here let me pause to regret the loss of the excellent literature which lies dead in our dead magazines. From 1824 literature has never been without a witness in our land. Some magazine, French or English, has stood as a living witness that we are not made to live by bread alone, and afterward fallen as a dead witness that bread also is necessary in order to live. This is a subject by itself and would require a separate paper to elucidate it fully.

Finally we reach the region of belles lettres, sometimes called "pure literature," and here we encounter a strong contrast between the English and French sides of our community. There are many volumes of *causeries*, *mélanges*, *revues*, *essais*, in French. Buies, Routhier, Marchand, Chauveau, and all the French writers of note are represented in this class. Such writing in English has seldom been published in the form of books.

I remember a book called "Trifles from my Portfolio," by Dr. Walter Henry, a retired army surgeon, published at Quebec by Neilson in 1839. The doctor had been stationed at St. Helena while Napoleon Bonaparte was confined there, and he had some interesting things to say about that. There were other army experiences, but his experiences in salmon-fishing took up a good share of the two volumes. Writing of this class will, however, be found abundantly in the contributions to the Saturday editions of the leading newspapers of the large cities. Much of it is exceedingly good, and while we read with pleasure the weekly contributions of Martin Griffin, John Reade, Bernard McEvoy, or George Murray, we feel regret that so much learning and cleverness should be in so ephemeral a form. I am glad, however, to recall in this connection Dr. Alexander's "Introduction to the Poetry of Robert Browning." For critical insight and appreciation the volume is worthy of remark.

One name must always be remembered when we take account of Canadian letters, and that is the creator of the inimitable Yankee peddler, "Sam Slick." Judge Haliburton unconsciously created a type to be as well known as Sam Weller, and while he was intent only upon quizzing his fellow Nova Scotians in the columns of a Halifax newspaper he woke up to find himself a favorite among the literary people of London.

But literature, in the opinion of the majority of the present day, consists mainly of fiction. More than three fourths of the books taken out from the public libraries are novels, and the world in its old age is going back to the story-tellers. Nor are we able to endure the long novels which held our parents in rapt attention. The stories must be shorter, and the more pictures the better. This last phase of literature is cultivated by all our younger writers, and, while the task is too extensive for anything but most imperfect performance, a few words on this branch of my subject are necessary.

One remark only I venture to make in the way of criticism, that, while in science we have produced some few men who stand in the very front of their respective subjects, we cannot boast yet of a novelist who has taken rank with the great masters of the craft, and none, perhaps, who have attained to the very forefront of the second class; but then it is only a few years since we made a beginning.

We cannot commence our review of Canadian fiction with the "History of Emily Montague," published in 1769. Even if it was written at Quebec the authoress was an Englishwoman not a permanent resident; nor even with "St. Ursula's Convent," for, although that story was publshed at Kingston in 1824, no one seems to know who wrote it, nor does there appear to be a copy now in existence.[1]

We must commence with Major Richardson's "Écarté," published in New York in 1829. In 1833 he published "Wacousta," a tale of Pontiac's war. It is really a good novel and contains an excellent picture of the siege of Detroit. The same author published at Montreal "The Canadian Brothers," in 1840, and afterward four or five other novels in New York. In 1833 two members of the Strickland family, Mrs. Moodie and Mrs. Traill, came to Canada and settled near Peterborough. They kept up their literary activity during their lives. Mrs. Moodie wrote many books, and from 1852 to 1860 she produced a number of fair novels. At the same time Mrs. Leprohon was writing stories. Her first novel appeared in the "Literary Garland" in 1848, and she followed it with a number of others.

The Hon. P. J. O. Chauveau, in 1852, led the way in French novel-writing with "Charles Guérin," and was followed in 1863, in "Les Anciens Canadiens," by Philippe Aubert de Gaspé, which has recently been translated and published in New York. It is thought to be the best French-Canadian novel, although it was its author's first book and was written when he was past seventy. Then followed Bourassa, Marmette, Beaugrand, Gérin-Lajoie, and others, but no important work was produced.

I do not recall anything in English of note until 1877, when William Kirby published "Le Chien d'Or." This was

---

[1] Kingsford ("Early Bibliography," p. 30) observes that "it is stated" that Miss Julia Beckwith, of Fredericton, wrote this book. The same statement has been repeated as a certainty in a recent issue of the "Montreal Star." No evidence of this has, however, been adduced. Dr. Kingsford never saw a copy of the book, and I have never met anyone who has seen it. Our knowledge of it is derived from a contemporary review.

long thought to be the best Canadian novel. It has met with much favor outside of Canada. The story, as given in the legend, is intrinsically of very exceptional interest, and it is told with considerable literary skill.

Since then writers of stories have become numerous in Canada. It will be impossible to mention more than a few. Miss Machar, of Kingston, has written some capital novels of Canadian life. Mr. James Macdonald Oxley is fully equal to the best writers of books of adventure for boys. Since 1877 he has produced a surprising number of books, published usually out of Canada, though all upon Canadian life and history.

Gilbert Parker is the chief name among Canadian writers of fiction, and he has won high position in the mother land. Although he now resides in England his subjects are Canadian and his books abound with local color and incident. He stands now among the leading novelists of the day.

During the last few years William McLennan has made a reputation far beyond the limits of Canada, not only by his dialect stories, but by his charming book, "Spanish John," a novel without a woman and yet full of interest. This book is remarkable for its singularly pure English style. "The Span o' Life," which he wrote in collaboration with Miss McIlwraith (a Hamilton lady well known as a contributor of bright essays and stories in British and American magazines) is a novel of the same period as the "Chien d'Or." It is written with the same charm of style as Mr. McLennan's other books. The plot is original and there is a very loveable heroine in it. The setting is historically true and the local color is faithful.

Miss Lily Dougall, not long ago, surprised the English public by a strong novel in an original vein, "Beggars All," published by Longmans. The subject was not Canadian, but her later books deal with more familiar scenes. Nor should we omit to count Miss Blanche Macdonald and Mrs. Harrison in the number of our novelists. We must not forget to make mention also of William Lighthall, whose two novels "The Young Seigneur" and "The False Repentigny" have met with much acceptance. Within the last few weeks Miss Agnes Laut, of Ottawa, has published "The Lords of the North," a novel upon the struggle between the two great fur companies which entitles her to an assured place among Canadian writers of fiction.

Mrs. Coates, now of Calcutta, formerly Sara Jeannette Duncan, of one of our Canadian cities, has written books, not only bright and interesting, but with a vein of most charming humor. One was a volume of travels around the world, another "The American Girl in London," an exceedingly clever story which appeared first in the "Illustrated London News," and the third "A Voyage of Consolation." She has written other books, but these are her best.

Robert Barr is a Canadian, now well established in England as a popular writer, whose first success was in Canadian story-writing. He has recently chosen other themes, and two of his later books, "Tekla" and "The Strong Arm," are historical novels of the Holy Roman Empire at the period of Rodolph of Hapsburg. His writings are sparkling and clever, but he has much to learn before he begins to understand anything of that complex institution, the Holy Roman Empire.

It is a far cry to Rodolph of Hapsburg, and the Rev. Charles W. Gordon, of Winnipeg (better known as Ralph Connor), has had the insight to find, among devoted missionaries on the outskirts of civilization, heroes who are fighting among the foothills of the Rocky Mountains as real a battle for civil order and righteousness as Rodolph ever fought. In "Black Rock" and the "Sky Pilot" are vivid pictures of life on the western plains and mountains. In that grand and solemn world which he describes with loving power his heroes labor and struggle and endure—true Galahads fighting the ceaseless battle of good against the evil and recklessness and profanity of border life. Stories these are—and good stories—but they are more, they are tonics for enfeebled faith, full of literary vigor, and instinct with highest truth.

The latest development of modern literature is the short story, and E. W. Thompson now on the staff of the "Youth's Companion" is a master in that art. There are many others, well known in the popular American magazines, among them Duncan Campbell Scott, better known as a poet, W. A. Fraser, and Dr. Frechette (whose French poetry was crowned by the Academy of France), who has achieved the success of writing a book of capital short stories in English and so of winning laurels in two languages.

Ernest Seton Thompson occupies a place by himself in his books "Wild Animals I have Known," "The Sand-Hill Stag," and "The Biography of a Grizzly." The sympathetic naturalist tells these stories from the animal's own point of view—a method which imparts much freshness into the narration. Mr. Thompson's skill as an artist adds charm to his books, and his wife, accomplished not only in the art of getting up pretty books, but also in the unconventional art of taking care of herself on the western prairies, has contributed another volume, "A Woman Tenderfoot," to our open-air literature.

Mr. W. A. Fraser has gone further in this direction, and his "Mooswa and Others of the Boundaries" makes the wild animals talk as they do in Kipling's "Jungle Book." His hero is a moose whose moral character has developed beyond that of the usual run of the Christians who hunt and trap in the spruce forests of the upper Athabasca. Our natural history is leading us back to Æsop and the dawn of literature, but our wild animals have not the keen wit and didactic brevity of the Greek creatures. They tend toward diffuseness and to the northwest superfluity of expletives.

Canadian history and scenery are beginning to make their appearance in novels by outside writers who, having no real knowledge of either, seek it in the pages of Francis Parkman with indifferent success. We may read with amused wonder (in a very successful American novel) of Daulac's wife—a Laval-Montmorenci—starting from Montreal in the year 1660 for Carillon on the Ottawa, with one Indian girl attendant, making a raft at Ste. Anne's with knives, and floating up the current to the north shore. We may follow her there to the seven chapels on the mountain where she and her attendant sleep and find food convenient for them in the bread and roasted birds which a pious devotee is accustomed to place upon the altar. It is only eighteen years since Maisonneuve landed, but Daulac has on Isle St. Bernard, at the mouth of the Chateaugay, a strong baronial castle built of stone with lancet windows, and we follow him also with wonder as he steps into his canoe at midnight and goes down to Montreal by the Lachine rapids, evidently his usual route to town; but this was his last trip down, for he was preparing for his fight at the Long Sault.

In like manner Dr. Conan Doyle, in the "Refugees," with much ingenuity rescues some Huguenots at Quebec from imprisonment for their faith. A fanatical Franciscan friar tracks them up the St. Lawrence and Richelieu rivers until they find refuge from persecution in the English colonies. This is hard to bear; for New France is the only region where there has never been persecution for the sake of religion. The only law relating to Huguenots was that they could not winter in the country without permission, or assemble for public worship. From such absurdities as these we must look to our native writers to protect us. It is enough for Edwin and Angelina to harrow our feelings with their woes without harrowing our geography and history also.

Apart from the choice of subject-matter the prospect for a distinctive Canadian school of literature is not bright; and in truth any provincial narrowness of style or language is not desirable. Our writers can reflect lustre on their country only when they venture into the broad world of our language and conquer recognition in the great realm of Anglo-Saxon letters. The great centres of our race, where are to be won the great prizes of life, must always attract the brightest and most ambitious spirits. One of our own people—a successful author now in London—writes in the "Canadian Magazine" to reproach us for underestimating ourselves. It is a good fault, even if uncommon among English speakers. Our youth are unlearning it; but they will not grow great by self-assertion, only by performance.

I have tried to set forth in detail the reasons of our retarded commencement—our growth of late years has been rapid. We have to guard against materialism and to watch lest literature be oppressed by the pursuit of practical science. We see the workers toiling and we hear the din, but the world is saved by the dreamers who keep the intellect of mankind sane and sweet by communion with the ideal. Canada must not regret her children if they achieve fame in other lands. John Bonner and William G. Sewell left Quebec long ago for the "Herald," and "Harper's," and the "New York Times." Lanigan wrote "The Akhound of Swat" one night waiting for telegrams in the "World" office. Nova Scotia lost John Foster Kirk, who completed Prescott's great task, and Simon Newcomb, of the United States Navy Department, astronomer and mathematician. From New Brunswick went Professor De Mille, the brilliant author of the "Dodge Club;" George Teall, the archivist and leading writer of South Africa; and May Agnes Fleming, a story-writer who for many years earned with her pen in New York an income as large as that of a cabinet minister at Ottawa. From Kingston went Grant Allen and Professor George Romanes—the latter a star of intellect in the regions of the higher science where it touches the realm of metaphysics. His premature death was lamented as a loss to Cambridge University. I could tell of many others if there were time—but I must close.

We read that in remote ages the followers of Pythagoras, and in mediæval times the adepts of the Rosy Cross had the power of separating at will their souls from their bodies, and then their spirits would travel away with the speed of thought and hover in the semblance of stars over far-off lands, but always a long trail of faint phosphorescent light connected the shining spirit with the quiet body in which its light was born.

So it is with us—we follow with interest the fortunes of our countrymen—we rejoice in their advancement, and star after star may leave us, but still we feel that their success is ours, and some faint lustre of their brilliance quickens with pride the heart of their motherland.

INGERSOLL

ROBERT GREEN INGERSOLL, a noted American lawyer, orator, and lecturer, was the son of a clergyman, and was born at Dresden, New York, August 11, 1833. He was educated in the common schools, studied law, and, after being admitted to the bar, settled first at Shawneetown, Illinois, but in 1857 removed to Peoria in the same State. In 1860 he was an unsuccessful Democratic candidate for Congress. He entered the Federal army in 1862 as colonel of an Illinois regiment and was for some months a captive in a Confederate prison. Resigning his commission in 1864, he resumed his law practice in Peoria, and, having now became a Republican, was appointed attorney-general of Illinois in 1866. In a since-famous speech delivered by him before the Republican Convention of 1876 he proposed the name of Blaine as the Republican nominee, alluding to him as "the Plumed Knight of Maine." From that time Ingersoll was in constant request as a campaign speaker. He was still more widely known, however, as a free-thought or agnostic lecturer. He removed to Washington after some years, and later to New York city, where he practised his profession with eminent success. His death took place at Dobbs Ferry, New York, July 29, 1899. He had great gifts as an orator, and the keenest wit and the deepest pathos were always at his command. A man of broad sympathies, he made friends even of those who dissented most heartily from his religious views. His published works include "The Gods" (1878); "Ghosts" (1879); "Some Mistakes of Moses" (1879); "Lectures Complete;" and "Prose Poems."

BLAINE, THE PLUMED KNIGHT

NOMINATING SPEECH IN THE REPUBLICAN NATIONAL CONVENTION AT CINCINNATI, JUNE 15, 1876[1]

MASSACHUSETTS may be satisfied with the loyalty of Benjamin H. Bristow; so am I; but if any man nominated by this convention cannot carry the State of Massachusetts I am not satisfied with the loyalty of that State. If the nominee of this convention cannot carry the grand old Commonwealth of Massachusetts by seventy-five thousand majority, I would advise them to sell out Faneuil

[1] From the "New York Times," June 16, 1876.

Hall as a Democratic headquarters. I would advise them to take from Bunker Hill that old monument of glory.

The Republicans of the United States demand as their leader in the great contest of 1876 a man of intellect, a man of integrity, a man of well-known and approved political opinion. They demand a statesman. They demand a reformer after, as well as before, the election. They demand a politician in the highest and broadest and best sense of that word. They demand a man acquainted with public affairs—with the wants of the people—with not only the requirements of the hour, but with the demands of the future.

They demand a man broad enough to comprehend the relations of this government to the other nations of the earth. They demand a man well versed in the powers, duties, and prerogatives of each and every department of this government.

They demand a man who will sacredly preserve the financial honor of the United States—one who knows enough to know that the national debt must be paid through the prosperity of this people. One who knows enough to know that all the financial theories in the world cannot redeem a single dollar. One who knows enough to know that all the money must be made, not by law, but by labor. One who knows enough to know that the people of the United States have the industry to make the money and the honor to pay it over just as fast as they make it.

The Republicans of the United States demand a man who knows that prosperity and resumption, when they come, must come together. When they come they will come hand in hand through the golden harvest fields; hand in hand by the whirling spindle and the turning wheel; hand in hand past the open furnace doors; hand in hand by the flaming forges;

hand in hand by the chimneys filled with eager fire by the hands of the countless sons of toil.

This money has got to be dug out of the earth. You cannot make it by passing resolutions in a political meeting.

The Republicans of the United States want a man who knows that this government should protect every citizen at home and abroad; who knows that any government that will defend its defenders and will not protect its protectors is a disgrace to the map of the world. They demand a man who believes in the eternal separation and divorcement of church and school. They demand a man whose political reputation is spotless as a star; but they do not demand that their candidate shall have a certificate of moral character signed by a Confederate Congress. The man who has in full-heaped and rounded measure all of these splendid qualifications is the present grand and gallant leader of the Republican party—James G. Blaine.

Our country, crowned with the vast and marvellous achievements of its first century, asks for a man worthy of her past—prophetic of her future; asks for a man who has the audacity of genius; asks for a man who is the grandest combination of heart, conscience, and brains beneath the flag. That man is James G. Blaine.

For the Republican host led by that intrepid man there can be no such thing as defeat.

This is a grand year: a year filled with the recollections of the Revolution; filled with proud and tender memories of the sacred past; filled with the legends of liberty; a year in which the sons of freedom will drink from the fountain of enthusiasm; a year in which the people call for a man who has preserved in Congress what our soldiers won upon the field; a year in which we call for the man who has torn from the throat of treason the tongue of slander—a man that has snatched the mask of Democracy from the hideous face of Rebellion—a man who, like an intellectual athlete, stood in the arena of debate, challenged all comers, and who, up to the present moment, is a total stranger to defeat.

Like an armed warrior, like a plumed knight, James G. Blaine marched down the halls of the American Congress and threw his shining lances full and fair against the brazen foreheads of every defamer of his country and maligner of its honor.

For the Republican party to desert a gallant man now is worse than if an army should desert their general upon the field of battle.

James G. Blaine is now, and has been for years, the bearer of the sacred standard of the Republic. I call it sacred because no human being can stand beneath its folds without becoming, and without remaining, free.

Gentlemen of the Convention, in the name of the great Republic, the only republic that ever existed upon this earth; in the name of all her defenders and of all her supporters; in the name of all her soldiers living; in the name of all her soldiers who died upon the field of battle; and in the name of those who perished in the skeleton clutch of famine at Andersonville and Libby, whose sufferings he so eloquently remembers, Illinois nominates for the next President of this country that prince of parliamentarians, that leader of leaders, James G. Blaine.

ORATION AT HIS BROTHER'S GRAVE

DELIVERED AT THE FUNERAL OF EBON C. INGERSOLL, IN WASHINGTON, JUNE 3, 1879[1]

MY FRIENDS,—I am going to do that which the dead oft promised he would do for me.

The loved and loving brother, husband, father, friend died where manhood's morning almost touches noon, and while the shadows still were falling toward the west.

He had not passed on life's highway the stone that marks the highest point, but, being weary for a moment, he lay down by the wayside, and, using his burden for a pillow, fell into that dreamless sleep that kisses down his eyelids still. While yet in love with life and raptured with the world he passed to silence and pathetic dust.

Yet, after all, it may be best, just in the happiest, sunniest hour of all the voyage, while eager winds are kissing every sail, to dash against the unseen rock, and in an instant hear the billows roar above a sunken ship. For, whether in mid-sea or 'mong the breakers of the farther shore, a wreck at last must mark the end of each and all. And every life, no matter if its every hour is rich with love and every moment jeweled with a joy, will, at its close, become a tragedy as sad and deep and dark as can be woven of the warp and woof of mystery and death.

This brave and tender man in every storm of life was oak and rock, but in the sunshine he was vine and flower. He was the friend of all heroic souls. He climbed the heights

---

[1] Copied from the New York "Tribune," June 4. 1879.

and left all superstitions far below, while on his forehead fell the golden dawning of the grander day.

He loved the beautiful, and was with color, form, and music touched to tears. He sided with the weak, and with a willing hand gave alms; with loyal heart and with purest hands he faithfully discharged all public trusts.

He was a worshipper of liberty, a friend of the oppressed. A thousand times I have heard him quote these words: "For justice all place a temple, and all seasons, summer." He believed that happiness was the only good, reason the only torch, justice the only worship, humanity the only religion, and love the only priest. He added to the sum of human joy; and were every one to whom he did some loving service to bring a blossom to his grave, he would sleep to-night beneath a wilderness of flowers.

Life is a narrow vale between the cold and barren peaks of two eternities. We strive in vain to look beyond the heights. We cry aloud, and the only answer is the echo of our wailing cry. From the voiceless lips of the unreplying dead there comes no word; but in the night of death hope sees a star, and listening love can hear the rustle of a wing.

He who sleeps here, when dying, mistaking the approach of death for the return of health, whispered with his latest breath: "I am better now." Let us believe, in spite of doubts and dogmas, and tears and fears, that these dear words are true of all the countless dead.

And now to you who have been chosen, from among the many men he loved, to do the last sad office for the dead, we give his sacred dust. Speech cannot contain our love. There was, there is, no greater, stronger, manlier man.

BRADLAUGH

CHARLES BRADLAUGH, an English reformer and socialist, was born in London, September 26, 1833, and until the age of eleven was sent to elementary schools in the East End of London. At fifteen he began to speak before street audiences and at nineteen was a lecturer on Free Thought. After a short experience in the army in Ireland he became a lawyer's clerk in 1853 and for a number of years subsequently lectured in various places, scoring many platform successes in spite of his hard, reckless, aggressive treatment of the themes which he handled. He edited successively "The Investigator" and "The National Reformer," and in 1868 began his endeavors to enter Parliament. After several unsuccessful contests for the borough of Northampton he was at length returned by that town in 1880, but his difficulties were by no means over. He claimed the right to take his seat by affirmation instead of by taking the oath of allegiance, and the House at once passed a resolution denying his right of entrance by either method. On February 21, 1882, he appeared before the House of Commons, and, taking out a Testament from his pocket, administered the oath to himself. After successive exclusions, ejections, and re-elections, he was allowed in 1886 to take his seat, and in 1888 moved and carried a bill allowing entering members desiring it to affirm instead of taking the oath. Bradlaugh's extreme views moderated very perceptibly after his entrance to Parliament, and he soon gained the respect and liking of his fellow members. He died in London, January 29, 1891, and during his last illness the House of Commons voted to expunge its resolution of June 22, 1880, denying Bradlaugh's right to affirm or take the oath. He published "The Impeachment of the House of Brunswick" in 1872.

AT THE BAR OF THE HOUSE OF COMMONS

MR. SPEAKER,—I have again to ask the indulgence of the House while I submit to it a few words in favor of my claim to do that which the law requires me to do. Perhaps the House will pardon me if I supply an omission, I feel unintentionally made, on the part of the honorable member for Chatham [Mr. John Gorst].

In some words which have just fallen from him I understood him to say that he would use a formal statement made by me to the Committee against what the Chancellor of the Duchy had said I had said.

I am sure the honorable and learned member for Chatham, who has evidently read the proceedings of the committee with care, would, if he had thought it fair, have stated to the House that the statement only came from me after an objection made by me—a positive objection on the ground that it related to matters outside this House, and that the House in the course of its history had never inquired into such matters; but I can hardly understand what the member for Chatham meant when he said that he contrasted what I did say with what the Chancellor of the Duchy said I said; for it is not a matter of memory, it is on the proceedings of this House, that, being examined formally before the committee, I stated "that the essential part of the oath is in the fullest and most complete degree binding upon my honor and conscience, and that the repeating of the words of asseveration does not in the slightest degree weaken the binding of the allegiance on me."

M

I now say I would not go through any form—much as I value the right to sit in this House, much as I desire and believe that this House will accord me that right—that I did not mean to be binding upon me without mental reservation, without equivocation. I would go through no form unless it were fully and completely and thoroughly binding upon me as to what it expressed or promised.

Mine has been no easy position for the last twelve months. I have been elected by the free votes of a free constituency. My return is untainted. There is no charge of bribery, no charge of corruption, nor of inducing men to come drunken to the polling-booth. I come here with a pure, untainted return—not won by accident. For thirteen long years have I fought for this right—through five contested elections, including this. It is now proposed to prevent me from fulfilling the duty my constituents have placed upon me. You have force: on my side is the law.

The honorable and learned member for Plymouth [Mr., afterward Sir, Edward Clarke] spoke the truth when he said he did not ask the House to treat the matter as a question of law; but the constituencies ask me to treat it as a question of law. I, for them, ask you to treat it as a question of law. I could understand the feeling that seems to have been manifested were I some great and powerful personage. I could understand it had I a large influence behind me. I am only one of the people, and you propose to teach them that, on a mere technical question, you will put a barrier in the way of my doing my duty which you have never put in the way of anybody else.

The question is, Has my return on the 9th of April, 1881, anything whatever to impeach it? There is no legal disqualification involved. If there were, it could be raised by petition. The honorable member for Plymouth says the dignity of this House is in question. Do you mean that I can injure the dignity of this House?—this House which has stood unrivalled for centuries?—this House, supreme among the assemblies of the world?—this House, which represents the traditions of liberty? I should not have so libelled you.

How is the dignity of this House to be hurt? If what happened before the 9th of April is less than a legal disqualification, it is a matter for the judgment of the constituency and not for you. The constituency has judged me; it has elected me; I stand here with no legal disqualification upon me. The right of the constituency to return me is an unimpeachable right.

I know some gentlemen make light of constituencies; yet without the constituencies you are nothing. It is from them you derive your whole and sole authority. The honorable and learned member for Plymouth treats lightly the legal question. It is dangerous to make light of the law—dangerous, because if you are only going to rely on your strength of force to override the law, you give a bad lesson to men whose morality you impeach as to what should be their duty if emergence ever came. Always outside the House I have advocated strenuous obedience to the law, and it is under that law that I claim my right. It is said by the right honorable baronet [Sir Stafford Northcote], who interposes between me and my duty, that this House has passed some resolution.

First, I submit that that resolution does not affect the return of the 9th of April. The conditions are entirely different; there is nothing since the date of that return. I submit next, that, if it did affect it, the resolution was illegal from the beginning. In the words of George Grenville, spoken in this House in 1769, I say, if your resolution goes in the teeth of the law—if against the statute—your resolution is null and void. No word have I uttered outside these walls which has been lacking in respect to the House. I believe the House will do me justice, and I ask it to look at what it is I claim.

I claim to do that which the law says I must. Frankly, I would rather have affirmed. When I came to the table of the House I deemed I had a legal right to do it. The courts have decided against me, and I am bound by their decision.

I have the legal right to do what I propose to do. No resolution of yours can take away that legal right. You may act illegally and hinder me; and unfortunately I have no appeal against you. "Unfortunately," perhaps, I should not say. Perhaps it is better that the Chamber that makes the law should never be in conflict with the courts which administer the laws that the Chamber makes. I think the word "unfortunately" was not the word I ought to have used in this argument.

But the force that you invoke against the law to-day may to-morrow be used against you, and the use will be justified by your example. It is a fact that I have no remedy if you rely on your force. I can only be driven into a contest, wearying even to a strong man well supported, ruinous and killing to one man standing by himself—a contest in which, if I succeed, it will be injurious to you as well as to me. Injurious to me, because I can only win by lessening your repute, which I desire to maintain. The only court I have the power of appealing to is the court of public opinion, which I have no doubt in the end will do me justice.

The honorable member for Plymouth said I had the manliness on a former occasion to make an avowal of opinions to this House. I did nothing of the kind. I have never, directly or indirectly, said one word about my opinions, and this House has no right to inquire what opinions I may hold outside its walls. The only right is that which the statute gives you; my opinions there is no right to inquire into. I shelter myself under the laws of my country. This is a political assembly, met to decide on the policy of the nation and not on the religious opinions of the citizens. While I had the honor of occupying a seat in the House, when questions were raised which touched upon religious matters I abstained from uttering one word. I did not desire to say one word which might hurt the feeling of even the most tender.

But it is said, Why not have taken the oath quietly? I did not take it then, because I thought I had the right to do something else, and I have paid the penalty. I have been plunged in litigation fostered by men who had not the courage to put themselves forward. I, a penniless man, should have been ruined if it had not been that the men in workshop, pit, and factory had enabled me to fight this battle. [An interruption.]

I am sorry that honorable members cannot have patience with one pleading as I plead here. It is no light task, even if you put it on the lowest personal grounds, to risk the ambition of a life on such an issue. It is a right ambition to desire to take part in the councils of the nation if you bring no store of wisdom with you and can only learn from the great intellects that we have. What will you inquire into? The right honorable baronet would inquire into my opinions. Will you inquire into my conduct, or is it only my opinions you will try here?

The honorable member for Plymouth frankly puts it, opinions. If opinions, why not conduct? Why not examine into members' conduct when they come to the table, and see if there be no members in whose way you can put a barrier?

Are members whose conduct may be obnoxious to vote my exclusion because to them my opinions are obnoxious? As to any obnoxious views supposed to be held by me, there is no duty imposed upon me to say a word. The right honorable baronet has said there has been no word of recantation.

You have no right to ask me for any recantation. Since the ninth of April you have no right to ask me for anything. If you have a legal disqualification, petition, lay it before the judges. When you ask me to make a statement you are guilty of impertinence to me, of treason to the traditions of this House, and of impeachment of the liberties of the people. My difficulty is that those who have made the most bitter attacks upon me only made them when I was not here to deal with them.

One honorable and gallant member recently told his constituents that this would be made a party question, but that the Conservative members had not the courage to speak out against me. I should have thought, from reading "Hansard," not that they wanted courage, but that they had cultivated a reticence that was more just. I wish to say a word or two on the attempt which has been made to put on the government of the day complicity in my views.

The Liberal party has never aided me in any way to this House. Never. I have fought by myself. I have fought by my own hand. I have been hindered in every way that it was possible to hinder me; and it is only by the help of the people, by the pence of toilers in mine and factory, that I am here to-day after these five struggles right through thirteen years. I have won my way with them, for I have won their hearts, and now I come to you. Will you send me back from here?

Then how? You have the right, but it is the right of force and not of law. When I am once seated on these benches, then I am under your jurisdiction. At present I am under the protection of the writ from those who sent me here. I do not want to quote what has happened before; but if there be one lesson which the House has recorded more solemnly than another, it is that there should be no interference with the judgment of a constituency in sending a man to this House against whom there is no statutory disqualification. Let me appeal to the generosity of the House as well as to its strength. It has traditions of liberty on both sides. I do not complain that members on that [the Conservative] try to keep me out. They act according to their lights, and think my poor services may be injurious to them. [Cries of "No!"] Then why not let me in? It must be either a political or a religious question.

I must apologize to the House for trespassing upon its patience. I apologize because I know how generous in its listening it has been from the time of my first speech in it till now. But I ask you now, do not plunge with me into a struggle I would shun. The law gives me no remedy if the House decides against me. Do not mock at the constituencies. If you place yourselves above the law, you leave me no course save lawless agitation instead of reasonable pleading. It is easy to begin such a strife, but none knows how it would end. I have no court, no tribunal to appeal to: you have the strength of your votes at the moment. You think I am an obnoxious man, and that I have no one on my side. If that be so, then the more reason that this House, grand in the strength of its centuries of liberty, should have now that generosity in dealing with one who to-morrow may be forced into a struggle for public opinion against it.

HARRISON

BENJAMIN HARRISON, the grandson of President William Henry Harrison, and great-grandson of Benjamin Harrison, signer of the Declaration of Independence, was born at North Bend, Ohio, on August 20, 1833. He graduated at Miami University in 1852, and practiced law in Indianapolis until the Civil War, in which he served from 1862 to 1865, first as the commander of a regiment, and then as the General of a brigade. He represented Indiana in the United States Senate from 1881 to 1887. In 1888 he was the candidate of the Republican party for the Presidency, and was elected. In 1892 he was renominated, but was beaten by Cleveland. Since his retirement from the White House he has appeared before the Board of Arbitrators at Paris as the representative of Venezuela in its boundary controversy with British Guiana. He has lately been appointed one of the representatives of the United States on the permanent Board of Arbitration established in pursuance of the Peace Conference at The Hague.

INAUGURAL ADDRESS

DELIVERED MARCH 4, 1889

Fellow Citizens.

THERE is no constitutional or legal requirement that the President shall take the oath of office in the presence of the people, but there is so manifest an appropriateness in the public induction to office of the Chief Executive officer of the nation that from the beginning of the government the people, to whose service the official oath consecrates the officer, have been called to witness the solemn ceremonial. The oath taken in the presence of the people becomes a mutual covenant. The officer covenants to serve the whole body of the people by a faithful execution of the laws, so that they may be the unfailing defence and security of those who respect and observe them, and that neither wealth, station, nor the power of combinations shall be able to evade their just penalties or to wrest them from a beneficent public purpose to serve the ends of cruelty or selfishness.

My promise is spoken; yours unspoken, but not the less real and solemn. The people of every State have here their representatives. Surely I do not misinterpret the spirit of the occasion when I assume that the whole body of the people covenant with me and with each other to-day to support and defend the Constitution and the Union of the States, to yield willing obedience to all the laws and each to every other citizen his equal civil and political rights. Entering thus solemnly into covenant with each other, we may reverently invoke and confidently expect the favor and help of Almighty God—that he will give to me wisdom, strength, and fidelity, and to our people a spirit of fraternity and a love of righteousness and peace.

This occasion derives peculiar interest from the fact that the Presidential term, which begins this day, is the twenty-sixth under our Constitution. The first inauguration of President Washington took place in New York, where Congress was then sitting, on the thirtieth day of April, 1789, having been deferred by reason of delays attending the organization of Congress and the canvass of the electoral vote. Our people have already worthily observed the centennials of the Declaration of Independence, of the battle of Yorktown, and of the adoption of the Constitution, and will shortly celebrate in New York the institution of the second great department of our constitutional scheme of government. When the centennial of the institution of the judicial department, by the organization of the Supreme Court, shall have been suitably observed, as I trust it will be, our nation will have fully entered its second century.

I will not attempt to note the marvellous and, in great part, happy contrasts between our country as it steps over the threshold into its second century of organized existence under the Constitution and that weak but wisely ordered young nation that looked undauntedly down the first century, when all its years stretched out before it.

Our people will not fail at this time to recall the incidents which accompanied the institution of government under the Constitution, or to find inspiration and guidance in the teachings and example of Washington and his great associates, and hope and courage in the contrast which thirty-eight populous and prosperous States offer to the thirteen States, weak in everything except courage and the love of liberty, that then fringed our Atlantic seaboard.

The Territory of Dakota has now a population greater than any of the original States (except Virginia), and greater than the aggregate of five of the smaller States in 1790. The centre of population when our national capital was located was east of Baltimore, and it was argued by many well-informed persons that it would move eastward rather than westward; yet in 1880 it was found to be near Cincinnati, and the new census about to be taken will show another stride to the westward. That which was the body has come to be only the rich fringe of the nation's robe. But our growth has not been limited to territory, population, and aggregate wealth, marvellous as it has been in each of those directions. The masses of our people are better fed, clothed, and housed than their fathers were. The facilities for popular education have been vastly enlarged and more generally diffused.

The virtues of courage and patriotism have given recent proof of their continued presence and increasing power in the hearts and over the lives of our people. The influences of religion have been multiplied and strengthened. The sweet offices of charity have greatly increased. The virtue of temperance is held in higher estimation. We have not attained an ideal condition. Not all of our people are happy and prosperous; not all of them are virtuous and law-abiding. But on the whole, the opportunities offered to the individual to secure the comforts of life are better than are found elsewhere, and largely better than they were here one hundred years ago.

The surrender of a large measure of sovereignty to the general government, effected by the adoption of the Constitution, was not accomplished until the suggestions of reason were strongly reinforced by the more imperative voice of experience. The divergent interests of peace speedily demanded a "more perfect Union." The merchant, the shipmaster, and the manufacturer discovered and disclosed to our statesmen and to the people that commercial emancipation must be added to the political freedom which had been so bravely won. The commercial policy of the mother country had not relaxed any of its hard and oppressive features. To hold in check the development of our commercial marine, to prevent or retard the establishment and growth of manufactures in the States, and so to secure the American market for their shops and the carrying trade for their ships, was the policy of European statesmen, and was pursued with the most selfish vigor.

Petitions poured in upon Congress urging the imposition of discriminating duties that should encourage the production of needed things at home. The patriotism of the people, which no longer found a field of exercise in war, was energetically directed to the duty of equipping the young Republic for the defence of its independence by making its people self-dependent. Societies for the promotion of home manufactures and for encouraging the use of domestics in the dress of the people were organized in many of the States. The revival at the end of the century of the same patriotic interest in the preservation and development of domestic industries and the defence of our working people against injurious foreign competition is an incident worthy of attention. It is not a departure but a return that we have witnessed. The protective policy had then its opponents. The argument was made, as now, that its benefits inured to particular classes or sections.

If the question became in any sense or at any time sectional, it was only because slavery existed in some of the States. But for this there was no reason why the cotton-producing States should not have led or walked abreast with the New England States in the production of cotton fabrics. There was this reason only why the States that divide with Pennsylvania the mineral treasures of the great southeastern and central mountain ranges should have been so tardy in bringing to the smelting furnace and to the mill the coal and iron from their near opposing hillsides. Mill fires were lighted at the funeral pile of slavery. The Emancipation Proclamation was heard in the depths of the earth as well as in the sky; men were made free, and material things became our better servants.

The sectional element has happily been eliminated from the tariff discussion. We have no longer States that are necessarily only planting States. None is excluded from achieving that diversification of pursuits among the people which brings wealth and contentment. The cotton plantation will not be less valuable when the product is spun in the country town by operatives whose necessities call for diversified crops and create a home demand for garden and agricultural products. Every new mine, furnace and factory is an extension of the productive capacity of the State, more real and valuable than added territory.

Shall the prejudices and paralysis of slavery continue to hang upon the skirts of progress? How long will those who rejoice that slavery no longer exists cherish or tolerate the incapacities it put upon their communities? I look hopefully to the continuance of our protective system and to the consequent development of manufacturing and mining enterprises in the States hitherto wholly given to agriculture as a potent influence in the perfect unification of our people. The men who have invested their capital in these enterprises, the farmers who have felt the benefit of their neighborhood, and the men who work in shop or field, will not fail to find and to defend a community of interest.

Is it not quite possible that the farmers and the promoters of the great mining and manufacturing enterprises which have recently been established in the South may yet find that the free ballot of the workingman, without distinction of race, is needed for their defence as well as for his own? I do not doubt that if those men in the South who now accept the tariff views of Clay and the constitutional expositions of Webster would courageously avow and defend their real convictions, they would not find it difficult, by friendly instruction and co-operation, to make the black man their efficient and safe ally, not only in establishing correct principles in our national administration, but in preserving for their local communities the benefits of social order and economical and honest government. At least until the good offices of kindness and education have been fairly tried, the contrary conclusion cannot be plausibly urged.

I have altogether rejected the suggestion of a special Executive policy for any section of our country. It is the duty of the Executive to administer and enforce in the methods and by the instrumentalities pointed out and provided by the Constitution all the laws enacted by Congress. These laws are general, and their administration should be uniform and equal. As a citizen may not elect what laws he will obey, neither may the Executive elect which he will enforce. The duty to obey and to execute embraces the Constitution in its entirety and the whole code of laws enacted under it. The evil example of permitting individuals, corporations, or communities to nullify the laws because they cross some selfish or local interest or prejudice is full of danger, not only to the nation at large, but much more to those who use this pernicious expedient to escape their just obligations or to obtain an unjust advantage over others. They will presently themselves be compelled to appeal to the law for protection, and those who would use the law as a defence must not deny that use of it to others.

If our great corporations would more scrupulously observe their legal limitations and duties, they would have less cause to complain of the unlawful limitations of their rights or of violent interference with their operations. The community that by concert, open or secret, among its citizens, denies to a portion of its members their plain rights under the law, has severed the only safe bond of social order and prosperity. The evil works from a bad centre both ways. It demoralizes those who practice it, and destroys the faith of those who suffer by it in the efficiency of the law as a safe protector. The man in whose breast that faith has been darkened is naturally the subject of dangerous and uncanny suggestions. Those who use unlawful methods, if moved by no higher motive than the selfishness that prompted them, may well stop and inquire what is to be the end of this.

An unlawful expedient cannot become a permanent condition of government. If the educated and influential classes in a community either practice or connive at the systematic violation of laws that seem to them to cross their convenience, what can they expect when the lesson that convenience or a supposed class interest is a sufficient cause for lawlessness has been well learned by the ignorant classes? A community where law is the rule of conduct and where courts, not mobs, execute its penalties, is the only attractive field for business investments and honest labor.

Our naturalization laws should be so amended as to make the inquiry into the character and good disposition of persons applying for citizenship more careful and searching. Our existing laws have been in their administration an unimpressive and often an unintelligible form. We accept the man as a citizen without any knowledge of his fitness, and he assumes the duties of citizenship without any knowledge as to what they are. The privileges of American citizenship are so great and its duties so grave that we may well insist upon a good knowledge of every person applying for citizenship and a good knowledge by him of our institutions. We should not cease to be hospitable to immigration, but we should cease to be careless as to the character of it. There are men of all races, even the best, whose coming is necessarily a burden upon our public revenues or a threat to social order. These should be identified and excluded.

We have happily maintained a policy of avoiding all interference with European affairs. We have been only interested spectators of their contentions in diplomacy and in war, ready to use our friendly offices to promote peace, but never obtruding our advice and never attempting unfairly to coin the distresses of other powers into commercial advantage to ourselves. We have a just right to expect that our European policy will be the American policy of European courts.

It is so manifestly incompatible with those precautions for our peace and safety, which all the great powers habitually observe and enforce in matters affecting them, that a shorter waterway between our eastern and western seaboards should be dominated by any European government, that we may confidently expect that such a purpose will not be entertained by any friendly power.

We shall in the future, as in the past, use every endeavor to maintain and enlarge our friendly relations with all the great powers, but they will not expect us to look kindly upon any project that would leave us subject to the dangers of a hostile observation or environment. We have not sought to dominate or to absorb any of our weaker neighbors, but rather to aid and encourage them to establish free and stable governments resting upon the consent of their own people. We have a clear right to expect, therefore, that no European government will seek to establish colonial dependencies upon the territory of these independent American States. That which a sense of justice restrains us from seeking, they may be reasonably expected willingly to forego.

It must be assumed, however, that our interests are so exclusively American that our entire inattention to any events that may transpire elsewhere can be taken for granted. Our citizens, domiciled for purposes of trade in all countries and in many of the islands of the sea, demand and will have our adequate care in their personal and commercial rights. The necessities of our navy require convenient coaling stations and dock and harbor privileges. These and other trading privileges we will feel free to obtain only by means that do not in any degree partake of coercion, however feeble the government from which we ask such concessions. But having fairly obtained them by methods and for purposes entirely consistent with the most friendly disposition toward all other powers, our consent will be necessary to any modification or impairment of the concession.

We shall neither fail to respect the flag of any friendly nation, or the just rights of its citizens, nor to exact the like treatment for our own. Calmness, justice, and consideration should characterize our diplomacy. The offices of an intelligent diplomacy or of friendly arbitration in proper cases should be adequate to the peaceful adjustment of all international difficulties. By such methods we will make our contribution to the world's peace, which no nation values more highly, and avoid the opprobrium which must fall upon the nation that ruthlessly breaks it.

The duty devolved by law upon the President to nominate, and by and with the advice and consent of the Senate to appoint, all public officers whose appointment is not otherwise provided for in the Constitution or by act of

Congress, has become very burdensome, and its wise and efficient discharge full of difficulty. The civil list is so large that a personal knowledge of any large number of the applicants is impossible. The President must rely upon the representation of others, and these are often made inconsiderately and without any just sense of responsibility. I have a right, I think, to insist that those who volunteer or are invited to give advice as to appointments shall exercise consideration and fidelity. A high sense of duty and an ambition to improve the service should characterize all public officers.

There are many ways in which the convenience and comfort of those who have business with our public offices may be promoted by a thoughtful and obliging officer, and I shall expect those whom I may appoint to justify their selection by a conspicuous efficiency in the discharge of their duties. Honorable party service will certainly not be esteemed by me a disqualification for public office, but it will in no case be allowed to serve as a shield of official negligence, incompetency, or delinquency. It is entirely creditable to seek public office by proper methods and with proper motives, and all applicants will be treated with consideration; but I shall need, and the heads of departments will need, time for inquiry and deliberation. Persistent importunity will not, therefore, be the best support of an application for office. Heads of departments, bureaus, and all other public officers having any duty connected therewith, will be expected to enforce the Civil Service law fully and without evasion. Beyond this obvious duty I hope to do something more to advance the reform of the civil service. The ideal, or even my own ideal, I shall probably not attain. Retrospect will be a safer basis of judgment than promises. We shall not, however, I am sure, be able to put our civil service upon a non-partisan basis until we have secured an incumbency that fair-minded men of the opposition will approve for impartiality and integrity. As the number of such in the civil list is increased, removals from office will diminish.

While a Treasury surplus is not the greatest evil, it is a serious evil. Our revenue should be ample to meet the ordinary annual demands upon our Treasury, with a sufficient margin for those extraordinary, but scarcely less imperative, demands which arise now and then. Expenditure should always be made with economy, and only upon public necessity. Wastefulness, profligacy, or favoritism in public expenditure is criminal. But there is nothing in the condition of our country or of our people to suggest that anything presently necessary to the public prosperity, security, or honor, should be unduly postponed.

It will be the duty of Congress wisely to forecast and estimate these extraordinary demands, and, having added them to our ordinary expenditures, to so adjust our revenue laws that no considerable annual surplus will remain. We will fortunately be able to apply to the redemption of the public debt any small and unforeseen excess of revenue. This is better than to reduce our income below our necessary expenditures, with the resulting choice between another change of our revenue laws and an increase of the public debt. It is quite possible, I am sure, to effect the necessary reduction in our revenues without breaking down our protective tariff or seriously injuring any domestic industry.

The construction of a sufficient number of modern warships and of their necessary armament should progress as rapidly as is consistent with care and perfection in plans and workmanship. The spirit, courage, and skill of our naval officers and seamen have many times in our history given to weak ships and inefficient guns a rating greatly beyond that of the naval list. That they will again do so upon occasion, I do not doubt; but they ought not, by premeditation or neglect, to be left to the risks and exigencies of an unequal combat. We should encourage the establishment of American steamship lines. The exchanges of commerce demand stated, reliable, and rapid means of communication; and until these are provided, the development of our trade with the States lying south of us is impossible.

Our pension laws should give more adequate and discriminating relief to the Union soldiers and sailors and to their widows and orphans. Such occasions as this should remind us that we owe everything to their valor and sacrifice.

It is a subject of congratulation that there is a near prospect of the admission into the Union of the Dakotas and Montana and Washington Territories. This act of justice has been unreasonably delayed in the case of some of them. The people who have settled these Territories are intelligent, enterprising, and patriotic, and the accession of these new States will add strength to the nation. It is due to the settlers in the Territories who have availed themselves of the invitations of our land laws to make homes upon the public domain that their titles should be speedily adjusted and their honest entries confirmed by patent.

It is very gratifying to observe the general interest now being manifested in the reform of our election laws. Those who have been for years calling attention to the pressing necessity of throwing about the ballot-box and about the elector further safeguards, in order that our elections might not only be free and pure, but might clearly appear to be so, will welcome the accession of any who did not so soon discover the need of reform. The National Congress has not as yet taken control of elections in that case over which the Constitution gives it jurisdiction, but has accepted and adopted the election laws of the several States, provided penalties for their violation and a method of supervision. Only the inefficiency of the State laws or an unfair partisan administration of them could suggest a departure from this policy.

It was clear, however, in the contemplation of the framers of the Constitution, that such an exigency might arise, and provision was wisely made for it. The freedom of the ballot is a condition of our national life, and no power vested in Congress or in the Executive to secure or perpetuate it should remain unused upon occasion. The people of all the congressional districts have an equal interest that the election in each shall truly express the views and wishes of a majority of the qualified electors residing within it. The results of such elections are not local, and the insistence of electors residing in other districts that they shall be pure and free does not savor at all of impertinence.

If in any of the States the public security is thought to be threatened by ignorance among the electors, the obvious remedy is education. The sympathy and help of our people will not be withheld from any community struggling with special embarrassments or difficulties connected with the suffrage, if the remedies proposed proceed upon lawful lines and are promoted by just and honorable methods. How shall those who practice election frauds recover that respect for the sanctity of the ballot which is the first condition and obligation of good citizenship? The man who has come to regard the ballot-box as a juggler's hat has renounced his allegiance.

Let us exalt patriotism and moderate our party contentions. Let those who would die for the flag on the field of battle give a better proof of their patriotism and a higher glory to their country by promoting fraternity and justice. A party success that is achieved by unfair methods or by practices that partake of revolution is hurtful and evanescent, even from a party standpoint. We should hold our differing opinions in mutual respect, and, having submitted them to the arbitrament of the ballot, should accept an adverse judgment with the same respect that we would have demanded of our opponents if the decision had been in our favor.

No other people have a government more worthy of their respect and love, or a land so magnificent in extent, so pleasant to look upon, and so full of generous suggestion to enterprise and labor. God has placed upon our head a diadem, and has laid at our feet power and wealth beyond definition or calculation. But we must not forget that we take these gifts upon the condition that justice and mercy shall hold the reins of power, and that the upward avenues of hope shall be free to all the people.

I do not mistrust the future. Dangers have been in frequent ambush along our path, but we have uncovered and vanquished them all. Passion has swept some of our communities, but only to give us a new demonstration that the great body of our people are stable, patriotic, and law-abiding. No political party can long pursue advantage at the expense of public honor or by rude and indecent methods, without protest and fatal disaffection in its own body. The peaceful agencies of commerce are more fully revealing the necessary unity of all our communities, and the increasing intercourse of our people is promoting mutual respect. We shall find unalloyed pleasure in the revelation which our next census will make of the swift development of the great resources of some of the States. Each State will bring its generous contribution to the great aggregate of the nation's increase. And when the harvests from the fields, the cattle from the hills, and the ores of the earth shall have been weighed, counted, and valued, we will turn from them all to crown with the highest honor the State that has most promoted education, virtue, justice and patriotism among its people.

BLAKE

EDWARD BLAKE, an eminent Canadian statesman, is the eldest son of the late Hon. William Hume Blake, a well-known Canadian statesman, who afterward became chancellor of Upper Canada, now Ontario. He was born at the present village of Cairngorm, Ontario, October 13, 1833, and was educated at Upper Canada College (Governor-General's prizeman) and at the University of Toronto. He was called to the bar in 1856 and entered into practice in the city of Toronto. In 1864 he was created a queen's counsel by Viscount Monck; became a bencher of the Law Society of Upper Canada in 1871; and treasurer of the Law Society in 1879. For a time he was one of the examiners in, and a lecturer on, equity for the Law Society; and was appointed an honorary member of the law faculty of Toronto University in 1888. He declined appointment as chancellor of Upper Canada under Sir John Macdonald in 1869; as chief justice of Canada under Mackenzie in 1875; and as chief justice of Ontario under Sir W. Laurier in 1897. His political career began in 1867, the epoch of confederation, when he was elected both to the House of Commons and the legislature. In 1869 he accepted the leadership of the Liberal party; and on the defeat of the Sandfield-Macdonald government in December, 1871 (an event largely due to his efforts), he was called on to form a new administration and succeeded in the task. He himself took the office of president of the council without salary. On the abolition of dual representation, some time later, he resigned the premiership with the view of devoting the whole of his attention to federal politics. He was one of the greatest champions in the contest over the Pacific Railroad scandal, which resulted in the downfall of Sir John A. Macdonald. When Mr. Mackenzie became prime minister of Canada Mr. Blake accepted a position in the cabinet without office. He was sworn of the privy council November 7, 1873. Owing to ill health he resigned in February, 1874. In May, 1875, he accepted office as minister of justice, and while such undertook an official mission to England. He was mainly instrumental in perfecting the constitution of the supreme court of Canada, and personally selected the first judges. After the defeat of the Mackenzie government at the polls in 1878, he was chosen leader of the Liberal party in the House of Commons, and remained in that position until after the general election of 1887, when he retired and was succeeded by Mr. Laurier. In June, 1892, he accepted the invitation of the leaders of the Irish parliamentary party to represent them in the British House of Commons. In 1894 he was elected a member of the executive committee of the Irish parliamentary party. In the same year he was included in the Royal Commission appointed to inquire into the financial relations between Great Britain and Ireland. In 1895 he was re-elected by acclamation for South Longford. In the same year he went to New Zealand to serve as arbitrator between the New Zealand government and the New Zealand Midland Railway Company, and made his award in December, wholly in favor of the government. In 1896 he was one of the committee of fifteen of the House of Commons, appointed to investigate South African affairs and the causes of the Transvaal raid. He received the honorary degree of LL.D. from his Alma Mater, in 1889, but declined a K.C.M.G. for his public services in 1876. He was a delegate to the third Commercial Congress, London, 1893. The "Globe" called him "the most powerful Canadian speaker whose voice has been heard by this generation;" and Lord Roseberry declared him to be "the most brilliant orator and one of the most capable statesmen of Canada."

SUFFRAGE FOR WOMEN

EXTRACTS FROM SPEECH DELIVERED IN THE CANADIAN HOUSE OF COMMONS, APRIL 17, 1885

LET me now look at one of the most important propositions, that to which I alluded a little while ago; look to the question of suffrage for women. Now, you found a marked difference in the language of the First Minister and that of the Secretary of State, with reference to that subject. The honorable Minister of Public Works was wisely silent; he said nothing about it. I do not know what he thought. Perhaps it was because he thought so much that he said so little; but at any rate he has kept a profound silence upon the subject of woman suffrage.

The honorable gentleman, however, upon some former occasions, was disposed, I remember, when a little badinage was passing across the House, rather to take credit for the woman-suffrage clause. I recollect he alluded to the ladies in the courteous and pleasant manner in which he speaks of the whole population, whether ladies or gentlemen, and spoke about the action of the right honorable gentleman with reference to it—so I presume that he favors it too.

But the First Minister declared himself strongly in favor of the woman suffrage; he declared the time was coming, and that soon, when it would be granted, and that he would be glad to see Canada take the first final step; and he referred to Mr. Gladstone, who, he said, was in favor of woman suffrage, and to Lord Salisbury and Sir Stafford Northcote, who had declared themselves in favor of it. Now, I think

I have read all that Mr. Gladstone has ever said on that subject—though I have not been able to refer to all his speeches since the honorable gentleman spoke—and my recollection is that Mr. Gladstone had not delivered an opinion in favor of woman suffrage.

I am quite certain that in the late debate, when he had to meet Mr. Woodall's motion, he did not express an opinion in favor of it. He declared he would not express an opinion on the subject. He took the line of the Secretary of State. But, if I do not greatly err, in a former debate upon the question he expressed the view that if the franchise was to be given to the other sex he saw no ground upon which it could be limited to unmarried women; he expressed the view, if I remember rightly, that it must be conferred upon married women if conferred at all. Now, the honorable gentleman says that he will adopt Mr. Gladstone's attitude, and that he will not imperil this bill on the question of woman suffrage.

But Mr. Gladstone's attitude was wholly different. Mr. Gladstone had not brought in a bill with woman suffrage in it. Mr. Gladstone had brought in a bill that did not give the franchise to women. It was a government bill, and he was handling that government bill with a government in which the question was an open question, avowedly. Some members of the government were in favor of it and others opposed to it. But what Mr. Gladstone, who had not committed himself upon the question, said, was:

"I will not imperil this bill by allowing you to add the question of woman suffrage to it at all. I will express no opinion. It is an open question so far as we are concerned, but we have a duty to discharge, and that is to carry this bill through; and those of us who are in favor of, as well as those who are opposed to woman suffrage, to take the ground that we are opposed to tacking it on to this bill."

But the honorable gentleman's view is different. He says:

"I have introduced a bill. I introduced it in 1883; I introduced it in 1884, and now in 1885; and I commend it to your attention as a government proposition. It is the government's proposition, but, forsooth, I will adopt Mr. Gladstone's views, and I will not imperil the bill."

The honorable gentleman had better have left it out, if he did not intend to carry it. But the honorable gentleman seems to be disposed to think that he will manage the matter. Having brought it in, in the former sessions, and having, presumably, taken the opinion of his friends upon it, he still proceeded, this session, with that clause in; and presumably he took some opinions again, and in the end he is to be forced to leave it out. It cannot be called an open question. Whoever heard of any ministerial measure being an open question. It is not an open question, but he has been forced to relax the tight bonds of party discipline and graciously to give his followers liberty to vote as they please on this question.

Well, the Secretary of State declared that he would not discuss the subject. He said that in different Provinces that question was not accepted in the same spirit, and that in Quebec public opinion was hostile. Now the question is no doubt a very important one. It is one of the most important that can be raised. I cannot conceive a more important political question than that which is raised by this clause of this bill, and I am free to say that I do not think the First Minister discharged his duty as a leader of the government by proposing such a clause in the bill if he did not mean to pass it, nor did he discharge his duty in the way of exposition of the views of the government in his speech. . . .

You talk of elevating the race—the race of women and of men. You say that it is for the good of the race that women should become political electors.

I grant your concession for argument's sake. But there is a law higher than your laws, that is the law under which we live and in which the appointed state of the great bulk of us is the marriage state; and that is not for the good of the race which tells us you are to elevate those who do not happen to be in the married state, and you are to disable them from the exercise of the elevating principle as soon as they assume that which is the ordinary condition of the race, both as regards men and women.

Will you be allowed, do you think, to say that the daughters may vote and the mothers shall not vote. Our laws are every day, and justly so, more fully recognizing the right of women to own property—the right of a woman to have her own property independent of her husband. These conditions of amelioration are being generally accepted, and they are becoming exceedingly wide—I do not know exactly how wide—in the different Provinces. They exist in Ontario, under the old codes, to a very large extent; they exist in Quebec, which for very many years has had more reasonable laws on this subject than formerly prevailed in others of the Provinces. We do not recognize the old doctrine that the husband may say to the wife that all she has is his.

This is no longer the doctrine. A woman's property may be her own. If a woman's property may be her own, why should we say that it is for the elevation of the woman that she should have a vote, and yet deny it to eight tenths of the women, the mothers and the wives, though they are property-owners, and give it to those who are spinsters or widows, and to those only. How can the question stop even the right to vote? On what principle will you grant the right to elect and deny the right to be elected? On what logical and political principle will you do that? I can apprehend inconveniences, of course, but, as to them, surely the people are to be the judges. If the people choose to elect a woman, and a woman is eligible to vote, why should she not be eligible to take her seat in Parliament? On what ground can we say that people shall not have the right to choose a woman as their representative if women have the franchise?

I did not see but that all these things are to be opened by this bill, and that we may some day or other, under the government's proposition when fully developed, have a Speaker in a gown, it is true, but of a different kind and framed on different plans from that which you, Mr. Speaker, wear. These questions are all opened by this bill; it is certain they are not closed. They are opened by this bill; and even the proposition brought forward is brought forward without popular approbation? Have we been told by the honorable gentleman at any election that this was his policy? The honorable gentleman says that he has always favored it. But he kept it, like many others of his favorites, in his bosom. He did not tell anybody of his secret affection for the female franchise; he did not disclose his hidden love:

"Concealment, like a worm i' the bud, preyed on his damask cheek."

He alone knew how devoted he was to the sex. Why did he not let us know; why did he not let them know? Why did he woo them so much in secret that they did not know he was wooing them at all? How did it happen that this unrequited attachment of the First Minister did not become known?

I maintain that if the honorable gentleman nourished those views, and nourished them not merely as theoretical views and ideas which he would like to see put in force, but did not intend to take the responsibility of bringing forward, but as practical ideas, in which he was going to legislate, he was bound to have told the people at large, and to have said, "I am in favor of woman suffrage, and I am not merely in favor of it, but I propose, if you elect me and my supporters, to use my influence and position to accomplish that which I conceive to be a great reform."

We did not know anything about this until the honorable gentleman was in office. Has there been any agitation on this question; has there been any discussion of it among the people? Yes, I think I hear the honorable gentleman say, "A petition or two was presented." But the greatest marks of surprise upon the subject were exhibited by the few agitators for the women's suffrage themselves, who met and passed a resolution of thanks to the honorable gentleman for having spontaneously and without request done so much more for them than they expected. Now, I maintain that that is not the way in which a great idea of this kind should germinate and ripen until it becomes an act of Parliament. I maintain that there ought to be suggestions by responsible statesmen, agitation and discussion, and fair opportunity for the people at large to decide what they will have upon such a subject, before you propose to legislate at all. . . .

I, myself, have not infrequently stated my earnest desire that my fellow country-women should take a more active interest them they do in public affairs; that they should acquaint themselves more thoroughly than they do with public questions, and I rejoice when I see them attending our political discussions and informing their minds on public questions. But while that is so, and while I believe there is a very satisfactory and progressive improvement in that department of this question, I ask the candid consideration of the House, and of the men and women of the country, to the question whether the women have as yet, as a class (if we are to call them so), as a sex, as a whole, taken up politics in the way we do.

I do not think the men pay sufficient attention to public affairs. I do not think that the electors give that attention which they ought to give to the current of public events. I do not think they do their full duty, or that they are fully alive to their responsibility as electors of this country. I think much has to be done in the way of informing them what that duty is, and enlisting from them a more active discharge of it. But, whatever the shortcomings of the men may be, it is clear, up to this time, that women have taken less steady and active interest in public affairs than those who are the electors. Now, do you wish to see them take that measure of interest that we do in politics? Unquestionably, yes, if you wish them to be voters. There is no more dangerous element in the voting community of the country than the mass which does not take a keen and active interest in public affairs, on one side or the other. I say the mass who do not inform themselves and keep their interest alive—and there are too many of them among the men of the country to-day—the mass who do not keep alive their interest in public affairs is a mass which is dangerous, and which impairs and sometimes imperils the stability of our institutions. Therefore, unquestionably, you do wish them to take an interest. Then, do you wish them to become delegates to your conventions; to become committee-women; to become canvassers? I say yes, if they are going to be voters. I say you cannot double the voting population of the country without danger if you do not hope that the added population will take the same degree of interest and activity in the formation of public opinion, the organization of public opinion, as the rest; and therefore you must wish these things.

Therefore it is, sir, that the question before you is a momentous question. The question whether you are to make electors of the women is a question not to be dealt with in a speech of one and a half minutes, even by a gentleman of the authority of the First Minister. It should not be settled without full and ample thought and deliberation; without full consideration of the people at large; without full consideration by the women of the country themselves; without an appreciation of what their wishes are,—which are important to the consideration of this question, because I think it would be a mistake to force the franchise on a reluctant portion of the population,— if they be reluctant to accept the franchise, as to which, again, one has no opportunity of forming an opinion except from the absence of application for the purpose.

I say we have got to consider, then, the whole bearings of this proposition in the extent to which, in my opinion it will inevitably lead. I do not believe the wives and mothers of Canada will be content to see the daughters and widows voting, and will support the proposition that they should vote,—the view that it elevates the sex that they should vote, and yet should find themselves relegated to the lower sphere of those who are debarred from voting because they are wives. I do not believe in that view at all. I do not think that we should in one breath say it is good for women; it is good for spinsters; it is good for widows; it is good for the race; it is for the elevation of women that they shall vote, but it is bad for the married woman. I do not think so at all;

and therefore I think the question of their opinion and of their condition must be taken into account on this subject. I do not intend, as I have said, to discuss what the present place of woman is and what the future of woman is to be, but if you will allow me I will read you what I think is some very good philosophy, couched in glorious poetry, on that subject, and which, although I do not agree with all it says, I think tells as much on the problem which the honorable gentleman has submitted to us as has been told in any time past in so short a space:

> "The woman's cause is man's: they rise or sink
> Together, dwarfed or Godlike, bond or free;
> For she that out of Lethe scales with man
> The shining steps of nature, shares with man
> His nights, his days, moves with him to one goal,
> Stays all the fair young planets in her hands.
> If she be small, slight-natured, miserable,
> How shall men grow? But work no more alone;
> Our place is much; as far as in us lies,
> We two will serve them both in aiding her,
> Will clear away the parasitic forms
> That seem to keep her up, but drag her down;
> Will leave her space to burgeon out of all
> Within her—let her make herself her own,
> To give or keep, to live and learn and be
> All that not harms distinctive womanhood.
> For woman is not undeveloped man,
> But diverse; could we make her as the men,
> Sweet love were slain; his dearest bond is this.
> Not like to like, but like in difference.
> Yet in the long years liker must they grow—
> The man be more of woman, she of man;
> He gain in sweetness and in moral height,
> Nor lose the wrestling thews that throw the world;
> e mental breadth, nor fail in childward care,
> lose the childlike in the larger mind;
> t the last she set herself to man,
> erfect music unto noble words;
> these twain, upon the skirts of time,
> by side, full-summ'd in all their powers,
> harvest, sowing the to-be,
> t each and reverencing each,
> ndividualities,
> other ev'n as those who love.
> statelier Eden back to men;
> orld's great bridals, chaste and calm;
> growing race of humankind.
> e!"

Yes; may these things be! But I believe that the philosophy which is indicated in those verses is a philosophy which requires deep study before you can decide that these things are to be by the honorable gentleman's proposal to confer the rights of voting upon spinsters and widows, and to leave out those to whom these verses are addressed—the married women.

Now, as I have said, the only safe process in this matter is discussion—gradual discussion, thorough discussion; and the result of that discussion may be—indeed probably will be, for we have to look far off—a diversity of opinion in the different Provinces. The Honorable Secretary of State to-day frankly admitted that on this branch of the Bill there are two opinions. There is the hostile opinion in the Province of Quebec; there is perhaps a favorable opinion in some of the other Provinces; I argue for leaving each Province to settle its own franchise. If you do not want woman franchise in the Province of Quebec, you are free not to have it; but leave the people to decide whether they shall have it or not. Woman franchise may be popular in the Province of Ontario; let the Province of Ontario pass a law to give women the franchise; that does not hurt Quebec, but give Ontario that which best suits her. And so with reference to the Provinces. Nc stronger argument for the adaptability and convenience of a independent franchise for each Province can be found th that provision of the bill, and the statement of the Secret of State with reference to the woman franchise.

INGALLS

JOHN JAMES INGALLS, an American politician and congressman, was born at Middleton, Massachusetts, December 29, 1833, and was educated at Williams College. He studied law and was admitted to the bar in 1857, and the next year removed to Atchison, Kansas, which continued thereafter to be his home. He was a member of the Wyandotte Convention of 1850, and entered the Kansas Senate in 1862. In the same year he was an unsuccessful Republican candidate for the lieutenant-governorship of Kansas, as also two years later. He was for some years editor of the "Atchison Champion," before his election to the United States Senate, where he took his seat in 1873. He served continuously in the Senate until his retirement from political life in 1891, and since that period engaged in journalism and lecturing. He was an able and eloquent debater, having at all times the courage of his convictions. He died August 16, 1900.

ON THE POLITICAL SITUATION

SPEECH IN THE SENATE OF THE UNITED STATES, JANUARY 14, 1891

MR. PRESIDENT,—Two portentous perils threaten the safety if they do not endanger the existence of the republic.

The first of these is ignorant, debased, degraded, spurious, and sophisticated suffrage; suffrage contaminated by the feculent sewage of decaying nations; suffrage intimidated and suppressed in the South; suffrage impure and corrupt, apathetic and indifferent, in the great cities of the North, so that it is doubtful whether there has been for half a century a presidential election in this country that expressed the deliberate and intelligent judgment of the whole body of the American people.

In a newspaper interview a few months ago, in which I commented upon these conditions and alluded to the efforts of the bacilli doctors of politics, the bacteriologists of our system, who endeavor to cure the ills under which we suffer by their hypodermic injections of the lymph of independent nonpartisanship and the Brown-Séquard elixir of civil-service reform, I said that "the purification of politics" by such methods as these was an "iridescent dream." Remembering the cipher dispatches of 1877 and the attempted purchase of the electoral votes of many southern States in that campaign, the forgery of the Morey letter in 1880, by which Garfield lost the votes of three States in the North, and the characterization and portraiture of Blaine and Cleveland and Harrison by their political adversaries, I added that "the Golden Rule and the Decalogue had no place in American political campaigns."

It seems superfluous to explain, Mr. President, that in those utterances I was not inculcating a doctrine, but describing a condition. My statement was a statement of facts as I understood them, and not the announcement of an article of faith. But many reverend and eminent divines, many disinterested editors, many ingenuous orators, perverted those utterances into the personal advocacy of impurity in politics.

I do not complain, Mr. President. It was, as the world goes, legitimate political warfare; but it was an illustration of the truth that there ought to be purification in our politics, and that the Golden Rule and the Decalogue ought to have a place in political campaigns. "Do unto others as ye would that others should do unto you" is the supreme injunction, obligatory upon all. "If thine enemy smite thee upon one cheek turn to him the other" is a sublime and lofty precept. But I take this occasion to observe that until it is more generally regarded than it has been or appears likely to be in the immediate future, if my political enemy smites me upon one cheek, instead of turning to him the other I shall smite him under the butt end of his left ear if I can. If this be political immorality, I am to be included among the unregenerated.

The election bill that was under consideration a few days ago is intended to deal with one part of the great evil to which I have alluded, but it is an imperfect, a partial, and an incomplete remedy. Violence is bad; but fraud is no better; and it is more dangerous because it is more insidious.

Burke said in one of those immortal orations that emptied the House of Commons, but which will be read with admiration so long as the English tongue shall endure, that when the laws of Great Britain were not strong enough to protect the humblest Hindoo upon the shores of the Ganges the nobleman was not safe in his castle upon the banks of the Thames. Sir, that lofty sentence is pregnant with admonition for us. There can be no repose, there can be no stable and permanent peace in this country under this government until it is just as safe for the black Republican to vote in Mississippi as it is for the white Democrat to vote in Kansas.

The other evil, Mr. President, the second to which I adverted as threatening the safety if it does not endanger the existence of the republic, is the tyranny of combined, concentrated, centralized, and incorporated capital. And the people are considering this great problem now. The conscience of the nation is shocked at the injustice of modern society. The moral sentiment of mankind has been aroused at the unequal distribution of wealth, at the unequal diffusion of the burdens, the benefits, and the privileges of society.

At the beginning of our second century the American people have become profoundly conscious that the ballot is not the panacea for all the evils that afflict humanity; that it has not abolished poverty nor prevented injustice. They have discovered that political equality does not result in social fraternity; that under a democracy the concentration of greater political power in fewer hands, the accumulation and aggregation of greater amounts of wealth in individuals, are more possible than under a monarchy, and that there is a tyranny which is more fatal than the tyranny of kings.

George Washington, the first President of the Republic, at the close of his life in 1799 had the largest private fortune in the United States of America. Much of this came by inheritance, but the Father of his Country, in addition to his other virtues, shining and illustrious, was a very prudent, sagacious, thrifty, and forehanded man. He knew a good thing when he saw it a great way off. He had a keen eye for the main chance. As a surveyor in his youth he obtained knowledge that enabled him to make exceedingly valuable locations upon the public domain. The establishment of the national capital in the immediate vicinity of his patrimonial possessions did not diminish their value. He was a just debtor, but he was an exact if not an exacting creditor. And so it came to pass that when he died he was, to use the expressive phraseology of the day, the richest man in the country.

At this time, ninety years afterward, it is not without interest to know that the entire aggregate and sum of his earthly possessions, his estate, real, personal, and mixed, Mount Vernon and his lands along the Kanawha and the Ohio, slaves, securities, all of his belongings, reached the sum total of between $800,000 and $900,000. This was less than a century ago, and it is within bounds to say that at this time there are many scores of men, of estates, and of corporations in this country whose annual income exceed, and there has been one man whose monthly revenue since that period exceeded, the entire accumulations of the wealthiest citizen of the United States at the end of the last century.

At that period the social condition of the United States was one of practical equality. The statistics of the census of 1800 are incomplete and fragmentary, but the population of the Union was about 5,300,000, and the estimated wealth of the country was between $3,000,000,000 and $4,000,000,000. There was not a millionaire, and there was not a tramp nor a pauper, so far as we know, in the country, except such as had been made so by infirmity, or disease, or inevitable calamity. A multitude of small farmers contentedly tilled the soil. Upon the coast a race of fishermen and sailors, owning the craft that they sailed, wrested their substance from the stormy seas. Labor was the rule and luxury the exception. The great mass of the people lived upon the products of the farms that they cultivated. They spun and wove and manufactured their clothing from flax and from wool. Commerce and handicrafts afforded honorable competence. The prayer of Agur was apparently realized. There was neither poverty nor riches. Wealth was uniformly diffused, and none were condemned to hopeless penury and dependence. Less than four per cent of the entire population lived in towns, and there were but four cities whose population exceeded 10,000 persons. Westward to the Pacific lay the fertile solitudes of an unexplored continent, its resources undeveloped and unsuspected. The dreams of Utopia seemed about to be fulfilled—the wide, the universal diffusion of civil, political, and personal rights among the great body of the people, accompanied by efficient and vigorous guaranties for the safety of life, the protection of property, and the preservation of liberty.

Since that time, Mr. President, the growth in wealth and numbers in this country has had no precedent in the building of nations. The genius of the people, stimulated to prodigious activity by freedom, by individualism, by universal education, has subjugated the desert and abolished the frontier. The laboring capacity of every inhabitant of this planet has been duplicated by machinery. In Massachusetts alone we are told that its engines are equivalent to the labor of one hundred million men. We now perform one third of the world's mining, one quarter of its manufacturing, one fifth of its farming, and we possess one sixth part of its entire accumulated wealth.

The Anglo-Saxon, Mr. President, is not by nature or instinct an anarchist, a socialist, a nihilist, or a communist. He does not desire the repudiation of debts, public or private, and he does not favor the forcible redistribution of property. He came to this continent, as he has gone everywhere else on the face of the earth, with a purpose. The 40,000 English colonists who came to this country between 1620 and 1650 formed the most significant, the most formidable migration that has ever occurred upon this globe since time began. They brought with them social and political ideas, novel in their application, of inconceivable energy and power, the home, the family, the State, individualism, the right of personal effort, freedom of conscience, an indomitable love of liberty and justice, a genius for self-government, an unrivalled capacity for conquest, but preferring charters to the sword, and they have been inexorable and relentless in the accomplishment of their designs. They were fatigued with caste and privilege and prerogative.

They were tired of monarchs, and so, upon the bleak and inhospitable shores of New England they decreed the sovereignty of the people, and there they builded "a church without a bishop, and a state without a king."

The result of that experiment, Mr. President, has been ostensibly successful. Under the operation of those great forces, after two hundred and seventy years, this country exhibits a peaceful triumph over many subdued nationalities, through a government automatic in its functions and sustained by no power but the invisible majesty of law. With swift and constant communication by lines of steam transportation by land and lake and sea, with telegraphs extending their nervous reticulations from State to State, the remotest members of this gigantic republic are animated by a vitality as vigorous as that which throbs at its mighty heart, and it is through the quickened intelligence that has been communicated by those ideas that these conditions, which have been fatal to other nations, have become the pillars of our strength and the bulwarks of our safety.

Mr. President, if time and space signified now what they did when independence was declared, the United States could not exist under one government. It would not be possible to secure unity of purpose or identity of interest between communities separated by such barriers and obstacles as Maine and California. But time and distance are relative terms, and, under the operations of these forces, this continent has dwindled to a span. It is not as far from Boston to San Francisco to-day as it was from Boston to Baltimore in 1791; and as the world has shrunk, life has expanded. For all the purposes for which existence is valuable in this world—for comfort, for convenience, for opportunity, for intelligence, for power of locomotion, and superiority to the accidents and the fatalities of nature—the fewest in years among us, Mr. President, has lived longer and has lived more worthily than Methuselah in all his stagnant centuries.

When the Atlantic cable was completed, it was not merely that a wire, finer by comparison than the gossamer of morning, had sunk to its path along the peaks and the plateaus of the deep, but the earth instantaneously grew smaller by the breadth of the Atlantic. A new volume in the history of the world was opened. The to-morrow of Europe flashed upon the yesterday of America. Time, up to the period when this experiment commenced on this continent, yielded its treasures grudgingly and with reluctance. The centuries crept from improvement to improvement with tardy and sluggish steps, as if nature were unwilling to acknowledge the mastery of man. The great inventions of glass, of gunpowder, of printing, and the mariner's compass consumed a thousand years, but as the great experiment upon this continent has proceeded, the ancient law of progress has been disregarded, and the mind is bewildered by the stupendous results of its marvellous achievements.

The application of steam to locomotion on land and sea, the cotton-gin, electric illumination and telegraphy, the cylinder printing press, the sewing machine, the photographic art, tubular and suspension bridges, the telephone, the spectroscope, and the myriad forms of new applications of science to health and domestic comfort, to the arts of peace and war, have alone rendered democracy possible. The steam-engine emancipated millions from the slavery of daily toil and left them at liberty to pursue a higher range of effort; labor has become more remunerative, and the flood of wealth has raised the poor to comfort and the middle classes to affluence. With prosperity has attended leisure, books, travel; the masses have been provided with schools, and the range of mental inquiry has become wider and more daring. The sewing-machine does the work of a hundred hands, and gives rest and hope to weary lives. Farming, as my distinguished friend from New York [Mr. Evarts] once said, has become a "sedentary occupation." The reaper no longer swings his sickle in midsummer fields through the yellowish grain, followed by those who gather the wheat and the tares, but he rides in a vehicle, protected from the meridian sun, accomplishing in comfort in a single hour the former labors of a day.

By these and other emancipating devices of society the laborer and the artisan acquire the means of study and recreation. They provide their children with better opportunities than they possessed. Emerging from the obscure degradation to which they have been consigned by monarchies, they have assumed the leadership in politics and society. The governed have become the governors; the subjects have become the kings. They have formed States; they have invented political systems; they have made laws; they have established literatures; and it is not true, Mr. President, in one sense, that during this extraordinary period the rich have grown richer and the poor have grown poorer. There has never been a time, since the angel stood with the flaming sword before the gates of Eden, when the dollar of invested capital paid as low a return in interest as it does to-day; nor has there been an hour when the dollar that is earned by the laboring man would buy so much of everything that is essential for the welfare of himself and his family as it will to-day.

Mr. President, monopolies and corporations, however strong they may be, cannot permanently enslave such a people. They have given too many convincing proofs of their capacity for self-government. They have made too many incredible sacrifices for this great system, which has been builded and established here, to allow it to be overthrown. They will submit to no dictation.

We have become, Mr. President, the wealthiest nation upon the face of this earth, and the greater part of these enormous accumulations has been piled up during the past fifty years. From 1860 to 1880, notwithstanding the losses incurred by the most destructive war of modern times, the emancipation of four billions of slave property, the expenses of feeding the best fed, of clothing the best clothed, and of sheltering the best-sheltered people in the world, notwithstanding all the losses by fire and flood during that period of twenty years, the wealth of the country increased at the rate of $250,000 for every hour. Every time that the clock ticked above the portal of this Chamber the aggregated, accumulated permanent wealth of this country increased more than $70.

Sir, it rivals, it exceeds the fictions of the "Arabian Nights." There is nothing in the story of the lamp of Aladdin that surpasses it. It is without parallel or precedent; and the national ledger now shows a balance to our credit, after all that has been wasted and squandered and expended and lost and thrown away, of between $60,000,000,000 and $70,000,000,000. I believe myself that, upon a fair cash market valuation, the aggregate wealth of this country to-day is not less than $100,000,000,000. This is enough, Mr. President, to make every man and every woman and every child beneath the flag comfortable; to keep the wolf away from the door. It is enough to give to every family a competence, and yet we are told that there are thousands of people who never have enough to eat in any one day in the year. We are told by the statisticians of the Department of Labor of the United States that, notwithstanding this stupendous aggregation, there are a million American citizens, able-bodied and willing to work, who tramp the streets of our cities and the country highways and byways, in search of labor with which to buy their daily bread, in vain.

Mr. President, is it any wonder that this condition of things can exist without exciting profound apprehension? I heard, or saw rather, for I did not hear it—I saw in the morning papers that, in his speech yesterday, the senator from Ohio [Mr. Sherman] devoted a considerable part of his remarks to the defense of millionaires; that he declared that they were the froth upon the beer of our political system.

[Mr. Sherman: I said speculators.]

Speculators. They are very nearly the same, for the millionaires of this country, Mr. President, are not the producers and the laborers. They are arrayed like Solomon in all his glory, but "they toil not, neither do they spin"—yes, they do spin. This class, Mr. President, I am glad to say, is not confined to this country alone These gigantic accumulations have not been the result of industry and economy. There would be no protest against them if they were. There is an anecdote floating around the papers, speaking about beer, that some gentleman said to the keeper of a saloon that he would give him a recipe for selling more beer, and when he inquired what it was, he said, "Sell less froth." If the millionaires and speculators of this country are the froth upon the beer of our system, the time has come when we should sell more beer by selling less froth.

The people are beginning to inquire whether, under "a government of the people by the people for the people," under a system in which the bounty of nature is supplemented by the labor of all, any citizen can show a moral, yes, or a legal, title to $200,000,000. Some have the temerity to ask whether or not any man can show a clear title to $100,000,000. There have been men rash enough to doubt whether, under a system so constituted and established, by speculation or otherwise, any citizen can show a fair title to $10,000,000 when the distribution of wealth per capita would be less than $1,000. If I were put upon my *voir dire* I should hesitate before admitting that, in the sense of giving just compensation and equivalent, any man in this country or any other country ever absolutely earned a million dollars. I do not believe he ever did.

What is the condition to-day, Mr. President, by the statistics? I said that at the beginning of this century there was a condition of practical social equality; wealth was uniformly diffused among the great mass of the people. I repeat that the people are not anarchists; they are not socialists; they are not communists; but they have suddenly waked to the conception of the fact that the bulk of the property of the country is passing into the hands of what the senator from Ohio, by a euphemism, calls the "speculators" of the world, not of America alone. They infest the financial and social system of every country upon the face of the earth. They are the men of no politics—neither Democrat nor Republican. They are the men of all nationalities and of no nationality; with no politics but plunder, and with no principle but the spoliation of the human race.

A table has been compiled for the purpose of showing how wealth in this country is distributed, and it is full of the most startling admonition. It has appeared in the magazines; it has been commented upon in this Chamber; it has been the theme of editorial discussion. It appears from this compendium that there are in the United States two hundred persons who have an aggregate of more than $20,000,000 each; and there has been one man—the Midas of the century—at whose touch everything seemed to turn to gold, who acquired within less than the lifetime of a single individual, out of the aggregate of the national wealth that was earned by the labor of all applied to the common bounty of nature, an aggregate that exceeded the assessed valuation of four of the smallest States in this Union.

[Mr. Hoar: And more than the whole country had when the constitution was formed.]

Yes, and, as the senator from Massachusetts well observes,—and I thank him for the suggestion,—much more, many times more than the entire wealth of the country when it was established and founded. Four hundred persons possess $10,000,000 each, 1,000 persons $5,000,000 each, 2,000 persons $2,500,000 each, 6,000 persons $1,000,000 each, and 15,000 persons $500,000 each, making a total of 31,100 people who possess $36,250,000,000.

Mr. President, it is the most appalling statement that ever fell upon moral ears. It is, so far as the results of democracy as a social and political experiment are concerned, the most terrible commentary that ever was recorded in the book of time; and Nero fiddles while Rome burns. It is thrown off with a laugh and a sneer as the "froth upon the beer" of our political and social system. As I said, the assessed valuation recorded in the great national ledger standing to our credit is about $65,000,000,000.

Our population is 62,500,000, and by some means, some device, some machination, some incantation, honest or otherwise, some process that cannot be defined, less than a two-thousandth part of our population have obtained possession, and have kept out of the penitentiary in spite of the means they have adopted to acquire it, of more than one half of the entire accumulated wealth of the country.

That is not the worst, Mr. President. It has been chiefly acquired by men who have contributed little to the material welfare of the country, and by processes that I do not care in appropriate terms to describe; by the wrecking of the fortunes of innocent men, women, and children; by jugglery, by book-keeping, by financiering, by what the senator from Ohio calls "speculation,"—and this process is going on with frightful and constantly accelerating rapidity.

The entire industry of this country is passing under the control of organized and confederated capital. More than fifty of the necessaries of life to-day, without which the cabin of the farmer and the miner cannot be lighted, or his children fed or clothed, have passed absolutely under the control of syndicates and trusts and corporations composed of speculators, and, by means of these combinations and confederations, competition is destroyed; small dealings are rendered impossible; competence can no longer be acquired, for it is superfluous and unnecessary to say that if, under a system where the accumulations distributed per capita would be less than a thousand dollars, 31,000 obtained possession of more than half of the accumulated wealth of the country, it is impossible that others should have a competence or an independence.

So it happens, Mr. President, that our society is becoming rapidly stratified—almost hopelessly stratified—into the condition of superfluously rich and helplessly poor. We are accustomed to speak of this as the land of the free and the home of the brave. It will soon be the home of the rich and the land of the slave.

We point to Great Britain and we denounce aristocracy and privileged and titled classes and landed estates. We thought, when we had abolished primogeniture and entail, that we had forever forbidden and prevented these enormous and dangerous accumulations; but, sir, we had forgotten that capital could combine; we were unaware of the yet undeveloped capacity of corporations; and so, as I say, it happens upon the threshold and in the vestibule of our second century, with all its magnificent record behind us, with this tremendous achievement in the way of wealth, population, invention, opportunity for happiness, we are in a condition compared with which the accumulated fortunes of Great Britain are puerile and insignificant.

It is no wonder, Mr. President, that the laboring, industrial, and agricultural classes, who have been made intelligent under the impulse of universal education, have at last awakened to this tremendous condition and are inquiring whether or not this experiment has been successful. And, sir, the speculators must beware. They have forgotten that the conditions, political and social, here are not a reproduction of the conditions under which these circumstances exist in other lands. Here is no dynasty; here is no privilege or caste or prerogative; here are no standing armies; here are no hereditary bondsmen, but every atom in our political system is quick, instinct, and endowed with life and power.

His ballot at the box is the equivalent of the ballot of the richest speculator. Thomas Jefferson, the great apostle of modern democracy, taught the lesson to his followers—and they have profited well by his instruction—that under a popular democratic representative government wealth, culture, intelligence were ultimately no match for numbers.

The numbers in this country, Mr. President, have learned at last the power of combination, and the speculators should not forget that, while the people of this country are generous and just, they are jealous also, and that, when discontent changes to resentment, and resentment passes into exasperation, one volume of a nation's history is closed and another will be opened.

The speculators, Mr. President! The cotton product of this country, I believe, is about 6,000,000 bales.

[Mr. Butler: Seven million bales.]

Seven million bales, I am told. The transactions of the New York Cotton Exchange are 40,000,000 bales, representing transactions speculative, profitable, remunerative, by which some of these great accumulations have been piled up, an inconceivable burden upon the energies and industries of the country.

The production of coal oil, I believe, in this country has averaged something like 20,000,000 barrels a year. The transactions of the New York Petroleum Exchange year by year average 2,000,000,000 barrels, fictitious, simulated, the instruments of the gambler and the speculator, by means of which, through an impost upon the toil and labor and industry of every laborer engaged in the production of petroleum, additional difficulties are imposed.

It is reported that the coal alone that is mined in Pennsylvania, indispensable to the comfort of millions of men, amounts in its annual product to about $40,000,000 of which one third is profit over and above the cost of production and a fair return for the capital invested.

That is "speculation," Mr. President, and every dollar over and above the cost of production, with a fair return upon the capital invested, every dollar of that fifteen or sixteen millions is filched, robbed, violently plundered out of the earnings of the laborers and operatives and farmers who are compelled to buy it; and yet it goes by the euphemistic name of "speculation," and is declared to be legitimate; it is eulogized and defended as one of those practices that is entitled to respect and approbation.

Nor is this all, Mr. President. The hostility between the employers and the employed in this country is becoming vindictive and permanently malevolent. Labor and capital are in two hostile camps to-day. Lockouts and strikes and labor difficulties have become practically the normal condition of our system, and it is estimated that during the year that has just closed, in consequence of these disorders, in consequence of this hostility and this warfare, the actual loss in labor, in wages, in the destruction of perishable commodities by the interruption of railway traffic, has not been less than $300,000,000.

Mr. President, this is a serious problem. It may well engage the attention of the representatives of the States and of the American people. I have no sympathy with that school of political economists which teaches that there is an irreconcilable conflict between labor and capital, and which demands indiscriminate, hostile, and repressive legislation against men because they are rich, and corporations because they are strong. Labor and capital should not be antagonists, but allies rather. They should not be opponents and enemies, but colleagues and auxiliaries whose co-operating rivalry is essential to national prosperity. But I cannot forbear to affirm that a political system under which such despotic power can be wrested from the people and vested in a few is a democracy only in name.

A financial system under which more than half of the

enormous wealth of the country, derived from the bounty of nature and the labor of all, is owned by a little more than thirty thousand people, while one million American citizens able and willing to toil are homeless tramps, starving for bread, requires readjustment.

A social system which offers to tender, virtuous, and dependent women the alternative between prostitution and suicide as an escape from beggary is organized crime for which some day unrelenting justice will demand atonement and expiation.

Mr. President, the man who loves his country and the man who studies her history will search in vain for any natural cause for this appalling condition. The earth has not forgotten to yield her increase. There has been no general failure of harvests. We have had benignant skies and the early and the latter rain. Neither famine nor pestilence has decimated our population or wasted its energies. Immigration is flowing in from every land, and we are in the lusty prime of national youth and strength, with unexampled resources and every stimulus to their development; but, sir, the great body of the American people are engaged to-day in studying these problems that I have suggested in this morning hour. They are disheartened with misfortunes. They are weary with unrequited toil. They are tired of the exactions of the speculators. They desire peace and rest. They are turning their attention to the great industrial questions which underlie their material prosperity. They are indifferent to party. They care nothing for Republicanism nor for Democracy as such. They are ready to say, " A plague on both your houses," and they are ready also, Mr. President, to hail and to welcome any organization, any measure, any leader that promises them relief from the profitless strife of politicians and this turbulent and distracting agitation which has already culminated in violence and may end in blood.

Such, sir, is the verdict which I read in the elections from which we have just emerged, a verdict that was unexpected by the leaders of both parties, and which surprised alike the victors and the vanquished. It was a spontaneous, unpremeditated protest of the people against existing conditions. It was a revolt of the national conscience against injustice, a movement that is full of pathos and also full of danger, because such movements sometimes make victims of those who are guiltless. It was not a Republican defeat. It was not a Democratic victory. It was a great upheaval and uprising, independent of and superior to both. It was a crisis that may become a catastrophe, filled with terrible admonition, but not without encouragement to those who understand and are ready to co-operate with it. It was a peaceful revolution, an attempt to resume rights that seemed to have been infringed.

It is many years, Mr. President, since I predicted this inevitable result. In a speech delivered in this Chamber on the 15th of February, 1878, from the seat that is now adorned by my honorable friend from Texas who sits before me [Mr. Reagan] I said:

"We can not disguise the truth that we are on the verge of an impending revolution. The old issues are dead. The people are arraying themselves upon one side or the other of a portentous contest. On one side is capital, formidably intrenched in privilege, arrogant from continued triumph, conservative, tenacious of old theories, demanding new concessions, enriched by domestic levy and foreign commerce, and struggling to adjust all values to its own standard. On the other is labor, asking for employment, striving to develop domestic industries, battling with the forces of nature, and subduing the wilderness; labor, starving and sullen in cities, resolutely determined to overthrow a system under which the rich are growing richer and the poor are growing poorer; a system which gives to a Vanderbilt the possession of wealth beyond the dreams of avarice and condemns the poor to a poverty which has no refuge from starvation but the prison or the grave.

"Our demands for relief, for justice, have been met with indifference or disdain.

"The laborers of the country asking for employment are treated like impudent mendicants begging for bread."

Mr. President, it may be cause, it may be coincidence, it may be effect, it may be *post hoc* or it may be *propter hoc*, but it is historically true that this great blight that has fallen upon our industries, this paralysis that has overtaken our financial system, coincided in point of time with the diminution of the circulating medium of the country. The public debt was declared to be payable in coin, and then the money power of silver was destroyed. The value of property diminished in proportion, wages fell, and the value of everything was depreciated except debts and gold. The mortgage, the bond, the coupon, and the tax have retained immortal youth and vigor. They have not depreciated. The debt remains, but the capacity to pay has been destroyed. The accumulation of years disappears under the hammer of the sheriff, and the debtor is homeless, while the creditor obtains the security for his debt for a fraction of what it was actually worth when the debt was contracted.

There is, Mr. President, a deep-seated conviction among the people, which I fully share, that the demonetization of silver in 1873 was one element of a great conspiracy to deliver the fiscal system of this country over to those by whom it has, in my opinion, finally been captured. I see no proof of the assertion that the Demonetization Act of 1873 was fraudulently or corruptly procured, but from the statements that have been made it is impossible to avoid the conviction that it was part of a deliberate plan and conspiracy formed by those who have been called speculators to still further increase the value of the standard by which their accumulations were to be measured. The attention of the people was not called to the subject. It is one of the anomalies and phenomena of legislation.

That bill was pending in its various stages for four years in both Houses of Congress. It passed both bodies by decided majorities. It was read and re-read and reprinted thirteen times, as appears by the records. It was commented upon in newspapers; it was the subject of discussion in financial bodies all over the country; and yet we have the concurrent testimony of every senator and every member of the House of Representatives who was present during the time that the legislation was pending and proceeding that he knew nothing whatever about the demonetization of silver and the destruction of the coinage of the silver dollar. The senator from Nevada [Mr. Stewart], who knows so many things, felt called upon to make a speech of an hour's duration to show that he knew nothing whatever about it. I have heard other members declaim and with one consent make excuse that they knew nothing about it.

As I say, it is one of the phenomena and anomalies of legislation, and I have no other explanation to make than this: I believe that both Houses of Congress and the President of the United States must have been hypnotized. So great was the power of capital, so profound was the impulse, so persistent was the determination, that the promoters of this scheme succeeded, by the operation of mind power and will force, in capturing and bewildering the intelligence of men of all parties, of members of both Houses of Congress, and the members of the Cabinet, and the President of the United States.

And yet, Mr. President, it cannot be doubted that the statements that these gentlemen make are true. There is no doubt of the sincerity or the candor of those who have testified upon this matter; and it is incredible (I am glad it occurred before I was a member of this body) that a change in our financial system, that deprived one of the money metals of its debt-paying power, that changed the whole financial system of the country, and, to a certain extent, the entire fiscal methods of the world, could have been engineered through the Senate and the House of Representatives and the Cabinet of the President, and secured Executive approval without a single human being knowing anything whatever about it. In an age of miracles, Mr. President, wonders never cease.

It is true, that this marvel was accomplished when the subject was not one of public discussion. It was done at a time when, although the public mind was intensely interested in financial subjects, and methods of relief from existing conditions were assiduously sought, the suggestion had never proceeded from any quarter that this could be accomplished by the demonetization of silver, or ceasing to coin the silver dollar. It was improvidently done, but it would not be more surprising, it would not be more of a strain upon human credulity, if fifteen years from now we were to be informed that no one was aware that in the bill that is now pending the proposition was made for the free coinage of silver.

Mr. President, there is not a State west of the Alleghany Mountains and south of the Potomac and Ohio rivers that is not in favor of the free coinage of silver. There is not a State in which, if that proposition were to be submitted to a popular vote, it would not be adopted by an overwhelming majority. I do not mean by that inclusion to say that in those States east of the Alleghanies and north of the Ohio and Potomac rivers there is any hostility or indisposition to receive the benefits that would result from the remonetization of silver. On the contrary, in the great commonwealths that lie to the north-east upon the Atlantic seaboard, New York, Pennsylvania, and the manufacturing and commercial States, I am inclined to believe, from the tone of the press, from the declarations of many assemblies, that if the proposition were to be submitted there it would also receive a majority of the votes.

If the proposition were to be submitted to the votes of the people of this country at large whether the silver dollar should be recoined and silver remonetized, notwithstanding the prophecies, the predictions, the animadversions of those who are opposed to it, I have not the slightest doubt that the great majority of the people, irrespective of party, would be in favor of it, and would so record themselves. They have declared in favor of it for the past fifteen years, and they have been juggled with, they have been thwarted, they have been paltered with and dealt with in a double sense. The word of promise that was made to their ear in the platforms of political parties has been broken to their hope. There was a majority is this body at the last session of Congress in favor of the free coinage of silver. The compromise that was made was not what the people expected, nor what they had a right to demand. They felt they had been trifled with, and that is one cause of the exasperation expressed in the verdict of November 4th.

I feel impelled to make one further observation. Warnings and admonitions have been plenty in this debate. We have been admonished of the danger that would follow; we have been notified of what would occur if the free coinage of silver were supported by a majority of this body, or if it were to be adopted as a part of our financial system. I am not a prophet, nor the son of a prophet, but I say to those who are now arraying themselves against the deliberately expressed judgment of the American people,—a judgment that they know has been declared and recorded,—I say to the members of this body,—I say, so far as I may do so with propriety, to the members of the co-ordinate branch of Congress,—and I say, if without impropriety I may do so, to the Executive of the nation, that there will come a time when the people will be trifled with no longer on this subject.

Once, twice, thrice by Executive intervention, Democratic and Republican, by parliamentary proceedings that I need not characterize, by various methods of legislative jugglery, the deliberate purpose of the American people, irrespective of party, has been thwarted, it has been defied, it has been contumeliously trodden under foot; and I repeat to those who have been the instruments and the implements,—no matter what the impulse or the motive or the intention may have been,—at some time the people will elect a House of Representatives, they will elect a Senate of the United States, they will elect a President of the United States, who will carry out their pledges and execute the popular will.

Mr. President, by the readjustment of the political forces of the nation under the eleventh census, the seat of power has at last been transferred from the circumference of this country to its center. It has been transferred from the seaboard to that great intramontane region between the Alleghanies and the Sierras, extending from the British possessions to the Gulf of Mexico, a region whose growth is one of the wonders and marvels of modern civilization. It seems as if the column of migration had paused in its westward march to build upon those tranquil plains and in those fertile valleys a fabric of society that should be the wonder and the admiration of the world; rich in every element of present prosperity, but richer in every prophecy of future greatness and renown.

When I went west, Mr. President, as a carpet-bagger, in 1858, St. Louis was an outpost of civilization, Jefferson City was the farthest point reached by a railroad, and in all that great wilderness, extending from the sparse settlements along the Missouri to the summits of the Sierra Nevada, and from the Yellowstone to the cañons of the Rio Grande, a vast solitude from which I have myself, since that time, voted to admit seven States into the American Union, there was neither harvest nor husbandry, neither habitation nor home, save the hut of the hunter and the wigwam of the savage. Mr. President, we have now within those limits, extending southward from the British possessions and embracing the States of the Mississippi Valley, the Gulf, and the southeastern Atlantic, a vast productive region, the granary of the world, a majority of the members of this body, of the House of Representatives, and of the Electoral College.

We talk with admiration of Egypt. For many centuries the ruins of its cities, its art, its religions, have been the marvel of mankind. The Pyramids have survived the memory of their builders, and the Sphinx still questions, with solemn gaze, the vague mystery of the desert.

The great fabric of Egyptian civilization, with its wealth and power, the riches of its art, its creeds and faiths and philosophies, was reared, from the labors of a few million slaves under the lash of despots, upon a narrow margin 450 miles long and 10 miles wide, comprising in all, with the delta of the Nile, no more than 10,000 square miles of fertile land.

Who, sir, can foretell the future of that region to which I

have adverted, with its 20,000 miles of navigable water-courses, with its hundreds of thousands of square miles of soil excelling in fecundity all that of the Nile, when the labor of centuries of freemen under the impulse of our institutions shall have brought forth their perfect results?

Mr. President, it is to that region, with that population and with such a future, that the political power of this country has at last been transferred, and they are now unanimously demanding the free coinage of silver. It is for that reason that I shall cordially support the amendment proposed by the senator from Nevada. In doing so I not only follow the dictates of my own judgment, but I carry out the wishes of a great majority of my constituents, irrespective of party or of political affiliation. I have been for the free coinage of silver from the outset, and I am free to say that after having observed the operations of the act of 1878 I am more than ever convinced of the wisdom of that legislation and the futility of the accusations by which it was assailed.

The people of the country that I represent have lost their reverence for gold. They have no longer any superstition about coin. Notwithstanding the declarations of the mono-metallists, notwithstanding the assaults that have been made by those who are in favor of still further increasing the value of the standard by which their possessions are measured, they know that money is neither wealth, nor capital, nor value, and that it is merely the creation of the law by which all these are estimated and measured.

We speak, sir, about the volume of money, and about its relation to the wealth and capital of the country. Let me ask you, sir, for a moment, what would occur if the circulating medium were to be destroyed? Suppose that the gold and silver were to be withdrawn suddenly from circulation and melted up into bars and ingots and buried in the earth from which they were taken. Suppose that all the paper money, silver certificates, gold certificates, national-bank notes, treasury notes, were stacked in one mass at the end of the treasury building and the torch applied to them, and they were to be destroyed by fire, and their ashes scattered, like the ashes of Wickliffe, upon the Potomac, to be spread abroad, wide as its waters be.

What would be the effect? Would not this country be worth exactly as much as it is to-day? Would there not be just as many acres of land, as many houses, as many farms, as many days of labor, as much improved and unimproved merchandise, and as much property as there is to-day? The result would be that commerce would languish, the sails of the ships would be furled in the harbors, the great trains would cease to run to and fro on their errands, trade would be reduced to barter, and, the people finding their energies languishing, civilization itself would droop, and we should be reduced to the condition of the nomadic wanderers upon the primeval plains.

Suppose, on the other hand, that instead of being destroyed, all the money in this country were to be put in the possession of a single man—gold, and paper, and silver—and he were to be moored in mid-Atlantic upon a raft with his great hoard, or to be stationed in the middle of Sahara's desert without food to nourish, or shelter to cover, or the means of transportation to get away. Who would be the richest man, the possessor of the gigantic treasure or the humblest settler upon the plains of the west, with a dugout to shelter him, and with corn meal and water enough for his daily bread?

Doubtless, Mr. President, you search the Scriptures daily, and are therefore familiar with the story of those depraved politicians of Judea who sought to entangle the Master in his talk, by asking him if it were lawful to pay tribute to Cæsar or not. He, perceiving the purpose that they had in view, said unto them, "Show me the tribute money;" and they brought him a penny. He said, "Whose is this image and superscription?" and they replied, "Cæsar's;" and he said, "Render unto Cæsar the things that are Cæsar's, and unto God the things that are God's."

I hold, Mr. President, between my thumb and finger, a silver denarius, or "penny," of that ancient time—perhaps the identical coin that was brought by the hypocritical Herodian—bearing the image and superscription of Cæsar. It has been money for more than twenty centuries. It was money when Jesus walked the waves and in the tragic hour at Gethsemane. Imperial Cæsar is "dead and turned to clay." He has yielded to a mightier conqueror, and his eagles, his ensigns, and his trophies are indistinguishable dust. His triumphs and his victories are a schoolboy's tale. Rome herself is but a memory. Her marble porticoes and temples and palaces are in ruins. The sluggish monk and the lazy Roman *lazzaroni* haunt the Senate House and the Coliseum, and the derisive owl wakes the echoes of the voiceless Forum. But this little contemporary disk of silver is money still, because it bears the image and superscripture of Cæsar. And, sir, it will continue to be money for twenty centuries more, should it resist so long the corroding canker and the gnawing tooth of time. But if one of these pages should take this coin to the railway track, as boys sometimes do, and allow the train to pass over it, in one single instant its function would be destroyed. It would contain as many grains of silver as before, but it would be money no longer, because the image and superscription of Cæsar had disappeared.

Mr. President, money is the creation of law, and the American people have learned that lesson, and they are indifferent to the assaults, they are indifferent to the arguments, they are indifferent to the aspersions which are cast upon them for demanding that the law of the United States shall place the image and superscription of Cæsar upon silver enough and gold enough and paper enough to enable them to transact without embarrassment, without hindrance, without delay, and without impoverishment their daily business affairs, and that shall give them a measure of values that will not make their earnings and their belongings the sport and the prey of speculators.

Mr. President, this contest can have but one issue. The experiment that has begun will not fail. It is useless to deny that many irregularities have been tolerated here; that many crimes have been committed in the sacred name of liberty; that our public affairs have been scandalous episodes to which every patriotic heart reverts with distress; that there have been envy and jealousy in high places; that there have been treacherous and lying platforms; that there have been shallow compromises and degrading concessions to popular errors; but, amid all these disturbances, amid all these contests, amid all these inexplicable aberrations, the path of the nation has been steadily onward.

At the beginning of our second century we have entered upon a new social and political movement whose results cannot be predicted, but which are certain to be infinitely momentous. That the progress will be upward I have no doubt. Through the long and desolate tract of history, through the seemingly aimless struggles, the random gropings of humanity, the turbulent chaos of wrong, injustice, crime, doubt, want, and wretchedness, the dungeon and the block, the inquisition and the stake, the trepidations of the oppressed, the bloody exultations and triumph of tyrants,—

> The uplifted ax, the agonizing wheel,
> Luke's iron crown and Damien's bed of steel,—

the tendency has been toward the light. Out of every conflict some man or sect or nation has emerged with higher privileges, greater opportunities, purer religion, broader liberty, and greater capacity for happiness; and out of this conflict in which we are now engaged I am confident finally will come liberty, justice, equality; the continental unity of the American republic, the social fraternity and the industrial independence of the American people.